Guide to Czechoslovakia

This book is dedicated to my mother

Guide to Czechoslovakia

Simon Hayman

BRADT PUBLICATIONS, UK
HIPPOCRENE BOOKS, USA

First edition published in 1987 by Bradt Publications, 41 Nortoft Road, Chalfont St Peter, Bucks SL9 0LA. Distributed in the U.S.A. by Hippocrene Books.

Second updated printing 1990.
Second edition published May 1991.

British Library Cataloguing in Publication Data
Hayman, Simon
   Guide to Czechoslovakia.
   1. Travel. Czechoslovakia
   I. Title
   914.370443

   ISBN 0 946983 62 3

Maps by Hans van Well
Photos courtesy of Čedok, London
Front cover photos: High Tatras (top) and Cheb (bottom)
Back cover photo: Skiing in Krkonoše
Typeset from the author's disc by Patti Taylor, London NW8 ORJ
Printed in Hong Kong by Colorcraft

ACKNOWLEDGEMENTS

In the first edition I did not mention any names of people who helped me with information, suggestions and hospitality in Czechoslovakia, as I was afraid they might get into trouble. Now that freedom of expression has been reintroduced in Czechoslovakia I would like to take this opportunity to express my thanks to those that have helped me on my travels both with the first and later editions: Ing. Peter Bealy, Ing. Ján Bobok (OSCR, Banská Bystrica), Eva Ďaďová, Košč Dušan (OSCR, Bardejov), Ing. Václav Dvořák (CKM), Zoltán Fazeka, Dr Iván Gály, Ing. Ladislav Girgasch (Reštaurácie, Štátny Podnik, Stará Ľubovňa), Oto Chudý (Horska služba), Ing. Viliam Jančík (OSCR, Bardejov), Vojtěch Jelínek (OK-Tours), Alice Klimova, Dagmar Kotlandová, Ing. Peter Krošlák, Vincent Kyšeľka (OSCR, Stará Ľubovňa), Ing. Lukáč (MOCR, Slovakia), Petr Marhoul (Čedok), Katařina Marušková, Elena Mončeková, František Morávek (Olympia), Marek Nalos, JUDr Ian Neoral, Ing. Petko Peter, Hana Povondrová (and Tony), Ing. Eva Skalová (MOCR, Prague, Department of Tourism & Public Catering), Vojtěch Skřivan, Jarmila Sládková, Rostislav Sliwka, Jozef Spišák (Podtatranské Restauracie), Ivor Šanek, Vít Šanek, Ján Šimún (OSCR Dolný Kubín), the Srameks (whose bookshelves introduced me to the most beautiful parts of the country), Anton Šteffek (Šport), Miroslav Valent, Paula Voleniková, and Ing. Milan Vondráček.

I would also like to thank those who have responded to my request and written letters, and especially to Ian Brewster, Robert Broughton, Fiona Bulmer, N. Fixsen, Ellie Howarth, Ann Johnston, Chris Mace, Peter Petrin, Carola Schwenold, John Skelton, Bob Swain, Philip Vickers and Hugo Vind.

My grateful thanks to Hugh Matthews for offering his word processor for the first edition, and for trying to help with my all too frequent word processing problems with this edition.

ABOUT THE AUTHOR

Simon Hayman was born in England, but emigrated to New Zealand with his parents. After completing a university degree in geography he travelled widely in Europe, Asia and the Pacific. He researched and wrote the second and third editions of *New Zealand — A Travel Survival Kit* for Lonely Planet Publications and co-authored the third edition of *Australia* in the same series. He has contributed to other guides and is the author of various newspaper articles in New Zealand, Australia and the UK.

Returning to Europe in 1983 for "a short visit", Simon has been travelling and working there ever since.

INTRODUCTION AND PREFACE

Czechoslovakia, lying in the heart of Europe, is a country with an immense variety to offer, but a country neglected by most travellers. Most people never go there. Those who do always want to return.

Czechoslovakia is not only a treasure-trove of all the attractions Europe is famous for (cathedrals, castles, and beautiful old buildings, to name but a few), but it also has fantastic natural scenery. In fact, as the Czechoslovak tourist authorities like to boast, Czechoslovakia has everything except the sea.

It would be an understatement to say that things have changed since the first edition of this book. A revolution has occurred. This edition has been longer under way than planned, as I have had to discard one draft after another as events have moved faster than my fingers on the keyboard.

Those familiar with the previous edition will notice that the book has been considerably expanded and (hopefully) improved, including the addition of both further historic towns and hiking route descriptions.

In Part 1 of the book I introduce many terms, so if you leap straight into (say) the section on Prague and find something you don't understand, the answer will be found earlier in the book.

I have tried to provide specific information and not just the general glossy descriptions you find in travel brochures. Although I have made every effort to keep my information as up to date as possible, a lot of changes are expected, so please bear with me if you find the situation is different from that I describe. It is now even more important that you, the readers, write and tell me if things have changed, or if you have further information or suggestions. Write to: Simon Hayman, c/o Bradt Publications.

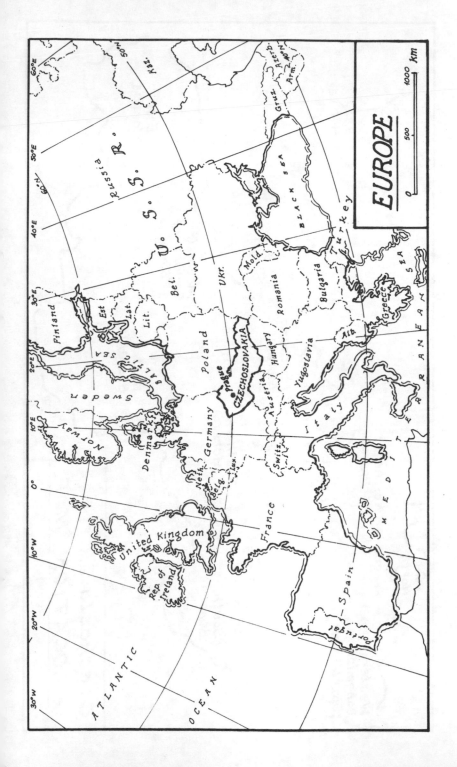

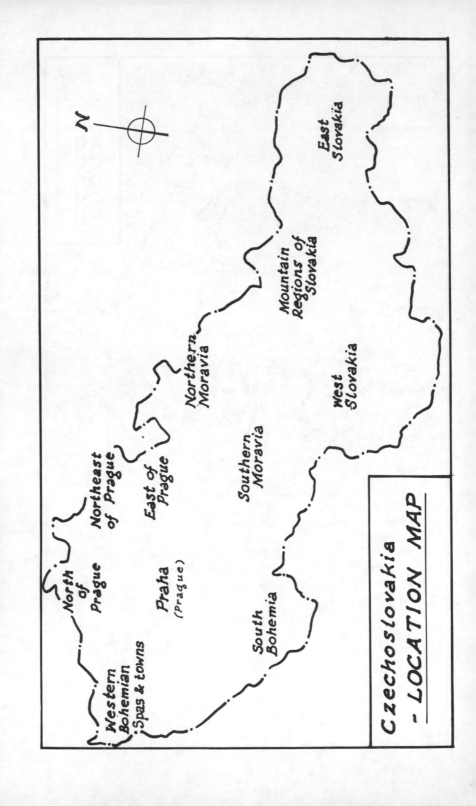

Czechoslovakia
- LOCATION MAP

TABLE OF CONTENTS

Land and people

BASIC FACTS

Czechoslovakia consists of Bohemia, Moravia and Slovakia. Situated in the centre of Europe, it is a long narrow country, about 800km from west to east. Its population of 15 million live in an area of 128,000 sq km. Since 1969 Czechoslovakia has been a federal state of two republics, the Czech republic (Bohemia and Moravia) with a population of about 10 million, and the Slovak republic with 5 million. The capital city is Prague.

The following public holidays are observed: January 1 (New Year's Day), Easter Monday, May 1 (May Day), May 9 (Liberation from fascism), July 5 (the coming of Christianity to Czechoslovakia), October 28 (National Holiday on the anniversary of the creation of Czechoslovakia in 1918) and December 24, 25, and 26 (Christmas). In addition July 6, the date Jan Hus was burnt at WHO the stake, is a public holiday in the Czech republic, while November 1, a Catholic holiday when one remembers the dead, is a holiday in Slovakia.

Time is CET: one hour ahead of Greenwich Mean Time, ie the same as most of western Europe. Summer time is synchronised with other European countries, ie from about late March until about the end of September.

HISTORY B.B. museum

There is archaeological evidence of habitation of Czechoslovakia from prehistoric times. Later, the Celts inhabited the land. One of the Celtic tribes, the Boi, gave that part of Czechoslovakia known as Bohemia its name. The Celts were driven out by Germanic tribes towards the end of the 4th Century AD.

The first Slavs, the predecessors of the present population of Czechoslovakia, arrived in the 5th Century. By the 9th Century, the Slav tribes had united to form the Great Moravian Empire, which included Bohemia, Moravia, Slovakia and part of Austria.

In 863 AD two monks from Thessaloníki, Cyril and Method (Metoděj), brought Christianity to Moravia. They were later canonised as saints by the Catholic church. They created a Slav alphabet based on Greek letters, and translated the Bible and Christian literature into what has become known as Old Church Slavonic. This alphabet became the Cyrillic alphabet, named after Cyril.

In 929 the first of the Přemyslid princes, Václav 1 (920 — 929), was murdered by his brother. He became the patron saint of the Czechs, and is the "King Wenceslas" of the carol we know so well.

In the beginning of the 10th Century the Magyars invaded Slovakia, putting an end to the Great Moravian Empire. Slovakia remained annexed to Hungary for the next thousand years.

In 995 the Czech lands were united under the rule of the Přemyslid princes. In the 14th Century, there remained no male Přemyslid successor to the throne, and the female successor, Eliška Přemyslid, married John of Luxembourg who annexed the Czech lands to the German Empire. Their son, Charles (Karel) IV, became the Holy Roman Emperor, and so for a period Prague became the capital of the empire. Charles has been remembered with a warm heart by the Czech people, as the father of their land. Many of the fine works in Prague date from his time, and it is said that he loved the Czech people and their language.

The 15th Century saw the rise of the Hussite movement. Jan Hus was a clergyman who tried to reform the church and society. Many view him as the first Protestant. Hus studied at Charles University, becoming a professor and even leading the university at one time. The High Priests didn't like him, as he criticised their wealth, and they forced him to leave Prague. In 1415, with both the Roman Catholic Church and the Holy Roman Empire against him, Hus was burnt at the stake at Constance as a heretic, after being called there under false pretext. When the news reached South Bohemia an armed uprising broke out, with the Hussite army being led by Jan Žižka. The Hussite movement lasted 20 years before it was finally crushed, and the Hussites were driven out to western Europe.

The 16th Century saw the beginning of a period of 400 years of Hapsburg rule over most of Central and South Europe. In 1618 the Czech nobility rebelled. This rebellion resulted in a crushing defeat for them at the Battle of White Mountain in 1620, and the loss of the Czech lords' independence. In 1621, 27 of the leaders of the rebellion were executed in the Old Town Square in Prague. The Hapsburgs forcibly re-Catholicised the land, and suppressed the Czech language and culture. Many left the country, including the famous philosopher Comenius (Jan Ámos Komesnský, the great teacher). 1618 also marked the beginning of the Thirty Years War, which saw the Swedes in Bohemia before it finished in 1648.

In 1805 Napoleon defeated the Russian and Austrian armies in the Battle of Austerlitz (Slavkov). Frightened by the French Revolution, Kaiser Franz II suppressed all freedom movements and put all public life under police surveillance. In 1866 war between Austria and Prussia took place on Czech soil, with the Czechs fighting loyally on the Austrian side. There was a lot of emigration, especially from Slovakia. At one time Chicago was the largest Czechoslovak city in the world.

During the First World War, the Czech and Slovak peoples' sympathies were on the Allies' side. In London, Paris and Washington, Tomáš Garrigue Masaryk, Beneš and others worked hard for the Czechoslovak cause. On October 28 1918, the Czechoslovak Republic was proclaimed. Masaryk (1850-1937) became its first president until Beneš succeeded him in 1935. Slovaks felt cheated as they had expected self-government after 1918.

Czechoslovakia suffered during the depression, with many unemployed and poor. Nevertheless in 1939 the country was the 10th strongest economic power in the world. *10th*

Hitler stirred up trouble in the Sudetenland, and encouraged Slovak separatism. In 1938 the British and French "sold out" Czechoslovakia to the Nazis, by agreeing that the border regions of Czechoslovakia had to be ceded to Germany. Chamberlain said he had obtained "Peace in our time". In March 1939, Germany invaded. Bohemia and Moravia became a German "protectorate", and parts of Slovakia and the whole of Carpathia were handed to Hungary. The rest of Slovakia became an independent country under German protection, led by president Josef Tiso (who was executed in 1947). Czech Jews were taken away to the Nazi concentration camps. (Those who survived were often treated badly on their homecoming, and it is said that some were even murdered by those who had taken over their houses.) Czechs living in Slovakia were forced to leave, and Slovakia fought on the German side in World War Two.

In 1942, the German "Protector", Reinhard Heydrich, was assassinated by Czechoslovak patriots. The Nazis razed the Central Bohemian village of Lidice *Again* to the ground, and shot all its men, in reprisal. The only large scale armed resistance during the war was an uprising in Slovakia in 1944, which was brutally crushed by the Nazis. The backbone of the Slovak National Uprising, *+* as it came to be known, was the communist resistance movement, and it was supported by the Soviet Union and the Allies.

On May 5 1945, there was an uprising in Prague. A few days later the Red Army reached the city. The US army had orders to stop at the demarcation line near Plzeň, according to the Yalta Agreement. During the war a government in exile was set up in London under Beneš. After the experience of 1938 there was not much trust of the West, and a treaty of friendship was signed with the Soviet Union in 1942. As part of this treaty, the Soviet Union agreed that its troops would not remain on Czechoslovak soil after the war. Carpathia was ceded to the Soviet Union.

A new government was formed at Košice in March 1945. Beneš was the head of a four party coalition until the Communists took over in 1948 during a Cabinet crisis. Beneš resigned and was succeeded by Gottwald. The foreign minister, Jan Masaryk (1886-1948, son of the country's first president), either committed suicide or was murdered while trying to flee the communists. An alleged witness to his death was killed in 1969 in a road accident caused when the driver of the vehicle he was in was shot.

Large-scale nationalisation of industry and of cultural institutions followed the Communist takeover. Agriculture was collectivised. Many people emigrated during this period. Then followed a Stalinisation period, when many were imprisoned, including leading Slovak communists, who resented centralised Prague rule, and including Gustáv Husák, who later became president. In 1960, Czechoslovakia was proclaimed a socialist republic.

In 1967 a liberalisation process commenced. In 1968, Novotný was succeeded as party secretary by Alexander Dubček on January 4, and as president by Ludvik Svoboda on March 31. The period known as the "Prague Spring" began, with an attempt to shape "socialism with a human face", as it was called. Censorship was removed, and a lively public debate started. On

August 21, 500,000 Warsaw Pact troops from the Soviet Union, Bulgaria, Poland and Hungary invaded Czechoslovakia, putting an end to the liberalisation. Since 1990 there has been some contention as to whether East German troops were also involved. Although the East German government supported the invasion, some say they agreed not to send troops over the border, so as not to remind Czechs of the Nazi invasion. But eye witnesses say they met East German troops in Czechoslovakia. The Soviet and allied troops were met by non-violent resistance. The official explanation for the troops was that the country was on the verge of a counter-revolution. There was another emigration wave before the border was again sealed. The Czechoslovak government reintroduced censorship, and increased party and police control. During autumn the Warsaw Pact troops withdrew, with the exception of the Soviet army, which remained in Czechoslovakia. On January 16 1969 Jan Palach, a student, burnt himself to death in Prague in protest against the occupation. stupid

In 1969 Czechoslovakia became a federal republic consisting of the Czech Republic and the Slovak Republic. In the same year Gustáv Husák became first secretary of the Czechoslovak Communist Party, and in 1975 he also became president, succeeding Ludvik Svoboda. With the winds of change blowing from Moscow, Milos Jakeš succeeded Husák as first secretary of the party in December 1987. Jakeš was the main person in charge of the exclusion of nearly half a million party members during the purges after the Dubček era. A limited edition of perestroika was introduced. But demonstrations in Prague and Bratislava in 1988 and 1989 were put down, often brutally, by the police.

Late in 1989 there was a peaceful revolution in Czechoslovakia. On 1989 November 17 some students held a legal demonstration in memory of Jan Opletal, a student killed by the Nazis on that date 50 years ago. This date has been commemorated as International Students' Day in the "communist" countries. The students decided to continue to Václavské náměstí, the traditional meeting place for demonstrations in Prague. The police blocked their way, and diverted them to Národní where a trap was laid. There was only one escape, and as the students were forced through this, they were beaten by the police.

A student strike resulted as a spontaneous protest against police brutality. There was no student organisation to organise the strike — it was just word of mouth. The rest of the country didn't believe or know what had happened — TV was forced to lie. So, at the risk of being beaten up by the local militia, students travelled to their home towns and villages to inform the people and gain their support. A great effort was made to ensure that everything happened peacefully, and to stop provocateurs. They decided to drink no alcohol until the revolution was won, to help them work harder and prevent provocation. They received support from artists and writers, Civic Forum was formed, and its backing spread rapidly. But the students were completely unprepared and extremely surprised when their strike and the reaction to it brought down the government, and Václav Havel, a dissident playwright who had frequently been jailed, became President, and Alexander Dubček the Speaker.

After a lot of argument and stirred up Slovak nationalism, Czechs and Slovaks agreed to change the country's official name from the Czechoslovak Socialist Republic (ČSSR) to The Czech and Slovak Federal Republic (ČSFR) in April 1990, the idea being to give more stress to *Slovak* than before

The Soviet troops who had been in Czechoslovakia since the invasion in 1968 began leaving in 1990, and the rest are expected to follow suit during 1991.

22 years after being taken there in handcuffs, Alexander Dubček made an official visit to Moscow in May 1990 as the guest of the Supreme Soviet of the USSR. The reforms the Dubček government tried to introduce are considered to be part of the foundation for Gorbachev's perestroika. When asked about the 1968 invasion by Soviet television, he answered that "there was no reason to cry over spilt milk". In Czechoslovakia a legal investigation to find out who was responsible for the invasion was undertaken, and on June 6 1990 Jakeš and others were arrested on charges under a law passed in 1950 by the Communist Party relating to national security.

In June 1990 the first free elections since 1946 were held in Czechoslovakia and won by Civic Forum and their Slovak sister party, Public Against Violence, with the Communist Party especially popular out in the villages and getting the second highest number of votes, with 14%. The plan is that the new parliament should sit for two years and prepare a new constitution and change the existing laws. By that time political parties would have time to establish themselves, and future elections would be held at normal intervals. On July 6 Václav Havel was re-elected president for a two year period.

On July 9 Miroslav Štěpán, the ex-leader of the Communist Party in Prague city, was jailed for four years for misuse of his position. He is thought to be responsible for the violence against the student demonstrators in November 1989.

MINORITY GROUPS AND CHANGING BOUNDARIES

Historically Czechoslovakia comprises Bohemia, Silesia, Moravia, Slovakia and Carpathia (Ruthenia or Podkarpatská Rus).

A lot of the old Silesia is in Poland, the rest is now part of Moravia and Bohemia.

Moravia itself is normally lumped together with Bohemia, as part of the Czech speaking part of the country (a fact that gets many Moravians' backs up). A party demanding more rights for the Moravian people has, since the 1989 elections, been represented in parliament.

Most of the so-called Ukrainians living in Czechoslovakia are actually Ruthenians (Ruthenians do not officially exist as a people). Labelling them Ukrainians helped excuse the Soviet takeover of Carpathia, where most of them live. This eastern part of the country was 12,000 sq km with 725,000 inhabitants, and bordered Romania. The Ruthenian minority in today's Czechoslovakia number 80,000, and live particularly in East Slovakia.

The Spiš region of Slovakia was devastated by the Tatars. The Hungarian rulers called new immigrants, mostly from Saxony, into the depopulated land.

There was a large German minority living in the border regions of Bohemia. They were Hitler's pretext to enter Czechoslovakia. After the war about 3 million Germans were deported to Germany, but a German minority of 80,000 remains, mostly in West Bohemia.

There is a large Hungarian minority (about 600,000) in Slovakia, especially in the south. During the Second World War part of Slovakia was handed over to Hungary, but returned to Slovakia after the war. The Communist government was accused of stirring up old animosity between Slovaks and Hungarians in autumn 1989 to try to stop Slovaks getting inspiration from the Hungarian reforms. Hungary has a minority of about 100,000 Slovaks.

There is a Gypsy minority of about 750,000, who live especially in Slovakia. They managed to escape the Nazi gas chambers, because Germany only truly occupied Slovakia from October 1944 until January to April 1945. Many have moved to Bohemia to areas where there was a shortage of manual labour. Ill-feeling towards Gypsies is widespread.

There is also a Polish minority of 100,000. Recently a lot of large construction projects have been undertaken by workers from Poland.

Since the Velvet Revolution Slovak nationalism has again flourished and the nationalists are being accused of oppressing the minority groups.

In more recent times there have been tens of thousands of foreign workers in Czechoslovakia, especially Vietnamese. The Velvet Revolution seems also to have freed a lot of aggressions and there have been many cases of gangs of skinheads and hooligans assaulting Vietnamese (as well as Gypsies). Vietnamese workers have complained that they are underpaid and made to work and live in bad conditions. The government has said that all foreign workers must leave by 1995. Czechoslovakia's relationship with Cuba has reached a low, and all Cubans should have left by the time this edition is published, though Czechoslovak student organisations have appealed for political asylum for Cuban students.

THE COUNTRY

Czechoslovakia offers a landscape varying from the Danube lowlands to the only alpine mountains between the Alps and the Caucasus, and almost everything you could think of in between.

Its central position in Europe is highlighted by the fact that it lies on the watershed between the Baltic, North and Black Seas. The main rivers are the Danube (*Dunaj*), Elbe (*Labe*) and the *Vltava* (Moldau in German).

One third of the country is covered in forests. Mountains and lakes abound. Many of the lakes, especially the larger ones, were created as storage areas for hydro-electric power stations, or as fishing dams. They are open for recreational use. In the mountains are beautiful natural tarns. Nearly 10% of the country has some type of nature protection status.

Bears There are still remnants of Europe's near extinct wildlife in Czechoslovakia, particularly in Slovakia, where 500 brown bears live in the mountains. Though your chances of seeing a bear may be rather slim, your chances of seeing wild deer in Slovakia are much better. There are also chamois, wild boar, wolves, lynx and foxes. Wildlife of a smaller kind abounds in some areas at some times of the year, so insect repellant can be very useful.

There are fascinating limestone areas with caves open to the public, areas **SEE** of sandstone carved into remarkable shapes by the elements, and even boiling mud-pools and geysers.

Most farming in Czechoslovakia is collectivised. Fields are very large by west European standards, and there is widespread use of machinery. Walking in the country in Czechoslovakia can be a delightful experience, and country roads are often lined with fruit trees.

Castle enthusiasts will be enthraled with Czechoslovakia, where there are several thousand castles and chateaux, ranging from those which have been restored and are now interesting museums, to ruins atop deserted rocky outcrops in the forest. What's more they are nearly all open to the public.

As well as the indescribable beauty of the heart of Prague, there are countless well preserved historical towns, with their fascinating old buildings and narrow cobble lanes. **NO KIDDING !**

On the negative side, rapid industrialisation has polluted air and water, and Czechoslovakia is suffering badly from the European-wide problem of acid rain. Firs are dying in all woods, but the problem is especially great in Bohemia. The Krušné Hory and Krkonoše are almost dead. A 1989 UN report lists Czechoslovakia as the European country worst affected by acid rain, with 70.5% of its forest affected, and 5.4% badly affected or completely dead (Britain is the second worst affected country.) As with other European countries, Czechoslovakia tends to blame its neighbours instead of getting to the root of the problem. The high sulphur content of the coal burned is one of the problems. Desulphurisation is expensive. But today there is a growing awareness of the problem of pollution.

LIFE AND PEOPLE

You meet people of all shades of political opinion, from ardent capitalist to ardent communist, and it can be very interesting talking with them (though while it was the ardent capitalists that were afraid to speak up before, it might now be the ardent communists). Before the Communist Party takeover in 1948, it had a lot of support in Czechoslovakia. There were many communists with idealistic visions that were crushed by the events to come. Although it is fashionable to criticise the old regime, it did guarantee the people work and social security. People did not have many of the human rights we take for granted, but had others we have never become acquainted with. Many ← Czechs and Slovaks tend to think in economic rather than political terms when comparing East with West (eg how well off people are). If you speak only English, communication can be difficult, but it is worth making the effort. Freedom of expression is a new right in Czechoslovakia. Before, people were often afraid to talk openly with strangers.

Many Czechoslovaks have a rather rosy picture of the West, and do not realise that many of the problems they blamed on "the system" are also endemic in the West. Now they are discovering that even the propaganda one hears in the West doesn't differ so much from the propaganda they are used to.

A Czechoslovak proverb repeated under the old regime was that if you don't steal from the state, you steal from your family. A lot of intellectuals feel that the moral rebuilding of the country is the most important and most difficult task ahead.

If you come from some out of the way place like New Zealand, as I do, you may cause a minor sensation in places where people are not so used to seeing foreigners.

Living standard: Before the Second World War Czechoslovakia had one of the highest living standards in the world. Though this has dropped, it is still one of the highest in "eastern" Europe, and it has the most egalitarian wage structure in Europe. Western ideas and technology are being copied, but also unfortunately are western ecological mistakes such as building motorways, increasing use of plastic packaging and throwaway cups etc. **YES !**

Work: Under the Communist Party there was no unemployment problem in Czechoslovakia, as everyone was guaranteed work. In fact everyone, except students and married women, had either to work or be able to show what they were living off. Czechoslovakia complained that it did not have enough workers, and many of the Vietnamese you'll undoubtedly notice in the country are working there on temporary work permits. (They must promise that they will not marry a Czechoslovak.) This has completely changed, and in 1991 the unemployment rate is expected to reach 15%.

Both husband and wife normally work, and get up very early in the morning to go to work. The working week is now Monday to Friday; until 1989 some Saturdays were designated as working Saturdays. The working tempo tends to be slower than in the West. I have been told that in Czechoslovakia you *go to work* from Monday to Friday, but you actually *work* at the weekend, when people are busy with private work. I mentioned this to others, who remarked, "How did you know our secret?" But with the strive after a market economy all this is changing. Now that private enterprise is allowed, many people are taking the plunge, though many others are loath to take the financial and political risks.

Under the Communists if someone had a foreigner visiting them at work, they were supposed to write a report on them.

Education: The education system was based on Marxism-Leninism and permeated by party propaganda, so a lot of changes are taking place. The philosophy students at Charles University found that once divorced from Marxism-Leninism there was not much left to their studies, so a whole new study programme was necessary.

Birth, marriage and death: Under the Communist Party there was tremendous social and governmental pressure to have children. The birth rate is high by European standards. In 1977 it was 18.7, as compared with 11.8 in Great Britain, but by 1988 it had fallen to 13.8 (12.7 in the Czech republic and 15.9 in Slovakia). You see babies everywhere, especially in Slovakia, and

YES ! – EXACTLY

buses have a place for prams. Contraception is available, and free abortion
was introduced in 1987, although the Catholic church and Slovak nationalists
are now fighting against it. There are about 75 abortions for every 100 births.
People marry young, especially in the country, where a girl is considered
an "old maid" if she is not married by her early twenties. The divorce rate is
high. Divorced women receive the family home, children and maintenance
from their ex-husband which is collected by the state. There is paid maternity
leave and mothers have the right to stay home if their children are sick.
Women are equal under the law, but feminism is almost unheard of.

The trend seems to be that people choose the civil alternative to baptism
and marriage, but select to have a Christian burial.

Name day: The Catholic tradition of having a name day has been kept alive
in Czechoslovakia. So as well as having a birthday, there is a specific day of
the year assigned to your name, which you also celebrate. On her name day,
you give a girl flowers, drink together and get the chance to kiss her. So,
men, this is your chance to kiss all the pretty girls. (I don't know if women get
the chance to kiss men on their name day.) When it is a common name like
Maria there are celebrations everywhere.

Housing: Flats are rented from the State or are collectively owned. Rent is
low by western standards. Some of the newer complexes are rather frightful.
Those who would like their own house usually build it themselves, though
they get financial assistance from the state. It is common for city people to
have cottages in the country. Many people must live in the city owing to their
work or study, but flee to the countryside whenever possible.

Travel: Before 1989 Czechoslovaks were not permitted to travel freely,
especially to the west. One of the easiest countries for them to travel to was
East Germany, while for a seaside holiday it was popular to go to Bulgaria.
They are subject to the same restrictions as western travellers if they wish to
travel to the Soviet Union. During most of the 1980s they were not even
allowed to travel to Poland unless invited by relatives living there. Now that
they are at last free to travel, buying the necessary foreign currency has
become their major problem.

Religion: Religion is frowned upon by communist ideology, but freedom of
religion is guaranteed by the Czechoslovak constitution. The Roman Catholic
church is the largest of the different sects. The proportion of the population
that are Christian varies from one part of the country to another. The Catholic
church is especially strong in Slovakia, and the demonstrations in Bratislava
before the fall of the Communist Party were organised by Catholics. Under
the old regime there was discrimination against Christians, for example when
it came to allotting places in educational institutions. The church was
controlled by the state. Disagreements with the Vatican led to many vacant
positions in the church hierarchy. Now there is talk of separating church and
state. In April 1990 the first ever papal visit to Czechoslovakia took place and,
what's more, the Pope addressed the huge crowd in Czech and Slovak. After
the Communist takeover many churches were closed or used as storehouses

etc. Now the church is getting back some of its confiscated property. From a tourist's point of view, many churches have a habit of only being open for mass.

Compulsory military training: Previously every male had to undergo compulsory military training for a period of two years, but from the beginning of 1991 this period was reduced to 18 months and conscientious objection was introduced. At the beginning of 1991 Czechoslovakia was short of soldiers, as over 40% of the country's young men were claiming the status of conscientious objector, which entails having to do a longer period of 27 months civil service. Previously people in the army were forbidden from having any contact with people from the West.

Health: Health care is normally free. The government has recently revealed that air pollution is so bad in some areas that it shortens people's normal life span by up to 11 years. School classes from the worst affected areas spend a part of the year in the mountains.

THE ARTS

Some of the famous names in Czech literature are Karel Čapek (1890-1938), an anti-humanist through whom the Czech word "robot" became internationalised, Franz Kafka (1883-1924), who lived in Prague but wrote in German, and Jaroslav Hášek (1883-1923), who wrote *The Good Soldier Schweik*. Schweik "is a small non revolutionary, half from proletariat half from small town, who is finding out in the army about capitalism. He is completely disoriented with what is presented to him as duty to the state. To save his sanity, he portrays the role of a fool who carries out orders ad absurdum. I see the book — as life — a tragicomedy. It's funny to those who understand Czech humour. It has been translated into English" (E. Hayman).

Jaroslav Seifert (1901-1985) received the Noble Prize for his writing in 1984. Famous living Czech writers include Václav Havel, Milan Kundera, Ivan Klíma and Bohumil Hrabal. Václav Havel is now world known as Czechoslovakia's new president. Kundera, who lived in exile, became known even outside literary circles when the film *The Unbearable Lightness of Being* was made, based on his book.

Slovakia didn't get its own codified written language until the middle of the 19th Century and its writers are not so well known outside the country. One of Slovakia's best known living poets is Lubomir Feldek, who has also written children's books and for theatre. Another living Slovak poet is Milan Richter. Andy Warhol was of Slovak origin. At the time of his death negotiations were under way to open a museum in his honour in Slovakia.

Many writers left Czechoslovakia in 1968, and an exile publishing house was set up in Canada.

The most famous Czech composers are Smetana, Dvořák, Janáček, Martinů and Friml. Bedřich Smetana (1824-1884) is especially well known for his series of six symphonic poems making up the cycle *Má vlast* (My Fatherland). The second of these was *Vltava* (Moldau in German), which follows the river Vltava from its source in Šumava, on its course across Bohemia, to its confluence with the Elbe. Antonín Dvořák (1841-1904) was a contemporary of Smetana, but came from much humbler origins. He was helped on his way by Brahms, and is best known for his *Symphony from the New World*. Leoš Janáček (1854-1928) remained in his native Moravia and, as Brno was an unknown dot on the artistic map, he was 60 years old before he became recognised in Prague. This recognition unleashed a stream of music, which continued until his death in 1928. Rudolf Friml was born in Prague in 1879 and lived in USA, where he received recognition, from 1906 until his death in Los Angeles in 1972.

International film festivals are held in Karlovy Vary. The well-known film director Miloš Forman is Czech, and other film directors worthy of note are Juraj Jadubisko and Jiří Menžel.

As far as theatre is concerned, Vlasta Burian, Jindřich Plachta, Stanislav Kostka Naumman and Hugo Hase (Osvobozené divadlo) were active in the 1930s, but all perished during the war. Other names are Jan Verich, who also wrote a few books, and Voskovec, a Jew who emigrated to America in 1940.

The wonders of Czechoslovak architecture of earlier centuries are around you all the time. In the interwar period there was a progressive school in Germany. Many of the members were Jews, so they came to Bohemia to avoid Hitler, helping to create good architecture in this period. After the Second World War art suffered under "socialist realism" and architecture tends to be either very drab and functional, or designed as showpieces. But many of the historically worthy buildings were restored in this period, while since the fall of the communists there has been talk of letting them fall into private hands because the upkeep is too expensive.

Art was subsidised in Czechoslovakia under the Communists, but was also under government control and censorship. As can be seen by the efforts the Communist Party went to to fetter free artistic expression, culture is very much alive and important in Czechoslovakia, and in fact today's president and many underground cultural personalities were those who surfaced in late 1989 as the leaders of the revolution. Czechoslovaks are often disillusioned if they come to the West where they find that culture is almost dead in comparison with their homeland.

FOLK TRADITION

Contrary to what is shown in the tourist brochures, you won't see people in traditional costumes wherever you turn, but in rural Slovakia, for example in the Spis region, you can see women wearing traditional wide skirts and headscarves. Folk costumes, dances and music are kept alive in annual festivals held in various parts of the country. Some of the better known festivals are the Chod festival at Domažlice in west Bohemia (mid August), Strážnice in south-west Moravia (June-July), Východná between the High and Low Tatras (first weekend of July), Detva near Zvolen (folk dancing, July) and Terchová near Žilina (August). There is an annual bagpipe festival in Strakonice, held around the end of August. In Gombasek (near Rožňava) is a Hungarian folk festival about the last weekend in June, and in Svidník a festival of Ukranian workers about the third or fourth weekend in June. See under the place where they are held for more information on some of these festivals. Check the dates before turning up. Otherwise there are some shows arranged especially for tourists.

In some places, especially in south Moravia and in Slovakia, *posviceni* (Czech), or *hody* (Slovak) is celebrated. This is a festival something like *fasnacht* in Switzerland. Its original intention was to chase the winter away and welcome the spring. There is a parade, drinking, folk costumes are worn, and a pig is killed and roasted.

There are still villages where you can see traditional local architecture. In villages such as Ždiar in the High Tatras and Čičmany near Žilina the houses have beautifully painted exteriors.

Some *skansens* (open air museums) have opened, where old buildings have been collected together. *Drevené Starby na Slovensku* by Eugen Lazišťan and Ján Michalov is a picture book of old wooden buildings.

Useful information

VISAS

Before the revolution every visitor from the West, except citizens of Finland, required a visa. The situation has since changed rapidly, and I advise you to check whether there have been further changes before you travel. (There is hope, for instance, that visas will be abolished for citizens of South American and Australasian countries.) Citizens of the following countries do *not* require visas for visits of up to three months: Canada, USA, USSR, plus all European countries except Portugal, Greece, Cyprus and Turkey. If that includes you, you need not read this section. The three month period begins again if you re-enter Czechoslovakia after a short visit to a neighbouring country. If citizens of these countries wish to stay longer than three months they should apply at a consulate for an entry visa which takes 15 days and cannot be obtained at the border. But it is possible to apply from within the country if you change your mind and wish to stay longer than three months.

Citizens of all other countries require visas. These are normally obtained in advance from a Czechoslovak embassy or consulate, but can now be obtained for a higher fee at *certain* border crossings (see section Travelling To and From Czechoslovakia: Border Crossings). Visas are usually issued very quickly from the embassies — in my experience between five and 45 minutes when you go to the embassy yourself. You can also apply by post, but in this case allow a few weeks. You'll need a passport which is valid for at least five months from the date of application, visa application forms, two passport photos (machine ones are OK, but make sure they are a current likeness), and about £20 (depending on which embassy you apply at) for the visa fee. If applying by post, enclose a stamped addressed reply envelope. You must enter Czechoslovakia within three months of the visa being issued by an embassy, or immediately if you get your visa at one of the border crossings where this is possible. Children under 15 who are included in their parent's passport don't need to apply for a visa. A double entry visa costs twice as much as a single entry.

The visa form has spaces for "Address in Czechoslovakia — District" and "Name of visited person — institution-hotel in Czechoslovakia". If you don't know where you will be staying you can write something like "Prague" and "camping" without being restricted to only staying there. If, when you apply for your visa at the embassy, you want more than one month, you'll probably get given only one month, and told you must apply for an extension of your visa once you are in Czechoslovakia. Czechoslovak transit visas must also be applied for in advance. If you require a visa to your country of destination, get that first. With a transit visa you are supposed to travel by the shortest route to your destination. A single transit visa costs the same as a tourist visa. A double transit visa costs twice as much. A single transit visa is valid for 24 hours, and does not normally give the right to sleep the night somewhere en route, so if you wish to do so, ask about this when you apply for your visa. With a double transit visa, it is possible to sleep en route.

Here are the addresses of some of the Czechoslovak embassies and consulates. The official title of Czechoslovakia's embassies is: *Embassy of the Czech and Slovak Federal Republic*.

Australia	Consulate General, 169 Military Road, Dover Heights, Sydney, NSW 2030,
Austria	Penzinger Strasse 11-13, A-1140 Wien
Belgium	152 Avenue A. Buyl, B-1050 Bruxelles
Canada	50 Rideau Terrace, Ottawa, Ontario, K1M 2A1
Denmark	Ryvangs Allé 14-16, DK-2100 København Ø, (tel. 31 29 16 64, open Monday-Friday 10.00am-11.00am)
Finland	Armfeltintie 14, SF-00150 Helsinki 15
France	15 Avenue Charles Floquet, F-75 007 Paris
Germany	5300 Bonn, Ferdinandstrasse 27 (also consulates in Berlin at 108 Berlin, Otto Grotewohl Strasse 21, in München, and plans to open further consulates)
Greece	Rue Séféris 6, Palaio Psychico, Athénes; (tel. 67 10 675).
Hungary	Népstadion út. 22, Budapest XIV
India	50/M Niti Marg, Chanakyapuri, New Delhi-110021,
Italy	Via dei Colli della Farnesina, 144-Lotto VI. I-00 194 Roma,
Japan	16-14, Horoo 2-chome, Shibuya-ku, Tokyo 150,
New Zealand	12 Anne Street, Wadestown, PO Box 2843, Wellington
Norway	Thomas Heftyes Gate 32, Oslo 2,
Poland	Koszykowa 18, Warszawa, Skr. poczt. 00-555
Sweden	Floragatan 13, Stockholm, S-114 31 (tel. 246153-8)
Switzerland	Muristr. 53, Bern (tel. 44 36 45)
UK	26 Kensington Palace Gardens, London W8 4OX
USA	3900 Linnean Ave NW, Washington DC 20008

Embassies are often open fairly limited hours only, usually in the morning. If you apply for your visa in an eastern European country, you must pay the visa fee in western cash.

As well as receiving a stamp in your passport, you'll be given some of the copies of the visa form to carry with you. You must produce these when you leave the country, so don't lose them.

Visa extensions

Visas can be extended at the discretion of the authorities, but they normally extend them automatically if you apply. Some Čedok offices will arrange a visa extension for you, or at least help you. Others will not. In Prague or Bratislava it is possible to extend a visa so that its total length is up to 180 days. In smaller towns, it may only be possible to get seven days, but you can extend it again once you come to Prague or Bratislava.

You extend your visa at ÚPSACA (*Úřad pro pasovou službu a cizineckou agendu*) or, if there is no such office in the town you are in, at the department of the local police station called *Pasové oddelini*. Both are closed at the weekend, so if your visa runs out at the weekend, extend it beforehand. In Prague go direct to ÚPSACA. In other towns it may be necessary to go through the following steps:

1. Find out from ÚPSACA (or the police) if you may extend your visa for the time you require, and how much it will cost.
3. Go to a *tabák* (*tabak* in Slovak) and buy special stamps called *kolky* (not postage stamps) that you use to pay the visa extension fee with. (Kčs 60 for a shorter extension, Kčs 120 for a longer one.) Some Čedok offices sell these stamps.
4. Return to ÚPSACA or the police and receive your visa extension.

Visas for other countries

British citizens don't require visas to cross any western European countries. But if crossing Poland or USSR as part of your travels, you need a transit visa for these countries. If visiting these countries, you need a tourist visa.

Polish visas are normally issued fairly quickly: you may be able to get one the same day. The compulsory minimum exchange has been abolished. For USSR you must have the complete trip booked (that is transport, hotels, etc) before you apply for your visa. If in Prague, first go to Čedok, and ask them to make arrangements for your trip through Intourist in Moscow. This step takes 10 days. Only after this can you apply for your visa, which takes seven working days. So it is best to apply before you leave home.

Addresses of foreign embassies in Czechoslovakia which you may need for visa applications are:

Hungary, 125 37 Praha 6, Mičurinova 1; tel. 36 50 41.

Polish Konsulat, Václavské nám. 49, Praha. tel. 26 44 64. Open 8.30-12.30. Consulate also in Ostrava.

Soviet Konsulate, Korunovačni 34, Praha 6. Tel. 37 37 97. Open Monday, Wednesday and Friday 9.30am-1.00pm only.

These three countries also have consulates in Bratislava (see section on Bratislava for addresses).

Passports

You are not obliged to carry your passport on you while in the country, but the authorities recommend that you do to ease identification should anything go wrong, and you will anyway need it when registering at any accommodation you use and to change money.

MONEY

Czechoslovak currency consists of crowns (Kčs) and hellers (h), with 100 hellers to one crown. It is non-convertible outside Czechoslovakia, which means it can not be freely changed to other currencies, and that it is illegal to take Czechoslovak money into or out of the country. Having a non-convertible currency has in the past protected Czechoslovakia from the inflation other countries have suffered and prevented its currency from becoming a plaything of speculators. The new government hopes to be able to make the Czechoslovak crown freely convertible at some stage. There are no restrictions on the import or export of convertible currency.

What was previously the bane of travellers to Czechoslovakia, the compulsory minimum exchange of DM 30 or the equivalent thereof per day, has been abolished.

At some border crossings there is no bank and at others they will only exchange cash, not travellers' cheques, which is rather a ridiculous situation considering that one may not bring Czechoslovak currency into the country. I had the following experience when crossing from Łysa Polana in Poland to Javorina in Czechoslovakia by bus. I had to change buses at the border, but as I could not bring Czechoslovak money into the country with me, and there was no bank at the border, I could not pay for the ticket. (If travelling to Poland via this crossing, there *is* a Polish bank at the border).

Some hotels also refuse to change travellers cheques (usually the smaller 1, 2 or 3 star hotels).

Not all bank branches change western currency. Apart from banks you can change money at many travel agents and hotels and at the new exchange offices which have begun appearing. If you have a visa, all your official money exchanges will be noted on one of the loose pages you were given, which you must not lose. You'll need your passport and this page of your visa every time you change money.

The following credit cards are accepted in Czechoslovakia: American Express, Diners Club, ACCESS, Master Card, Eurocard, VISA, JCB and Carte Blanche. They can be used only: to pay Čedok; in more expensive hotels and restaurants; and in some speciality shops. Credit cards are not widely used, so it is necessary to have travellers cheques or cash as well. The only places in Czechoslovakia where you can receive cash with your credit card are at Čedok, Na příkopě 18, Prague, and Živnostenská Bank (in Prague at Na příkopě 23), and you can only draw Czechoslovak cash, not foreign currency.

In an attempt to put a damper on the thriving black market, there has been a radical adjustment in the official exchange rates. The previous myriad of different exchange rates has disappeared, to leave just one rate, as in

Western countries. The following rates of exchange are subject to currency fluctuations:

Deutschmark	DM 1	=	Kčs 18
Pound Sterling	£1	=	Kčs 50
U. S. Dollar	$1	=	Kčs 28
Australian Dollar	$1	=	Kčs 27
Danish Kroner	Dkr 1	=	Kčs 4.50
French Franc	FRF 1	=	Kčs 5
Swiss Franc	CHF 1	=	Kčs 21
Swedish Kroner	SEK 1	=	Kčs 5
Norwegian Kroner	Nkr 1	=	Kčs 4.50
Belgian Franc	Bfr 100	=	Kčs 84
Italian Lire	Itl 1000	=	Kčs 25
Canadian Dollar	C$ 1	=	Kčs 28
Dutch Guilder	NLG 1	=	Kčs 16

The official rate is higher for travellers cheques than for cash. But have some small denominations, because if they don't add up to the exact amount you have to change, you can't get change in foreign currency. If changing cash — if you're insistent enough — it is possible to get change in foreign currency.

Prices in Czechoslovakia were very stable until the "Velvet Revolution". Since then there have been big increases, but these are compensated for by the better exchange rate now received for convertible currency, so Czechoslovakia is still a cheap country for most people to travel in. Accommodation, car rental, telephoning and postage are some of the areas where prices are at western European levels. In most other areas, such as museum and castle entrance fees, food, public transport, books, maps and stationery you'll find prices very cheap.

If you're a student, take an ISIC (International Student Identity Card) with you, as there are many student discounts available, especially in admission fees. The new plastic ISIC has replaced both the old "capitalist" ISIC and "socialist" IUS (International Union of Students) cards and is recognised in Eastern Europe.

I advise you to change just enough money for your stay. If you haven't spent all your Czechoslovak currency when you leave, it is theoretically possible to change it back to convertible currency at the border or airport up to 50% of what you have officially changed. You may be required to show your currency exchange receipts to prove that you have obtained your crowns legally. The exchange office will only very rarely have £ sterling to return to you. Your money is more likely to be returned in US$ orDEM, but instead of cash you may be given a receipt which you can either send in asking for the money to be sent to you, or produce when you return to Czechoslovakia to claim your money back. In the latter case you must return within three years. During the first year you can draw it out again at any border crossing point. During the next two years you must draw it instead from Živnostenská banka. Remember that at some border crossings there is no bank.

If you want money transferred to Czechoslovakia, have it sent to Československa obchodní banka. There are branches in Prague, Plzeň, Brno and Bratislava, amongst other places. Have the sender give your name and passport number, and if you have one, your address. If given an address, the bank will contact you when the money arrives. If not, the bank will hold the money, and wait for you to call.

Using the official exchange rate, making any comparison with local people over prices in Czechoslovakia and prices in your home country is meaningless unless you look at the price as a proportion of one's income after tax instead of converting. I mention this as a caution, as I've often been asked to compare living costs with people I have met.

Fiona Bulmer writes that in car parks used by foreigners she got mobbed by children demanding "Eine mark" (one mark) or cans of cola.

REGISTRATION

Those who do not require visas need no longer register if they stay in Czechoslovakia no longer than 30 days. Visa holders staying over 48 hours (weekends excluded) are obliged to register with the police within 48 hours of arrival in Czechoslovakia. This can wait until the next working day if you arrive at the weekend or on a public holiday. If you stay in a hotel, camping ground or hostel, registration will normally be taken care of for you. But if you stay with friends or people you meet along the way, you are supposed to go to the police yourself and register. In theory you should have stamps on your visa form to account for every night you were in Czechoslovakia. But in practice, particularly if you stay in many different places, your visa form becomes such a maze of stamps that no-one checks it properly. Many places don't even bother to stamp it. So as long as you have some stamps on your visa form, it shouldn't matter if you are not registered for some periods along the way if registering at that particular address becomes a problem for some reason.

If you need to do something official, such as extending your visa, you must be registered in the town you are doing it in. This can land you in a bureaucratic circle in the following situation: If you try and prolong your visa on the day it is due to run out in a town you have just arrived in, the police won't prolong it until you are registered, and the place you are staying in won't register you until you have prolonged your visa.

If you plan to be in Czechoslovakia for a longer time (two months or more), it is a good idea to contact your own embassy.
Some foreign embassies in Prague:

Austria: 125 43 Praha 5, Viktora Huga 10, tel. 54 65 50
Belgium: 125 24 Praha 1, Valdštejnská 6, tel. 53 40 51
Canada: 125 33 Praha 6, Mickiewiczova 6, tel. 35 69 41
Denmark: 120 21 Praha 2, U Havlíčkových sadů 1, tel. 25 47 15
Finland: 125 01 Praha 2, Dřevná 2, tel. 20 55 41
France: 125 27 Praha 1, Velkopřevorské nám. 2, tel. 53 30 42
Germany: 118 00 Praha 1, Vlašská 19, tel. 53 23 51

Great Britain:	118 00 Praha 1, Thunovská 14, tel. 53 33 47
Italy:	125 31 Praha 1, Nerudova 20, tel. 53 26 46
Netherlands:	125 40 Praha 1, Maltézské nám. 1, tel. 53 13 78
Norway:	125 41 Praha 2, Žitná 2, tel. 29 88 56-58
Portugal:	160 00 Praha 6, Slunná 12, tel. 32 14 22
Spain:	160 00 Praha 6, Pevnostní 9, tel. 32 71 24
Sweden:	125 52 Praha 1, Úvoz 13, tel. 53 33 44
Switzerland:	160 00 Praha 6, Pevnostní 7, tel. 32 04 06
USA:	125 48 Praha 1, Tržiště 15, tel. 53 66 41 (open 8.00am to 1.00pm, 2.00pm to 4.30pm).

HEALTH AND INSURANCE

If you want any type of travel insurance, you must organise it before you arrive. No insurance can be purchased in Czechoslovakia. The only exception is if you join a ski school. People on work camps are provided with insurance cover. British citizens have the right to free first aid treatment on production of their passport (though in smaller towns doctors will not always know this). Some other countries have agreements with Czechoslovakia, or have arrangements where they repay their citizens' medical expenses abroad (eg Denmark). There is only a very small charge for medicines on prescription.

Though hygiene standards are not quite as high as in the West, you should normally have no problems. If you need a doctor, go to a hospital. All towns have a 24-hour emergency service. Most doctors do not speak English. In Prague there is a special clinic for foreigners where doctors and dentists speak English (see section on Prague for address).

If you are using any medicaments take enough with you, as not all those we are used to are available, and there can be shortages. Although buying ordinary toiletries is no problem, if you use such things as special shampoo for dandruff, dental floss, desensitising toothpaste etc take them too as they can't be bought.

Spas

Spa treatment used to be considered a luxury affordable only by the rich and famous. But in Czechoslovakia it has become a way of life for all the people. People recuperating from accidents or surgery are often given a stay in a spa, all expenses paid. This privilege has not been extended to foreigners, who must pay a price of between US$25 and $65 a day, depending on the standard of the accommodation. The price includes food, lodging and basic treatment. If sharing a double room it is a bit cheaper, and if accompanying someone and not undergoing treatment you will have a slightly cheaper price again. The normal length of stay is three weeks.

For information and bookings for spas in Bohemia and Moravia contact Balnea, Pařížská 11, 110 01 Praha 1 (tel. 232 19 38, telex 12 22 15); and for Slovakia contact Slovthermae, Radlinského 13, 812 89 Bratislava (tel 572 75, telex 092238, fax 580 59). Their agent in Britain is Čedok, London.

Many of the foreign visitors to spas are older people. Sixty per cent of patients come regularly. Foreigners usually ask for the older accommodation,

which they find nicer and more homely. Most foreigners come from Germany and Austria, but there are also many Americans and Arabs.
There are many spas in Czechoslovakia. Some of the more famous are:

Františkovy Lázně: West Bohemia. Specialising in women's disorders. Dates back to 1707. Beautiful parks and gardens.

Karlovy Vary: West Bohemia. Founded in the 14th Century. Its prominent guests have included Tsar Peter the Great, Beethoven, Chopin and Goethe. Specialising in disorders of the digestive system, metabolic disorders and disorders of the endocrine glands.

Mariánské Lázně: West Bohemia. Second largest spa in Czechoslovakia, built in Empire style and set in parks and woods. Specialises in diseases of the kidneys and urinary tract, metabolic disturbances, ailments of the skin and of the upper respiratory tract.

Nový Smokovec: High Tatras. Climatic spa. Non-specific disorders of the respiratory organs, etc.

Piešťy: Slovakia. In the warmest region of Czechoslovakia. Rheumatism, sciatica, gout, post-injury conditions.

Štrbské Pleso: High Tatras. Climatic spa. Bronchial asthma and allergic colds.

Trenčianské Teplice: Slovakia. The springs were known to the Romans, but development was after 1800. Diseases of the motor organs, of the upper respiratory tract, rheumatism, post-injury conditions.

Whether you intend to have treatment or not, and whatever your views on spas are, these spas are worth a visit as tourist attractions, especially the three west Bohemian spas with their beautiful surroundings and old buildings.

TOURISM IN CZECHOSLOVAKIA

Until the Wall fell, by far the main group of tourists in Czechoslovakia came from East Germany, as it was the only country East Germans could freely travel to. Now tourists are streaming in from the West. Western visitors come mostly from West Germany, followed by Austria. Many Germans come because they have relatives in Czechoslovakia. The language of tourism tends to be German, especially in the west of Czechoslovakia. But although this may occasionally lead to difficulties if you don't speak German, Czechoslovaks often become very interested when they find out that you are one of the few who are not German. English-speaking tourists are uncommon outside Prague, Bratislava and the High Tatras.

Czechoslovakia is very much a land of package tourism — the Henry Ford system of mass production — and it was a difficult country for individual travellers. But the centralised system is changing, making it easier than before to travel around on you own — which I recommend because, instead of being treated like a "tourist", you are more likely to be treated like a real person by the people you come in contact with. Get away from the tourist places and you'll find people are more helpful and friendly, even if they don't speak English.

INFORMATION

Information in English is hard to come by in Czechoslovakia. If you require more information than given in this book I recommend you visit or write to an office of Čedok, a Czechoslovak travel agent with offices abroad.

Čedok Offices Abroad

Austria	Čedok, Tschechoslowakisches Reisebüro GmbH, Parkring 12, A-1010 Wien 1, tel 520199, 524372
Belgium	Čedok, Tsjechoslowaakse dienst voor toerizme, Stromstraat 19, 1000 Bruxelles, tel 5116870
	Čedok, Office du Tourisme Tchécoslovaque, Rue d'Assaut 19, 1000 Bruxelles
Denmark	Čedok, Tjekkoslovakisk Turistbureau, Vester Farimagsgade 6, 1606 København V, tel 33 12 01 21
France	Čedok, Office Tchécoslovaque de Tourisme, 32 Avenue de l'Opéra, 75002 Paris 2, tel 47428773, 47423845, 47421811
Germany	Čedok, Tshechoslowakisches Verkehrsbüro, Strausberger Platz 8/9, 1017 Berlin-Friedrichshain, tel 4394113, 4394135, 4394157
	Čedok Reisen GmbH, Spezialbüro Für Reisen in die Tschechoslowakei, Kaiserstr. 54, 6000 Frankfurt am Main, tel 232975-7
Great Britain	Čedok London Ltd, Czechoslovak Travel Bureau, 17-18 Old Bond Street, London W1X 4RB, tel (071) 629 6058, 491 2666
Hungary	Čedok, Csehszlovák Utazási Iroda, Kossuth Lajos tér 18, 1055 Budapest, tel 128233, 119855
Italy	Čedok, Ufficio per il Turismo Cecoslovacco, Via Piemonte 32, 00187 Roma, tel 483406
Netherlands	Čedok, Tsjechoslowaaks Reisinformatiebureau, Leidsestraat 4, 1017 PA Amsterdam C, tel (020)220101, (020)222788
Sweden	Čedok, Tjeckoslovakiska Turistbyrån, Sveavägen 9-11, 111 57 Stockholm, tel. 207290, 210790
Switzerland	Čedok, Tschechoslowakisches Verkehrsbüro, Urania-Strasse 34/2, 8025 Zürich, tel 2114245, 2114246
USA	Čedok, Czechoslovak Travel Bureau, 10 East 40th Street, New York, NY 10116, tel 212/689-9720
Yugoslavia	Čedok, Čehoslovačka putnička agencija, Strahinjića bana 51/111, 110 00 Beograd, tel 629543, 628416

Prague and Bratislava have tourist information offices, and in many towns in Slovakia you will find Slovakotour tourist offices. Apart from these there are no tourist offices as such in Czechoslovakia, so once in the country you could try the following for information: the hotel, camping ground or whatever you are staying in; Čedok or other travel agents such as Rekrea, Sportturist, Slovakoturist or Tatratour; the travel department (*odbri cestovníhr ruchu*) of the District National Committee (*Okresní národní Výbor* or *ONU* for short). In some centres Čedok has an office specialising in dealing with foreigners, and usually one of the staff in each of these will be able to speak English. Čedok are usually open longer hours than the other travel agents, but their opening hours are shorter in winter than in summer.

Books

Czechoslovakia Prague, published by Olympia, Prague, 1989, Kčs 40 in Czechoslovakia or £9.93 in UK, gives an alphabetcial listing of places in Czechoslovakia.

In the last year several new guide books on Prague and Czechoslovakia have been published. Stanfords in London (Tel: 071-836 1321) or Collets (Tel: 0933 224351) can provide a complete list.

For information on guide books to particular areas or subjects, see under the relevant section in this book.

Maps

You may be able to get a free map of Czechoslovakia from Čedok. Much more detail can be found in *Auto Atlas ČSSR*, which can be bought in bookshops in Czechoslovakia for Kčs 29. More detail still can be found in a new series of 17 maps called simply *Automapa* (Road Map), which include accommodation listings, information for motorists, and town plans showing main through roads. Another edition of the same maps includes information in various languages, including English, about places on the map with maps of historic town centres instead of the accommodation and motoring details. This series is called *Poznáváme Československo* (Getting to Know Czechoslovakia).

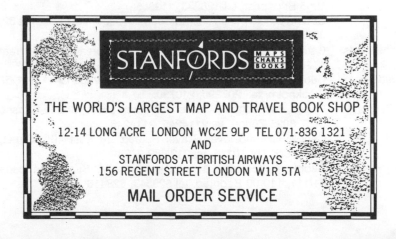

SEASONS AND WEATHER

Czechoslovakia has a climate midway between maritime and continental, with four distinct seasons. In summer it is often fine for long periods, but broken by violent thunderstorms with very heavy rain. Average summer temperatures are around 20°C, but it can be much hotter. In the mountains it can be quite cold, even in summer. Southern Slovakia is the warmest part of the country, where the temperature is often above 25°C in summer. In winter the average temperature is about -5°C, but it can be in the -20s in the mountains. Autumn starts in late August. Early autumn can be beautiful, with still clear days, and the chance of an "Indian summer". Late autumn tends to be foggy and cold.

The mountains have more rain and snow than the rest of the country. Bohemian mountains have more rain than Slovakian ones, because they are further west and catch the fronts from the Atlantic. The Krkonoše, for example, have about 200 days a year with precipitation. This means it is wet there in summer, but good for skiing in winter, because it gets snow earlier than other areas, and the snow stays longer than elsewhere. Spring comes later to the mountains than to the lower areas, and autumn starts earlier. The climate in Slovakia is more continental and 2000m above sea level in Slovakia corresponds to 3000m in the Alps.

But no matter what *should* happen the weather in Czechoslovakia is of course just as unpredictable as anywhere in the world.

If you are the sort of person that doesn't like to plan your travel too much, it is much easier to travel in Czechoslovakia in the summer, when the camping grounds are open and you don't have to worry so much about finding somewhere to sleep. From the last week of August you'll suddenly find yourself alone: the Czechoslovak holidays are over. But there are disadvantages travelling outside the main holiday period: to visit such attractions as castles and caves you must be guided around in a group and there may not be enough people to make up a group (can be easier at weekends); many buses to scenic areas stop running; and there is no traffic left for hitchhiking to out of the way places. Although cold, winter can be very beautiful, and opens possibilities for winter sports. But many interesting places to visit, eg nearly all castles, are closed in winter. Autumn can be a nice time of year to be in the mountains, and is also the grape harvest season.

LUGGAGE

What you take and how you carry it depends a lot on how you plan to travel. Here are some hints:

Rucksack: A day-pack (small rucksack) is very useful if you're planning hikes, or for carrying extra clothing, camera etc around in towns during the day. It's possible to buy very light cheap day-packs that you can stuff into your rucksack when you're not using them.

Clothes: As a general rule, take just enough so you have something to change into while you wash what you are wearing. Remember that it can be cold in the mountains, even in summer, so be prepared. It can also be almost unbearably hot at times. Slovaks and more particularly East Slovaks tend to dress up and dress conservatively. But if you are living out of a pack, it is not very practical to dress according to local norms. If camping, showers are sometimes rather filthy, so take some footwear you can wear in them (eg flip-flops, "jandals", "thongs", plastic sandals).

Rainwear: A folding umbrella may be useful in towns in the summer, and can easily be bought in Czechoslovakia, but if you intend spending time in the country or mountains bring a parka from home, as good parkas are not available.

Toilet gear: Take just what you need. Soap, toothpaste, shampoo and toilet paper are easily available, except for occasional local shortages. Have some toilet paper on you, as although you get given a little as you enter public toilets, it is often not enough, and on trains it often runs out.

Sleeping bag: If camping you will need a sleeping bag. In hostel style accommodation bedding is provided. When deciding what type of sleeping bag to take, remember that even in summer it can be quite cool in the mountain areas.

Camping: In summer, smaller tents can be an advantage, as camping grounds can get very full. Open fires are normal, and canvas or cotton tents are at less risk from cinders and sparks than light synthetic fibres. White spirit — *benzínový čistič skvrn* (Czech), *bezínový čistič škvrn* (Slovak) — is available in *drogéria*, as is the Slovak solid fuel, *pevný lieh*, or the Czech make "Hexa" which is sold in larger pieces. Solid fuel cookers are called *vařík* in Czech and are sold under the brand name "Koliba". Neither "camping gaz" (the blue French gas canister) nor meths for cookers are available in Czechoslovakia.

Hiking/climbing gear: For what to bring on a hiking or climbing trip, see section on *Tramping*.

Other: Writing paper: Air mail paper is sometimes difficult to buy in Czechoslovakia. Insect repellant: very handy in summer and purchasable in Czechoslovakia. A good pocket knife (for example a Swiss army knife) obviates the need to take scissors, bottle opener, cork screw, table knife etc.

Theft
Theft on the whole it is not too much of a problem in Czechoslovakia, but it has become a problem in Prague, and there has been a dramatic increase in criminality since the Velvet Revolution. Watch your possessions if you are out in the evening in a big city, and be wary of prostitutes.

Left luggage
There is normally a left luggage service at railway stations, and sometimes at bus stations. If you are carrying a pack around with tent, sleeping bag etc a

big problem is the frequent weight limit of 15 kg. This rule was brought in because it was considered the maximum women working in these places should have to lift. You can explain that you will carry it in yourself in some places, but in others, especially larger towns such as Prague, Bratislava, Brno and Žilina, this won't help — it makes no difference if it is men or women working there. Another problem is that left luggage depots can be full (eg Bratislava in summer). If you can leave your luggage, it is cheap, and it is possible to leave it there for a long time. There are lockers in many places, but they are only large enough for smaller bags.

LANGUAGE AND COMMUNICATION

Czechoslovakia has two official languages, Czech, spoken in Bohemia and Moravia, and Slovak, spoken in Slovakia. They are both Slav languages, and Czechs and Slovaks can understand each other. They have a similar relationship to each other as Norwegian, Swedish and Danish do, and probably grew apart because the two parts of the country had different foreign rulers for such a long time.

Hungarian is spoken in parts of southern Slovakia, Polish in Český Těšín and a small area around it, German by some in West Bohemia and a few older people in the Spis region, and Ruthenian (a sort of Ukrainian with a strong Slovak influence) by some people in East Slovakia. In regions of Slovakia with a very large minority group, the language of that group can also be used officially, a fact that Slovak nationalists protest against.

As far as foreign languages are concerned, German is fairly widely understood in the western part of the country, but rather less so the farther east and the farther from the tourist spots one goes. Russian is the main foreign language in the east, and Slovak is closer to Russian than Czech is, but you may not be popular if you approach people in Russian. Russian is more commonly understood amongst young people throughout Czechoslovakia, because it was a compulsory subject in school under the Communists.

Neither English nor French are commonly understood, particularly in the east and away from the main centres. But don't let this put you off. Some travellers have written that a knowledge of German is necessary. This assumption comes from an attitude among many English-speaking people that if another person doesn't speak the same language, communication is impossible. But the problem is in approach, rather than language *per se*. With a bit of ingenuity and a phrasebook and dictionary, you can get by on a practical level (deep political discussions are another question!). Learn from the Italians who can communicate with their arms alone. If asking for directions, have a map to ease communication, or if you don't have one, hand the person you ask paper and pencil so they can draw one for you instead of giving you instructions you don't understand. If you want to know where the square is, show someone the word in a dictionary, then point around with a questioning look on your face. If you are looking for somewhere to sleep rest your head on one side on your hands. Try and learn a few useful words in Czech, Slovak or German — in any case you'll find you pick some up along the way. The expensive hotels in the main tourist places usually have staff that can speak English. Since 1990 Russian has no longer been compulsory in school and the free choice between English, German, French and Spanish, has led to more pupils learning English. In the late 1980s there was a comeback in English, especially in the larger cities, and helped by the advent of computers. A lot of Czechs speak German, and a lot of Germans speak English, so Germans can be useful interpreters.

Certain English words are regularly used wrongly in "Czech and Slovak English", eg when someone says "tourist" they mean tramper (hiker), "your" means his or hers, "the wonderful achievements of socialism" used to refer to anything built after 1948. There is now even a book addressing itself to this problem (*English or Czenglish?*, Don Sparling, Státní pedagogické nakladatelství, Kčs 19).

Most English speaking people find Czech a very difficult language. One difficulty is the strings of consonants sometimes encountered. Once you can say the following tongue-twister, you can consider yourself pretty good at Czech: *Strč prst skrz krk*, which means "Thrust finger down throat". And this doesn't even contain the hardest letter of all for English speakers: *ř*, which is pronounced something like "rzh". Czech grammar is incredibly complicated compared to English. Slovak is more mellow than Czech. Most of what you pick up of Czech you can use in Slovakia, and vice versa. You'll quickly discover what is different.

It is useful to have a phrase-book before you arrive in Czechoslovakia, so you can begin to prepare. If you can get hold of it (it is available in some bookstores in England at least), I recommend you buy a copy of *Say it in Czech* by Alois Krušina, published in Prague in 1963 by the State Pedagogical Publishing House, (UK price: £2.50). It is written for English-speaking people, and has a mass of useful phrases and a detailed pronunciation section. *Travellers' Czech* published by Collets in Britain or Orion in Prague is more compact than the above, but is not as thorough. If you want to get into more depth, try *Colloquial Czech* by James Naughton and published by Routledge in London and New York in 1987. There should also be a book called *Basic Slovak*, but I've never been able to find it. Try asking around in Bratislava if you are interested.

Czech-English and Slovak-English dictionaries are sold in Czechoslovakia: *Anglicko-Český a Česko-Anglický Kapesní Slovník* (English-Czech, Czech-English Pocket Dictionary), by Dr Karel Hais, Statni pedagogické nakladatelství, Praha (ie the same publishers as *Say it in Czech*), 1974, Kčs 30; *Anglicko-Slovenský Slovensko-Anglický Vreckový Slovník* (English-Slovak, Slovak-English Pocket Dictionary) published in 1984 by Slovenské pedagogické nakladateľvo, Bratislava, Kčs 26. These dictionaries are useful for translating signs, menus etc, and for looking up words when trying to communicate with people, but they are not quite as pocket-size as their names would suggest.

A Czech/English, English/Czech dictionary has been published by Hippocrene (the US distributors of this book) and is available in England through Bradt Publications. There was such an increase in interest in learning English after the Velvet Revolution, dictionaries were unobtainable in 1990, so it might pay to buy this one before you travel.

Slav languages bear no resemblance to English, though the odd borrowed word is recognisable for the English-speaker. There is at least one word that English has borrowed from Czech: "robot". It means to work, make or do. Karel Čapek first used the word in his writing, and English borrowed it from him.

THE GLOBETROTTERS CLUB

An international club which aims to share information on adventurous budget travel through monthly meetings and *Globe* magazine. Published every two months, *Globe* offers a wealth of information, from reports of members' latest adventures to recent travel bargains and tips, plus the invaluable 'Mutual Aid' column where members can swap a house, sell a camper, find a travel companion or offer information on unusual places or hospitality to visiting members.

London meetings are held monthly (Saturdays) and focus on a particular country or continent with illustrated talks.

Enquiries to: The Secretary, Globetrotters Club, BCM/Roving, London WC1N 3XX.

Notes on the Czech alphabet:
"č" comes after "c"
"ch" comes after "h"
"ř" comes after "r"
"š" comes after "s"
"ž" comes after "z"
The same holds true for Slovak, except that there is no "ř" in Slovak.

Notes on pronunciation
"c" = ts, "č" = ch, "š" = sh, "ř" = rzh, "r" is rolled, "ž" = je, as in the French "Je t'aime".
Stress normally comes on the first syllable of a word, or if the word is preceded by a preposition, on the preposition.

Some words and expressions

Czech	Slovak	English
Ahoj	*Ahoj*	General informal greeting and goodbye (comes from English.)
Dobrý den	*Dobrý deň*	How do you do (more formal greeting)
Dobrý večer	*Dobrý večer*	Good evening
Dobrou noc	*Dobrú noc*	Good night (on going to bed)
Sbohem	*Zbohem*	Good-bye (literally means "go with God" — not used so much now)
Na shledanou	*Do videnia*	Rather like the French "au revoir" (difficult to translate to English)
Ne	*Nie*	No
Prosím	*Prosím*	Please
Děkuji	*Ďakujem*	Thank you
Ejakuji	*Éjakujem*	Ejaculate (so be careful how you pronounce thank you!)
Díky	*Ďekju*	Thanks
Děkuji pěkná	*Ďakujem pekne*	Thank you very much
Mluvíte anglicky?	*Hovoríte po anglicky?*	Do you speak English?
Kde?	*Kde?*	Where?
Kde je autobus do. . . ?		Where is the bus to. . . ?
Vlak	*Vlak*	Train
Nádraží	*Stanica*	Station
Tramvaj	*Električka*	Tram
Náměstí	*Námestie*	Square (in a town)
Pošta	*Pošta*	Post office
Hlavní pošta	*Hlavná pošta*	Main post office
Banka	*Banka*	Bank
Směnárna	*Zmenáreň*	Exchange (money)
Potraviny	*Potraviny*	Grocer's
Knihy	*Knihy*	Books
Lékárna	*Lekáreň*	Chemist
Nemám	*Nemán*	I have not (common response when you ask for something in a shop)

Zítra	*Zajtra*	Tomorrow
Vcera	*Vcera*	Yesterday
Pozor	*Pozor*	Look out (a warning sign)
Hranice	*Hranice*	Border (beware when you see a sign with this on it. It may mean it is a border area you are not allowed to enter)
Máte tu volno	*Máte tu voľné*	What you say if you want to ask if a seat is free in a bus, train or restaurant (it is normal practice to ask before you sit down in such situations in Czechoslovakia)
Pitná voda	*Pitná voda*	Drinking water
Nepitná voda	*Nepitná voda*	Non-drinking water

Numbers

Note that Czech and Slovak have three genders — masculine (m), feminine (f) and neuter (n).

	Czech	Slovak
1	jeden (m), jedna (f), jedno (n).	
2	dva (m), dvě (f, n)	
3	tři	tri
4	čtyři	štyri
5	pět	päť
6	šest	šesť
7	sedm	sedem
8	osm	osem
9	devět	deväť
10	deset	desať
11	jedenáct	jedenásť
12	dvanáct	dvanásť
13	třináct	trinásť
14	čtrnáct	štrnásť
15	patnáct	pätnásť
16	šestnáct	šestnásť
17	sedmnáct	sedemnásť
18	osmnáct	osemnásť
19	devatenáct	devätnásť
20	dvacet	dvadsať
21	dvacetjedna	
22	dvacetdva	
100	sto	sto
200	dvě stě	
300	tři sta	
400	čtyři sta	
500	pět set	
1000	tisíc	tisíc

For food see the *Food and Drink* section. Other words and phrases are mentioned under the appropriate sections of the book.

I have used anglicized names where these names are in common English usage (eg Czechoslovakia, Bohemia, Slovakia and Prague). Otherwise I have used the correct Czech or Slovak names. Note that while in English we write Charles Bridge, October Square etc, in Czech and Slovak one writes Karlův most, Októberové námestie etc – ie in names such words as bridge and square do not (with some exceptions) have a capital letter.

TRAVELLING TO AND FROM CZECHOSLOVAKIA

Czechoslovakia is easily accessible by air, rail and road. Czechoslovakia has two international airports, one in Prague and one in Bratislava. There is also a customs post in Bratislava for those entering Czechoslovakia by boat on the Danube.

The following is given as a guide, but bear in mind that things change, and fares tend to go up. If purchasing a ticket from Czechoslovakia to any other country, including east European countries, you must pay in western currency. To purchase student fares an ISIC (International Student Identity Card) is normally required.

By air

Czechoslovakia has its own national airline, ČSA, which has a network stretching west as far as North America and Mexico, and east as far as Indonesia. In some countries it is possible to buy very cheap ČSA tickets from travel agents (eg in Singapore). In others they are sold for full price only (eg Czechoslovakia itself). Many other airlines also fly to Czechoslovakia. The following fares are *not* the same if you buy your ticket in Prague, and are subject to change.

From London

From London (Heathrow) there is a direct flight to Prague with either British Airways, ČSA or both every day. Flying time is about two hours. An ordinary one way fare costs £251, return £502, and the ticket is valid for one year.

The Eurobudget Economy Fare is £211 single, £422 return. You must book and pay at the same time, and cannot change the booking without paying the difference between this fare and a normal full fare. There is a 20% cancellation charge.

PEX (public excursion) fares are much cheaper: £222 return in the low season; about £254 return from July 1 to September 30. It is not necessary to purchase PEX tickets in advance, but availability is limited at some periods of the year. Full payment must be made on booking, outward and homeward journey must be booked, reservations cannot be altered and no refund is possible. The period in Czechoslovakia must include at least one night between Saturday and Sunday, and must not be longer than three months.

APEX fares are cheaper again at £194 return. Apart from the fact that tickets must be purchased at least two weeks before departure, the restrictions are the same as for PEX fares.

Student fares cost between about £182 and £253. It can be worth trying student travel companies even if you are not a student. For example in 1990 Campus Travel had a return ticket for £167 available to anyone. Youth fares for those over two and under 26 years old cost £108 one way, £216 return. Bookings cannot be made earlier than 24 hours before departure. You must pay and reserve at the same time, and can't change your booking or get a refund, even if there are medical grounds.

There are connections to other centres in Britain. London is one of the world's best cities to buy discounted air tickets, and although Prague is not a popular destination you could try the back street travel agents.

From Scandinavia

From Copenhagen their are eight flights a week, but there is not a flight every day. The cheapest return air tickets are APEX, which must be bought 14 days in advance and cost Dkr 2485 including tax. For those under 25 there are youth tickets for Dkr 1618 if you book the outward trip same day or the day before. The return leg is open, and must be booked in Prague the day before.

The same types of tickets with the same restrictions are sold from Oslo and Stockholm, and flights from these cities are via Copenhagen. From Oslo APEX return tickets cost Nkr 2825 and youth tickets Nkr 2160, and from Stockholm Skr 2985 and Skr 2280 respectively.

From North America

An ordinary return ticket from New York to Prague costs US$1848, and a one month excursion ticket US$1248. This means that it is much cheaper to take advantage of one of the cheap deals available to London or another European city, and so continue on to Czechoslovakia from there.

A one way full price ticket from Montreal to Prague costs C$1,611. Shop around for something cheaper, remembering that it might prove cheaper to fly to another European destination and travel on to Czechoslovakia from there. It might even pay to go to New York and make use of the cheap flights from there to Europe.

From Southeast Asia

In Singapore cheap ČSA tickets can be bought at Airmaster, 36-G Prinsep Street, Singapore 0718 and some other travel agents — eg a ticket to London, with a stopover in Prague, so that you could travel around Czechoslovakia, then fly on to Britain afterwards, costs about S$700 (£230).

To Berlin

Full price tickets between Prague and Berlin with ČSA costs DM218. 75 one way or DM439.50 return. One month excursion fares cost DM315.50 return. It's best to book a week ahead, but it's possible to get a seat the day before.

By rail

Czechoslovakia is connected with the international European railway system. There are frequent trains on the route Berlin-Dresden-Prague-Bratislava-Budapest, with some continuing to Romania and Bulgaria, but there are also regular trains from western Europe (eg Paris-Frankfurt am Main-Prague). From Scandinavia there is a new direct train from Sweden in summer and plans for one from Denmark – otherwise you must change trains in Berlin.

Other lesser known international routes are: Dresden to Košice via northern Czechoslovakia including Poprad; and Berlin-Leipzig-Karlovy Vary.

From Britain you travel via Dover-Ostende and must change trains, in Germany. You can for example catch a train leaving Victoria Station in London at about 1.00pm daily and arrive in Prague at about 5.00pm the next day, having changed trains in Mainz or in Cologne and Frankfurt.

Another route is via Hoek v. Holland with changes in Amsterdam, Cologne and Nürnberg. For fares and times you could contact one of the following: European Rail Travel Centre, PO Box 303, Victoria Station, London SW1V 1JY (tel. 071-834 2345); European Rail Passenger Office, Room E211, Departure Side Offices, Paddington Station, London W2 1FT; or Thomas Cook.

From 1990 Inter-Rail was valid in Czechoslovakia. This pass gives one month's unlimited travel in most European countries. To buy an Inter-Rail pass you must (in theory anyway) have been resident in one of the countries in which it is valid for the last six month, and for travel in your home country pay 50% of the normal ticket price. It is now available for all ages, costing about £235 for adults, and £155 for those under 26. Eurorail is not valid in Czechoslovakia.

Youth fares for those under 26 are available from many countries. From London Eurotrain tickets to Prague cost £70 one way or £135 return while a Eurotrain Eastern Explorer (London-Amsterdam-Berlin-Prague-Budapest-Vienna-Salzburg-Zurich-Luxembourg-Brussels-London) costs £172.50.

Students travelling to Czechoslovakia from another east European country can get discounted tickets. Discount varies between about 25% and 50%.

In Czechoslovakia international train tickets must normally be bought at Čedok and paid for in convertible currency, but you can pay as far as the border in Czechoslovak currency. Some international tickets are available from some stations. When leaving Czechoslovakia it is much cheaper and simpler to buy a ticket to the border at a railway station, paying in Czechoslovak crowns, and then buy a ticket for the rest of the trip from the conductor.

When buying international train tickets in Czechoslovakia, there are two different price structures, one for tickets to destinations in east European countries, and one for destinations in west European countries. It is much cheaper to buy a ticket to a destination in eastern Europe, and what's more it is cheaper *per kilometre*. So if you are travelling to the West via another east European country, the answer is to buy two tickets. Buy a ticket to the point you will leave eastern Europe. Then buy a ticket from there or from the conductor to where you are actually going. If you are a student, this also means you can get a student price on the first ticket (there are no student prices to the West).

International train tickets sold in Czechoslovakia are valid for two months. This means that you can stop as often as you like between the station you bought the ticket from and your final destination, as long as you complete your journey within two months.

It is possible to send baggage ahead to the West, but it is very expensive.

By road

From Britain there are a multitude of possible routes to Czechoslovakia by road. One of the simplest routes to follow is via Belgium and West Germany: take the Dover-Ostende ferry (3¾ hours); then drive to Nürnberg via Brussels, Cologne and Frankfurt; from Nürnberg the E 50 leads directly to Prague via Plzeň. London to Prague is about 1300km (about 800 miles) by road. For information on what documents you need and on driving in Czechoslovakia see section *Getting Around in Czechoslovakia*.

Since the Velvet Revolution many new international bus services have begun operation. There are bus services to Czechoslovakia from Britain, Germany, Austria, Finland, Sweden, Denmark, Hungary, Switzerland and Italy but many don't run very frequently, and some are seasonal. Many of them run to Prague or to spas or tourist resorts. Although they don't run as often as trains, they are generally cheaper. The Czechoslovak agents for most of these buses is Bohemiatour, Praha 1, Zlatnická 7, tel. 23 12 589 or 23 53 877.

There are now two weekly bus services from London to Prague. The state bus company, ČSAD, has a service via Brussells costing £50 one way or £95 return from London or a bit under half that price from Brussells. It leaves from outside the Czechoslovak embassy in London on Saturday at 6.30pm arriving at Florence bus station in Prague at 7.00pm the next evening. From Prague it leaves Wednesday at 5.30pm arriving in London at 4.00pm the next day. For information in Britain phone (071) 5870955. Kingscourt Express, a private company, run the other service, and tickets cost £45 or Kčs 2400 one way and £83.50 or Kčs 4380 return. Their bus departs from Victoria Coach Station, London on Saturday evening, with the return trip leaving Prague on Friday from Švermovy sady near Florenc. They are expecting to begin operating twice weekly in summer 1991. For information in Britain call (0860) 791 754. Their Prague address is Poleškova 93, Praha 10, tel. 75 24 22.

From Germany there is a service from the main railway station in Munich to Plzeň (bus station) and Prague (Florence bus station) stopping for passengers at the railway stations in Regensburg, Cham, and Furth i. W. Tickets from Munich to Prague cost DM57 one way or DM102 return and to Plzeň DM43 and DM78 respectively. The bus leaves both ends at 9.00am and takes about eight hours. For information, tickets and reservations in Munich contact Autobus Oberbayern GmbH, 8 – Munich 2, Lenbachplatz 1, tel. (089) 558061. There is a weekly night bus service from Hamburg to Prague via Berlin leaving the central bus station in Hamburg at 8.00pm on Wednesday, Hotel Stadt Berlin at 12.30am Thursday and arriving at ul. Na Florenci in Prague at 6.15am Thursday morning. The return trip leaves Prague at 8.00pm on Tuesday, arriving in Berlin at 2.00am and Hamburg at 6.45am Wednesday. Fares from Hamburg are Kčs 570 one way or Kčs 1050 return, and from Berlin Kčs 300 one way or Kčs 550 return. There is a seasonal Munich-Piešťany-Trenčianske Teplice service.

There is a weekly night bus service from Zürich to Prague which also takes passengers from Stuttgart and Nürnberg. It leaves from Ausstellungstr. (about 200m from the main station) in Zürich at 7.00pm on Saturday and Florenc bus station in Prague at 6.00pm Friday and takes 25 hours. Single fares are Kčs 550 from Zürich, Kčs 400 from Stuttgart and Kčs 250 from Nürnberg.

Wasatrafik have a weekly bus service from Stockholm to Prague, via Norrköping, Jönköping, Helsingborg, Malmö, Trelleborg and Sassnitz. It leaves Stockholm at 7.30am on Fridays and Prague at 8.45pm Saturdays and takes about 25 hours. The Prague agents for this bus are Čedok, not Bohemiatour.

DSB and Pan Bus began a night bus service from Copenhagen to Prague in late 1990, leaving Copenhagen Thursday and departing from Prague on Saturday. The only scheduled stop is Nykøbing-Falster, and the fare from both Copenhagen and Nykøbing is Dkr 435 one way. Smoking is allowed on Pan's buses, but not on DSB's. Being a new service it may change depending on its success. From summer 1991 a Czech bus will join the route, departing Prague Monday evening and departing Copenhagen Tuesday evening, and the route will be extended to Vienna. The operators plan these further developments if they can get the necessary permits: to have stops in Berlin and Dresden; for Pan to drive direct from Jylland, instead of via Copenhagen, and to continue to Brno and Bratislava, with the timetables synchronised with the bus form Copenhagen so that it will be possible to change buses for onward travel in Prague. Information in Prague from Bohemiatour, and in Denmark from DSB Rejsebureau, Pan Bus (Vestergade 16, 8800 Viborg, tel. 86 62 58 77) or by phoning 31 16 66 33.

There were some bus services between Poland and Czechoslovakia, but after the advent of Solidarity Czechoslovaks were no longer allowed to travel as individuals to Poland, so these services were suspended. Where there is no service between the two countries, it is usually possible to get a local bus to one side of the border, walk over, then continue in another local bus.

There are many bus services between Hungary and Slovakia. In summer there are buses between Yugoslavia and Czechoslovakia.

There are various bus services between Vienna and Czechoslovakia. A daily service to Prague costs US$28. For the Vienna to Bratislava service see under Bratislava. From Vienna to Brno via Mikulov takes three hours, costs about ÖS200, and is run by ČSAD and Post-u. Telegraphendirektion, Wien. ČSAD also run a weekly service from Vienna to Piešťany (ÖS200) and Trenčianske Teplice (ÖS260).

Hitchhiking over the border is not all that easy, though it's possibly improved now that citizens of Czechoslovakia's neighbouring countries no longer require visas. If you have a visa and are hitchhiking out of the country, make sure you don't get stuck and finish up overstaying your visa. People do try hitching the relatively short hop between Vienna and Bratislava, but even that is not very easy. Even being on an "E" road or a thick line on the map won't necessarily guarantee you much traffic over the border. I've tried hitching in on the E 55 via Salzburg and Linz in Austria for example. It has less and less traffic as you near the border, and I eventually had to catch a bus to the border post at Wullowitz, to be greeted by rather amazed Austrian customs officials ("Who'd want to come all the way from New Zealand to walk into Czechoslovakia at a God forsaken place like this?"). Then a long walk over no man's land, past beautiful raspberries which I was too afraid to pick because I was being watched by Czechoslovak border guards (this was 1983), to the Czechoslovak control. This is one possibility on this route. Otherwise catch the train before the railway and the road part company.

By boat

In summer there is a boat service between Budapest and Bratislava on the Danube. It takes 3½ hours downstream (towards Budapest) and 4¼ hours upstream. There is also a hydrofoil service between Vienna and Bratislava (ÖS 115 one way). In Vienna get tickets from DDSG on the Danube at Handelskaj 235, Vienna 1020. The boat is often booked up with package tours, when the only way you can get on it as an individual is to ask the captain if he can take you when he is in port. It leaves Bratislava at 5.00pm daily. It's not as nice a trip as it may sound, as it's a fast, closed-in boat.

Tours

Čedok has a wide range of tours. From Britain most of Čedok London's tours fly to Czechoslovakia, although the odd trip uses coach transport and they also have packages for those travelling in their own car. Some sample tours offered by them are: 2 weeks grand tour by air to Czechoslovakia, then coach, about £450; Prague and Karlovy Vary, 1 week, about £340; Prague and Slovakia 1 week by air, about £330; all with hotel and half board. Čedok also arrange more specialised tours, eg for those interested in music, castles or skiing. (See *Information* for Čedok's addresses.)

I will be organising tours myself according to demand, so please write to me (c/o Bradt Publications) telling what your interests are and enclosing an international postal reply coupon. I can organise tours to Prague and the

main attractions of Czechoslovakia, but I am also keen on organising them to more out-of-the-way places and to mountain areas.

Other companies offering tours from Britain are Regent Holidays, Thomson Holidays (skiing tours to the Tatry by charter aircraft), Sovereign (British Airways) Holidays (Prague), Saga, Wallace Arnold, Cosmos, Global, Trafalgar, Miki Travel, Insight, International, Creative Tours, Ohshu Express and Harry Shaw Travel.

Other established Czechoslovak travel agents are not very interested in dealing with individuals. Rekrea (Czech) and Tatratour (Slovak, and the second largest travel agent in ČSFR) are cooperatives, and deal mostly with hotels in the middle price bracket, while Čedok deal more with the higher price bracket. Sport-Turist (Czech) and Slovakoturist (Slovak) specialise in arranging tours for sports teams. They can organise training camps including matches with local teams if required. Sport-Turist's address is Národní 33, 112 93 Praha 1, tlf. 26 33 51, telex 122664. Slovakoturist's is Volgogradská 1, 816 15 Bratislava, telex 92321. Since the Velvet Revolution many new travel agencies have opened.

Border crossings

The following border crossings are open to foreigners. They are listed in clockwise order, starting from the meeting point of the German, Austrian and Czechoslovak borders. The numbers refer to numbers on the map. The border crossings are often at small villages with names most people are unfamiliar with, so nearby larger towns or main centres are in brackets to help with orientation. All crossings are open 24 hours, unless mentioned otherwise. The only four crossings where it is possible to obtain a visa at the border are marked with an asterisk, though there is talk of allowing this at some other crossings.

New border crossings are being opened, but at the time of writing these and any other crossings I don't mention were open only for citizens of Czechoslovakia and the neighbouring country in question. Some of the new ones are open for cars, and some pedestrians only (eg between two villages or in mountain areas). There are plans to open these walking crossing points to all citizens. Work is underway to reopen old closed rail crossings, but this will take some time due to having to lay the tracks again.

Rail

With Germany

1.	Domažlice	Furth im Walde
2.	Cheb	Schirnding (main line: Prague-Nürnberg)
3.	Vojtanov	Bad Brambach
4.	Děčín	Bad Schandau (main line: Prague-Berlin)
5.	Hrádek nad Nisou	Zittau

With Poland

6.	Lichkov	Miedzylesie
7.	Petrovice u Karviné	Zebrzudowice (near Ostrava)
8.	Plaveč	Muszyna

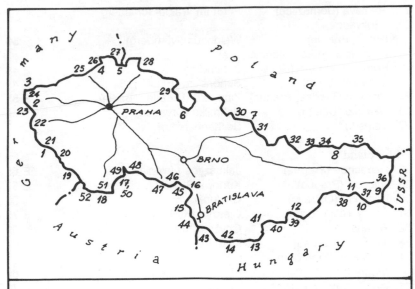

Czechoslovakia

– BORDER CROSSINGS

With USSR
9. Čierna nad Tisou   Čop

With Hungary
10. Slovenské Nové Mesto   Sátoraljaújhely
11. Čaňa   Hidasnémeti
12. Fiľakovo   Somosköújfalu
13. Štúrovo   Szob
14. Komárno   Komárom

With Austria
15. Devínska Nová Ves   Marchegg (Bratislava-Vienna)
16. Břeclav   Hohenau (Brno-Vienna)
17. České Velenice   Gmünd-Schiel
18. Horní Dvořiště   Summerau

Road

ČSFR control	Foreign control	Road number
With Germany		
19. Strážný (Strakonice)	Philippsreut (Passau)	4
20. Železné Ruda (Klatovy)	Bayerisch Eisenstein (München)	E 53, 27

21. Folmava (Domažlice)   Furth im Walde-Schafberg
22. *Rozvadov
    (Plzeň, Prague)   Waidhaus (Nürnberg)   E 50
    (there is a photo machine here)
23. Pomezi nad Ohří (Cheb)   Schirnding   E 48
24. Vojtanov (Cheb)   Schönberg (Plauen)   E 49
25. Cinovec (Teplice, Prague) Zinnwald (Dresden, Berlin)   E 55
26. Hřensko (Děčín)   Schmilka (Dresden)
27. Varnsdorf   Seifhennersdorf

With Poland
28. Harrachov (Prague)   Jakuszyce (Jelenia Góra)   E 65
29. Náchod (Prague)   Kudowa Slone (Wrocław)   E 67
30. Bohumín (Ostrava)   Chalupki   58
31. Český Těšín (Brno)   Cieszyn (Kraków)   E 75
32. Trstená   Chyžne (Kraków)   E 77, 59
33. Javorina (Poprad)   Łysa Polana (Zakopane)   67
34. Mníšek n. Popradom
    (Poprad)   Piwniczna (Nowy Sacz)   89
35. Vyšný Komárnik (Prešov)   Barwinek   73

With USSR
36. Vyšné Nemecké (Košice)   Užgorod   E 50
    (open April 1-Sept. 30: 8.00am-10.00pm,
    Oct. 1-March 31: 7.00am-9.00pm)

With Hungary
37. Slovenské Nové Mesto   Sátoraljaújhely
38. Hraničná pri Hornáde
    (Košice)   Hidasnémeti (Miskolc)   E 71
39. Šiatorská Bukovinka   Somoskóújfalu
40. Slovenské Ďarmoty   Balassagyarmat
41. Šahy (Banská Bystrica)   Parassapuszta (Budapest)   E 77
42. Komárno   Komárom
43. Rusovce (Bratislava)   Rajka (Györ)   E 75, E 65

With Austria
44. *Bratislava-Petržalka   Berg (Vienna)   E 58
45. Mikulov (Brno)   Drasenhofen (Vienna)   E 461
46. Hevlín   Laa an der Thaya
47. *Hatě (Znojmo)   Klein Haugsdorf (Vienna)   E 59
48. Nová Bystřice
    (Jindřichův Hradec)   Grametten
    (Open April 1-Sept. 30: 7.00am-11.00pm,
    Oct. 1-March 31: 6.00am-10.00pm.)
49. Halámky (Třeboň)   Neu Nagelberg
50. České Velenice   Gmünd-Schiel (Vienna)   E 49
    (Open April 1-Sept. 30: 9.00am-12.00am & 3.00pm-7.00pm,
    Oct. 1-March 31: 8.00am-11.00am & 2.00pm-6.00pm.)

51. *Dolní Dvořiště
    (České Budějovice)   Wullowitz (Linz)   E 55
52. Studánky u V. Brodu
    (Vyšší Brod)   Weigetschlag (Leonfeldon)
    (Open April 1-Sept. 30: 7.00am-11.00pm,
    Oct. 1-March 31: 8.00am-8.00pm.)

GETTING AROUND IN CZECHOSLOVAKIA
Public transport

Czechoslovakia has a good, cheap, public transport network. The backbone of it is provided by rail and bus routes, but there is also a domestic air service and the occasional ferry service.

Timetables are displayed at all bus stops and railway stations. It is possible to buy timetables if you want to lug them around with you. New timetables are usually issued annually, so it is possible that there have been changes, but this book should be a good guide. There tends to be a lull in public transport in what is late morning by Czechoslovak standards, ie between about 9.00am and 11.00am, so it pays to make an early start.

Arrivals = *příjezd* (Cz.) = *príchod* (Sl.)
Departures = *odjezd* (Cz.) = *odchod* (Sl.).

As a general rule trains are cheaper than buses. The exception can be with fast (*rychlík*) trains, where you pay a set surcharge no matter what the distance. If your choice is between using these trains for a *short* distance or using a bus, the bus may well be cheaper. Trains are more comfortable when travelling longer distances.

When you have luggage it is much easier to travel by train, as you can take your luggage in with you and there is plenty of room for it. Buses have storage for luggage underneath, but on short distance buses the driver won't normally open the luggage compartment, while on long distance buses they often force you to put all your luggage underneath, including your treasured photographic equipment etc.

It is normal practice to ask if a seat is free in a bus or train, before sitting down next to someone (see *Some words and expressions*).

Whether you travel by train, bus or city transport doesn't make any difference — you'll get pretty filthy from the dust and dirt.

By train

Trains are operated by ČSD, the Czechoslovak state railways.
Train = *vlak*
Reservation = *místenka*
Sleeper = *lůžko*
Couchette = *lehátko*

There are ordinary trains (*osobní*) and fast trains (*rychlík*) or the even faster *expres*, which stop at very few stations. There is no smoking in *osobní* trains. *Rychlík* and *expres* are shown in red on notices. Another type of train that is not so common is *spěšný*. These are trains to mountain areas which are faster than the normal trains. They miss some of the many stations found in these areas, and stop a shorter time at others.

Although Czechoslovakia is an "east-west" country, the railways often tend to run in a north-south direction, reflecting the period of foreign rule during which they were built.

Train tickets are normally valid until the end of the day after you buy them. If the ticket is for more than 200km, it is valid for three days (the dated day is counted as the first day, and it is valid until midnight on the third day). This means that you can stop along the way during this period of time.

Fares are very reasonable, and although they have recently doubled, recent changes in the exchange rate mean you receive twice as much Czechoslovak currency for your foreign money, making the relative price the same. The uncertainty over what will happen with fares means that I unfortunately have had to stop listing specific fares as in the first edition. There are standard surcharges for *expres*, *rychlík* and *spěšný* no matter what the distance, and expres train fares are the same as *rychlík*. First class fares are 50% higher than second class, but are not available on some trains, particularly small local ones. If you are a student, and are entering from another east European country, you can buy all your tickets there at student price. No student discount is available on domestic train tickets once you enter Czechoslovakia.

Tickets are normally bought at the station, but in the case of unmanned stations, you pay the conductor. If you don't buy your ticket at a manned station, it will cost both a reprimand and extra money on the train. Advance reservations are compulsory on some trains, optional on some, and not available on others. Reservations can be made at a station, or for an extra charge, at Čedok.

Domestic sleepers are available only on trains travelling over 300km. International sleepers are booked at Čedok, not at railway stations. First class compartments sleep two, second class sleep three, and couchette compartments sleep five. If you haven't managed to book a sleeper, you can try asking the staff in the sleeping cars if there is any space left, but don't get your hopes up.

Symbols from train timetables
First find the route number on the map of the railways, then the timetable for that route. *Rychlík* and *expres* trains are printed in red or heavy print.

◻ = tickets issued on train only at that station. Luggage checked or received on train.
✕ = dining car
☉ = train doesn't wait for any connections
D = carriage for passengers with children up to 10 years old
☎ = border station with customs and passport control
(☎) = border station with customs and passport control in the train
◊ = can't check in luggage
⊠ = can't check in luggage, prams possible as hand luggage
◯ = see notes
Ⓡ = seat reservation necessary (Kčs 40 fine if don't have)

⟨b⟩R⟨r⟩= seat reservation necessary for the indicated carriages
🛏 = sleeping car
🛏 = couchette carriage, 2nd class only unless otherwise indicated
| = train doesn't stop here [thin line in middle of column]
◖ = setting down only
◗ = picking up only
> = (before a time) means train runs certain days or periods only
1 = Monday
2 = Tuesday
    etc.
L = summer
Z = winter
✕ = working days
† = holidays
N = last day of rest before working day
P = first working day following a holiday
S = Saturday except holiday
A = last working day before "S" or holiday

By bus

The excellent bus service is operated by ČSAD. Since the first edition of this book, many new long distance bus routes have started, and these are often faster than trains, especially when they run via motorways. But these services get very full on Friday and Sunday afternoons and evenings. One problem with bus services is that they are organised on a district basis, so services between districts may be sparse or non-existent, especially on country roads. For example, if two neighbouring villages happen to lie in different districts, there may be no, or only a very infrequent, bus service between them.

(Although there should be timetables displayed at all stops, bored people sometimes peel them off.) Villages in Czechoslovakia were grouped so one village has medical and other services for all the villages in the area. Timetables use the same grouping, creating problems for travellers, because the village you want might well be listed under another village. The problems are compounded by the fact that villages now have the right to leave these groupings if they wish. Bus timetables are published in a series of books under regions, but if one region runs a bus which enters another region, the timetable will be shown only in the book of the region which owns the bus. It is also possible to buy one book for all of the long-distance buses in Slovakia. I feel they are too heavy to carry around.

Unlike trains, with buses in Czechoslovakia you cannot break your journey. Even if you have to change buses along the way, you need a new ticket.

Normally tickets are bought from the driver, but on some routes prior reservations are possible, and on certain routes, particularly in peak periods, they are advisable.

Fares increased 50% in late 1990. They are calculated according to tariff zones, based on distance. There is no extra charge for *rychlík* buses, but there is for express buses on the Prague-Brno-Bratislava route. You may get charged extra for luggage — it depends on the driver. In my experience this was the case only occasionally in Slovakia, but usually in Bohemia and Moravia.

Symbols from bus timetables
Workday = Monday to Friday
Holiday = Sundays and Public Holidays
X   =   workdays
b   =   workdays and Saturdays
g   =   daily except Saturday
a   =   Saturdays and holidays
V   =   work day before a Saturday or holiday
S   =   Saturday
+   =   holidays
N   =   holiday preceding a workday
P   =   workday after holiday
c   =   schooldays
w   =   not July-August, nor Xmas-New Year period
h   =   school holidays
y   =   daily except workdays after holidays
d   =   daily except "V"
•   =   priority to pupils
r   =   not 24/12 and 31/12
k   =   not Xmas and 30/3
L   =   summer
Z   =   winter
A   =   on work day before Saturday or holiday
1   =   Monday
2   =   Tuesday
3   =   Wednesday
4   =   Thursday
5   =   Friday
6   =   Saturday
7   =   Sunday
Ⓡ   =   reservation possible
R̄   =   reservation necessary
| instead of a time means the bus goes past that stop.
<   =   the bus goes in another direction (it doesn't pass that stop)
◖   =   alighting only at that stop
◗   =   boarding only.
x   instead of a time means that the bus stops if signalled or requested
MHD   means that the stop is located in the area of mass urban transportation
        (ie local city buses etc).

Local transport
Public transport in towns is provided by trams, buses, and, in Prague, the metro. Tickets cost Kčs 1 (from April 1st tickets will increase to Kčs 4), and must be purchased beforehand at a PNS kiosk or from a machine. You punch them yourself as you enter the tram or bus or metro. At the moment a 7-day travel past costs 3034 kr but this will also increase after 1 April. Once

when I was checked, I was told I should have an extra ticket for my luggage. The same tickets are used on all forms of transport, but if you change buses or trams you need a new ticket. Tickets from one town are valid only in that town. This is a fact that has been criticised for years, but nothing has been done about it.

Taxis are also available, but the drivers are unlikely to speak English and, especially in Prague, are likely to rip you off.

By air

Domestic air services are operated by ČSA. There are services to Prague, Bratislava, Piešťany, Poprad, and Košice. In winter there should not be much problem getting a seat, but in summer it's best to book one week in advance. There is a 20kg free luggage allowance, with excess baggage at 1% of the ticket price per extra kilo.

By motor vehicle

Check with your local automobile association for up to date information before driving to Czechoslovakia.

Documents, insurance and accidents

UK and many other drivers' licences are accepted but some nationalities may require an international driving licence. You must have the vehicle's original registration papers with you. If the driver is not the owner of the car, he/she must have the owners' written permission attested by an automobile association. Insurance documents must be produced upon entry to Czechoslovakia. The licence plates of motor vehicles from the following countries are recognised as valid insurance documents, along with the green card: Austria, Belgium, Denmark, Finland, West Germany, Ireland, Italy, Luxembourg, Liechtenstein, Netherlands, Norway, Sweden, Switzerland, the UK and Yugoslavia. If a driver cannot show he has insurance cover for the time he will be in Czechoslovakia, he must purchase Czechoslovak insurance. The police must be notified of all accidents, and damages inflicted to foreign drivers in car accidents must also be notified to Kancelář zákonného pojištění motorových vozidel na území ČSSR, Praha 1, Spálená 14. Contact ČSP, Dept Pojištění pro cizinu at the same address if you require information on car insurance. Drivers involved in accidents are normally taken into custody until it is established who was the guilty party. No customs documents are necessary for taking a car in. International SOS cards are recognised. Note: petrol coupons must be purchased in advance. See *Fuel*.

Driving conditions

Main roads and country roads are both generally in a good state of repair. The motorway network is not very developed yet, but is rapidly expanding. Although motorways are a quick way from A to B, you'll need to get on to the smaller country roads if you want to appreciate the countryside and see the small picturesque villages. Owing to complicated one way systems, the almost invisible traffic lights, and the fact that there are always detours because of road works, many foreigners prefer to park their vehicles in towns and use the excellent public transport instead. This also allows the driver to sample Czech beer.

Winter driving

"Cars equipped with tyres with anti-skid spikes are not allowed to enter Czechoslovakia". Chains may be used only when the road is covered with a thick layer of snow. Normally all roads remain open in winter.

Road rules

* As in the rest of Europe, (apart from some strange islands out to the west), one drives on the right-hand side in Czechoslovakia.
* Keep to the right, also on multi-lane roads, unless overtaking.
* Indicators must be used.
* Always have your driver's licence, passport and technical certificate with you when driving.
* Drink *absolutely no* alcoholic beverages before and while driving.
* Safety belts in front seats must be used at all times, except in built-up areas.
* Motorcyclists and passengers must wear helmets and goggles.
* Children under 12 years old must not sit in the front seats.
* Lanes marked "BUS" may not be entered, except to avoid an obstacle or to turn.
* At tram stops without a safety area, remain stationary behind the tram for as long as passengers are getting on and off.
* Speed limits for cars: motorways 110kph; normal maximum 90kph; built-up areas 60kph from 5.00am to 11.00pm, 90kph from 11.00pm to 5.00am.
* Speed Limits For Motorcycles: Built-up areas 60kph from 5.00am to 11.00pm; Otherwise 80kph.
* Speed limit crossing a level crossing is 30kph.
* As well as at dusk and night, headlights must be used when visibility is reduced owing to weather conditions. It is illegal to use only side lights.
* Motorcycles must use dipped lights during the day.
* The most frequent offence committed by foreign drivers in Czechoslovakia is illegal stopping or standing. One must not stop in the following situations:
  - where signs prohibit it
  - before the top of gradients
  - within 5 metres of a pedestrian crossing
  - before intersections
  - before bus or tram stations without a safety zone
  - on bridges
  - within 15 metres of a level crossing
  - within 3.5 metres of tram rails (in this case you must not even be temporarily stationary)

Fuel

Foreigners can no longer pay for petrol in Czechoslovak crowns, but must buy petrol coupons for foreign currency. These are available from: Čedok in London; Zivnostenska Banka, 104-106 Leadenhall Street, London EC3A 4AA; certain automobile associations outside Czechoslovakia; border control points; most branches of Státní banka československá (Czechoslovak State Bank); most branches of Čedok in Czechoslovakia (but only one of their many Prague offices, the address of which keeps changing); the more expensive hotels; and some Tuzex shops. Diesel (called NAFTA) can be purchased only with special coupons obtained from Zivnostenska Bank in London or any branch of Státní banka československá in Czechoslovakia. Coupons are not refundable, unless you buy them from Zivnostenska Banka in London and return them there, nor can you get change if you should, for example, buy 35 litres but only have 10 litre coupons.

Petrol stations are probably fewer and farther between than you are used to, usually have queues, and with some exceptions are also open shorter hours than might be expected. A list of them and their opening hours is often included on road maps. Only 80 petrol stations sell diesel to foreigners, and only 32 outlets sell lead-free petrol (called "Natural" — a map of them, with addresses and opening hours on the back, may be available from petrol stations).

Breakdowns and spare parts

The emergency breakdown telephone number is 154 throughout the country. On motorways only, this is a direct line. Autoturist have a list of emergency breakdown service addresses in the back of their magazine (if they haven't run out of them). Letters of credit issued by AIT (Alliance Internationale de Tourisme) are accepted as payment for car repairs at those garages displaying the AIT emblem.

Spare parts can be very difficult to obtain. They are sold by Mototechna. As well as the Czechoslovak Skoda, the Ford Escort 1300, Fiat 127, Fiat 125, Lada and Renault are sold in Czechoslovakia, so parts for these are sold. Other parts can be imported if necessary, but it is a complicated procedure. All vehicles must carry a first-aid kit, warning triangle and spare bulbs.

Rental cars

There is a huge price difference between what a local pays for a rental car and what a foreigner must pay, making renting a car in Czechoslovakia an expensive proposition. So some people get their Czech friends to rent them a car. Rental for foreigners must be paid for in hard currency or by credit card. There are connections with Avis, Hertz, Europcar, Budget and Inter-Rent so that their cars can be driven across the border and picked up or dropped off in Czechoslovakia. Cars may be rented from Pragocar in Prague and many other towns, Brnocar in Brno, and Čedok or Slovakotour in Bratislava. (See sections on Prague, Brno or Bratislava for further details.) Outside peak periods it is usually possible to get a car on the spot, but to be sure it is best to make a reservation. This can be done before you travel, through a travel agency or through Hertz, Avis etc throughout the world.

By bicycle

Long distance cycling is not common in Czechoslovakia, but I have received a surprising number of letters from cyclists, all of whom praise Czechoslovakia as a good country for cycling. Personally I have enjoyed cycling in the countryside, but the traffic, tram rails, state of the streets and lack of cycle lanes put me off cycling in the cities. There are hills, especially in Slovakia, but the magnificent scenery makes them worth putting up with. N. Fixen writes that: "It is a good country for cycling. All the roads are tarmacadam and one can usually avoid the main roads by using secondary roads. It is true that there are no special cycle tracks, but the volume of traffic is not great, except on the mainer roads, ... motorists ... were nearly always courteous to bikes." With the exception of the South Bohemia to South Moravia stretch, the scenery is very varied. Břeclav district is delightful for cycling. You can take your bicycle with you on most trains. A cycling and camping trip is a very cheap way to see Czechoslovakia.

Hitchhiking

Hitching in Czechoslovakia is rather erratic. I've found good hitching in country areas in Slovakia, but I've heard of people taking three days to get from Prague to Bratislava! It is easier to hitch on country roads than on highways, and it is definitely easier hitching into towns than out of them. Hitching alone and with a small pack helps. Škodas, the all pervasive Czech car, are not all that big, and they are usually full. The working day begins very early in Czechoslovakia, so if you want to catch the morning traffic you need to be out on the road between 6.00am and 8.00am.

The hitchhiking sign is not a thumb, but a downward wave of the arm with your open hand facing the traffic. Hitching on motorways is forbidden.

Hitchhiking is, of course, a good way to meet people. You are likely to get a better impression of the people than if the only people you meet are hotel employees etc. It's handy to have a phrase book and/or dictionary to try and communicate — very few people speak English. Girls I have spoken with report that hitching for women in Czechoslovakia doesn't carry nearly so much fear of danger as in many countries. But as in most countries, there has been the odd case where a hitchhiker has come to grief.

Walking

YES In towns take care, as drivers don't stop for pedestrian crossings. Sightseeing in towns tends to be much more pleasant at the weekend, when there is not so much traffic, though many town centres are now closed to vehicles.

There is a good network of marked tracks and walking routes in Czechoslovakia, so a walking holiday is quite possible. See chapter on *Tramping* (hiking) for more details.

Signposting and finding addresses

Although main routes are generally adequately signposted, it is not always easy to find street name signs. Since the Velvet Revolution many streets, stations and even towns have changed their names from "Marxova", "Leninova", "Gottwaldov" etc back to their original names or to new names, making it a little difficult for you to find your way around. Some streets are numbered with even numbers on one side and odd on the other, while others are numbered consecutively going up one side then down the other so that the first and last numbers are opposite.

ACCOMMODATION

For every type of accommodation except YHA youth hostels there are two price categories: one for Czechoslovak citizens and the other for foreigners. Foreigners must pay the normal price plus a surcharge of between 100 but more normally 160%. This brings prices up to west European levels. The surcharge can be a little less if the accommodation is booked from abroad. The prices in this book are what you pay if you haven't pre-paid from home.

Prices vary according to category and how much extra foreigners are charged, and are cheaper in the less "touristy" places. Be warned that if you take a room without bath there is often a whopping great extra charge (for foreigners) for using the shower or bath. In larger towns it is much cheaper to go to the railway station, where foreigners pay the same as Czechoslovaks. You will often have to pay for all the beds in a room or bungalow, and if camping the greatest price is for the tent, rather than the person, making it more expensive the fewer people there are.

Organised group tourism is encouraged in Czechoslovakia and all types of accommodation are regularly booked up by groups or travel agents, making it difficult for individuals to get a bed. The worst time to get accommodation is during the Catholic holidays. Outside the peak season some establishments close and others in mountain areas are taken over by school groups escaping the pollution of the large cities for a term. The situation could well now improve for individual travellers, as travel agents are expected to loose their stranglehold on beds. In popular tourist places hotel employees often keep some rooms empty for someone willing to slip them some a few dollars. Gloomy as this sounds, I have always managed to come up with something in the end without either booking or resorting to slipping anyone dollars, even if it's a hotel receptionist moonlighting by illegally letting out rooms in her house. But if you'd rather be sure, make prior reservations.

Prior bookings for the expensive international class hotels can be made through Čedok (see *Information* for addresses). By telex it takes only a few hours to receive a confirmation. For other bookings you could try another travel agent or you can contact the establishment yourself. If you can't write in Czech or Slovak it helps to write in German, but even if you write in English most people can find someone to translate for them. But as with everything else in Czechoslovakia, you can't depend on an answer. For summer and Christmas it is best to book two to three months in advance.

Once in Czechoslovakia you can also book through Čedok or other travel agencies, although some may refuse to make bookings for individual foreigners. Čedok have some offices specialising in dealing with foreigners, but for westerners they will often only book the higher priced accommodation categories, even denying the existence of cheaper alternatives. You could ask the receptionist at places you stay to telephone the next place and book for you, thus saving you language problems.

Some maps include a listing of accommodation. *Kempink v Československu* (Olympia, Praha, 1990, Kčs 33) is a complete guide to cabins, motor camps and camping sites in Czechoslovakia, in Czech only. There are no plans to republish the other comprehensive guidebooks to accommodation once available.

Types of accommodation

It is important that you read this section in order to understand my accommodation listings in the text. Most travel agents will try and steer you into the more expensive hotels and motor camps. There are many other types of accommodation in Czechoslovakia, but you may have to go out and find them yourself.

Hotels

Hotels are categorised C, B, B*, A* or A* de luxe. Sometimes extra stars are added to the B* category, B** meaning with private bathroom, and B*** meaning with private bathroom separate from private toilet. Some hotels are classified under a star system in an attempt to be more international. The following table shows what they are equivalent to; the prices in Kčs are only a very rough guide. If prices have increased a lot, at least you can work out what you should multiply by.

Category	Star system	Single	Double
C	*	100	190
B	**	150	280
B*	***	300	630
A*	****	420	830
A* de luxe	*****	600	1,000

Higher category hotels may demand that guests pay in foreign currency. Economic liberalisation may see the hotel category system begin to disappear.

Motels

There are a few motels with prices similar to B* category hotels.

Botels

Botels are boats moored on the river Vltava in Prague used as hotels.

Pensions

A new category of accommodation, private pensions, began appearing in Prague and other places with a shortage of accommodation in 1990.

Ubytovací hostinec (UH)

This is an inn or pub with a bedroom, but often no bathroom. It's just a place to sleep for the night, and costs about Kčs 100.

Turistická ubytovna (TU)

Literally "tourist accommodation". These are hostels with dormitories. They are the closest thing to a YHA hostel found in Czechoslovakia, though they have no connection with YHA. You'll have to persevere if you want to stay in them, as visitors from the West are generally directed towards the more expensive hotels and receptionists are even less likely to speak foreign languages than their hotel counterparts. TU tend to be a bit different from YHA hostels, in that they are hardly more than just a place to sleep for the night, with little social interaction. There is normally somewhere to wash oneself, but rarely anywhere to cook. They come in two grades, depending on how many beds there are to a room: TU A cost about Kčs 80; and TU B about Kčs 60. TU are often only open seasonally. There are sometimes dormitories in hotels.

Chatové osady (CHO)

These are "chalet colonies" or cabins, found particularly in Slovakia. One often must pay for all the beds in the cabin (typically 2 or 4 beds), so they are less practical for those travelling alone. There are three grades: A* about Kčs 100 per bed; A about Kčs 80 per bed; and B about Kčs 50 per bed.

Horské hotely

Mountain hotels.

Horské chaty (Cz), turistické chaty (Tur. ch.) (Sl)

Mountain huts or chalets costing about Kčs 80 per person. Singular is *chata*.

YHA hostels

There are no real YHA hostels in Czechoslovakia in spite of the fact that the International Youth Hostel Handbook lists hostels in Czechoslovakia. The hostels listed can be divided into three types: Juniorhotels; summer hostels; and SSM hostels. CKM, the Czechoslovak youth and students' travel agent, administer this system. They don't really cater for individuals, and although they say they will do their best to reply if you write to them, they may not have time in the busy season. Their address is: Klub mladých cestovatelů, CKM, Žitná ulice 12, 121 05 Praha 2 (tel. 294587, 299941-9, telex 122299CKMC, telefax 02-2351297). The following YHA prices are not available if booking from abroad, when the price leaps to several times as much.

Juniorhotels have a special price of about Kčs 45 to Kčs 90 for those who can show a YHA or international student card, both of which can be bought from CKM, but Juniorhotels are nearly always booked up by groups.

Summer Hostels. In the summer in the large cities CKM take over student hostels and run them as summer hostels, with a reduced price of about Kčs 55 for those with a youth hostel or student card. Non-YHA members pay about Kčs 150 at these hostels.

SSM Hostels are situated in the country and are usually occupied by groups. You may be able to stay there in exceptional circumstances although not if there is a children's group there. If there is no group there, it will probably be closed. So, in theory YHA members can sleep there, but in practice it's difficult. If you want to try, go direct to the hostel. These hostels were owned by the socialist youth movement, and at the time of writing their ownership was in doubt.

Autokempinky (ATC) (motor camps)

These come in two categories, A and B, and cost around Kčs 15 to Kčs 30 per tent, plus Kčs 8 to Kčs 30 per person, plus charges for vehicles, caravans etc. Some also have cabins (chalets, huts). Kitchens are very rare, but there is often some sort of food or drink on sale. Showers and toilets are usually not terribly clean (though the authorities have been trying to tighten up on hygiene), there is usually no hot water (whatever any camping guide you may have says to the contrary), and there can be water shortages. On the other hand they can be good places to meet other travellers, with a couple of beers and a guitar, sitting around the campfires, which are a part of camping life in Czechoslovakia. Campfires are also the most common means of cooking. But beware if you have a nylon tent: a stray spark on the heavy canvas tents used in eastern Europe doesn't do much harm, but if it lands on your nylon tent it will. For details on fuel for cookers, see the Luggage section. Most camps are open only for a short season, typically May to September.

Czechoslovakia Camping is a camping guidebook published in 1983 in English, French and German. Don't count on a camp having all of the facilities listed in it. Auto Kempinky CS is a camping map with some information on the back, also in English, and costs Kčs 8.

Stanový tábor (camping sites)

These are primitive camp sites, with toilets and water supply, and occasionally cold showers. They are cheaper than motor camps, and can be better value than some of the large autokempinky. Other details are the same as for ATC. Camp sites are not listed in the above guidebook or marked on the camping map, but you'll find them in the previously mentioned Kempink v Československu. Many camp sites marked on maps no longer exist. You may be greeted instead with a "No Camping" sign. Camp sites are normally open seasonally, but when they are closed it may still be possible to camp although there will be no facilities.

Private accommodation

There is private accommodation available in Czechoslovakia in guest houses or with people letting out rooms in their home. Previously westerners were not allowed to use it, but if this law still applies it is now flagrantly violated. The established travel agents will book private accommodation in places where there is a shortage of accommodation, but in this case one must pay the usual inflated price for foreigners, putting the price up to around the same as a hotel room. In Prague new small agencies are offering private accommodation and, especially near Čedok's accommodation office, there are often people in the street offering private accommodation to foreigners.

Staying with friends or people you meet along the way is another story. This is fine, but those liable to register with the police are supposed to do so. (See section on Registration). When staying with people in this way, their hospitality can be embarrassingly overwhelming. The idea of "crashing" with friends or people you meet along the way, and being left more or less to your own devices, is alien to most Czechoslovaks, or at least the older generation. Many people are very interested in meeting foreigners, helping them, and talking with them.

THE MEDIA

Censorship was abolished in 1990 in Czechoslovakia. Before this the news media was strictly controlled and foreign newspapers were not available in Czechoslovakia, with the occasional exception of foreign communist party newspapers.

Radio Prague's Interprogramme (on medium wave) has special programmes in foreign languages including English. Write to Interprogramme Radio Prague, Praha 2, Vinohradská 12, 120 99 Czechoslovakia for further information. Radio Prague also has a shortwave service in English, as does the BBC World Service.

There are two television channels. Foreign programmes are normally dubbed, but on Monday evening foreign films are shown in their original language with sub-titles. Until recently Russian television was broadcast to Czechoslovakia. This channel has been changed to a mixture of several western channels, including the American CNN.

MAIL, TELEPHONE, ETC

Mail can be sent to you c/o post offices. It should be addressed as follows:

your name,	eg	Simon HAYMAN
"Poste Restante",		Poste Restante
post office		Hlavní pošta
street & no.		Jindřišská 14
post code, town, post district		110 00 Praha 1

Often the town is written before the street. If you don't know the address, and want your mail to go to the main post office, write "Pošta 1" as the post office, and your mail should find you. In large towns you should have no problem, but in smaller towns you may have trouble making yourself understood when you ask for "Poste Restante", in which case try pronouncing it the Czechoslovak way as separate syllables: "Pos-te Re-stan-te". Local mail is held for two weeks, and foreign mail for one month. Some embassies may allow you to have your mail sent c/o them.

Although slow, in my experience letter post is fairly reliable, but sending packages is *not*. Packages sent to Czechoslovakia often don't turn up unless they are registered. Parcels to be sent abroad must be taken to Customs, not the post office, if they weigh over 1kg (5kg for printed matter). If sending something airmail, make sure it is obvious that it is airmail, and that you are sold the correct stamp for airmail — I have had postcards turning up on the other side of the world months after I have sent them. The post office by the railway station is the fastest place to send mail from (it's usually "Pošta 2").

Local telephone calls from public telephones cost Kčs 1 for an unlimited period. For calls to other districts you'll need to find a phone that takes Kčs 1, 2 and 5 coins (most take only Kčs 1), or go to a post office. Larger post offices may have these coin phones, but normally you place your call through a telephonist and pay afterwards. In larger towns you'll probably have to pay a deposit. Calls to other countries are *very expensive*. Place them from a post office as you won't be able to feed a coin phone fast enough. Hotels charge extra for the use of their phone. Telegrams within Czechoslovakia are fast and reasonably priced and are also sent from post offices.

Post office = *pošta*
Registered = *dopuručené*
Printed matter = *tlačivo*
C/o = *u*
Telephone = *telefon*
Telegrams = *telegramy*

SHOPPING

Shopping hours vary, but on weekdays shops tend to open between 6.00am and 9.00am, and close at 6.00pm. Small shops are often closed for lunch. Some shops are closed all or part of Monday. On Saturday food shops and most others are open till noon, while department stores are open till about 4.00pm. Shops tend to close earlier than the specified time, or if they are still open you won't get any service in the last half hour or so because the people who work there are itching to get home. Everything is closed on Sundays and holidays. If a sign on the door says *Inventura* the shop is closed for several days for stocktaking.

In self-service shops you often must have a basket to enter, and if there are none left you must queue. Supermarkets are not common outside Prague.

Tuzex are a chain of shops which accept only foreign currency or Tuzex vouchers. They sell export quality Czechoslovak goods and imported goods not available from normal shops, and not subject to duty.

Beautiful "coffee table" style picture books of Czechoslovak scenery are available if you have the means to carry them. Avoid bookshops on Thursdays, which is the day new books come out, resulting in long queues of people. The queues became even longer in 1990 as many previously banned books were published for the first time in Czechoslovakia.

Other possibilities for shopping are Czech glass, porcelain, leather goods, embroidery, weaving, lace, classical records, the famous beers, *slivovice* (plum brandy), and Becher liqueur. But many of these can only be taken out of the country legally if they were bought at Tuzex.

Chocolate is good. Western brands of cigarettes are available, but they are much more expensive than local ones.

PHOTOGRAPHY

Most of the film currently available is made in the former eastern Bloc countries. There shouldn't be any problem processing local black and white film in the West, but if buying colour make sure it can be processed in the West, as the processes used are different. Normally having a film processed in Czechoslovakia takes a very long time, but there are now some fast labs in the cities, addresses of which you will find in this book. These labs are expensive, but they can process western film.

Don't photograph near the border, and be careful not to photograph anything which could be construed as a military target.

FOOD & DRINK

Although prices have increased a lot, eating out in Czechoslovakia can still be cheap thanks to the good exchange rate people from western countries get. Every eating and drinking establishment has a class (skupina) from I to IV. Cheapest are the class IVs, which are usually stand-up and self-service. Some class Ivs are more like workers' cafeterias, with good cheap meals in the middle of the day. At class III you are more likely to be able to sit down and have service. Class II are more like a western restaurant, but the prices aren't so high. Class I are expensive. This class system may start disappearing with privatisation of restaurants. A lot of eateries are much of a muchness, so in many cases it is not worth mentioning specific places, other than those which are particularly good, or to show what is available. Restaurant food is generally rather fattening with little fresh fruit or vegetables, so it's best if you have the chance to prepare your own food sometimes, or can eat with friends.

Menus in restaurants usually spell out exactly what you are getting, the weight of the meat, and exactly what accompanies it, rather than giving a name of a dish. This makes them more difficult for foreigners, simply because there is more to read. In tourist places, beware of waiters who suggest something instead of bringing you the menu, as they are often about to rip you off. Ask the price first, as their suggestion will often be the most expensive thing on the menu, or some sort of fiddle.

Here is a little to help you:

Czech	English	Slovak
Jídelní lístek	The menu	*Jedálny lístok*
Breakfast		
šunku s vejci	bacon and eggs	*šunku s vajcom*
čaj	tea	*čaj* (pronounced the same as the Indian word)
káva	coffee	*káva* (*káva turecka* is Turkish coffee, with the grinds in the cup)
chléb	bread	*chlieb*
máslo	butter	*maslo*
džem	jam	*džem*

Ways of cooking

dušené	stewed	*dusené*
smažené	fried	*vyprážané*
vařené	boiled	*varené*
pečene	roast	*pečené*

Cold and Hot

studený	cold	*studený*
horký	hot	*teplé*

Soup, meat, egg

polévky	soup	*polievka*
maso	meat	*mäso*
hověčí	beef	*hovädzie*
roštěnka	roast beef	*roštenka*
svíčková	sirloin of beef	*sviečková*
telací maso	veal	*teľacie mäso*
vepřové maso	pork	*bračové mäso*
vepřová pečeně	roast pork	*bračová pečienka*
žebírko	rib	*rebierko*
kachna	duck	*kačica*
kuře	chicken	*kura*
slepice	fowl	*sliepka*
ryby	fish	*ryby*
omeleta	omelette	*omeleta*

Vegetables

zelenina	vegetables	*zelenina*
brambory	potatoes	*zemiak*
okurka	cucumber	*uhorka*
rajská jablíčka	tomatoes	*paradajky, rajčiny*
zelí	sauerkraut	*kyslá kapusta*
knedlík	dumpling	*knedlík*

Dessert and Drinks

palačinky	pancakes	*palačinky*
zmrzlina	ice-cream	*zmrzlina*
ovoce	fruit	*ovocie*
kompot	stewed fruit	*kompot*
nápoje	drinks	*nápoye*
limonáda	soda water (flavoured)	*limonáda*
pivo	beer	*pivo*
víno	wine	*víno*
víno bílé	white wine	*víno biele*
víno červené	red wine	*víno červené*

A typical meal when eating out is soup followed by pork with dumpling and sauerkraut, and accompanied by beer. Another common dish is *segedinský guláš* (from Hungary), pork stew with sauerkraut. What one can buy when eating out is not always a good reflection of what people eat in their homes. Geese are raised everywhere, but you won't find them on many menus. They are stuffed with *šišky* to enlarge their livers prior to killing them. *Bryndzové halušky*, sheep's cheese with pasta, is a national Slovak dish, especially in north and central Slovakia. *Žinčica*, sheep's whey, is often drunk with it. It is supposed to be good for your stomach, enabling you to drink alcohol without any bad effects. But the hygiene with these sheep milk products is not always so good, with many cases of salmonella poisoning (of which I had first hand experience).

Note that food is often measured by weight. Sausages may cost Kčs 'x' per 100gm, but one sausage may weigh 200gm. *Párek* (frankfurters) with mustard and bread are sold in many places as takeaways. In season (around August-September) piping hot fresh corn on the cob is available, often in the street. What for Czechoslovaks is foreign and exotic food, such as pizza and hamburger, is starting to creep in.

Cakes and sweets look more tempting than they taste, but the ice-cream (*zmrzlina*) is delicious, at around Kčs 2 a cone. Occasionally dumplings filled with plums are available (*švestkové knedlíky* in Czech, *slivokové knedle* in Slovak). *Pirohy* are a batter of flour, egg and water with sheep's cheese or jam filling which are boiled in water and eaten with melted butter.

Czechoslovakia produces some of the best beer in the world, at prices one can afford. The original Pilsener beer (Plzeňský Prazdroj) comes from Plzeň, and the original Budvar (Budweiser) from Česke Budějovice. American Budweiser tastes nothing like the real Budvar, and Czechs are angry that an ex-brewery employee from Česke Budějovice who emigrated to USA has stolen their beer's name. Staropramen 12° is a good Prague beer. The most famous Slovak beer is Zlatý Bažant (Golden Pheasant) from the little village of Hurbanovo. Beer comes in different strengths: 10° is weak and 12° strong. Some years ago beer prices shot up. Schweik once said that the government which puts up beer prices must fall. The prophecy has been fulfilled!

Wine is also produced locally, especially in Moravia and Slovakia. In fact there are vineyards on the hills around Bratislava. Although Czechoslovak wine is good, you can't rely on the wine in two bottles with the same label tasting the same. During the grape harvest in autumn, *burčák* (Cz) or *burčiak* (Sl), a young wine that is still fermenting, is available for a short period in wine producing areas such as Bratislava. Two stronger drinks worth knowing about are *slivovice*, a plum brandy most common in Moravia, and the ever-pervading *borovička* in Slovakia, made from the cones of the juniper (*juniperus comunis*) tree. It's hard to compare *borovička* with any other drink. It is often translated as gin, but it tastes nothing like gin. Juniper brandy is a better attempt. Slovaks tend to live on it, and knock back the glass in one go. It's also drunk as a beer chaser. On my last visit I saw three-litre souvenir bottles of *borovička*. Another drink you might come across is *stará myslivecká*, commonly known as *myslivec*. It is said that Bohemia has the best beer, Moravia the best wine, and Slovakia the best spirits.

There are deposits on beer and soft drink bottles. Beware the trick sometimes played against tourists, of charging for the bottle even when they drink there.

Tea is normally tea-bag tea. Coffee is usually Turkish coffee, with the boiling water poured onto the ground coffee in your cup. Espresso coffee is also available in some places. Coffee costs upwards of Kčs 6 a cup.

Here is a rough guide to the various types of eating and drinking establishments (with Slovak in brackets):

restaurace (reštaurácie)	restaurant
restaurace samoobsluhou	cafeteria
hospoda or hostinec	local pub (snacks such as hard-boiled
(hostinec or krčma)	eggs and rolls often also available)
pivnice	beer cellar (sells food that goes with beer)
vinárna (vináreň)	wine bar (sells food that goes with wine)
občerstvení (občerstvenie)	refreshments
cukrárna (cukráreň)	sell cakes and sweet things (open only in daytime)

If you enter any type of establishment within one hour of closing time, you are likely to be studiously ignored by the waiter/waitress, until you eventually grab them, by which time you will probably be told that there is nothing left. But I have heard it is rather different at the new private restaurants. A lot of eating places in Czechoslovakia are non-smoking for at least some of the hours they are open.

A few hints if you are preparing your own food:

Potravniny = grocery
Lahůdky (Cz), lahôdky (Sl) = delicatessen

Though supermarkets are becoming more common, most food shops are not self-service. You must ask for what you want, which makes for language difficulties. But normally everything is on display, so you can point. What's not on display is on the black market. Grocery stores are closed on Saturday afternoon or Sunday. Many shops also have a half day on Monday. There are queues, especially for fresh food.

Western brand-names, such as Coca-Cola and Tang, are much more expensive than the local equivalents. Delicious canned peach juice is available.

Watch that things packed in plastic and polythene are sealed properly.

It can be a problem to buy fresh fruit and vegetables, and people go to extraordinary lengths to protect the fruit they grow, with high fences and walls. It's better to buy from fruit stalls and the markets than from shops. In the country you can find wild berries (raspberries, blackberries and blueberries). Good *kompot* (stewed fruit) is available everywhere in jars.

Salami is good. Packet soups and milk powder are easily available, and handy for travelling.

Yoghurt can be bought in the cities. *Bio-kys* is drinking kefir (which for those not familiar with it, is a another sour milk product).

Muesli is not usually available outside Slušovice, but you can sometimes find rolled oats (*ovesné vločky* (Cz), *ovsené vločky* (Sl)), sultanas (*rozinka* (Cz), *hrozienka* (Sl), milk powder, yoghurt or fresh milk, *kompot*, and fresh fruit and berries, and make your own.

Bread is sold in large oval loaves (*chléb*). It is usually possible to ask for a half or quarter loaf. Be careful you are not sold stale bread. *Rohlík*, white rolls, are nice when fresh, but they are often not fresh. Filled wafers are the most common type of biscuit. *Křupky arašidové* are peanut flavoured snacks. *Arašidky v cukru* are delicious peanuts coated in sugar. *Perník* is gingerbread.

If you find you get a taste for Czech cooking, get hold of a copy of the book *Czech Cuisine* by Joza Břízová and Maryna Klimentová. Published by Avicenum in Prague in 1986, it's distributed in North America by Czech Cottage, 100 16th Avenue SW, Cedar Rapids, Iowa 52404.

ENTERTAINMENT AND EVENINGS

Prague is famous for its classical music and opera, but be warned that seats are hard to come by, and often must be booked far in advance. The other cities also have a rich cultural life.

Rock and modern music were rather frowned upon by the previous administration, but with a rock fan as president its situation is improving. Heavy metal is very popular. Concerts get booked out. Student functions and other club functions are a better bet than the public nightclubs, which tend to have closed doors and hassling doormen to get past, and staff who often treat you with disdain. Some nightclubs don't allow jeans or sneakers. Come early. A musician I met was complaining that a new law banning alcohol from dances for young people meant that no-one was turning up.

Pubs close early. Smaller towns are dead after 10.00pm, while in the cities you have to go on to nightclubs after this time.

A lot of foreign films are shown. Some are dubbed (*česká verze, slovenská verzia*) while others are shown in the original language with Czech or Slovak subtitles (*české titulky, slovenská titulky*). In summer there are many outdoor cinemas.

Devín. Abandoned and graffiti-covered police look-out post across the confluence of the Danube and Morava rivers. (photo by John Skelton)

Tramping (hiking) and other outdoor activities

TRAMPING

I am using the word "tramping" in its New Zealand sense, not only because I am a New Zealander, but because for some reason that I have not been able to discover, the word has a similar meaning in New Zealand as it has in Czech. For those of you not familiar with the word, its meaning is similar to "rambling", "hiking", "trekking", "back packing", or "bush-walking". Some more New Zealand-Czech terminology: a person who tramps is called a "tramper" (*tramp* in Czech); the actual trip is called a "tramp" (same word in Czech); "tramping" is the activity; the verb is to "go tramping" (*jít na tramp* in Czech).

Whatever you like to call tramping, Czechoslovakia is one of the best countries in Europe for it, so a lot of space in this book is devoted to information and route guides. The High Tatras are the highlight for many, with their highest peak towering 2655 metres above sea level. This alpine area is a national park. There are many other mountain areas, especially in Slovakia. There are also forest areas, areas with fantastic limestone and sandstone formations, or just pleasant walking through typical countryside and interesting villages (where dogs are usually kept under control, but geese can get rather aggressive).

Altogether there are about 40,000 km of marked paths, tracks and routes in Czechoslovakia. Unlike Britain, where public footpaths have a habit of disappearing in the middle of a farmer's field, or New Zealand where one needs to be an experienced route finder, tracks are (with occasional exceptions) easy to follow in Czechoslovakia. They are marked for ordinary people, by volunteers from sports clubs. The track markers are normally repainted every three years, or every two years in the mountains. This tradition of track marking goes back 100 years.

The tracks are marked in the same way throughout the country, by coloured markers on trees, walls, rocks, fences etc. The colour of the markers corresponds to the colour the track is marked on maps. Principal routes are marked in red. Others in blue, green, and the least important in yellow. The tracks are marked in three stripes, one the colour of the track, and a white stripe above and below it:

Some other markings you may come across are:

▧   local marking, eg a short round trip from a car park

▧   instructional tour

⊙   side track to water source

◬   side track to summit or lookout point

▣   side track to ruins or castle

◎   end of track

⏚   side track to interesting point

Good hiking maps (*turistické mapy*) are sometimes available for some areas. They tend to be in bookshops for a few months, then disappear for a few years until the next edition is produced. So, if you see any for areas you expect to walk in, grab them. The keys are in several languages, but not always in English.

Symbols vary, but here is a guide to help you:

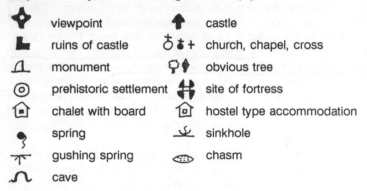

✤	viewpoint	♠	castle
▙	ruins of castle	♁♠✝	church, chapel, cross
⚲	monument	♀♣	obvious tree
◎	prehistoric settlement	⌗	site of fortress
⌂	chalet with board	⌂	hostel type accommodation
♦	spring	⚐	sinkhole
⚵	gushing spring	⬭	chasm
⌒	cave		

There are a few long distance tracks with some educational aim. For example the Česta Hrdinov SNP from Bratislava to Dukla. This is the track of the heroes of the Slovak National Uprising, and many people walk it on the anniversary of the uprising.

Long distance hikes are possible, whether or not you actually follow a track marked as a long distance track. There is a good enough network of marked routes to be able to plan your own trip, using camping grounds, hostels, or hotels to sleep in along the way. In Slovakia there are plans to build huts in which one can sleep overnight along the way. These will be unmanned, and probably have mattresses and somewhere to cook. The sites have been decided, and they should be built over the next few years.

Horska Sluzba is the mountain service for the whole of the country. It is a professional organisation involved in rescue and research work.

It used to be permissible to camp out anywhere, but this is no longer the case. People still do so, but discreetly. You can ask to camp on somebody's land, but in national parks even this is forbidden. The mountain areas are generally small enough to allow for you to use an official camp site as a base, and tramp on day trips. In national parks lighting fires is prohibited. Outside national parks, one may light fires if there is a place provided for that purpose. The water from mountain streams can be drunk. On hot still summer days there is a strong likelihood that you will meet some of Czechoslovakia's insect life. Widespread use of insecticide has held mosquitoes down, but horseflies (in the wheat season) and wasps (in the apple season) are worse, owing to increasing monoculture.

The most important word you need to learn for tramping in Czechoslovakia is *Ahoj!*, the common greeting, or you can use *Dobrý den*. But when there are lots of tourists around people probably won't bother.

If you are interested in joining an organised group to go tramping in Czechoslovakia, either for the company or because you lack experience to set off into the mountains yourself, write to me c/o Bradt Publications, enclosing an international postal reply coupon. I can also make arrangements for rambling clubs and other groups planning to visit Czechoslovakia.

Good day-packs (rucksacks) made of canvas with leather straps are made in Czechoslovakia. Good boots are made in Czechoslovakia, but you may have trouble finding the right size.

Preparations to preserve and waterproof your boots are sold, including "Elaskon" in a plastic bottle for Kčs 4.50, and "Jelení Loj", which I was told was better, for Kčs 1.50.

Bring a water bottle from home — they can't be bought in Czechoslovakia.

What to take in the forest and countryside

Boots are recommended, though in many areas any reasonable footwear will suffice. If you don't have boots, buy them well in advance so you have time to wear them in. Good boots can, subject to availability, be bough in Czechoslovakia, but then you won't have time to wear them in. I have been warned to buy a pair made with foreign glue, as Czechoslovak glue doesn't hold. In addition you will need: a day pack to carry things in; parka; sweater; waterbottle or thermos (light waterbottles cannot be bought in Czechoslovakia); your lunch; insect repellant; basic first aid especially something for blisters if you are not used to boots; map; protection from the sun (hat, suncream, sunglasses); puttees (gaiters) are useful in some areas to keep stones, twigs, etc. out of your boots.

What to take in the mountains

For high altitudes add the following to the above list: woollen mitts; balaclava or woollen hat; woollen trousers or knickerbockers; waterproof over-trousers; and some quick energy food such as chocolate, raisins or sweets. Good walking boots with ankle support and vibram soles protect your ankles and are more comfortable to walk in, as long as they are worn in first. Puttees (gaiters) can be very useful, so you don't have to keep stopping to get stones out of your boots. For those of you not used to mountains, the main thing to remember is that the weather can change very rapidly. So be prepared with a good parka and something warm. Wool clothing keeps you much warmer than other clothing if it should become wet.

Above the tree line you must have good visibility. Here tracks are not marked with poles, though there may occasionally be painted markers on rocks to help you find the way. Don't go above the bushline in bad weather, and if the clouds begin to close in on you while you are up there, get down quickly. Snowstorms can occur at higher altitudes even in summer.

CLIMBING

The Tatry are the best climbing area in Czechoslovakia — see the Vysoké Tatry section for more details. Other areas are used more for training. Good training areas are found near Bratislava, in the Slovensky Raj, and in Malá Fatra. There is a guide book to smaller climbs in Slovakia, but it is available only in Slovak.

In Bohemia the climbing is in sandstone, eg in Český Raj (the Czech Paradise) and České Švýcarsko (Bohemian Switzerland). Some of the climbs are very difficult.

Take your own climbing gear: it is difficult to get good gear locally. You can get ropes, karabiners and helmets, but the quality is not good.

Climbing in national parks and reserves without a guide is only allowed for members of climbing clubs with a membership card. Climbing in some special nature reserves is forbidden for everyone.

Czechoslovak climbers have had expeditions to the Himalaya, as well as USA, Canada and South America.

CAVING

Czechoslovakia is a wonderland for caving. For the uninitiated there are many limestone caves open to the public with guided tours. These include Dobšinská Ľadová Jaskyňa (Dobšiná Ice Cave) in East Slovakia, one of the most beautiful ice caves in Europe, and the Moravský Kras, north of Brno, where the attractions include a boat trip on the underground river Punkva. During the high season there are many tours, otherwise you'll probably only be taken around if enough people turn up (try and latch on to a bus tour) and in winter many caves are closed. In summer it is likely to be a lot colder underground than above ground, so take some warm clothes. (Ice caves, obviously, are very cold.)

If you wish to visit caves that are not open to the public you must be a member of a caving club, or be conducting research. You first need permission from the government centre for nature conservation. In Slovakia the address is Ústredie Štátnej Ochrany Prírody, 1 mája 38, Liptovský-Mikuláš. There is another office for Bohemia and Moravia. The Czech speleological society is Česká speleologická spoločnost, Ústřední výbor

Handwritten margin note: CAVES ✳✳ MUST GO !!

[= central committee], Valdštejnské náměstí 1, CS-118 01 Praha 1. There is also a Slovak Speleological Society.

SKIING

Downhill skiing facilities are not up to western European standards. There are long waits, and it is difficult to hire good quality gear. But cross country skiing is good in Czechoslovakia.

The main winter sports area of Czechoslovakia is Vysoké Tatry (High Tatras). Here the skiing season can last from December to May, but between January and April is the best time. There is one valley in the Vysoké Tatry where skiing is possible all year: Zmrzla dolina (Frozen Valley); and another where it is possible for 10 to 11 months of the year: Studena dolina. Other important centres are the Nízke Tatry (Low Tatras) and Malá Fatra (Little Fatras). Jasná, in the Nízke Tatry has hosted international skiing championships. In fact there is skiing in all the Slovakian mountains, though not so much in west Slovakia, as well as little local ski-fields all over Slovakia. In Bohemia, Krkonoše (Giant Mountains) have a long season because they receive more snow. They also receive many day and weekend trippers from Prague. A good cross country ski area is the Orlické Hory, by the Polish border, not so far from Hradec-Králové. More information on skiing in particular areas is included under that area in this book.

Skiing package tours are offered from Britain.

Skiing maps are available for some of the skiing areas.

Tatra poma lifts are made under licence to the French poma company.

It is wise to have insurance cover. This should be taken out at home before you leave. If you join a ski school, insurance is included.

WATER SPORTS

Water sports are one of the lesser known attractions of Czechoslovakia which has everything from white water rivers to calm peaceful lakes. Usually it is not possible to hire boats of any sort, but you may take your own boat with you. The only other real possibilities are to make a group arrangement through Slovakoturist, or if you are travelling independently, to ask at clubs if you could hire a boat. Slovakoturist's address is Volgogradská 1, 816 15 Bratislava (telex 92321). They can arrange (for groups only) yachting at Piešťany and Senec, and rowing at Nitra, Piešťany and Púchov.

Slovakia offers the best possibilities for kayaking. Some of the most attractive Slovak rivers are in the mountain regions. They are best in spring, when the snow melt raises their level. The following are especially suitable. See the map on page 65 for their location.

Belá: Navigable only in spring and the beginning of summer, when snow and ice are thawing in the mountains. An exacting river, with plenty of rocks in the upper reaches, and gravel shoals in the lower reaches. In favourable conditions navigable for 22 km, from Podbanské to where it enters the Váh at Liptovský Hrádok. Fabulous mountain backdrop.

Rafting on the Dunajec river

Čierny Váh (The Black Váh): Navigable when the water level is high, from Biely potok foresters' lodge for 20km to Kráľova Lehota, where it joins the Biely Váh (the White Váh) to form the Váh, Slovakia's longest river. The river flows through the forests of an almost uninhabited valley. Good camping.

Váh: Its upper mountain reaches extend from Kráľova Lehota for 120km down to Žilina, but this is broken by hydro dams and below Ružomberok it is too polluted.

Hron: In its upper reaches from Pohorelá to Brezno (about 35km), the Hron is fast flowing over a gravelly river bed. Many possible camp sites.

Orava: Especially suitable for those with less experience. 60km from the Orava dam to the Váh at Kraľovany. As well as mountain scenery, the trip is interesting from a cultural and historical point of view. The river passes below the fantastic Orava castle.

Poprad: Navigable from Poprad to the border with Poland (80km). Best in April and May. A less well known river.

Dunajec: Really a Polish river, but it flows along the border for 16km through a very interesting area. The international "Pieniny slalom' is held here annually. Raft trips for tourists.

Hornád: One of the most beautiful and one of the fastest Slovak rivers. The most interesting stretch is the Hornád Break, starting from Hrabušice and ending 16km downstream at Smižany. Here the river flows through a canyon only a few metres wide in places, with cliffs towering up to 150m above the water. Best in April and May, or when flooded. Permission is needed. It is also possible to walk through here (see section Slovensky Raj).

For non-mountain rivers try the lower reaches of the Hron, Váh or Hornád. Water sports are also possible on the many dam lakes. Near Liptovský Mikuláš an artificial river has been created for kayaking. There is a windsurfing school at Liptovský Mikuláš. This seven-day course can be booked through Slovakoturist, but you'll need a group of 30 in order to get an English-speaking instructor.

Then there is of course the Danube, but this is full of international shipping and not as nice a trip as it may sound. The Maly Dunaj (little Danube) is popular with people from Bratislava, because of its closeness to the city.

Outside Slovakia the Sázava is pleasant, because it is not as polluted as other rivers. It is not surrounded by factories, but has lots of castles etc along its banks. It runs from Moravia westwards to the Vltava. Other suitable rivers in Bohemia are: the Lužnice; the upper Vltava (the common starting point is Vyšší Brod); and the Otava from Šušice, or if the water is high from Rejštejn.

Permission is not needed for kayaking, except in nature reserves (eg on the Hornád). Camping is allowed only at special camp sites, and you can be fined if you camp outside these. If a group wants to camp outside official camp sites, permission is needed from the authorities.

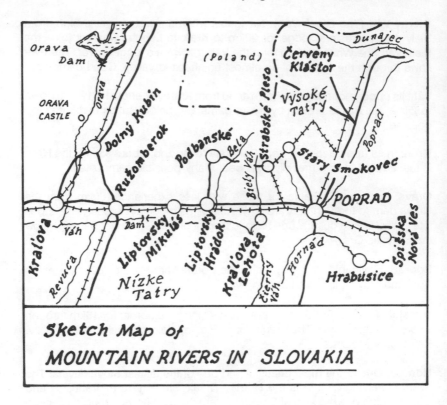

Sketch Map of
MOUNTAIN RIVERS IN SLOVAKIA

In 1956 water-sportsmen from Bratislava arranged a joint Czechoslovak-Hungarian trip down the Danube from Bratislava to Budapest. This was the foundation for what today is called TID, the "Tour International Danubien", which now begins in Ingolstadt in West Germany and finishes in Silistra in Bulgaria. The whole trip is 2082km, but most choose only one part of it. The trip is organized in sections: Ingolstadt (West Germany) — Linz (Austria) — Bratislava (Czechoslovakia) — Budapest (Hungary) — Belehrad (Yugoslavia) — Vidin (Bulgaria) — Silistra (Bulgaria). To participate, contact the club at the place you would like to begin from. For Linz-Bratislava contact Österreichischer Kanu-Verband, Bergasse 16, 1060 Wien. For Bratislava to Budapest contact SÚV ČSZTV Zväz turistiky, Vajnorská 100, 832 80 Bratislava.

TID is held in summer-early autumn. Most of the participating boats are canoes and kayaks. Typically there are about 300 entries per section. It is *not* a race. For many people it is not just the trip itself that attracts them, but the camping on the riverbanks, and the companionship of people from so many countries. It's said that the language barrier has been overcome by a sort of Danubian Esperanto that has developed.

Maps for canoeists are available for some of the rivers, eg the Danube and Lužnice.

For those who cannot hope to get involved in anything as ambitious or adventurous as the above, there are chances in some places for tourist trips on rivers and lakes. In season there are boat trips on the Vltava from Prague. There are raft trips for tourists on the Dunajec, not very far from the High Tatras (see section on Pieniny).

HUNTING AND FISHING
Hunting (shooting)

Foreigners wishing to hunt in Czechoslovakia must arrange this in advance through CCL Tour, Elišky Krásnohorské 10, 110 00 Praha 1; tel. 231 21 26, 231 05 89, 231 05 15; telex 123079 cedo c; fax 236 71 21. They quote their prices in German currency.

A licence and liability insurance are compulsory and cost DM 70 for a month, or DM 145 for a year. There is an organisational fee of DM 52 per day. One must be accompanied by a guide-interpreter appointed by the travel agency. 1000 shotgun cartridges and 50 rifle cartridges can be imported duty free. Shotgun cartridges cost DM 59 per 100, and rifle cartridges DM 2 each. Then there is a whole string of charges ranging from DM 13 for shooting a duck, to charges for shots that miss, to a DM 6,850 trophy fee for a brown bear! These charges must be paid after the hunt. In short, it is expensive and not for the average tourist.

Hunting in Czechoslovakia has a long tradition. There is planned breeding and protection of game, some of which is provided with food during the winter months. In Slovakia alone there are about 26,000 red deer, 1,800 fallow deer, 67,000 roebucks, 3,000 moufflon, 15,000 wild boar, 500 brown bears, 180,000 pheasants, 160,000 hares, 30,000 wild ducks, as well as wolves, lynx and foxes. The intention is to keep numbers at the level they are today.

Hunting of a rather less bloodthirsty kind is also possible. Bear hunters in the Oravská Magura and Beskydy mountains may photograph the protected wood-cock and wood-grouse. In April and May photographing of the mating rituals of the bustard, the largest bird in Europe, can be arranged in the shooting grounds of Žitný ostrov (Wheat Island) and the West-Slovak Lowland.

Accommodation is in mountain hotels or accommodation belonging to the forestry service.

Fishing

Fishermen must have a licence. For foreigners this is only available in advance through a travel agency, and must be paid for in western currency. The cost for one day is DM 35, one week DM 55, one month DM 85, or one year DM 195. You need to bring your own gear with you, or buy gear in Czechoslovakia. Fishermen can also use forestry accommodation.

There is a wide variety of fishing in Czechoslovakia, everything from the calm of dams and lakes to gushing mountain streams and rivers. Among the fish to be caught (with closed season in brackets) are carp, tench, bream, chub, barbel (1/1-30/6), roach, nose-fish, pike (1/1-30/6), perch, sheet-fish (1/1-30/4), eel, trout (1/9-15/4), rainbow trout (1/12-15/4), grayling (1/12-31/5), Danube salmon (rare, and suffering from pollution, 1/12-30/9) and even crayfish (1/10-30/4).

WORK CAMPS

Each year, mostly in July and August, International Work Camps are held in Czechoslovakia. Participants work as unpaid volunteers for two or three weeks, usually for eight hours a day for a five-day week. There are about 20 camps organised every year. The work is of various kinds, eg work in forests, gardens, and helping with construction projects.

The aim of the camps is to bring together young people from different countries to work on a project of benefit to the local community, and in so doing help shape understanding and friendship between people and nations.

The number of participants varies between 15 and 25, with a restriction that there should not be more than three of the same nationality. Applicants should be aged between 19 and 35. English tends to be the language used for communication.

Simple accommodation and food are provided. Lectures, discussions, outings and meetings are organised in evenings and weekends.

The work camps are organised by CKM, the Czechoslovak youth and students travel bureau. Their postal address is CKM, Žitná 12, 121 05 Praha 2. But it is not possible to apply directly through them. You must apply through organisations *in your home country*. Some of these organisations are:

UK: International Voluntary Service, 162 Upper New Walk, Leicester LE1 7QA, tel. (533) 549 430; Quaker International Social Projects (QISP), Friends House/Euston Road, London NW1 2BJ, tel. (071) 387 3601-55; Christian Movement for Peace, CMP Bethnal Green URC, Pott Street, London E2OEF, tel. (071)729 7985; Concordia, 8 Brunswick Place, Hove BN3 1ET, tel. 11 20 86; Great Georges Community Cultural Project, Great George Street, Liverpool 1, (051) 70 95 109; United Nations Association of Wales International Youth Service, UNA Wales Temple of Peace, Cathays Park, Cardiff CF1 3AP, tel. (0222) 223088.

USA: CIEE, 205 East 42nd Street, New York, NY 10017, tel. (212) 661 1414; Service Civil International (SCI), c/o Innisfree Village Route 2, Box 506 Crozet, Virginia 22932; Volunteers for Peace (VFP), 43 Tiffany Rd, Belmont, Vermont 05730, tel. (802) 259 2759

Canada: CBIE, 85 Albert Street, Ottawa, Ontario K1N 7N8. Or Christian Movement for Peace, Toronto.

Germany: Internationale Jugendgemeinschaftsdienste (IJGD), Kaiser Strasse 43, 5300 Bonn 1, tel. (228) 22 10 01; SCI, Blücherstrasse 14, 5300 Bonn 1, tel. (228) 21 20 86/87; and many other organisations.

Netherlands: Internationale Christen Vredes Dienst (ICVD), Postbus 377, 1000 Amsterdam AJ, tel. (20) 253 150; SIW International Volunteer Projects, Willimstraat 7, 3511 RJ Utrecht, tel. (30) 317 721; Vrijwillige Internationale Aktie (VIA), Bethanienstraat 20, 1012 CA Amsterdam, tel. (20) 258 393

Denmark: Mellemfolkeligt Samvirke, Afdeling for International Ungdomsudveksling, Borgergade 14, 1300 København K, tel. 33 32 62 44 (they charge a Dkr 645 administration fee)

New Zealand and Australia: apply through the Youth Hostel Association.

You should apply about April or May. For citizens of some countries (eg UK) it may be difficult to get a place, while for others (eg Denmark) it isn't difficult.

Participants from countries requiring visas still need to obtain one, but may stay on in Czechoslovakia for the rest of the month.

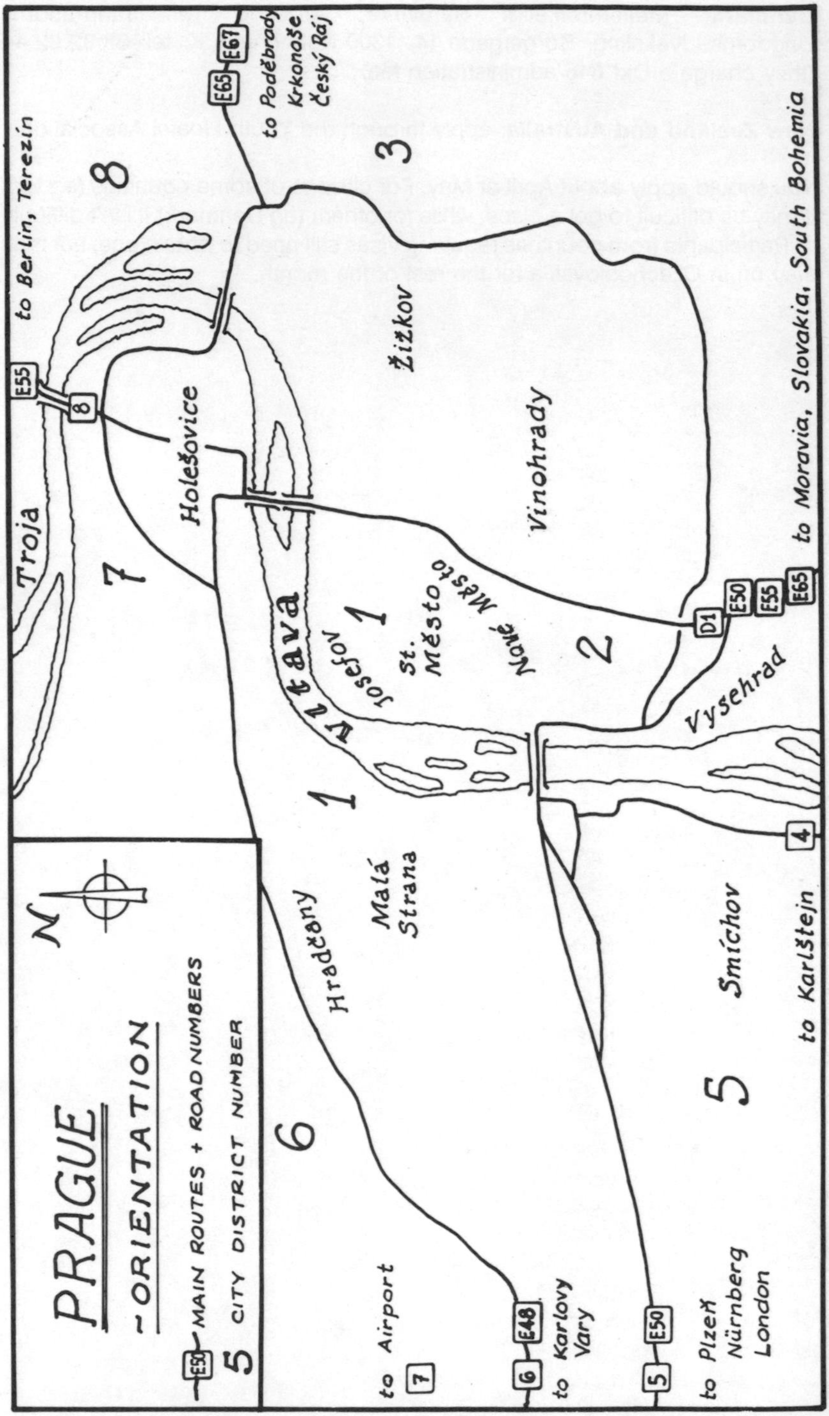

PRAGUE
~ORIENTATION

— E50 MAIN ROUTES + ROAD NUMBERS
5 CITY DISTRICT NUMBER

N

to Airport
7

E48
6
to Karlovy Vary

5
to Plzeň
Nürnberg
London

6
Hradčany

Malá Strana
1

Vltava

Josefov
St. Město
1

Nové Město

Smíchov
5

to Karlštejn

Vyšehrad

4

2

Vinohrady

Žižkov

D1
E50
E55
E65
to Moravia, Slovakia, South Bohemia

Holešovice

Troja
7

E55
8

8

to Berlín, Terezín

E65
E67
to Poděbrady
Krkonoše
Český Ráj

3

Prague in winter

Astronomical clock, Prague

Main street and river, Karlovy Vary

Lidice Memorial

PART 2: CZECHOSLOVAKIA: FROM WEST TO EAST

Prague (Praha)

Prague for me and for many other travellers I have spoken with is the most beautiful city in Europe. The city was not bombed much during World War Two, so its Gothic and Baroque heritage was not destroyed. The newer outer suburbs are a ghastly jungle of ugly apartment blocks, but the old central city has retained its character over the centuries. A wander anywhere in the old parts of Prague is likely to uncover beautiful old churches, narrow cobbled streets and a medieval atmosphere that is very hard to find in European cities today. Words cannot describe Prague; it is a city you must see.

Prague straddles both sides of the river Vltava (Moldau in German), made famous by Smetana. Sixteen bridges connect the two sides of the river, by far the most famous and most beautiful of them being Karlův most (Charles Bridge). Hradčany, Mala Straná, Josefov, (the Jewish town), Stará Mešto (the old town) and Nové Mešto (the new town) were once independent towns each with their own character. Today they have coalesced to form the centre of a city whose suburbs spread far beyond them; (a city of 1,194,900 inhabitants.)

Many people say that spring is the best time to visit Prague. The blossoms are out in April and May. In summer it is warm, and the evenings can be delightful. Prague's residents flee to the countryside to escape the pollution and get some fresh air, and Prague fills up to bursting point with tourists. In autumn it begins to get cold again, though it can be beautiful with the first snow. The average temperatures in °C for Prague are:

	max.	min.		max.	min.
January	1	-4	July	25	14
February	3	-2	August	25	14
March	7	1	September	18	11
April	13	9	October	12	6
May	18	9	November	5	2
June	22	13	December	1	-1

Those of you who knew the Prague of before, with its rather sombre atmosphere and the ever present hassling police on Václavské náměstí will be very surprised by the city's new face. Since the "Velvet Revolution" Prague is overrun by tourists, and really can't cope with them.

HISTORY

The first Slav tribes settled in the area in the 5th Century AD on the site of Prague Castle and at Vyšehrad, to the south on the opposite side of the river. The vicinity of the Old Town Square was a busy meeting place of long distance trading routes. Here Frankish, Byzantine, Arab and Jewish merchants bartered their goods for agricultural produce, textiles, leather goods and slaves. Prague Castle was first built in the 9th Century by the Přemyslid rulers. Vyšehrad was for a time the main residence of the Přemyslids, but it was destroyed in 1420, and later developed as a fort to protect Prague from the south. The first stone bridge was built over the Vltava in the 12th Century, roughly on the site of present day Charles Bridge. By the 13th Century Staré Město had developed into its present form and shape and in 1257 King Přemysl Otakar II founded Mala Straná. The town of Hradčany was founded at the beginning of the 14th Century.

Much of the attraction of modern day Prague can be attributed to Charles IV, who became King of Bohemia in 1346. In 1349 he became Holy Roman Emperor, and Prague was for a period the capital of the Holy Roman Empire. During his reign the first university north of the Alps was founded in Prague, Nové Město (the new town) was founded, the building of St Vitus's Cathedral began as well as many other church buildings, and a new stone bridge, the present day Charles Bridge, was built across the Vltava. Charles IV is known as the founder of "Prague Gothic". At this time with a population of 40,000, Prague was one of the largest towns in Europe.

The preacher and founder of the Hussite movement, Jan Hus, preached in Bethlehem Chapel in the Old Town. Battles with the Hussites meant that the Renaissance came late to Prague. Baroque was at first an expression of the victory of the re-Catholicisation process. The first gigantic Baroque works were Wallenstein Palace and the Klementinum. Maybe the most splendid Baroque building in Prague is the Church of St Nicholas, in Malá Strana. In the 18th Century Prague Castle was extended into the complex it is today, and in 1784 the four townships were officially united.

At the turn of this century the Jewish Ghetto was sacrificed to a slum clearance project. In 1918 Prague became the capital of newly independent Czechoslovakia.

TO AND FROM PRAGUE

There are international air services to Prague from all over the world. See section on *Travelling to and from Czechoslovakia*. Internally there are direct flights to Bratislava, Ostrava, Piešťany and Sliač near Banská Bystrica, and flights via Bratislava to Košice and Poprad. Latest check-in times at the airport: 20 minutes before domestic flights; 40 minutes European flights; 50 minutes intercontinental flights; 90 minutes Moscow, Hanoi or Havana. See section *Getting Around* below for transport between airport and city.

If arriving by car try to avoid rush hours and Sunday nights, when driving in Prague's traffic can be quite an ordeal. Even if you have a good map, you will often find closed roads and badly marked detours.

There are many train and bus stations, so make sure you know which one you are arriving at or departing from. The main bus station is Florenc (metro line B or C to Florenc). Hlavní nádraží is the main railway station, and under it, on line C, is the metro station of the same name. Many international trains, especially those from "eastern" Europe, go to Praha-Holešovice (metro line C, Nádraží Holešovice). Trains for Karlštejn, Plzeň and places west leave from Nádraží Praha-Smíchov (metro station Smíchovské nádraží, line B).

Advance bookings are best on the most popular bus routes, and can be made at Florenc or Čedok's office at Na příkopě 18. There are frequent express buses to Brno: Čebus have a service for Kčs 69 leaving from Švermovy sady (metro Florenc). Express buses to Bratislava take 4 hours 40 minutes, but there are not many of them. *Rychlík* trains to Bratislava are cheaper than the bus and most of them take about 6 hours. There are long queues for tickets and information at Hlavní nádraží in the summer holidays, so it pays to learn to read the Czech timetables. The office for seat reservations (*místenky*) here is open all night. The best way to Karlovy Vary is by express buses, which leave about every 1½ hours, take two hours, and don't usually require booking if you travel midweek.

There are frequent trains from Berlin and Budapest, as well as trains from West Germany and Austria. For more information on international train and bus connections see section on *Travelling to and from Czechoslovakia*.

For hitching towards East Germany take the metro to Fučíkova and the country bus from there to Zdiby. Get off at the first stop in Zdiby, and walk back 50 metres from the stop to the top of a rise. For hitching towards Brno, Bratislava, Tábor or České Budějovice take the metro to Pražského povstání. Cross nám. Hrdinů to 5. května, the highway out of Prague. For hitching towards Plzeň and West Germany take metro line B to Mostevská, then head out along Plzeňská by tram, bus or foot.

GETTING AROUND

Parking in the historic centre is discouraged, in fact prohibited outside special parking places. You must not enter Václavské náměstí (Wenceslas Square) by private car unless you are residing in a hotel there. You can park outside the centre, and then use public transport.

The best time for walking around the city is at the weekend when there is not so much traffic and pollution. Conditions for pedestrians have improved with the recent creation of pedestrian precincts and the best way to sightsee in the centre of Prague is to walk.

There are three complementary forms of public transport in Prague: trams, buses and the fast, efficient metro. The metro operates from 5.00am to 12.00pm. There is quite a confusing network of trams and buses. Whatever map you have is probably out of date, as the lines are constantly changing as streets are closed or reopened. But it is fun finding out, and there is an excellent public transport system if you can work it out. All tram, bus and

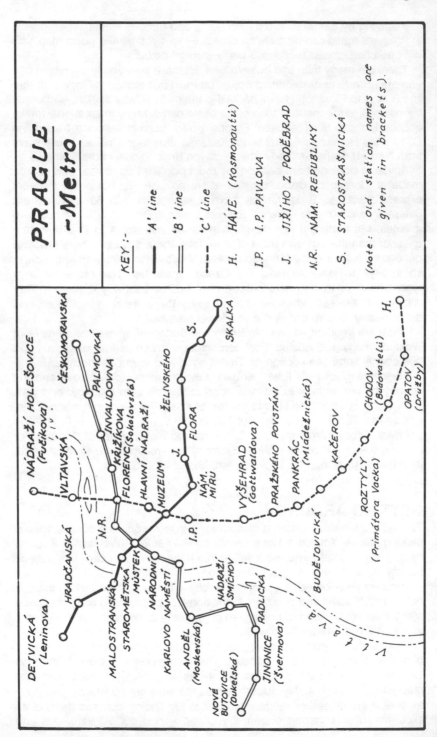

metro stops have names. Many of these were changing at the time of writing, and I have included the new metro station names. Night trams have blue numbers. There are route maps on the timetables at the night tram stops. There are also night buses. The section *Getting Around in Czechoslovakia* describes the basic ticket system, but note in addition the following: that you can travel on the metro for 90 minutes without a new ticket if you don't leave the underground; 24-hour tickets (from the time of purchase) are available from red automats as well as five-day tickets; the fare is expected to quadruple to Kčs 4 shortly.

There are three alternative bus services between the airport and city. A shuttle bus service between the airport and the most expensive hotels cost Kčs 100. It is necessary to book it at your hotel at least one hour before departure. The normal ČSA bus service to the airport runs according to a seasonal timetable. Tickets cost Kčs 6 for international flights, but for domestic flights the bus is free. The downtown terminal is at Revoluční 25, but the bus also stops at Dejvická metro station. Otherwise take the city bus number 119 from the airport to Dejvická metro station, from where you can take the metro into the centre. If travelling out on bus 119 make sure you don't get off at the old airport, which you pass on the way to the new.

Taxis are cheap by west European standards. You can find them on Václavské náměstí at night. Be wary, as some drivers try to rip you off. The fare from the airport should be about Kčs 100 (December 1990). "Hotel taxis" are more expensive as you have to pay the return fare to the hotel.

MAPS AND GUIDES
A map is a must. The *Praha Town Plan* for Kčs 10 is probably the most useful, showing the whole central area and much of the suburbs on a single sheet. If you are staying in the centre and confining yourself to this area, Prague Information Service had a free map of the centre last time I was there, otherwise buy *Praha, Plan of City Centre* for Kčs 6. This is simply an enlargement of the centre part of the first map with some important landmarks drawn on. It is worth having anyhow as it is much easier to follow when sightseeing in the centre. A new map, *Praha Cultural Monuments* (Kčs 18), covers the city centre and includes information in English, but doesn't show tram and bus routes. There is also a map in book form of the whole of Prague costing Kčs 34. For trips out of Prague in south and westerly directions the map *Okolí Prahy* is excellent. It includes Karlštejn, Koněpruské Caves and Slapy. These maps are not always available.

Olympia has published a new guidebook to Prague in English. (*Prague*, by Michal Flegl, 1988, Kčs 45.) It is strong on history and architecture, but can be rather dry reading. There are now several guidebooks to Prague published in the West.

A good bookshop for maps and travel books on Czechoslovakia is Melantrich on Na příkopě at the corner of Václavské náměstí. Another is at Staroměstské nám. 16. There is a bookshop on Václavské náměstí (on the right hand on the way up) specialising in Slovak literature and maps.

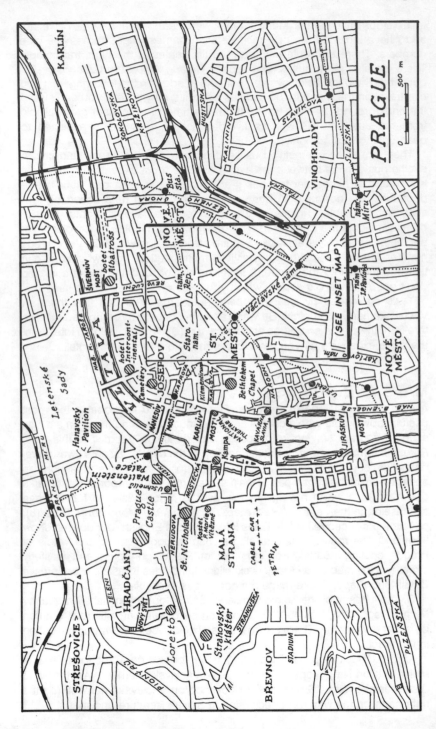

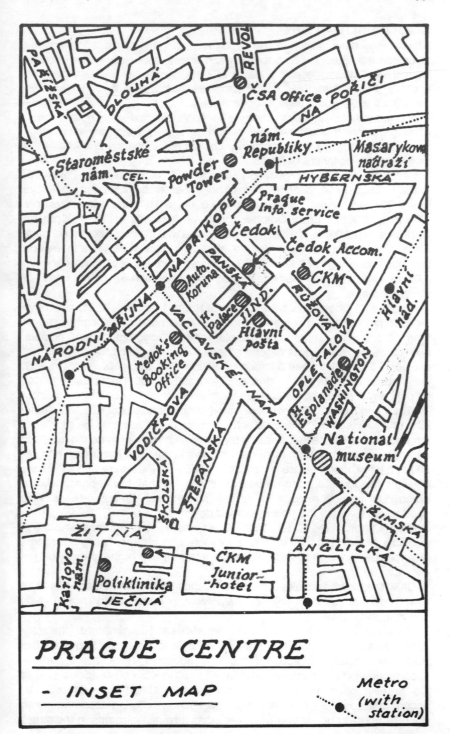

PRAGUE CENTRE

- INSET MAP

Metro
(with
station)

ACCOMMODATION

It has always been difficult to find accommodation in Prague, and since the revolution the situation has become even worse, especially in the cheaper price bracket, and especially in May and June, September and October, and at Christmas and New Year, Easter and the Whit holidays. If you know when you will be in Prague it pays to book ahead.

Accommodation in private homes is easier to find than hotel rooms. Although accommodation in the centre is usually full, there is a quick turnover, so you may find something. On the houseboats it is a little easier as it is on the periphery of Prague.

Čedok have an accommodation service for foreign visitors at Panská 5, Praha 1; tel. 22 70 04, 22 56 57. From April to September it is open weekdays from 9.00am to 9.45pm, Saturdays from 9.00am to 6.00pm and Sundays from 9.00am to 4.30pm. From October to March it closes earlier: 8.00pm on weekdays and 2.00pm at weekends. They deal with the more expensive price bracket, starting at Kčs 500 a double. You can't book in advance there, and they don't usually know before 10.00am where there are free rooms. Between 9.00am and 2.00pm they can also book hotels in other parts of Czechoslovakia.

Pragotur, U Obecního domu 2, 110 00 Praha 1, tel. 231 72 81, also have an accommodation service and tend to deal with cheaper accommodation than Čedok. They can book hotels, private accommodation, hostels, bungalows and camping. Pragotur's hotel rooms are in the "C", "B" and "B*" classes. To give an idea of prices a double without bath or breakfast in a "B" class costs from Kčs 280, and in a "B*" class Kčs 336. Commission is Kčs 10 per person per night. Hotels give them information on free rooms at about 10.00am and 5.00pm. Rooms in private houses or flats cost Kčs 130 single, Kčs 180 double and 230 double with an extra bed. They may be situated a *long way* out of the centre, and are for a minimum stay of three nights. They can book accommodation in student hostels in July and August for Kčs 46-80 per person, though there is very little for Kčs 46. Persevere with asking for different categories of accommodation if they say they have none available. When booking accommodation of any sort through Pragotur, there is no need to register with the police as they do this for you.

Rekrea, Pařížská 26, tel. 232 27 51, have student accommodation available all year, but they tend to deal more with groups. These are rooms with four beds, with hot and cold water and free use of the shower on the corridor.

CKM, the Czechoslovak youth travel agency, have a new office at Žitná 10 (next door to their hotel) to help young people find hostel type accommodation.

There are now three accommodation offices at Hlavní nádraží, the main railway station. The original office may be able to book you into a student hostel for around Kčs 250. Of the new agencies Vesta offers pension accommodation out in the suburbs for Kčs 460 to Kčs 600 per double, while Co-op Tour offers private accommodation for DM20, as well as hotel accommodation. A lot of other small new agencies offering accommodation are now popping up, or you may see signs advertising rooms in the street.

People sometimes approach foreigners in the street asking if they are looking for private rooms, and recently cars have been waiting at the motorway exits to Prague with "Zimmer frei" (Room Available) signs displayed. Prices I have heard range from DM15 for a whole flat to DM25 per person sharing a room, but one thing they all have in common is that they want to be paid in convertible currency.

Camping

Even camping grounds get full in Prague in the summer holiday period. Addresses are:

Caravan Camp Motol, A, Praha 5, Plzeňská, Post code 150 00; tel. 52 47 14. Open 15/5 to 15/9. People I have spoken with who have stayed there say it is a terrible, unfriendly place. On the E50, the main road in from Plzeň.

Sportcamp Motol, A, Praha 5, V Podhájí, post code 150 00; tel. 52 18 02. Open 1/4 to 31/10. Tent camping and bungalows.

Troja, A, Praha 7, Trojská 171, post code 171 00; tel. 840 505. Open 15/6 to 15/9. Bungalows and tent camping. Full in summer. The residents on Trojská have people camping in their gardens when the camping ground is full. This is not as idyllic as it sounds, as the garden is likely to be packed with tents, and there will probably be long queues to use the inadequate sanitary facilities. You can approach people directly, but you may have to pay at Pragotur.

Slavoj Suchdol, Praha 6-Suchdol, Za sokolovnou 440; tel. 34 23 05. Tents only. Perhaps the most likely camp to have some space left, but check to see if it's open as it has been under reconstruction. Open June to September.

Camping Aritma, Praha 6, Nad lávkou 3; tel. 36 85 51. Tents only, and a little better chance than some other camps to find a space. From Dejvická metro station take bus 119, 218 or 216, or tram 20 or 26. Don't be fooled by Aritma's position beside a lake — it is not nice to swim in — but the camp is beside Džbán swimming pool.

Na Vlachovice Autocamp, Rudé Armády 217, tram 5 or 17 from the centre, or tram 5, 17 or 25 from Holešovice station. A highly recommended camp without tents. You sleep in beer barrels for about Kčs 150 a double. Open May to September, but the excellent restaurant is open all year.

Březiněves, A, U parku 6, 182 Praha 8-Březiněves; tel. 85 91 85 2. A camping ground 10km north of Prague (10 minutes by car). Nice clean rooms also for Kčs 750 a double, less if you pay in foreign currency. Good, plain food served. Open May to September, but rooms open all year.

Arrangements for YHA members

YHA members can in theory stay at the centrally located CKM Juniorhotel, Žitná 12, 121 05 Praha 2, tel. 29 99 41, for the YHA price of Kčs 90 if there happens to be a free bed, but in practice it's impossible.

There is now a hostel in Prague open all year (Ubytovna Admira, U skolske zahrady, Praha 8.) which can be booked from abroad through CKM, Žitná 12, 121 05 Praha 2 for DM18 (or the equivalent in another convertible currency) per night including breakfast. They recommend you book 40 days in advance. On receipt of your letter, they reply giving you a bank account number to pay the money into. When you arrive in Prague go first to CKM's accommodation office. You can stay in the hostel without booking from abroad for Kčs 90, but you risk that it is full. Take metro C to Nádraží Holešovice then tram 17. The price is the same for non-YHA members. Otherwise YHA members and students may stay in some student hostels in July and August for Kčs 50. There are two to three beds to a room, with use of a bathroom shared between two rooms included in price. Addresses with directions using public transport are: Spartakiádní 5, 160 00 Praha 6 – Strahov, tel. 35 44 41 (metro A to Devické then bus 143 or 217, or metro B to Korlovo náměstí then bus 176 to its terminus); Kolej VŠCHT, ČVUT Praha, Kosmonautů 950, 148 28 Praha 4 – Jižni město (metro C to Kočerov then bus 114); Vysoká škola zemědělská, Kamýcká ul, 165 00 Praha 6 — Suchol, tel. 34 41 10 (metro A to Dejvické then bus 147); Vysoká škola ekonomická, Koněvova 193, Praha 3 – Žižkov, tel. 824 604 (metro C to Hlavní nádraží then tram 9). You can go the hostels directly, but you could first check with CKM's accommodation office in Žitná ul, as the hostels in use could change from year to year, and they may know where there is space. The price for those without a YHA or student card is Kčs 127.

Other hostels (turistické ubytovny)

Ubytovna TJ Spartak Karlín Dukla, TU B, 186 00 Praha 8, Malého 1; tel. 22 20 09. Open 6.00pm to 8.00am only: in daytime you must be out. By the bus station Florenc. Handy but noisy situation. Crash pad type of place, but friendly. Communal (m & f together) hot showers. Groups have priority, so you may only know from one night to the next if you can sleep there. If full and you have a sleeping bag, you may be able to sleep on the floor.

TU Stadión, TJ Viktoria, Žižkov. A football stadium where you can sleep for Kčs 210. Tram 9.

Turistická ubytovna TJ Slovan Bohnice, TU A, Praha 8, středisko Na pískovně, post code 181 05; tel. 85 52 62 8. Take metro C to Nádraží Holešovice, then bus 102 to nám. Stare Bohnice (the last stop). 3 to 6 beds to a room.

TJ Dolní Měcholupy, Na paloučku 223. Kčs 65 per night per person. Metro A to Želivského, then bus 229 to Měcholupy. 30 minutes from centre. Last connection 00.20. Kitchenette. Possible to use sports facilities.

At the time of writing new *turistická ubytovna* were opening in Prague.

Motel

Club Motel Pruhonice, A*; tel. 72 32 41. Just outside Prague on the road to Brno. Reopening 1991. Sports facilities.

Botels

To help ease the accommodation shortage Prague has some "botels" — hotels on houseboats on the river Vltava.

Botel Albatross, B*, Praha 1, nábř. L. Svobody, post code 110 00; tel. 23 13 63 4, 23 13 60 0, 23 16 99 6. Close to centre. Doubles only: 542 kčs including breakfast. Little private shower & toilet. Not worth the money. If you do stay, try and get a room on the river side of the boat, which has a nice outlook at least. Night club.

Hotels

The most expensive hotels in Prague are another world, with better service than elsewhere, luxury, and staff who speak foreign languages.

A* deluxe (*****)

Intercontinental, 110 15 Praha 1, nám. Curieových; tel. 28 99 or if ringing from outside Prague 2311812; telex 122681 ihc c. Centrally located near the Vltava. Singles £110, doubles £140. Must be paid in foreign currency.

Esplanade, 110 00 Praha 1, Washingtonova 19; tel. 22 25 52-4, 22 60 56-9; telex 011067. £70 single, £120 double. Very flash. Near main railway station.

Hotel Palace, 110 00 Praha 1, Panská 12; tel. 235 93 94, fax 235 93 73, telex 123 337 IHPPC. The new Palace Hotel, built inside the walls of the old, opened in 1989. Opposite the main post office.

Atrium, by the river, north of Florenc. Expected to open summer 1991.

A* (****)

Forum, Praha 4, Kongresová ul. ; tel. 41 01 11 1. Opened 1988. By Vyšehrad metro station (line C). A special "4* superior" category, because at £90 single, £110 double, their prices are higher. Another world!

International, Praha 6, nám. Družby 1; tel. 33 91 11, telex 12 10 55. A large hotel a little outside the centre. Singles about US$80, doubles about US$140.

Diplomat, Eduarda Beneše 15, Prague 6, tel. 34 21 75, 231 15 91, by Dejvická metro station at the end of line A.

Panorama, Praha 4, Milevská 7; tel. 41 61 11. Again outside the centre. Singles Kčs 735, doubles Kčs 956.

B* (***)

Centrál, 110 00 Praha 1, Rybná 8; tel. 23 19 284, 23 14 240. Central, close to Powder Gate. Some rooms with bath or shower.

Paříž, Praha 1, U Obecního domu 1; tel. 23 22 05. Flash facade. Centrally situated by nám. Republiky metro station.

Hotel Tatran, Praha 1, Václavské náměstí 22. Right in the centre.

Hotel Ungelt Garni, near Tyn Church, singles Kčs 317, doubles Kčs 496.

B

Hotel Adria on Václavské náměstí is available only for groups.

Erko, 197 00 Praha 9, Kbely, Luštěnická 723; tel. 89 21 05. 40 minutes by tram and bus. Double only, extra beds available.

Hybernia, 115 44 Praha 1, Hybernská 24; tel. 22 04 31. Very central, can walk to the bus and train stations.

Juniorhotel, 121 05 Praha 2, Žitná 12; tel. 29 99 41, telex 122299. 2 to 3 bed rooms with private facilities. Kčs 346 per person. Usually full. YHA members see above.

Kriváň, Praha 2, nám. I. P. Pavlova 5; tel. 29 33 41-4. Centrally situated by I. P. Pavlova metro station.

Juventus, 120 00 Praha 2, Blanická 10; tel. 25 51 51. Small student hotel. Singles and doubles. Metro to nám. Miru.
Meteor, Praha 1, Hybernská 6; tel. 22 92 41 or 22 42 02. Central. Doubles Kčs 270.
Modra hvězda, 190 00 Praha 9, Jandova 3; tel. 83 02 91-2. Doubles only with extra beds available. Half hour by tram.
Solidarita, 100 00 Praha 10 – Strašnice, Soudružská 1; tel. 77 84 41-5, reception 77 71 45. Large modern type hotel. Singles and doubles, extra beds available. Tram 7, 11 or 14.
Union 128 00 Praha 2, Jaromírova 1; tel. 43 78 58-9. Singles and doubles. Tram 7,18 or 24.

C
Balkán, 150 00 Praha 5, Svornosti 28/218; tel. 54 07 77. In Smichov. Tram 4, 7 or 16 to Lidicka stop.
Moravan, 170 00 Praha 7, Dimitrovovo nám. 22; tel. 80 29 05, 80 24 49. 2 and 3 bed rooms. Tram 12 or 25 to U Uranie stop.

Other
For further hotels, the booklet *Prague, the Heart of Europe, Guide Book,* which you can buy in bookshops or at Prague Information Service (Kčs 15) has a list of hotels, motels and motor camps without any details or prices.

ADDRESSES AND INFORMATION

Prague Information Service, Praha 1, Na příkopě 20; tel. 54 44 44. A rarity in Czechoslovakia: a real tourist office. Open Monday to Friday 8.00am to 8.30pm in summer, or to 7.00pm in winter, Saturday 8.00am to 3.00pm, Sunday closed. They now also have information booths at Hlavní nádraží (open 8.00am to 8.00pm every day all year), Staroměstské náměstí (8.00am to 6.00pm, weekends 9.00am to 5.00pm, includes an exchange office) and Hradcanská metro station. Their free booklet *The Month in Prague* has a wealth of information, but the English edition was out of print on my last visit. There are also a few computer information screens around the town, difficult to get to use owing to the queue of people playing with them.

Čedok, Praha 1, Na příkopě 18; tel. 22 42 51. Open Monday to Thursday 8.15am to 4.15pm, Friday 8.15am to 3.45pm, Saturdays from June 1 to September 30 8.15am to 1.00pm and Saturdays for the rest of the year closing at 12.00am. Large Čedok office for foreign tourists. Here you can exchange money, book flights and trains, and find someone who speaks English to help you with other problems. Čedok's accommodation service is at Panská 5.

Pragotur. See above under *Accommodation*.

Rekrea, Praha 1, Pařížská 26, tel. 232 27 51, is the Rekrea travel agency office for foreigners.

Sport-Turist, Národní 33, 112 93 Praha 1; tel. 26 33 51, telex 122664. Make arrangements mostly for sports groups, but can also do so for individuals. They do not arrange skiing. Can accommodate in dorms etc, so could be cheaper than Čedok.

Autoturist, at Ječná 40 on the corner with Kateřinska. A travel agency office for motorists. Won't make accommodation bookings for individuals. Open Monday to Wednesday 8.30am to 11.30am and 1.00pm to 4.00pm, Thursday 8.30am to 11.30am and 1.00pm to 6.00pm, and Friday from 8.30am to 2.30pm.

CKM, Žitná 9, Praha 1, tel. 29 85 87. The youth and student travel bureau. For international student identity cards go to their office at Jindřišská 28 from Monday to Friday between 10.00am and 12.00am or 2.00pm and 4.00pm. ISIC cards cost 50 kčs and YHA 40 kčs.

IUS (International Union of Students), Pařížská 25.

Balnea (for spas), Pařížská 11, Praha 1, tel. 232 19 30. Open Monday to Friday 8.00am to 3.00pm, Tuesdays to 6.00pm.

Hlavní pošta (main post office), 110 00 Praha 1, Jindřišská 14. Has desks and pens. Open 24 hours, but poste restante is open weekdays 7.00am to 8.00pm, Saturday 7.00am to 2.00pm only. When poste restante is closed, someone from a nearby counter will *sometimes* oblige and check your mail for you. Telephone and telegram office in same building.

Changing money: At the airport, banks, exchange offices, Čedok, and the more expensive hotels. The exchange office (*Směnárna*) at Hlavní nádraží is open every day from 8.00am to 6.00pm, and after it is closed you can change cash only at the station's accommodation booking office. Another exchange office is on Celetná, just off the Old Town Square. Obchodní bank (see below) is slow, but is much faster and more efficient than the other banks. They also have counters labelled in foreign languages, and their staff speak foreign languages. Čedok at Na příkopě 18 and Živnostenská banka are the only places you can draw cash on your credit card (see introductory section, *Money*). Živnostenská banka at Na příkopě 23 are open 8.00am to 7.00pm Monday to Friday (closed for lunch 1.00pm to 1.30pm). *Chequepoint* have opened exchange offices at Václavské nám. next to Hotel Ambassador, Hlavní nádraží, Na příkopě, the Old Town Square, Prague Castle and Nádraží Holešovice, all open 9.00am to 9.00pm every day of the week, but their commission, which they don't advertise, is very high. Other exchange offices are sprouting up around the centre.

Sending money to Czechoslovakia: send to Československá obchodní banka, Na příkopě 14, 115 20 Praha. Swift-telex: CEKO CS PP. Open Monday to Friday 9.00am to 12.30pm, 1.00pm to 2.00pm (Mondays to 6.00pm).

ÚPSACA (the office of the police for registering and visa extensions), Olšanska 2. Open Monday to Friday 8.00am to 12.00am, 12.30pm to 3.30pm, except Wednesday when it is closed in the afternoon.

Left luggage. At Florenc bus station. Must be under 15kg. Closed 11.00pm to 4.00am. At Hlavní nádraží (the main railway station), 15kg maximum, maximum 45 days. Also lockers, which people have trouble working out how to use. You choose your own combination and set the interior combination to the one you chose, put in Kčs 1 and close the door. Remember the combination *and* the locker number or the number you set on the outside. Open 24 hours. Also left luggage at the ČSA terminal.

Shavers are available at Praha-Holešovice railway station.

Airlines. ČSA, Praha 1, Revoluční 1; tel. 21 46. By Kotva. ČSA Terminal is at Revoluční 25 near the Vltava. Phone number at the airport is 33 41 11 1. British Airways, Praha 1, Štěpánská 63; tel. 23 60 353-4.

Medical. There is a medical and dental clinic for foreigners at the Fakultni poliklinika, Karlovo nám. 32, 3rd floor. First aid for UK citizens is free. Otherwise you must pay in western currency.

Foreign press: There is a foreign press shop at Jungmannova 5 (near the end of the street nearest Vodičkova), Praha 1. Melantrich on Na příkopě at the bottom of Václavské náměstí sell the Guardian.

American Embassy: Has a library with books, periodicals and newspapers open to the public, and shows videos of US news in the afternoon. Address: Tržiště 15, 125 48 Praha 1. Tel. 53 66 41, ext. 238. Open Monday to Thursday 11.00am to 6.00pm and Friday 11.00am to 3.00pm. Recently an "American Hospitality Center" and "American Tourist Services" office has opened at Malé náměstí 14 (tel. 236 7486).

Rental Cars: Pragocar, Praha 1, Štěpánská 42, tel. 24 52 809, 23 52 825, telex 122 641. Also at the airport (tel. 36 78 07, telex 122 729), Hotel Forum (tel. 41 02 13) and Hotel Intercontinental (tel. 231 9595). Rates (set in US$) from US$28 to US$50 per day, US$171 to US$305 per week, plus 26c to 44c per kilometre. Unlimited mileage rates US$88 to US$154 per day, US$327 to US$569 per week. 15% tax is added to all these rates. Petrol US$0.70 per litre. Insurance: driver pays first US$120 in case of damage to vehicle. This can be waived on payment of an extra US$5 per day or US$30 per week. Passenger insurance US$2 per day. Delivery fee US$0.20 per kilometre. One way rentals: up to 200 km free, 201 to 500 km US$50, 501 to 1000 km US$80, over 1000km US$150. If between Pragocar stations, no extra charge. Tie ups with international rental car companies, so cars may be taken out of Czechoslovakia or vice versa. Caravans can also be rented. Small caravans cost US$8 per day and sleep two adults and one child. Larger caravans cost US$11 per day, and sleep two adults and two children. Plus 15% tax again. Mostly Czechs rent caravans.

Film processing: There are now labs that can process C41 colour negative film (Kodak, Agfa, Sakuracolour and Fuji) in Prague: Minilab, at Na příkopě 24 (in the arcade) and at Rytířská 22. It takes 48 hours, or 24 hours express, and is quite expensive. They *can not* process slides.

WHAT TO SEE

A coronation route has recently been reconstructed from Na příkopě via the Powder Tower, Old Town Square, and Charles Bridge to the castle, connecting many of the sights described below. It has been criticised because, while the building facades along it have been carefully restored, in the streets behind, away from foreign visitors' eyes, everything has been left to decay.

Staré město (the old town)

Staré Město, the Old Town, centres on **Staroměstské náměstí**, the Old Town Square, a beautiful place by day, and a haunting place by night. Staroměstské nám.'s most famous tourist attraction is the **astronomical clock** on the Old Town Hall. First built in 1410, it has undergone modifications through the centuries. Damaged by the Nazis in 1945, it was operational again by 1948. Every hour the skeleton, the symbol of death, rings the bell, nodding his head at the Turk, the miser and the figurine representing vanity. But the others nod their heads back, showing that they are not ready to die. As the bell strikes, two windows in the top of the clock open, and the twelve apostles parade between them. The performance is completed by a crowing rooster.

The **Old Town Hall** itself is a complex of several buildings erected between the 14th and 19th Centuries. Founded by King John of Luxembourg in 1338, it was formed by joining the existing buildings together. The area was often flooded by the river Vltava, so the streets were raised, and the Town Hall's ground floor became its cellar. A large part of the complex was destroyed in World War Two. The Old Council Chamber is the most beautiful part remaining. The Old Town Hall is open daily from 8.00am to 6.00pm from March to October, and 8.00am to 5.00pm during the rest of the year. There are tours each hour immediately after the clock performs. The tower provides a good view of Prague and is not difficult to climb (a lift is available for the handicapped and elderly).

In 1621 Staroměstské nám. saw the execution of 27 of the leaders of the uprising of the Czech nobility against the Habsburgs, after the Habsburgs defeated them at the Battle of White Mountain. The square was a meeting place during the Hussite period, and has a **monument to Jan Hus** which was unveiled in 1915 on the 500th anniversary of his burning at the stake. The large Gothic church with its two steeples just back off the square is the **Church of Our Lady of Týn**. Begun in 1380 and completed in 1511, it was the main church of the town, and the seat of the archbishop, during the Hussite period. The towers are said to represent Adam and Eve. It is now open to the public again after restoration. The building in front of the church

Domažlice (Photo by S. Hayman)

Český Krumlov

Dining room, Hluboká castle

is the old Týn School. On the same side of the square, **Dům u zvonu**, the Gothic building with the bell at the corner, has reopened as a gallery. The narrow little streets around Staroměstské nám., with their quaint old buildings, date from medieval times, while the broad Pařížská has an atmosphere of elegance.

Another church worth visiting is **Sv Jakub** with its Minorite monastery in Malá Štuparská. The building of this church was started by Václav I (King Wenceslas I) in 1232. Work on the large Gothic form of the church was started by King John of Luxembourg and completed under the reign of Charles IV in 1374. Even in today's Baroque form, it has preserved some of the High Gothic influence. It differs from other Prague churches, for example with its very long nave. Just inside, high up to the right, hangs the arm of a man who took something from the church and wouldn't let go of it. Because of its good acoustics the church is often a venue for concerts.

The **Powder Tower (Prašná brána)** at the northeast end of Na příkopě is one of Prague's landmarks. This Gothic tower dates back to 1475 and it was used for a time as a magazine for gunpowder; hence its name. A remnant of the city's medieval fortifications, it is open for its museum and view on Wednesday, Saturday, Sunday and public holidays during the following hours: May to September 10.00am to 6.00pm; April and October 10.00am to 5.00pm; November to March closed. Near the Powder Tower, at nám. Republiky 5, is **Obecní dům**, a beautiful building in Art Nouveau style, dating from 1910. It houses the Smetana Concert Hall, which is worth a look at if it is open.

It's almost worth changing money at **Živnostenská banka** at Na příkopě 20 just to see inside the building. Look up!

The **Karolinum** (Železná 9) is the oldest building of Charles University, dating from the 14th Century. It was adapted to the Baroque style in 1718.

On Husova opposite Karlova is Clam Callasův palác, built in Baroque style in 1713-19, and today housing the Prague archives. They are open only in the summer if there is an exhibition. There is beautiful sculpture by M. B. Braun, and the frescoes on the stairway depict the Triumph of Apollo. It is possible to look in during working hours (ie weekdays 9.00am to 12.00am, 1.00pm to 3.00pm).

The **Klementinum** is the second largest building complex (after the castle) in Prague, and fills the block between Karlova, Seminářská, Platnéřská and Křižovnická. In 1232 the Dominicans built a monastery here. This was later acquired by the Jesuits, who gradually bought up the surrounding buildings. The Baroque form of their Jesuit college dates from the 17th Century. The Klementinum was a centre of the counter-Reformation. Father Koniáš burnt 30,000 "heretical" Czech books here. Today it houses the State Library, the Slav Library, the University Library (which includes a collection of rare manuscripts starting from the 14th Century) and the oldest meteorological station in Czechoslovakia. **Kostel Sv. Kimenta**, one of the churches in Karlova, was a centre for the Dominicans from 1232, but from 1556 became part of the Jesuit college. Today it is a Greek Catholic church. The present form is from 1711-15, and the sculptures by M. B. Braun. The whole church is Baroque, from the peak of Czech Baroque, rather than the mixture of styles that is normal.

Powder Tower and Obecní dům, Prague

Johannes Kepler, the German astronomer, lived at Dům U francouzské koruny (house at the French crown) at Karlova 4. The elliptical chapel across the street gave him the idea that the planets "circled" the sun in an ellipse. The original **Bethlehem Chapel (Betlémská kaple)** was built in Gothic style in 1391. The Czech reformer Jan Hus taught and preached here in the Czech language (which was not allowed) from 1402 to 1412. In the late 18th Century the chapel was demolished, but part of the walls survived and it was reconstructed from 1949 to 1954. It doesn't look anything much at first, but find a guide to explain the history to you. Open daily April to September 9.00am to 6.00pm, October 9.00am to 5.00pm, rest of year closed. On the same square as Bethlehem Chapel is **Náprstkovo muzeum** with a collection relating to American Indian, Asian and African culture. The museum has been under reconstruction, but should reopen about the time this edition is published. The Asian collection is in the branch museum at Liběchov, near Mělník.

Nearby at Husova 8 is **Kostel sv. Jiljí (Church of St Giles)**, a little known, but very interesting church. Mention of it is found back to 1238. In 1626 the Dominicans took over, and their adjoining monastery survived until 1950. The present church has to a large extent preserved its Gothic exterior, though the interior was changed to Baroque style in the 18th Century. The interior, especially the frescoes, are beautiful. (The small door to the left of the entrance to the church is open in daytime, and leads to the very peaceful former courtyard of the monastery.)

Mention the name Bartolomějská to anyone, and they will know what you are talking about. This is the headquarters of the secret police (STB) as well as the normal police (VB).

The **Bedřich Smetana Museum** is situated by the river at Novotného lávka 1, just south of Karlův most (Charles Bridge). It's open daily except Tuesday 10.00am to 5.00pm. From outside the museum there is a beautiful view across the river and Karlův most to the castle, especially at night.

Just before Karlův most there is a fantastic Baroque church on the right, founded by the Order of the Knights of the Cross in the 17th Century. Its patron saint is St Frances of Assisi. In the square outside it is a statue of Charles IV.

By the next bridge down river, Mánesův most, is the square, **Palachovo nám.**, named in memory of the student Jan Palach who burnt himself to death in 1969 in protest against the Soviet invasion of 1968. Although the square had been unofficially known by this name, the official name until after the Velvet Revolution was Náměstí Krasnoarmejců (Red Army Square).

Prague's historic bridges

Karlův most (Charles Bridge) is one of the main attractions of Prague. Named after Charles IV, this beautiful bridge is open for pedestrians only. At both ends are towers, and the bridge is lined with statues. From it you can gaze up at Prague Castle and St Vitus's Cathedral. The bridge itself and the tower at the Staré Město end of the bridge were built in the 14th Century. The tower at the Malá Strana end of the bridge was added in the 15th Century. The other smaller Malá Strana tower is Romanesque, being the only relic of the 12th Century Judith Bridge, which was destroyed by a flood in 1342. At that time Judith Bridge and the stone bridge at Regensburg were the only stone bridges in Europe. (There were earlier wooden bridges spanning the Vltava.)

strange

There is a legend that Charles Bridge was to be the strongest bridge in the world, so the builder used mortar mixed with eggs and wine. As there were not enough eggs in Prague, all towns in Bohemia were ordered to contribute. But the citizens of Velvary, not understanding properly, were afraid the eggs would break, so they hard-boiled them first. The citizens of Unhošť wanted to help even more, so they sent curd and cheese as well.

Charles Bridge was originally called Stone Bridge, or simply Prague Bridge. Its name was changed last century. Until 1841 it was the only bridge in Prague. Today's statues were added at various times between the 17th and 19th Centuries. The tower at the Malá Strana end was restored in 1969-70, and you can climb it from April to October inclusive from 10.00am to 6.00pm (Kčs 2, Kčs 1 children and students). These days the bridge is lined with people selling paintings, jewellery etc to the tourists.

The next bridge to be built was a chain bridge named after František I. Built in the first half of the 19th Century, tram passengers had to alight and walk across, continuing their tram trip from the other side.

The second oldest bridge still in use is **Železniční most (the railway bridge)** linking Holešovice and Karlín. It was designed by Alois Negrelli, the designer of the Suez Canal. Opened in 1849, parts of the bridge are original and unrepaired.

The shortest of the bridges is **most Svatopluka Čecha**, an iron bridge named after the Czech writer. Built early this century in Art Nouveau style, its original road surface was made of the Australian timber, jarrah, which lasted up to 1961.

Malá Strana

Malá Strana developed as a noblemen's suburb. The nobility and church wanted to be close to the castle. After the Battle of White Mountain in 1620, whole blocks of houses, streets and gardens disappeared to make room for palaces for the nobility. When the political administration moved to Vienna, there was a decline in the importance of Malá Strana. The dominant feature of the suburb is the dome and bell-tower of St Nicholas Church. Today Malá Strana is still a "posh" suburb, with many foreign embassies. It is an interesting part of Prague to wander around.

Stepping off Karlův most to the left before you come to the end of it takes you to **Kampa**, a peaceful island with a park and an embankment, and an old watermill on Čertovka, the branch of the river Vltava separating the island from Malá Strana. At the end of the bridge, there is an interesting herb and spice shop "U Salvatora". Nearby to the north are the pleasant gardens, Vojanovy sady.

Continuing straight ahead from Karlův most up Mostecká leads you to Malostranské nám. In the centre of this square stands the Malá Strana landmark, **St Nicholas Church, the culmination of Bohemian Baroque**. It was built from 1704 to 1755 and the architects included K. I. Dienzenhofer. The ceiling paintings have recently undergone a thorough restoration. Open daily November to February 9.00am to 4.00pm, March and April 9.00am to 5.00pm, May to September 9.00am to 6.00pm, and October 10.00am to 5.00pm.

Wallenstein Palace (Valdštejnský palác), the first monumental building of Prague Baroque, was built between 1623 and 1630. To clear the site for this palace alone, 23 houses, a brick kiln, and three gardens were demolished. General Albrecht Wallenstein is said to have plotted with the Swedes during the Thirty Years War to become king of Bohemia. But he changed sides, and became very wealthy after the Battle of White Mountain. But later intrigues and accusations led to Emperor Ferdinand II arranging for Wallenstein's assassination at Cheb. Today the palace houses a government ministry, but the gardens, which are surrounded by an enormous wall, are open to the public between May and September from 9.00am to 7.00pm (access from Letenská). In the gardens are copies of the original statues by Adrian de Vries (1626-7) which were carried off as war bounty by the Swedes in 1648.

The famous wax statue, the **Infant of Prague**, is found on a marble altar to the right in **Kostel P. Marie Vítězné (Church of Our Lady Victorious)** at Karmelitská 13. It came from Spain, and was presented as a gift in 1628. The Infant is a Catholic icon that was said to have brought the Habsburgs good luck, and even today is used as a luck and get well symbol. Copies of it are found all over the world. The church itself was built by German Lutherans in 1611-13, but was taken over and reconstructed by the Carmelite order in 1624. A stroll around Malá Strana will uncover many other palaces and churches, mostly from the 17th and 18th Centuries.

In the southern part of Malá Strana is the hill **Petřín**. A cable car operates up it between 5.00am and midnight, or you can walk up one of the many paths. On top is a 60m lookout tower, built in 1891 as a miniature Eiffel Tower. The tower has been closed for some time. There is also a diorama painting of Prague's citizens fighting the Swedes on Charles Bridge, a mirror maze (open April to September 9.00am to 6.00pm, October 9.00am to 5.00pm) and an observatory. The wall by the tower is the so-called Hunger Wall, built by Charles IV as part of Malá Strana's fortifications. Legend has it that during a period of drought Emperor Charles IV had a large crowd of poor people assembled in the castle courtyard. He fed them well, and then gave them the task of building a long wall from the castle fortifications over Petřín Hill and down to the river. They worked for two years, unpaid, but were provided with clothing and food for themselves and their families, which saw them over the worst of the drought. Petřín is a pleasant area to walk, with good views. Behind Petřín is the huge stadium, built in 1933.

Hradčany

One of Prague's dominating landmarks is **Pražský hrad (Prague Castle)** which you can walk up to from Malá Strana. Today's castle is an incredible mixture of architectural styles. Now 1100 years old, the castle has undergone constant transformation. Inside the complex is the amazingly intricate structure of **St Vitus's Cathedral (Katedrála sv. Víta)**.

The castle was founded in the 9th Century as a fortress, rebuilt as a Romanesque palace in the 12th Century, extended in Gothic style by Charles IV, and extended and adapted at various times later. On May 23 1618, a large group of noblemen demanded an audience with the two Habsburg vice regents. There was a dispute over who should be the next monarch. The noblemen didn't want the Habsburgs, and became so het up that the meeting ended with the two ministers and their secretary being thrown out of the window. Their lives were saved by the large heap of sweepings which had accumulated under the same window through the years. This is known as the second Prague Defenestration and it marked the beginning of the Thirty Years' War. The oldest part of the castle, including the famous window, is open to the public. Noblemen were said to ride their horses into the large hall here. In the 18th Century Maria Theresa had the unfinished parts of the castle completed. From the 9th Century until 1918 Prague Castle was the official seat and place of coronation of Czech sovereigns. Now it is the seat of the president of Czechoslovakia.

St Vitus's Cathedral replaced a Romanesque basilica, which itself replaced a rotunda built in the 10th Century. Construction of the cathedral began under the rule of Charles IV in 1344 and was finally completed in 1929! The stained glass windows are relatively modern. The most important chapel is that of St Wenceslas, built by Peter Parler in the 14th Century, decorated with frescoes and semi-precious stones. Czech kings were crowned here. The coronation jewels are kept in a special chamber, and only on special occasions moved for exhibition purposes.

St Georges Church (Bazilika sv. Jiří) is a simple Romanesque basilica founded in 920 AD and completed in the 12th Century, without later additions. There is a relief of St George fighting the dragon over the side entrance. The adjoining nunnery was adapted between 1963 and 1974 to house the Old Czech Art Collection of the National Gallery, Open daily except Monday, 10.00am to 6.00pm. madonnas...

At the end of the 16th Century, and especially in the 17th Century, Prague Castle became a place of refuge for those wishing to evade the jurisdiction of the Prague authorities, which reached only to the castle ramparts. So many, especially tradesmen and artisans, who for various reasons wished to elude the Prague authorities, built parasite dwellings in all sorts of places around the castle. Because of the numerous improvised fireplaces the fire risk was high, so in the 18th Century the parasite dwellings were demolished. For some reason **Zlatá ulička** Golden Lane was overlooked and here remain tiny little dwellings built into the castle wall. At the end of the street stands **Daliborka**, a prison used mainly for debtors.

In the 1960s the castle stables were converted into a gallery (**Obrazárna Pražského hradu**) housing paintings of Prague Castle. Open daily except Monday 10.00am to 6.00pm.

Tours of the castle and cathedral are not conducted in English, but it is worthwhile hiring an English speaking guide if you would like to learn more. It is best to book in advance at the tour office at the castle. The whole complex is open all year. The castle is open daily except Monday, November to March 9.00am to 4.00pm, April to October 9.00am to 5.00pm.

Hradčany was the third of the Prague towns to be founded. It arose around the castle in about 1320. Charles IV extended and fortified the town. Hradčanské nám., just outside the castle, is surrounded by palaces. From the square there is access to Sternberk Palace (Baroque, 1698-1730), which **GO** today houses a **Collection of European art**. A must for art lovers, it is one of the collections of the **National Gallery**, and open 10.00am to 6.00pm, closed Mondays. The Archbishop's Palace is also on Hradčanské nám., and in the **Schwarzenberg Palace** on the south side of the square is a **military museum**.

Following up Loretánská from Hradčanské nám. brings one to Loretánské Náměstí and the **Loretto**. The Loretto are pilgrimage churches built as copies of the original Santa Casa, in the Italian town of Loretto, which was supposed **B.S.** to be the dwelling of the Virgin of Nazareth, conveyed by angels from Palestine to Italy in the 13th Century. The Czech Loretto was built as part of the re-Catholicisation process after the victory of the Habsburgs at White Mountain; as Catholic propaganda to win back the Czechs. The Loretto Church was built during the Thirty Years War. The Loretto itself was built from 1626-31 and stands in the yard.

Nový Svět (which means "New World") was formerly the quarter of the poor. Despite later alterations the area still retains something of its atmosphere of simple little houses. **POOR**

Strahovský klášter (Strahov Monastery) was founded in 1140, but rebuilt many times in different styles. It now houses a **museum of Czech literature**. The ceiling of the Philosophical Hall of the library has a Rococo fresco from 1794 by Anton F. Maulbertsch, while the Theological Hall has frescoes by S. Nosecký. Traces of the original Romanesque structure can be seen in places. In the richly decorated Church of the Virgin Mary, Mozart played the organ. Outside there is a good view of Prague. Closed Mondays. From here there is access to Petřín. **By Swedish Embassy**

Josefov (the Jewish quarter)

On the other side of the river again from Hradčany is the Jewish quarter. Jews have lived in Prague for 1000 years. But in 1896 the whole quarter **1896** except the synagogues, cemetery and town hall was demolished in a large scale urban renewal project.

From the mid 15th Century the main Jewish cemetery which lay outside the bounds of the Jewish town was closed for burials and the **Old Jewish Cemetery** arose. This cramped area was not big enough, so the old graves **1439 →** were covered over and new ones laid above them. The last burial here was **1787** in 1787. The oldest preserved tombstone is dated April 25 1439. The reliefs on the tombstones often symbolise the name of the deceased (eg stag, cock) and his profession (eg doctor's instruments, tailor's scissors).

In the former ceremonial hall, the building by the entrance to the cemetery, are haunting reminders of the Nazi occupation in the form of a display of drawings by children in the concentration camp of Terezín. This exhibition was not respected enough to be untainted by communist propaganda.

The **Staronová (Old-New) Synagogue** is one of the oldest synagogues in Europe still in use. Dating from about 1270, it was one of the first Gothic buildings in Prague. The Klausen Synagogue was built in Baroque style at the end of the 17th Century. The Maisel Synagogue was built in Renaissance in the 1590s, and rebuilt in Baroque after the great fire in the Jewish town in 1689. The High Synagogue was built in Renaissance style in 1568 as a part of the Town Hall, and separated from the Town Hall in the 19th Century. It now houses a collection of tapestries, ornaments etc.

The cemetery, the collection of drawings, Staronová Synagogue, and the other synagogues which house various collections of Jewish significance comprise the State Jewish Museum. Many of the exhibits were collected under orders from Hitler so that he could set up a museum of "decadent Jewish culture" when there were no more Jews left. A ticket to any part of the museum gives access to all of the others. Open daily except Saturday, from 9.00am to 5.00pm (or 4.30pm out of season). The Staronová Synagogue closes to the public at 3.00pm on Fridays. There are services here on Saturdays, and daily at dawn and dusk.

Nové město (the new town)

Once a Hussite stronghold, Nové Město fared badly during the religious wars. Today it forms the commercial centre of Prague. At its heart lies **Václavské náměstí (Wenceslas Square)**, which has been a site of protests since Hussite times. It was here Jan Palach burnt himself to death in January 1969. After the brutality with which the 1989 demonstration in his memory was put down, it is a wonder there remained people brave enough to carry out the later demonstrations which eventually led to the "Velvet Revolution". Although the square looks relatively modern, it was in fact Charles IV who had it built in 1348 in connection with the creation of Nové Město. Earlier it was the site of horse markets and was known as Koňský trh (Horse Market) until it received its present name in 1848. Václavské náměstí is a long wide street lined with elegant hotels and shops, and dominated by the **National Museum, which was built 1885-90.** Unless you have a particular interest in any of its subjects (geology, palaeontology, zoology, mineralogy, pre-history) you may not find the museum very interesting. It is open 9.00am to 4.00pm Monday and Friday, 9.00am to 5.00pm Wednesday and Thursday, closed Tuesday. The statue at the top of the square is of St Wenceslas (Sv. Václav), and is a common meeting place. Dating from 1912, it is the work of Josef Václav Myslbek.

Just off the bottom end of Václavské náměstí, to the south, is Jungmannovo náměstí. At number 18, back off the square, is **Kostel Panny Marie Sněžné (Church of Our Lady of the Snows)**, which Charles IV started building in 1347. The present church dates from 1375-97, while the interior dates from the 17th and 18th Centuries. The church was designed to reach as far as the present day Jungmannovo náměstí, and even though this never happened, it is still the biggest church building in Prague, its nave reaching a height of 33 metres. Fotochema have a small photo gallery on the same square, with changing exhibitions. (The sign over the door says *výstavní síň*.) Another gallery with changing exhibitions is Galerie Mladých (U Řečických) at Vodičkova 10 (tel. 22 59 02).

The place on the street Národní demonstrating students were forced through and beaten at by the police in November 1989 was still marked by burning candles a year later, and is now marked also by a memorial plaque.

The house of Slovak culture (**Dům slovenské kultury**) at Purkyňova 4, by Národní třída metro station, has Slovak exhibitions, films and food.

The **New Town Hall (Novoměst. radnice)** is presently under reconstruction. It's on Karlovo nám., which, named after Charles IV, is the second largest square in Prague. On the river at the bottom of Myslíkova is the art gallery and restaurant **Mánes**, named after the Czech painter. This was one of the centres of activity during the demonstrations and strikes in late 1989.

The old part of the present **Hlavní nádraží, the main railway station** was built in Art Nouveau style in 1901-09 on the site of an older station building, and may be worth a look if you are passing through. The new station dates from 1980. Nearby at Jeruzalémská 7 is the Jubilee Synagogue, built in pseudo-Moorish style in 1906. It is closed, but is a colourful and interesting sight from the outside.

The author Franz Werfel was born in Prague and there is a memorial plate on his house in Havlíčkova.

For rainy days, you could try the first floor of Varieté Praga, Vodičkova 30, where you can play cards, chess and billiards. *maybe fun !*

Vyšehrad

Just south of Nové Město, situated high on a bluff overlooking the Vltava, is Vyšehrad, the former seat of the Přemyslid princes. The Church of St Peter and St Paul, the Romanesque rotunda of St Martin, the deanery, and gardens and cemetery are there today. A peaceful spot to relax, it offers a beautiful view of the Vltava and Prague.

Smíchov

W A Mozart lived for a time at **Betramka** (Mozartova 169), a villa belonging to Josefina Dušková. He composed many works here, and the villa is now a Mozart museum. Open every afternoon except Monday, mornings also at the weekend.

Vinohrady

Just east of the centre of modern Prague, Vinohrady was covered in vineyards in Charles IV's time and takes its name after the stately home which still exists as a children's and young people's home in the park, Havlíčkovy **?** sady, a small area of which is covered in vines today (behind a high fence). Before World War Two the nearby street U Havlíčkových sadů, which houses the Danish Embassy, was the most expensive in Prague.

Žižkov

Národní památník na Žižkově (Žižkov National Monument) stands on the hill where the Hussite army defeated the "crusaders" in 1420. The name of the hill was changed from Vítkov to Žižkov, in honour of the Hussite

commander. The remains of leading members of the Czechoslovak
Communist Party lie here, and there is a memorial to the Soviet army.

Troja

In the northern suburb of Troja is Prague's zoo and *Trojský zámek* (Troja
Chateau), which was recently opened to the public (bus 112 from Nádraží
Holešovice metro station).

Roztoky

At Roztoky, in the northern suburbs of Prague, is a castle with a very nice
garden. Take a bus from Dejvická metro station, or a train from Masarykovo
nádraží. Open 9.00am to 5.00pm, closed Monday.

Out of Prague

One of the main attractions in the vicinity of Prague is Karlštejn Castle.
Charles IV had Karlštejn built in the 14th Century to house the royal jewels.
The foundation stone was laid in 1348 and the castle was finished in record
time, Charles IV taking possession in 1355. The present appearance of the
castle reflects two major periods of reconstruction: from 1575 to 1597, and
from 1887 to 1897. In 1420 the treasures were removed from the castle. In
1422 Karlštejn was under seige by the Hussites for seven months. Swedish
attacks badly damaged the castle in 1648, and from then on it lost its political
importance. The restoration work commenced in 1887 was intended to
restore its Gothic appearance.

The exterior of the castle is perhaps more impressive than the interior. The
exterior walls are six metres thick, and the interior two metres. The tower
which dominates the castle houses the Chapel of the Holy Rood, which is
decorated with precious stones.

From Prague, Karlštejn is 28km by car. Take Highway 4 towards Zbraslav,
Dobřichovice. Trains leave from Praha Smichov station, and take about 40
minutes — pleasant trip. The village of Karlštejn itself is also nice, and the
castle looks quite imposing above it. Open 9.00am to 4.00pm, May to
September 8.00am to 6.00pm, may be closed in January and February.
Closed Mondays. Entrance Kčs 10, Kčs 5 children. Tours in Czech and
German, but good displayed multilingual information. There are attractive
walks in the area (see map *Okolí Prahy*).

Near Karlštejn, but a bit difficult to get to without a car, are the **Koněprusy
Caves**, the largest stalactite caves in Bohemia, where there have been many
archaeological finds from Palaeolithic times. In the 15th Century there was a
coin counterfeiting centre here. Open April to October Monday to Sunday
8.00am to 3.00pm.

In the summer **Slapy Dam**, on the Vltava south of Prague, is a popular
destination, accessible by boat (3 hours) or bus.

Konopiště is a chateau with a wonderful big park, 44km south-east of
Prague near Benešov. Once owned by the Austrian Crown Prince Ferdinand
d'Este, who was assassinated at Sarajevo in 1914, it houses a large collection
of medieval weapons. Open May to August 9.00am to 6.00pm; September
9.00am to 5.00pm; April and October 9.00am to 4.00pm; closed Mondays.

Entrance fee Kčs 10. Train to Benešov, then local bus to Konopiště. Nice motel & restaurant.

South of Prague in **Jílové u Prahy** is a museum (*Okresní Muzeum v Jílovém u Prahy*) with permanent <u>exhibitions on tramping</u> and the history of **?** the region, as well as changing exhibitions. Open 9.00am to 12.00am and 1.00pm to 4.00pm, closed Monday. Tel. 995 17 36.

Lidice was razed to the ground by the Nazis after the assassination of Reinhard Heydrich by Czech and Slovak patriots who were parachuted into Czechoslovakia. Hitler said that one Czech town must be "wiped off the face of the Earth". Lidice was chosen. The men of the village were shot, and the women and children taken to concentration camps. Lidice was left as it was, and a new village built a little north of the old. Lidice was a mining village, and British miners from Birmingham decided that "Lidice shall live". A movement was started with contributions from all over the world. A large rose garden was planted on the site of the village, and many other villages were renamed "Lidice".

A film was taken by the Nazis of the destruction of the village. The memorial ground is open daily throughout the year, and the museum Oct. to March 8.00am to 4.00pm, April to Sept. 8.00am to 5.00pm. Lidice is 22km north-west from Prague. If driving take highway 7 towards Kladno. Public transport: metro to Dejvická, then take the Kladno ČSAD bus (Lidice is before Kladno).

Between Prague and Plzeň there are a lot of woods. Brdy is pleasant for hiking.

To the north and east of Prague, around the Elbe, fruit and vegetables are grown.

BOATING ON THE VLTAVA

In summer there are boat trips on the Vltava if the water level is high enough. They depart from Palacký bridge roughly hourly between 10.00am and 4.00pm daily except Monday. One trip is around central Prague, another north to Roztoky, and another south to Slapy (see above). In summer you can hire small boats by the National Theatre or by the House of Artists on Slovanský ostrov, but you may have to queue for them.

SIGHTSEEING TOURS

Prague Information Service arrange <u>three-hour walking tours of Prague.</u> GOOD!
Čedok's sightseeing tours can be booked at their office opposite Hotel Intercontinental at Bílkova 6, Praha 1, (tel. 2318255, 2316619). Most of their tours leave from this office, though with many it is possible to get picked up at an earlier time from Hotel Panorama (tel. 416 679) or the Čedok office at Václavské náměstí 24 (tel. 235 6356).

Sightseeing tour of Prague. Three-hour guided tour beginning 10.00am daily all year, with extra tours during the summer. Bus tour of main sights and visit to Prague Castle. Kčs 320.

Prague at Night. Five hours. One hour sightseeing tour followed by folklore show, dinner and night club. May 15 to October 15 Wednesday and Friday 7.00pm. Kčs 700.

Excursions from Prague

<u>Karlovy Vary</u> — Lidice, whole day. April to October Monday, Wednesday and Friday 8.45am. Kčs 820.

<u>Karlštejn</u> — <u>Konopiště</u>, whole day, April to October, Tuesday, Thursday, Saturday, and Sunday, 8.45am. Kčs 650.

<u>Southern Bohemia</u>, visits České Budějovice and Hluboká, whole day. Mid-May to mid-October, Wednesday, Friday, and Sunday, 8.45am. Kčs 790.

Czech Wine Tour. Tour to Mělník and Veltrusy. Mid-May to mid-October, Saturday, 1.30pm. Half day. Kčs 420.

Other tours include <u>Kutna Hora</u>, Bohemian Paradise and Plzeň. Consult the table of contents and index to find more information on these destinations.

EVENTS

Mostly in May, but running a bit into June, an International Spring Music Festival is held in Prague. You are advised to book at least six months in advance for accommodation.

EATING

Prague eateries can get crowded, and it can be very hard to find a seat somewhere. Expensive restaurants are sprouting around the tourist areas and it is more difficult to find cheaper ones now. But in neither category, is there likely to be any room. Most of the hotels have their own restaurants. If you're not too fussy about what you want, and don't mind standing, your best bet may be to go to one of the large *bufet* around Václavské náměstí and choose the shortest queue. If there are two of you, one can queue for the drinks while the other queues for the food. Or buy sausages from one of the stalls on Václavské nám., or *bramborák*, the potato pancakes you can often buy on the street, and sit on the benches in the middle of the square to eat.

The old town and Jewish quarter

U Prince is a sk.II restaurant open till 10.00pm on the Old Town Square, near the clock. Another on the same square is Staroměstská Restaurace (sk.III) at no 19, open 9.00am to 11.00pm (10.00pm in winter)

In Malé Náměstí, behind the town hall, is a busy crowded sk.III restaurant called U Radnici with better than average food. But it closes at 6.00pm (4.00pm on Friday).

Vegetarka is a Prague rarity: a vegetarian restaurant. Open weekdays 11.00am to 2.30pm only, you'll find it on Celetná, just off Staroměstské nám. Otherwise some of the more expensive restaurants may prepare vegetarian dishes for you if you ask.

In the Jewish Quarter at Maislova 18 is a kosher restaurant (košer jídelna rest.) open 11.30 to 13.00 only, but it is often reserved by groups.

Next to the old synagogue, but on Pařížská, is the restaurant U Staré Synagogy, a better than average sk.III in surroundings and food. Open 9.00am to 10.00pm. No smoking.

In Obecní dům, the building by the Powder Tower, Plzeňská Restaurace (not to be confused with the better known restaurant of the same name on Karlovo nám.) has a good uncrowded sk.III restaurant in the cellar. Because tourists don't come here you get treated a lot better than in other places. Find it by going right through the entrance hall and inside the building, then downstairs to the right past the *vratna*. Open 12.00 to 4.00pm, as in the evening it becomes a disco. In the same building on ground floor level there is a nice sk.II restaurant to the right of the entrance hall, and a pleasant sk.II kavárna to the left.

Pivnice U Medvídků (sk.II**) at Na perštýně 7, off Národní, includes a non-smoking dining room which you'll find by going as far as you can to the left after entering. Open 9.00am to 11.00pm.

Václavské náměstí and nearby streets

At the bottom of Václavské náměstí, on the corner with Na příkopě, is Automat Koruna. This is a huge, cheap stand-up place with many counters offering different types of food, and long queues. A little way up the street on the other side is another stand-up place, open later in the evening than Koruna.

Blaník, near the top end of Václavské náměstí on the right hand side if you face the statue, is a *gril* open until midnight for, by Prague standards, late night snacks and drinks. The cheaper *bufet* closes at 9.00pm.

Dům Potraviny at the top of Václavské nám. is a very fine restaurant, and one can normally find a seat.

On Štěpánská, just off Václavské náměstí, is the Indian restaurant Mayur (sk.II). Reservations are usually necessary. Don't eat the cashews or whatever is put on the table unless you want to pay for them. Open 12 noon to 4.00pm and 6.00pm to 11.00pm. Next door is an Indian snack bar open from 11.00am to 11.00pm every day in the summer. On the same street beside Hotel Alcron Plzeňská Restaurace has good food, but is better known for its good draft beer.

Bistro na Můstku on Na můstku at the bottom of Václavské náměsti has *palačinky* (pancakes) and the famous but hard to come by *švestkové knedlíky* (plum dumplings) on the menu, but you'll be lucky if they actually have them. You might have more luck with their spaghetti and pizza. Open daily 9.00am to 8.00pm.

U Šuteru vinárna at Palackého 4 is Moravian. Not bad, usually not full. Sk.III. Open 11.00am to midnight, Saturday 4.00pm to midnight, closed Sunday. Upstairs there is a more expensive restaurant, with mains at around Kčs 50. I preferred the food downstairs.

Slovak specialities can be found at the restaurant in DSK (Dům slovenské kultury, the house of Slovak culture) at Purkyňova 4, by Národní třída metro station.

Others on same side of Vltava

The restaurant on the third floor of Slovensky Dům on Na příkopě is open from 11.00am to 2.00am and has good food.

Nearby at Na příkopě 29 is the new McDonald's style Arbat. Upstairs is a Russian restaurant.

At Hlavní nádraží there are *bufets*, a sk.III restaurant with terrible service and a sk.II restaurant.

I would recommend avoiding the restaurant (sk.II*) in the new national theatre, as the food etc, in my opinion, is not up to standard.

Opposite CKM at Žitná 15 is U Pravdů, has a bar on the right and a sk.III restaurant to the left with good, cheap food and filthy toilets. Open 10.00am to 10.00pm, you can usually get a seat.

If shopping for your own groceries the underground *potraviny* at Kotva has a larger selection than other places and is open longer hours.

Malá Strana

U Schnellů (sk.II**) is popular both for eating and for a beer. Meals cost around Kčs 60, but I much preferred the bar to the right than the pseudo-ritzy restaurant to the left. Open daily 9.00am to 11.00pm, you'll find it on the corner of Tomášská and Letenská, just off the square Malostranské nám.

U Mecenáše on Malostranské nám. is a very good sk.II+20% restaurant, but it has become expensive. Open 5.00pm to 1.00am, closed Saturdays. Booking advisable.

Vinárna U Kolovrata (sk.II) is small, nice and rather different with good food. It is popular with diplomatic staff and the waiters speak English. Open 11.30am to 10.00pm, closed Sunday and Monday, it is best to reserve. At Valdštejnská 18, just off Valdštejnská nám. in Malá Strana. Cheaper than U Mecenáše.

If you head up Mostecká from Charles Bridge (Karlův most) you'll find a cheap *bufet* on the left, just before Malostranské nám.

On the way up the cable car to Petřín is the new and very expensive restaurant Nebozízek.

Other

There is a selection of both cheap and expensive restaurants around the castle area.

Praha Holešovice railway station's restaurant may look tempting with its terrace and courtyard garden, but I got ripped off by the waiter and was sick for several days after eating there.

CAFÉS

Kavárna Slavia at Narodní 1, near the river and opposite the National Theatre, is a famous and popular old coffee bar. It was the hangout of Bohèmes and snobs. Last time I was there they had introduced music and a cover charge to keep out the punks who drank only tea and didn't spend enough. Open 8.00am to midnight.

U zlatého hada at Karlova 18 is the oldest café in Prague. Established by an Armenian, the inside has now been modernised. Open till midnight. Malostranská kavárna, in the middle of Malostranské nám. in Malá Strana, ← is another famous Prague café.

By one of the stairways down to the metro at the bottom of Václavské náměstí is an *expresso* with drinks and snacks.

PUBS AND WINE BARS

Personally I avoid the well-known tourist spots of Prague, but many like to visit them, so I'll start with a couple so you can try them for yourself:

U Kalicha at Na Bojišti 12 was Švejk's pub. This is a tourist attraction; few Prague people come here. It's difficult to get in, as it is full of German package tourists who are shuffled in, then kicked out again to make room for the next bus load, almost before they have time to drink anything.

U Fleků, Praha 1, Křemencova 11, is famous for its dark beer, (which may be watered down!). In a nice building with a large beer garden, it has an international clientele, but unfriendly staff who rip you off. Open 8.30am to *yes!* 11.00pm. Tours of U Fleků's brewery can be booked through Čedok.

U. sv. Tomáše (sk.II) at Letenska 12 in Malá Strana is also popular with tourists, but has a much nicer atmosphere than the above two. Open 11.00am to 3.00pm, 4.00pm to 11.00pm. Good beer, but I wouldn't recommend the food.

Malá Strana has a collection of pubs popular with Prague's young people. If you are a beer drinker, the most popular is U Kocoura at the bottom of Nerudova (open daily 11.00am to 11.00pm). Others in the same street are U Bonaparta (about half-way along) and U Tří Sluncủ. U dvou srdcí (At the Two Hearts) is a famous pub at U lužického semináře 38 selling Staropramen 12° beer. Na Kampě hostinec at Na Kampě 14 is a typical little crowded local pub where people come to sink some suds. There are frescoes on the walls. Find it on Kampa near Charles Bridge. Closes 8.00pm.

On Karlova, near the bridge, is the *pivnice* U Malvaze (sk.III), with a barrel over the door. Here you can taste black beer from 10.00am to 10.00pm. This small, lively pub with its good atmosphere is popular with Germans, but smoky. Black beer is also sold at the railway station.

Plzeňská pivnice: u zlatého tygra (at the golden tiger) is a crowded popular pub at Husova 17. Closed Sunday.

Still in the Old Town, but a bit off the tourist trail, are U Medvíků at Na Perštýně 7 which, apart from its peaceful non-smoking room (see above), is a noisy bar frequented by locals, and U Vejvodů at Jilská 4 (sk.III), a beer hall like the popular tourist spots, but without their prices.

If you want to get away from the pseudo-ritzy places around Václavské náměstí to a more typical Czech pub, try Bránický Sklípek on the corner of Voldičkova and V jámě. It closes at 11.00pm, which of course means 10.30pm!

Vinárna ve Štěpánská is a cosy little wine bar which also sells food. On the street of the same name, you can normally get a seat here.

JZD Blatnicka on Michalská is a cheap wine place, and there are other good cheap ones in the same area.

The *vinárna* at Melantrichova 5 and T-club on Jungmannova are unofficial gay hangouts.

There is a *vinárna* to the left in the basement of Obecní dům open 10.00am to 3.00am.

Outside Florenc bus station on Křižíkova is the small smoky Denní bar Florenc, where you can get a late night drink on the way home. Open 8.00am to 2.00am, but the kitchen closes at 9.00pm.

Some of the establishments mentioned above under eating are also suitable for an evening drink. Otherwise just head out and find yourself a *pivnice* or *vinárna*.

DISCOS, NIGHT CLUBS ETC

There are a variety of places in Václavské náměstí and the surrounding streets, so try the following or find something else for yourself. Prague used to be a very safe city to be out in at night, but these days it's not just pickpockets you need to watch out for, robberies are also becoming commonplace. Václavské náměstí seems also to have become popular with prostitutes in recent years. YES

Video Discotek Zlata Husa (sk.I*+20%) on Václavské náměstí is very expensive — no jeans or running shoes. Open 7.30pm to 2.00am; come early on Saturday night or you won't get in.

Tatran at Václavské náměstí 22 also has a video disco. Open 9.00pm to 3.00am, Kčs 20 entry.

Luxor is a new disco (with telephones on the tables) Also on Václavské náměstí; Kčs 25 entry.

Disco Alfa on Václavské náměstí has a Prague speciality: unfriendly doormen. Otherwise a fairly popular, but ordinary, sort of place.

Barbara's at Jungmannovo nám 14 near the bottom of Václavské náměstí is a small bar with disco and dancing open from 9.00pm till 4.00am.

Jalta Club, in Jalta Hotel at Václavské nám. 45, has live music, disco, and a show, but is expensive. Open 9.00pm to 4.00am, closed Tuesday. Tel. 26 55 40-9. You must be "decently dressed".

Alhambra: variety show in Ambassador Hotel, Václavské náměstí 5. Kčs 50.

Vinárna U tří bílých beránků at ul 28. října 11, near Václavské náměstí, is less pretentious than the other nightclubs and is open 9.00pm to 4.00am every day. Wine and spirits are served, and old-time music played.

You can dance at Split in Štěpánská without paying a cover charge from 7.00pm to 2.00am. The café and restaurant open at 4.00pm.

The Plzeňská Restaurant in Obecní Dům becomes a disco from Tuesday to Saturday from 10.00pm to 4.00am, but it is not popular. Kčs 10 entry.

THEATRE, MUSIC, ETC

The best cultural season is spring. To find out what's on in Prague visit Prague Information Service, Čedok's booking office at Václavské náměstí 24, or one of the "Sluna" booking offices which you'll find in Lucerna, Alfa Arcade (Václavské náměstí 28) and Černá Růže arcade (off Na příkopě). It has been a major problem to get tickets in Prague for many years now, but recently it has become a little easier because Prague people go out less because they are worried about their finances with the new economic liberalism, and the increasing crime, and because theatre is not as interesting for them now that it no longer plays hide and seek with the censor, and they can now for the first time sit at home and watch western television. Nevertheless it is advisable to book well in advance.

Apart from classical concerts, the best entertainment available in Prague is possibly traditional jazz. Rock music was not popular with the old regime, and so has only recently "come out of the closet" and is not as common as in the West; keep your eyes open for posters about what is on in workers' and students' clubs etc.

Prague is famous for its Laterna Magika, a sort of blending of cinema, ⟵ ✳ theatre, pantomime and music. It was previously performed at Národní 40, which became known for another reason in November 1989, as the headquarters for Civic Forum. Theatre is still performed at this address, but Laterna Magika is closed until September 1991 when you can see it at Nová Scéna further down the same street.

Varieté Praga (commonly known by its old name of "U Nováků") is a variety show at Vodičkova 30, open daily except Monday. The ticket office is open 10.00am to 5.00pm, Tuesday to Saturday — after 5.00pm you can buy tickets for the same evening only. The programme changes monthly. The variety show is in the basement. On the ground floor is a sk.II restaurant, and on the first floor you can play cards, chess and billiards.

Národní divadlo, the old National Theatre, is at Národní 2, (tel. 20 53 64), while Nová Scéna, the new one, is next door at Národní 4 (tel. 20 62 60). Another theatre is Na zábradlí at Anenské nám. 5, near Charles Bridge (tel. 236 0 49).

There is pantomime at Branické divadlo, Praha 4, Branická 63, tel. 46 05 07, which is a long way out in Braník and hard to find.

In summer there are outdoor events in courtyards around the city. Mime is especially good, and no knowledge of Czech is required to understand it.

Laetitia, a group of singers and musicians specialising in Baroque and Renaissance music, give occasional concerts in the summer at the National Museum. Look for posters on Koncert Na Schodech Narodniho Muzeum at stations to find out when.

In Zrcdlová síň in the Klementinum there are more often concerts than at the National Museum.

There is jazz and folk at Malostranská Beseda, on Malostranské nám. Advance bookings are handled by Sluna, but you can try phoning 539024 or 532357 on the same day to see if there is any room. The door opens at 7.00pm, and the programme is from 8.00pm to about 10.00pm.

Press Jazz Club (so-called because it uses premises in the press centre) is a new jazz club operated by jazz musicians. Open Monday to Saturday from 9.00pm to 2.00am, entry is Kčs 25 to Kčs 30. The address: Syndikát novinářů ČR, Pařížská 9, Praha 1.

Reduta at Národní Třída 20 has good jazz, beat and theatre. Across the street is a new video disco. There was talk at the time of writing of introducing background jazz in Slavia (see Cafés).

Junior Klub na Chmelnici, outside the centre at Praha 3, Koněvova 219, tel. 82 85 98 has good rock music.

Divadlo Hudby on Opletalova shows audiovisuals of such artists as Michael Jackson, Barbra Streisand, Bob Marley and Frank Zappa, but what with television and the fact that such artists can now often be seen in person, interest is dwindling, so it will probably change.

Classical music venues include Hudební divadlo in Karlín (metro Florenc), the Smetana Hall in Obecní dům, and Smetanovo divadlo (Smetana Theatre, not to be confused with Smetana Hall) on Wilsonova tř (Vítězného února on old maps) near the National Museum. All of these are situated in the centre of Prague.

You'll find most of Prague's cinemas in the arcades off Václavské náměstí.

Various concerts and exhibitions are held in Julius Fučík Park from May to September.

St John the Baptist, Karlštejn Castle

CHOMUTOV

KARLOVY
VARY

Františkovy
Lázně

CHEB

Mariánské
Lázně

PLZEŇ

TACHOV

DOMAŽLICE

KLATOVY

WESTERN BOHEMIAN
SPAS and TOWNS

Western Bohemian spas and towns

CHEB

Cheb is a small medieval town, close to the German border. The centre of Cheb has recently been restored — or at least the front of the buildings that the tourists see. On the main square is a group of restored Gothic merchants' houses known as **Špalíček**, behind which is the building where Albrecht Wallenstein, the Thirty Years War military commander, was murdered. It now houses a **museum** (open Tues. to Fri. 8.00am to 12.00am, 1.00pm to 4.00pm; weekend 9.00am to 12.00am, 1.00pm to 3.00pm; closed Monday). The former New Town Hall on the square was built in the 18th Century, and now houses an **art gallery** (open 9.00am to 12.00am, 1.00pm to 5.00pm; closed Monday; Kčs 4, Kčs 2 child, student).

The **Church of St Nicholas** below the square is a huge forbidding rectangular building from the outside. It was built in the 13th Century, and has original Romanesque features. The **Church of St Bartholomew** has a group of Gothic statues, and during reconstruction after 1945 frescoes were discovered here.

Cheb Castle was built by Emperor Friedrich Barbarossa in the 12th Century on the site of a Slav fort. The tower was added in the 13th Century, and from 1665 to 1700 the castle's Baroque fortifications were built. The castle features in Schiller's work *Wallenstein*. Open April to October only, closed Monday.

There are other churches of historical interest, as well as old houses from various ages.

Cheb is small enough to walk around.

Out of Cheb

Komorní hůrka, is the youngest extinct volcano in Czechoslovakia. Last century tunnels were dug into the hill to ascertain its origin and the entrance to one of these has been preserved on the southern slopes. Lying between Cheb and Františkovy Lázně, Komorní hůrka is accessible by road, or you can walk there by following the red or blue markers from Cheb. The blue marked route is longer, as it takes you over Špitálský hill on the way. The red markers continue to Františkovy Lázně.

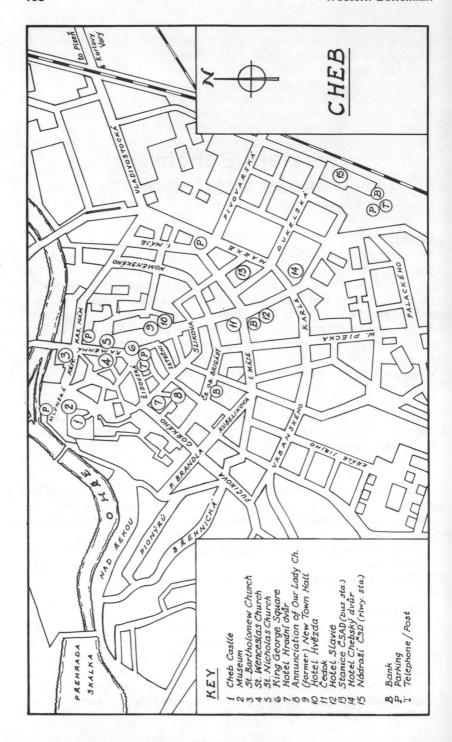

KEY
1 Cheb Castle
2 Museum
3 St. Bartholomew Church
4 St. Wenceslas Church
5 St. Nicholas Church
6 King George Square
7 Hotel Hradní dvůr
8 Annunciation of Our Lady Ch.
9 (former) New Town Hall
10 Hotel Hvězda
11 Čedok
12 Hotel Slavie
13 Stanice ČSAD (bus sta.)
14 Hotel Chebský dvůr
15 Nádraží ČSD (rlwy. sta.)

B Bank
P Parking
T Telephone / Post

Soos is a thermal area with springs and mud pools. It is nothing by New Zealand or Icelandic standards, but an interesting area nevertheless. Some of the plants are normally only found by the sea, but grow here owing to the salt in the ground from the springs. From Cheb take the Luby train and get off at the third stop, Nový Drahov. The only convenient trains leave at 13.22, 16.00 and 18.50, returning at 14.56, 17.34 and 20.26. There are a few more trains from Tršnice. Walking to Soos from Cheb is 16km via Komorní hůrka (short detour) and Františkovy Lázně (red markers).

There are recreational areas on the nearby **Skalka** and **Jesenice** dam lakes.

To and from Cheb

Cheb is within daytripping distance by bus or train of the spa towns of Karlovy Vary, Mariánské Lázně and of course the nearby Františkovy Lázně. From Karlovy Vary trains are quicker, taking about one hour as against one hour 40 minutes by bus. From Mariánské Lázně both take ¾ hour. There are regular buses to Františkovy Lázně — buy tickets from the special automat or the driver. The train leaves much less often but is quicker.

International trains stop in Cheb on their way to and from Nürnberg in West Germany. Both trains and buses to Prague take about 4½ hours. The bus and railway stations are beside each other. There is also a bus stand nearer the centre.

Information and orientation

Money can be changed at the railway station, but the exchange office is not always open at the time international trains depart and arrive. Walking straight ahead from the railway station (the route veers slightly to the right) brings you to the centre of town. On the way you pass Čedok at 1. máje 31; tel. 339 51. Money can be changed at Čedok and Hotel Hvězda on the square.

Orientační Plán Města Chebu is a useful little free map of the town with addresses in Czech and information in English on the back. Detailed map of the surrounding area: *Západočeské Lázně* (Kčs 8).

Accommodation

It is difficult to get accommodation at all times of the year. Book through Čedok, Cheb.

Hotels

Hotel Hvežda, B*, nám. Krále Jiřiho 4-6, tel. 225 49. On the square.
Hotel Slavie, B, ul. Čs. -sovětského přátelství 32; tel. 332 16. Near Čedok.
Hotel Chebský Dvůr is not normally available for travellers, as it is usually full of workers, Vietnamese when I was there.

Private

A little private accommodation is available through Čedok.

Camping

There is a good camp out at Dřenice on Jesenice lake, though it's huge and a long way out if you don't have a car. Open May 15 to September 15. Swimming, boats for hire.

Eating

There is a restaurant (open 9.00am to 10.00pm) and stand-up *bufet* (6.00am to 6.00pm) at the railway station, both sk.III. Hotel Slavie has a restaurant open 7.00am to 11.00pm, and a *vinárna* open from about 8.00pm to 2.00am (closed Sunday and Monday), both sk.II. Hotel Hvežda has a nice sk.II restaurant open 7.00am to 11.00pm. In the same hotel is a good value sit-down sk.IV *jidelna* for workers, with a good variety of food, but get in before they begin to run out of things. Fortuna is a sk.II *vinárna* and *cukrárna* on the square.

FRANTIŠKOVY LÁZNĚ

One of the three famous West Bohemian spa towns, Františkovy Lázně, with its peaceful atmosphere, large parks, and elegant white buildings, is a lovely place to stroll around. The spa was founded last century — named after the Austrian Emperor Franz I — with buildings in Empire style. Many famous people have visited here, including Beethoven and Goethe. Gynaecological diseases (particulary sterility), heart diseases and rheumatism are treated at the spa.

Komorní hůrka (see Cheb section) is a 3.5km walk from Františkovy Lázně (red markers).

Although closer to Františkovy Lázně, by public transport Soos (see Cheb section) is more easily accessible from Cheb. From Františkovy Lázně you must change trains at Tršnice, with the likelihood of a long wait, or take the bus to Cheb and the train from there. By car to Soos, drive to Hájek via Nový Drahov. Soos is a 7.5km walk on the red marked route. Hitching is useless.

By train to Karlovy Vary change at Tršnice. There are regular buses to Cheb.

There is a map of the town, *Františkovy Lázně*, costing Kčs 5.50.

Accommodation

Hotel Slovan, Národní třída 5, 351 01 Františkovy Lázně, tel. 94 28 41, is opposite Čedok on the main street.

It is sometimes possible to stay in pensions by booking through Čedok, Františkovy Lázně.

At Amerika, 1.5km from the centre, is a good camp with bungalows. Tel. 94 25 18. Open 1/5 to 30/9.

KARLOVY VARY

Karlovy Vary is the best known of the many spas towns in Czechoslovakia. The resort is tucked in the valley of the River Tepla, and surrounded by forest covered hills. It was founded in the 14th Century by the Bohemian king and

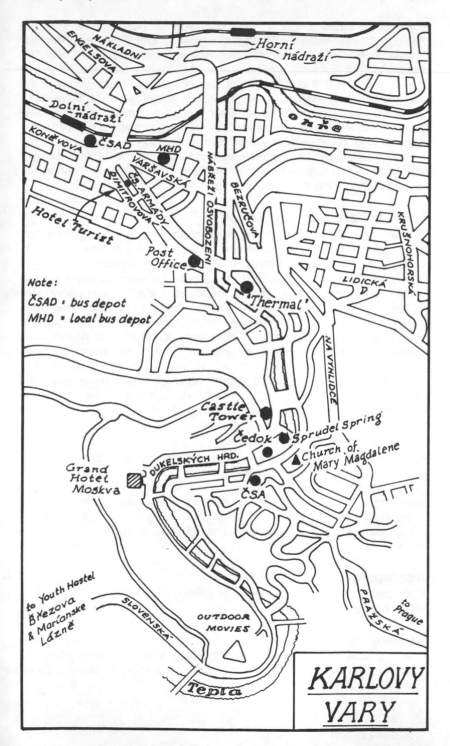

Note:
ČSAD = bus depot
MHD = local bus depot

KARLOVY VARY

Holy Roman emperor Karl IV, who bestowed his name on the town. Its previous famous visitors include Tsar Peter I, Empress Maria Theresa, Goethe, Schiller, Beethoven, Chopin, Brahms, Bismarck and Marx. The Karlovy Vary of today still preserves an air of Victorian grandeur.

Here your ears ring to the sound of German, and your eyes goggle at the expensive clothes, unaffordable in Czechoslovakia, that people are wearing. This is the "West" Germans' resort. "East" Germans complain that they can't afford the hotels. The shops are stocked with things that are difficult to buy elsewhere in Czechoslovakia — especially in the food and drink line.

Karlovy Vary could be dubbed a giant sized pick-up joint! Czechoslovaks usually go on spa cures without their husband or wife, and many find a "spa husband/wife" for the time they are here.

To and from Karlovy Vary

The quickest and most convenient means of transport between Karlovy Vary and Prague is bus. These buses run frequently, but it is wise to book in advance, especially in peak season. There are some trains.

International services include a bus service between Karlovy Vary and Vienna, and one train a day to Berlin at 7.40am (compulsory seat reservation). To/from West Germany, Paris and Britain, change trains at Cheb.

Trains to Cheb run roughly hourly. *Rychlík* take just under an hour, and *osobní* just over an hour. There is one direct connection per day to Děčín (Liberec train, *rychlík*), otherwise change at Chomutov and/or Ústí nad Labem. There is a direct daily train all the way to Slovakia. There are two railway stations in Karlovy Vary — Horní nádraží, the main station where the above services leave from, and Dolní nádraží, which is the terminal for the service to Mariánské Lázně, which takes 1¾ to 2 hours.

Getting around

From the main railway station you can cross the road and catch a bus one stop to the local bus station, or walk down the hill and across the bridge. The middle part of the valley is closed to traffic. The main way of getting around is walking, and it's a lovely area to walk in. There are buses to the upper part of the valley from the bus station. They climb along the hill on the east side of the valley, before dropping down higher up and doubling back to Leninovo náměstí.

Accommodation

It is difficult to get accommodation in Karlovy Vary in the summertime. In winter it is okay, except at New Year.

Camping and motel

Camping is at an A category camp in Březová, a few kilometres up the valley from Karlovy Vary. Phone 252 24-5. This is also an A* category motel. Open from about May to September.

Youth hostel
CKM's Juniorhotel Alice has a separate building they use as a hostel. The YHA price is also given to those with ISIC cards, but if booking from abroad you'll get charged hotel price. There are two dorms with 13 beds in each. Linen is provided, use of the shower is included in the price, but there is no kitchen. In the summer it's usually full. Juniorhotel is located up the valley in Březová. Local bus no. 7 runs up there about once an hour, or there is an occasional ČSAD bus. The hotel restaurant is open 8.00am to 8.00pm. Postal address: Pětiletky 1/147, 360 08 Karlovy Vary. Tel. 248 48-9.

Turistické ubytovny
Ubytovna TJ Slavia, TU B, Lidická 12, tel. 252 35. 25 beds in 2 to 6 bed rooms. Food from Hotel Slavia, 50 metres away. Much more central than Junior Hotel. Hugo Vind writes that Slavia was excellent and friendly and cost Kčs 54 per person.
Ubytovna TJ Slovoj, TU B, Školní 21, tel. 252 35. 50 beds. 1 or 2 beds to a room. Open 1/5 to 31/8.

Hotels
Grandhotel Moskva *** & ****, Mírové nám. 2, tel. 221 21-5, telex 156220. THE hotel in town! 300 metres above Čedok, at the upper end of the spa area. Founded in 1701, it is one of the oldest extant hotels in the world. Singles from US$25 to US$50 depending on season and whether the room has a private bath or shower. Doubles US$40 to US$80.
Hotel Central, Leninovo nám., has reopened after renovation and has been recommended.
Atlantic Hotel **, Tržiště 23, tel. 247 15 is in the same building as Čedok. Singles Kčs 125, doubles Kčs 178, without bath.
Juniorhotel Alice. Double rooms with shower: Kčs 234; with an extra bed: Kčs 291. Booked up in the summer. If booked from UK price is £12.20 per person full board, £9.90 half board. Showers extra and cost a fortune. See under Youth Hostel for further details.
Slavia, B, Lidická 12, tel. 272 71-3.
Turist, C, Dimitrovova 18, tel. 268 37. Near the bus station, and a bit cheaper.

Information
Left Luggage: at Horní nádraží, usually without problems with weight limits.
Post: The main post office, pošta 1, is open every day. Post code for Karlovy Vary is 360 00.
Changing Money: at the bank, or at the following: Grand Hotel Moskva (7.00am to 9.00pm); Atlantic Hotel (7.00am to 7.00pm); the Motel at Březová (anytime).
Maps: A town plan of Karlovy Vary including an enlargement of the main spa area costs Kčs 10. For a detailed map of the area of the three spas, with marked walking routes, look for a map called Západočeské ázně (Kčs 8).
Čedok: There are two Čedok offices. Go to the one in the resort area, not the one near the bus station which is not for foreigners.

To see and do

The lower part of the town, along the river Ohře, is not very interesting. The spa area lies along the river Tepla, and it is to here you should head. Don't expect to see springs in natural surroundings; they have been tamed, and you can see them gurgling out of pipes in various places as you walk up the valley. The 12 springs together produce about 3 million litres of mineral water per 24 hours. You'll see the patients on their drinking cures.

Near the bottom of the valley is the modern spa building "Thermal", which I would dub "The Monstrosity", built to house spa patients. As one walks up the valley, Pramen Svobody (Freedom Spring) is on the right, as is the Colonnade. Around the bend in the river, one comes to the Sprudel Spring Colonnade, where water shoots up as a geyser. It is a good spring to visit on a cold day, as it is warm inside the building, a much-admired steel structure, finished with Bulgarian marble, and completed in 1975. It was named the Yuri Gagarin Colonnade, after the first astronaut stayed here in 1961 and 1966. His statue stands in front of the colonnade.

Just behind Sprudel Spring is the Church of Mary Magdalene, designed by K. I. Dienzenhofer and built in Baroque style between 1732 and 1736. On the other side of the spring is the castle tower, built is 1608 in place of an older hunting lodge which belonged to Charles IV. In the 18th Century it was reconstructed in Baroque form. Today it's a vinárna. There are many old buildings in Karlovy Vary. Just walk around and you'll find them as you soak in the spirit of the place. A lot of the sanatoria are under reconstruction, but they are in any case not open for tourists.

There are many paths in the woods around the valley, most of which are not marked on the town map. If you want to do more than stroll, there are signposts marking longer distance routes outside Čedok and outside the main post office.

You can swim at Bazen thermal pool for Kčs 5 from 2.30pm to 9.30pm.

Eating and drinking

In the castle tower is a sk.I vinárna. Open 7.00pm to 2.00am. Closed Wednesdays & Thursdays. Otherwise there are the hotels, and plenty of other restaurants etc.

There are 12 mineral water springs in Karlovy Vary. People say that the 13th is Becherovka, a herb liquor from the town. The distillery was founded by Jan Becher, and the liquor in the special shaped bottle is reputed to be made from 123 plants.

Culture and entertainment

Karlovy Vary has a reputation for an active cultural life. The many events include an annual International Film Festival held in about July. In 1990 the programme included nearly 30 previously banned films made by exiled Czechoslovak film people. Higher up the valley there are open air movies in the summer. The place to go at night is the Disco at the Grand Hotel Moskva (open every night).

MARIÁNSKÉ LÁZNĚ

Mariánské Lázně is the second most famous of Czechoslovakia's spas. Founded last century with buildings in Empire style, Mariánské Lázně's famous visitors included Gogol, Kafka, Ibsen and Goethe, whose *Marienbader Elegie* was about the love he felt for Ulrika von Levetzow here. (Marienbad is the German name for Mariánské Lázně). There are 140 springs in the area, 39 of which are used for therapeutical purposes. It is worth seeing the colonnade housing Křížový and Rudolph Springs. The town's new attraction is the Singing Fountain, with synchronised jet, music and illumination effects.

The Municipal Museum (Městské Muzeum) at náměstí Klementa Gottwalda 11 has exhibitions on the history of the town and spa, Goethe and West Bohemia. Goethe stayed in this house, one of the oldest in Mariánské Lázně, in 1823. Chopin was in Mariánské Lázně in 1836, in the house called u. Bílé Labutě. There is a Chopin Museum (Památník Fryderyka Chopina) at Dům Chopin, Tř. Odborářů 47, open Tuesday to Thursday 10.00am to 12.00, 2.00pm to 4.00pm. Every year around August-September a Chopin Music Festival is held in Mariánské Lázně.

Pravoslavný kostel sv. Vladimira (St Vladimir Orthodox Church) was built in 1901 and has noteworthy icons.

The summer golf course is used for skiing in winter. At the lake Lido-koupaliště (take bus 17 to the last stop) is swimming, rowing boats and a restaurant.

To and from Mariánské Lázně

International trains from Frankfurt and Nürnberg to Prague pass through Mariánské Lázně. Buses and trains to Prague operate via Plzeň — most of the trains are *rychlík*. Many trains and some buses to Plzeň and Cheb.

One bus a day to Karlovy Vary (not in Xmas-New Year period), leaving Mariánské Lázně 12.30, and leaving Karlovy Vary at 5.00pm. Otherwise several trains a day, but they are much slower than the bus.

One bus a day to České Budějovice, two a day to Domažlice.

Buses leave from outside the railway station.

Getting around

There are parking places at the north and south ends of town. The local bus service is useful for getting from the station into the centre. Routes 2, 5, and 6 are trolley buses which operate from 3.00am to about 12.30am. Other buses operate from about 6.00am to about 10.30pm. On all buses you must have the exact change.

Accommodation

For accommodation during the season you should reserve two months in advance. The area code for phoning Mariánské Lázně is 0165. All the following have post code 353 01 Mariánské Lázně unless mentioned otherwise.

Autokemp Luxor, 354 71 Velká Hleďsebe, open May to September. Bungalows or private tents. 5km from Mariánské Lázně. Trolley bus no. 6,

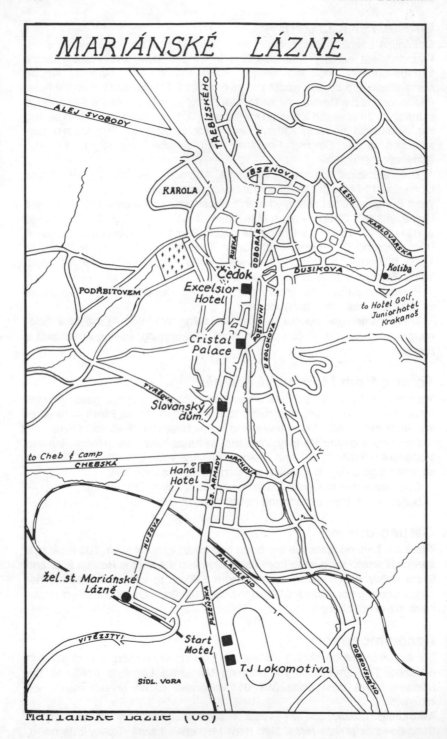

MARIÁNSKÉ LÁZNĚ

then walk 1km south on highway 21. Tel. 3504.
Autokemp Start, Plzeňská 729/7A., tel. 2062 (camping, bungalows and motel). Close to station. Open April to October. 20 bungalows sleeping 2, 2 sleeping 4; Kčs 47 per person. Tent camping, 5 sites only, tent Kčs 21, car Kčs 21, adult Kčs 10.50, child Kčs 5. Kitchen. Camping is by a noisy road. Motel, 45 beds, 2 beds to a room, 2 rooms to a bathroom, Kčs 91 per person. Noisy on the street side of building. Restaurant (sk.III). Parking. If it's the same manager as in 1985, he can read English.
Ubytovna TJ Lokomotiva, TU, Plzeňská 9, tel. 39 17. Near "Start". Dorms all year, and bungalows 1/5 to 31/10. No tent camping.
Juniorhotel Krakonoš, 353 34 Mariánské Lázně, tel. 26 24-5. Two hotels, B & a B* dependence. YHA hostel on the top floor, but YHA price not available if booked from abroad. Bus no. 12, which runs roughly hourly between 5.00am and 11.00pm.

The following hotels can be booked through Čedok: **Corso**, B, Odborářů 61, tel. 30 991, central; **Excelsior**, B*, Odborářů 121, tel. 27 05-6, central; **Esplanade**, ***, Karlovarská 438, tel. 21 62-4, towards the golf course; **Hotel Golf**, A* de luxe, 353 00 Mariánské Lázně, tel. 26 51-5, on the outskirts of town by golf course, and the flashiest hotel in Mariánské Lázně.

Robert Broughton recommends **Hotel Cristal** as being good quality at a reasonable price. It's at ul. Čs. armády 61.

There is accommodation in Tepla at **Hotel Flora** (class C, tel. 923 30).

Information
Čedok is in Hotel Excelsior. A map of the town is available for Kčs 9. For the surrounding area use the map *Západočeské Lázně*.

Out of Mariánské Lázně
All of the following are accessible by car or by walking routes. **Kladská zamek** is a small wooden hunting castle. **Lázně Kynžvart** is a small spa for children. The chateau there is closed. In **Teplá** is a monastery founded in 1193. If you are keen, you can walk there by following the red marked route east from Mariánské Lázně, otherwise take the train towards Karlovy Vary. Mariánské Lázně lies on the edge of Slavkovský les, a large area of woods offering numerous hiking possibilities.

Organised tours
A walking tour of Mariánské Lázně leaves from the Čedok office at 1.30pm every Wednesday 3 hours, US$3.60, refreshments included.

A whole day tour of Karlovy Vary, Františkovy Lázně and Cheb leaves from Cristal Hotel at 8.00am on Tuesdays. US$10.70.

Both tours operate from mid-May to mid-September only.

Eating and evenings
There are sk.II and III restaurants at the railway station.

The following have been recommended to me. Grill at Hotel Slunce, Vrchlivkého 30. Koliba on Dusíkova. The best restaurant in town is Hotel Golf's, sk.I, expensive. Lunapark: restaurant (with music) in daytime, disco at night when it becomes a young peoples hangout, out of town to the north, get there by car, taxi or walk. Good disco (sk.I) at Hotel Corso. Lil Club, U Sokolova 336, sk.I nightclub, open all night.

PLZEŇ

Everyone has heard of Plsener lager. Plzeň is its original home. In 1295 King Václav (Wenceslas) II gave the town the right to brew beer and 25 breweries were built. In 1839 the inhabitants got together and built a large modern brewery, and since then "Pilsener Urquell" (Plzeňský prazdroj) has been exported all over the world. Plzeň is also well-known for its Škoda engineering works, originally called Wallenstein Engineering Works. (Škoda cars are not made here.)

It was a problem to build here as the rivers keep moving. The old town was not on the same site and no-one is certain when the first settlement developed.

Today with a population of 170,000 Plzeň is the sixth largest town in Czechoslovakia, and the capital of West Bohemia. Easily accessible from Germany, at the weekends it is full of German groups.

To and from Plzeň

Plzeň lies on the E50 between Prague and Nürnberg. International trains pass through here. There are direct trains to Prague, Cheb via Mariánské Lázně, Domažlice, Železné Rudy and České Budějovice (*osobní* and *rychlík*). The main station is just outside, but within walking distance, of the town centre.

Accommodation

Camping

Intercamp Bílá Hora, ul. 28. října, 301 62 Plzeň-Bílá Hora; tel. 356 11. Tent camping and 4-bed chalets. Bus no. 20 from nám. Republiky. Open 1/5 to 30/9.

Autokemp Ostende, tel. 520 194. Tent camping and 2, 3, and 4-bed chalets. Pleasant location right on a lake, but facilities a bit primitive. Well signposted from centre. Bus no 13 A, 1km walk from the last stop at Bolevec. Open May to September.

Pod zám. Kozel is a camp by the river below Kozel with tent camping and cottages, but unless you have a car the above two are easier to get to. Open May 15 to September 15.

Turistická ubytovna

Ubytovna TJ Lokomotiva, TU A, Úslavdká 75, 301 59 Plzeň; tel. 480 41. 2 to 6 to a room. Tram 2, towards Světovar.

Hotels

Ural, A*, Nám. Repuliky 33, 305 31 Plzeň; tel. 226 757. Right on the square. Parking for guests on square. Posh sk.II restaurant. Many German weekenders.

Škoda, A, nám. Českých bratří 10; tel. 275 252. Short way out of centre.

Interhotel Continental, ***, Zrojnická 8. Central.

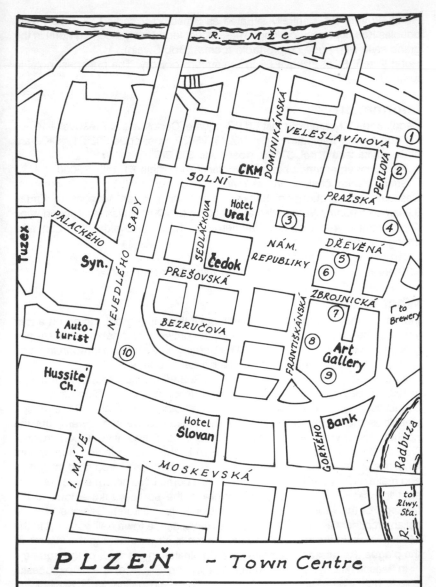

PLZEŇ – Town Centre

KEY

1 Pivovarské Museum
2 Plzeňská Historické Podzemí
3 St. Bartholomew's Ch.
4 Masné krámy
5 Gerlachovský dům

6 Národopisné (Ethnographic) Museum
7 Hotel Continental
8 Franciscan Ch.
9 Zapadoceske (W. Bohemian) Museum
10 Divaldo J. K. Tyla

Hotel Slovan, B*, centrally situated as Smetanovy sady 1, 305 28 Plzeň, doubles Kčs 302, easy parking, "magnificent faded elegance; old hotel in the grand style with huge comfortable rooms" (Bob Swain).
Hotel Plzeň, B, at Žižkova 66 in the suburb of Bory. The cheapest hotel in town.

Information

Čedok and CKM are both just off the square. Čedok are at Prešovská 10, on the corner with Sedláckova (tel. 36243, 35639, post code 303 21). CKM are at Dominikánská 1 (tel. 37585, post code 305 36).

Autoturist emergency breakdown service, 1. maje 61, tel. 276000.

Státní banka československá are in the new building at Gorkého 1. Československá obchodní banka, Tomanova 5, open Monday to Friday 8.00am to 1.00pm, Wednesday also 3.00pm to 5.00pm. Use the second bank if you want to have money transferred to Czechoslovakia. You can also change money at Čedok.

Tuzex are at Kollárova 1.

There is a town map in book form with information in Czech.

What to see

Individuals may not tour the brewery, but if there is a group going on a tour you may be able to tag on. Go out to the brewery and ask if there are any groups coming (weekdays only). The brewery was closed for reconstruction on my last visit, so check first to see if it has reopened.

In the main square, nám. Republiky, is St Bartholomew's Church, founded in 1292. Today's Gothic sandstone construction has a very high nave, good acoustics, and beautiful glass windows and other decor. Its 103-metre high steeple is the highest in Bohemia. There used to be two towers, but the northern tower was destroyed by lightning in 1525 and never reconstructed. Outside there are angels on the iron gate of the church facing Supraphon. Only one is clean; the others are black. This is because if you hold this angel and make a wish it will come true. Students come here before exams and the spot is a popular meeting place. While in the square, take a look at the frontage of the *radnice* (town hall, not open for visitors). Designed by the Italian architect Giovanni de Statio, the Renaissance town hall was built in the 1550s. Between the *radnice* and the church is a monument to the victims of the plague. Renaissance architecture dominates in the area of the square.

In Masné krámy, the old butcher shop on Pražska, the Západočeská galerie holds temporary art exhibitions. The main gallery is at Kopeckého sady 2 (see below). Opposite Masné krámy is the old watertower which has recently been restored.

Around the corner on Perlová is the entrance to a network of passages under the town (Plzeňské Historické Podzemí). They were opened to the public in 1985. Open all year Wednesday to Sunday, 9.30am to 12.00am, 12.30pm to 5.00pm. No children under 6 years old. The underground passages were used to store food, wine and beer. Later they were used by the brewery to store beer in 1,000 litre barrels.

Nearby again is the Pivovarské muzeum at Veleslavinova 6, an interesting museum of beer brewing in a beautiful old house. Open Tuesday 1.00pm to 4.30pm, Wednesday to Sunday 9.00am to 4.30pm.

Other museums are the Západočeské (West Bohemian) museum and gallery (under reconstruction at the time of writing, and expected to reopen in 1991 or 1992), and the Národopisné (Ethnographic) museum at nám. Republiky 13, which has changing exhibitions (closed Monday).

Gerlach House (Gerlachosvký dům) on Dřevěná ul. dates from the 14th Century. On Františkánská is the Františkánský (Franciscan) church. It has good acoustics, and its organ is the oldest in Plzeň. There are sometimes organ concerts here. There was also a monastery here, now partly destroyed.

The synagogue on Nejedlého sady is large, impressive, forlorn and closed. On the corner of Leninova, diagonally opposite Divadlo J. K. Tyla (theatre), is a small Hussite church.

The new House of Culture by the Radbuza river is known by the locals as "the horror of the Radbuza"!

The suburb of Bílá Hora has lakes and woods and is the nicest part of town.

Out of Plzeň

Starý Plzenec is the old settlement, but there is not so much of the old left. You can reach it by bus or train from Plzeň. From the village you can climb to the ruins of the castle Radyně (567m, yellow markers), where there is also a restaurant. Charles IV founded the castle in the 14th Century. Fires here warned the people when enemies invaded the country.

Kozel is a hunting chateau and park near Šťáhlavy. You must go around with a guide, and there is an English text you can borrow. Open April and October 9.00am to 3.00pm, in May and September till 4.00pm, and in June, July and August till 5.00pm. Get there by taking a train towards České Budějovice or Nepomuka as far as Šťáhlavy station (one station past Starý Plzenec, and not to be confused with Šťáhlavice station), from where you can see the chateau in the woods. To reach it, go to the end of the platform farthest from the village, then walk about 40 minutes, following the path across the fields. Follow the blue markers to the bridge, then turn left and follow the yellow markers. There is also an occasional bus from Plzeň on weekdays.

In the same direction, but a lot further from Plzeň, is **Žlinkovy zamek**, a 17th Century chateau rebuilt in Neo-Gothic style in 1916. It is not open to the public, but the grounds are a reserve with botanical gardens, water plants, swimming and boating.

You'll find other walks in the surrounds of Plzeň on the map *Plzeňsko*.

Tours

Čedok have tours of Plzeň on Saturdays leaving from Hotel Continental at 2.00pm in July and August.

Events

Every year in about the first week of July a five day festival of folk and tramping songs called PORTA is held at Ex Plzeň Výstavisté, the exhibition grounds at nám. Palackeho, and at the open air theatre in the suburb of Lochotín.

Eating and evenings

There are lots of restaurants and places for cakes and snacks etc around the centre, but nothing to write home about.

You can taste Plsener beer at the restaurant at the brewery entrance, "Prazdroj".

Svazáček, tř. 1. máje 125, tram 1 or 4, has a pub downstairs and dancing upstairs via a different entrance.

Two pubs with black beer are U Žumbery, Bezručova 14, with reasonably priced food, and Na Rychté, near the south railway station.

Next door to CKM is Kavárna Dominik, popular when there is something good on.

Moravská vinárna, Bezručova 2, is open 10.00am to 10.00pm and has wine in carafe brought in bulk from Moravia. Go early, or if it's full try Jadran vinárna at Bezručova 9.

U námořnika has sailing decor and is near the bus station.

There's dancing at Hotel Continental (Zbrojnická 8), Slávie (nám. Republiky 28), Ural, Beseda (centre of town), Sport (near the ice skating rink), Svazaček (see above) and Sputnik (U Borského parku 20).

KLATOVY

Klatovy is a town of 22,000 inhabitants located 42km south of Plzeň and 41km north of the Železná Ruda / Bayerischer Eisenstein road border crossing with Germany. Beneath the town is a network of catacombs which in the Middle Ages had passages leading out beyond the town walls. The town's main attraction are the catacombs below the church in the square, with their mummified monks, which are open to the public. The town's landmark, the 76m high Black Tower, is also on the square, as is the Renaissance town hall. The town's historical core has a Gothic layout, while the styles of its buildings range from Gothic to Baroque to Empire.

Klatovy can be used as an access point to the northwestern end of Šumava (see South Bohemia), or to Domažlice, 37km to the west.

There are four B category hotels, one of which, Bílá růže, is right on the square. TJ Klatovy (TU) is 1km from the centre at Pod Hůrkou.

DOMAŽLICE

A southwest Bohemian town, not far from the West German border, Domažlice is the centre of the Chod region. The Chods are an ethnic group of unknown origins who were given special privileges by the Přemyslids and the Luxemburgs in return for guarding the western borders. No-one knows if they were brought here for the task or if they are indigenous to the area. Their culture has survived, and in the second weekend in August (from Friday to Sunday) the Chodsko Region Folklore Festival is held in Domažlice.

Domažlice is one of the nicest towns in Bohemia. It was founded in 1262 on the site of an older settlement. At the end of the 13th Century a royal castle was built. You can climb to the top of the round castle tower which has been preserved in its 13th Century form. There is a Chod museum, which, when I visited, had information sheets one could borrow in English. A really nice town to wander in.

Hotels and *turistická ubytovna*. Camping at Babylon, a few kilometres towards the border. The nearby Folmava / Furth im Wald-Schafberg road border crossing is open 24 hours.

Madonna and Child, Cheb museum

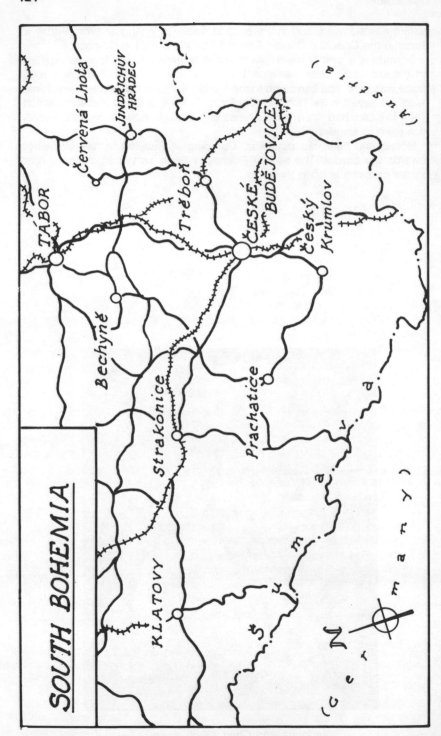

South Bohemia

ČESKÉ BUDĚJOVICE

České Budějovice is the capital of the picturesque South Bohemian region. It was founded in 1265 by King Přemysl Otakar II, as a fortress protecting the Crown's interests in the south of Bohemia. The town grew through the trade in salt and wine from Austria. During the Renaissance České Budějovice owned silver mines in the area but the town was impoverished during the Thirty Years War. In 1641 České Budějovice was almost completely destroyed by fire, resulting in a lot of Baroque reconstruction. There were just as many Germans as Czechs living here before the Second World War. The inhabitants usually spoke both languages, and got on well together. There was also a Jewish minority.

The first horse-drawn railway in continental Europe was constructed from České Budějovice to Linz in Austria in 1825-1832. It operated until 1872, when it was reconstructed for steam engines. Goods trains had the right of way over passenger trains. Giving way consisted of going back to the nearest station, or if that was too far, the drivers used jacks to take the carriage off the tracks. In the heyday of the horse-drawn railway, around 1868, the railway company owned 662 horses, 1092 goods wagons, and 65 passenger wagons. Some remnants can be seen from today's railway, which by and large follows the same route.

The highlight of the town is its magnificent **square**, one of the largest in Europe. The houses surrounding it have Renaissance gables and arcades. In its centre stands the Baroque **Samson's Fountain**, designed by Josef Dietrich in 1727. The **town hall** on the south-west side of the square is also Baroque, replacing an earlier Gothic town hall in 1731. At one corner of the square is the recently reconstructed 16th Century **Černá Věž** or **Black Tower**. At 72 metres high it provides a good view. It's open from 9.00am to 5.00pm daily except Monday, and you pay at the top. The tower was originally built as a combined bell tower for the church and sentry tower for the town. On the way up the steep climb, you can see the clock mechanism. Adjoining Černá Věž is **St Nicholas Cathedral**, founded in the 13th Century, but rebuilt many times. Its present style dates from restoration work undertaken in the middle of the 17th Century. During the Thirty Years War, one of its chapels was converted into a strongroom to house the coronation jewels.

One of the oldest buildings in České Budějovice is the early Gothic **Dominican monastery**, dating from 1265. What remains of the town walls dates from the 15th Century. A couple of the more interesting streets to stroll along are Česká and Kněžská. The **museum of South Bohemian history** at Dukelská 1 is open daily except Monday from 9.00am to 12.00am and 1.00pm to 6.00pm. The other highlight of České Budějovice is Budvar beer, better known to some by its German name, Budweiser. České Budějovice is the home of the original Budvar beer, which to my palate is the best in Czechoslovakia. Unfortunately the brewery is not open to the public, but you can buy its product around the town.

There is a local bus service in České Budějovice. There is also a night bus service which consists of one bus running once an hour to all parts of the town via a complicated route.

To and from České Budějovice

There is still a rail service to Linz, but the horses are gone. České Budějovice is the first main town on the E55 after it enters Czechoslovakia from Linz. The E55 is the main route from Salzburg to Prague. There is a bus service to the border (you might have to change buses in Kaplice). There are trains from Prague and Tábor, and buses to Třeboň. Four times daily there is a direct bus to Bratislava. Reservations are not compulsory, but I recommend you book at weekends and holidays.

The bus station is beside the train station in České Budějovice. Both have a left luggage service, although the bus station's is only open limited hours. Both have a 15kg weight limit. The road opposite the railway, but a bit to the right, Maršála Malinovského, later becoming Kanovnická, leads to the square.

Accommodation

Camping

Autokemping Dlouhá louka, A class, tel. 383 08. Bungalows and tent camping. Dirty and primitive, but lot of friendly East Germans (at least before the wall fell!). Restaurant and bar. Bus no. 6. Open all year.

Autokempink Stromovka, B, tel. 288 77. Open 1/4 to 31/10. Bus 6. Largely booked up by Autoturist for their package holidays for Czechs. Also bungalows.

ATC Křivonoska is 6km from Hluboká. Open May 15 to Sept. 30. Tel Č. Bud. 96 52 85.

Student hostel

It's best to check first at CKM's office for the current situation. During the summer holidays you can try directly at Vysoká škola zemědělská Juniorstředisko CKM, Čtyři Dvory, Sinkuleho ul. 13-19, post code 370 05; tel. 414 25. But it is nearly always full.

Other places to try are Domov mládeže KNV Čes. Bud., Holečkova ul. 2, 370 00 České Budějovice, tel. 337 64 and Restaurace Perla, Třída míru 17, tel. 337 65.

Hotels

Gomel, **, tř.** Míru, tel. 289 41, 279 49. Skyscraper 10 minutes walk north of the square towards Prague, with a "G" on top. 469 beds, mostly in double rooms.

Hotel Zvon, A* and B, Žižkovo nám. 28, tel. 353 61-62. On the square. Prices start from a single with washbasin for Kčs 225. The more expensive rooms have a bath. Breakfast is available in your room, or from 6.00am in the restaurant. Full in the summer; at other times of year you should be able to get a room. Exchange office.

Malše, B, Nádražní 31, tel. 276 31, opposite the railway station. Sleazy.

Hotel Grand, B*, tel. 365 91, also in Nádražní near the station.

Parkhotel, B class hotel in Hluboká nad Vltavou. Tel. 96 52 81, 96 53 41.

Interhotel Slunce was closed and being renovated by Polish workers at the time of writing.

Information

Fiona Bulmer writes that there is now "a sort of tourist information office ... in the main car park".

Čedok, Žižkovo nám. 35, tel. 323 81. From May 15 to September 30 open weekdays 9.00am to 6.00pm, Saturdays 9.00am to 12.00am. During the rest of the year, open 9.00am to 5.00pm, Wednesdays 10.00am to 6.00pm, Saturdays 9.00am to 12.00am.

CKM, tř. Osvobození 14, 370 21 České Budějovice, tel. 36 138 or 37 751.

Šport Turist, Malinoského (near station). **Autoturist,** Kanovnická 11 (near the square).

Post and telephone. The main post office, Pošta 1, is near Hotel Gomel, just off třida Míru. Collect poste restante at the parcels counter downstairs. If you are travelling by public transport, Pošta 2 by the station is handier. Telephone area code (038).

Rental cars. From Pragocar.

Maps can be bought at the bookshop on the south side of the square. There is a town map for Kčs 9.

What to see

South of České Budějovice at Římov is a Baroque church.

Hluboká nad Vltavou

Hluboká Castle in its present form is a small replica of Windsor Castle set in a magnificent park on a steep hill above the Vltava. Founded by King Přemysl Otakar II, it was originally built in Gothic style in the 13th Century. Hluboka was at this time considered a strategic point. During its life-time it has been owned by various noble families, and has undergone reconstruction at various times. One of its prior owners, Záviš of Falknštejn, was executed in 1290 below the castle in Execution Meadow, as a result of court intrigue and politics. During the Hussite period the castle was a stronghold of the Catholics. After the Battle of White Mountain, the castle was confiscated by the Emperor and sold to the Spanish general Balthasar Marradas, in recognition of the services he rendered to the Habsburgs in the suppression of the revolt. In 1661 the castle came into the ownership of the Schwarzenberg family. Between 1840 and 1871 the Schwarzenbergs had it rebuilt in neo-Gothic style and it became the centre of the Schwarzenberger domains, the largest private property in Bohemia. In 1945 the entire Schwarzenberger holdings were nationalised.

The castle is open to the public from April to October from 9.00am to 12 noon, and 1.00pm to 5.00pm. It closes one hour earlier in April, September and October, and is always closed Mondays. The last entry is one hour before closing time. A tour in English is unlikely, but maybe you could find someone on the tour who could translate for you. The castle contains various collections, eg Bohemian and Venetian glass, works of art, hunting trophies. The riding school houses the Aleš Art Gallery, named after the popular Czech painter Mikulás Aleš. It contains works of South Bohemian Gothic, and 17th Century Dutch and Flemish art, and is open the same hours as the castle.

At Ohrada, 2km south of Hluboká, in an old hunting mansion, is an interesting museum of hunting, milling and fishing. The last bear killed in the Šumava is exhibited here. It is open the same time as Hluboká Castle. Some of the exhibits are labelled in English. There is also a little zoo at Ohrada.

There are fishing lakes everywhere in the area. Pleasant walks can be made among the lakes and forests.

There are buses from České Budějovice to Hluboká nad Vltavou, but the service is slack at weekends. By train it takes 10 minutes. There are two Hluboká railway stations, one on the České Budějovice-Plzeň line, and one on the České Budějovice-Tábor line, but both are out of town, especially the one on the Plzeň line. From Hluboká to Ohrada is a pleasant 2km walk among trees and lakes (follow the yellow markers). One can also drive. From Ohrada one can walk back to the main road, or walk in the opposite direction to the railway station on the Plzeň line (ask for directions).

Mydlovary
A few kilometres northeast of Hluboká n. Vlt. is Mydlovary where there is today a large area that has been polluted by radioactivity. Uranium was processed here by prisoners for export to the Soviet Union.

Eating and drinking
Masné Krámy ("Butcher Shop"), 23 Třida 5 Května. Sk.III restaurant with large alcoves. More a pub, but has food as well. Good place to taste the local suds. Women a distinct minority.

Železná Panna ("Iron Virgin"), restaurant on the corner of Biskupská and Široká.

Otherwise there are various snack bars, including one near the above restaurant, or the hotels.

ČESKÝ KRUMLOV
Český Krumlov is one of the most picturesque towns in Czechoslovakia. A medieval town on the banks of the Vltava, with cobbled streets, little back lanes, and arch covered footpaths, Český Krumlov is overlooked by what is

considered to be the second most outstanding castle in the country.

The old town covers a large area. Entering it via Horní, you cross a very high viaduct, and can see that the Vltava almost cuts off the old town as an island here. Many old houses are falling down, but an effort is underway to reconstruct them.

To and from Český Krumlov

There are buses roughly once an hour from České Budějovice on working days, but the service is slack at the weekend. There are also trains, but they are not as frequent and don't drop you in as central a place as the buses. Český Krumlov is within easy daytripping distance of České Budějovice.

Accommodation
Camping
There is a camp site 2km upstream from the centre of Český Krumlov: **Veřejné Tábořiště Nové Spolí**. It is a site only, not a fully fledged camping ground, and is popular with canoeists. Open 1/5 to 31/10.

Hostels
Turistická ubytovna Panská ulice, A and B class, 91 beds, 3 to 14 beds to a room. Open summer season only, from 6.00pm. In the old centre, 50m from the square. Partly permanently booked by Čedok Český Krumlov.

Český Krumlov

Turistická ubytovna Slavoj I and **II**, A class, Chvalšinská silnice, tel. 22 11. 135 beds altogether, mostly 3 bed rooms, one 12 bed room. Most beds in No. II. Open 1/5 to 30/9. Just outside the old town, with a summer outdoor cinema beside it. Often full.

Hotels
It is difficult to get a hotel room in the summer, and best to reserve before you come to Czechoslovakia.
Hotel Růže, B*, tel. 22 45. Nice hotel in the old centre. Reception open 24 hours. Restaurant and vinárna. Double rooms or larger only.
Interhotel Krumlov, B*, Gottwaldovo nám. 13, tel. 22 55. On the square in the centre of the old town. Not as nice as Růže. Doubles Kčs 300 to Kčs 500. You could try asking if there are still any of the cheaper B class rooms left. From June to September you need a reservation. The rest of the year is not so bad. Reception open day and night.
Hotel Vyšehrad, B*, tel. 23 11, 23 51 or 30 70. In the newer part of town to the north.
There are no other hotels in Český Krumlov.

Private
Because of the accommodation shortage, private rooms may be rather expensive here.

Information
Čedok is on the square at Gottwaldovo náměstí 15, tel. 3444.
There is a **bank** on the square.

What to see
The whole old town is worth seeing, just stroll around. Sv. Vít kostel, the main church of the town, is magnificent, even under restoration. The back alleys can also be worth exploring. For example from Radniční, just before the bridge, walk back towards Horní bridge along the lane near the river. Go under the arch at the end of the lane. To the right is Horní viaduct. To the left is an old mill. If the river is low enough go down to the river and rock hop to the left and you can see the remains of the waterwheel etc. If you head directly towards the castle viaduct on the other side of the river from the square, there is another old mill before the little footbridge.

The museum is on Horní, opposite Hotel Růše. Open Tuesday to Saturday 9.00am to noon, 12.30pm to 4.00pm (to 6.00pm on Wednesday). Sunday 9.00am to noon only.

The castle is situated on a hill on the opposite side of the river to the old town centre. The lower castle was built in the 13th Century, and the upper castle in the first half of the 14th Century. The entire complex was rebuilt in Renaissance style by Italian architects in the 16th Century. There were once bears in the moat. From May to August it is open to the public from 8.00am to 5.00pm, and in April, September and October from 9.00am to 4.00pm. Closed during the rest of the year, on Mondays, and between 12.00am and 1.00pm. When the castle is closed it is still possible, and worth while, to walk up through the courtyards. Up the hill above the castle are the gardens (open until 7.00pm) in which is an open air theatre where the audience's seats move to follow the actors. Plays are performed in the summer holidays only. There is also a Baroque theatre from the 18th Century, presently under reconstruction.

On the same side of the river as the castle is the monastery. It was rebuilt in Baroque style in the 17th Century, but the cloister with the Stations of the Cross is Gothic, dating from 1491. The monastery is not open, but one can walk around the outside of the buildings.

Eating and drinking

Restaurant U hroznu, sk.III, on the square. Sk.II *vinárna* (open 8.00pm to 2.00am, closed Tuesday and Wednesday) in the same building. **Pub of Peter of Rosenberg**: the Czech family, Rosenberg, possessed Southern Bohemia: the five leaf rose symbolises the five families of Rosenberg. Restaurant **U mešta Vidné** ("at the town of Vienna"), sk.III, okay. Otherwise try the hotels.

Out of Ceský Krumlov

The map *Českobudějovicko* covers the area around Český Krumlov in detail, but it took me over five years to find a copy in a shop.

Kleť

Kleť (1008m above sea level) is the highest peak in the area. On top is the oldest lookout tower in Bohemia, built in the 1830s, as well as a rather more modern TV tower and a pub (Horská chata Kleť, 382 03 Křemže, tel. 32 89) with dorm accommodation for 14. In good weather you can see the Alps from here, but usually only in autumn or winter. There is a green marked track up Kleť from the castle in Český Krumlov. The 8km climb takes two to three hours. There is also a chairlift up from Krasetín which is a 2.5km bus trip from Holubov, on the Český Krumlov-České Budějovice railway line. The chairlift operates all year, except Mondays, but may be closed in October/November for maintenance. One can also walk up from Holubov (green marked track).

Zlatá Koruna

At Zlatá Koruna is a former Cistercian monastery founded in 1263. Built in Gothic style, there was major reconstruction in the 18th Century, and restoration after the Second World War. The library of theological literature is open to the public from April 1 to October 31 from 9.00am to 4.00pm, closed Mondays. There are buses to Zlatá Koruna from Český Krumlov. The railway station is up the hill 1.5km out of the town, and there are not many trains. Kleť can also be climbed from here by the red marked route which leads up past the railway station. There is a good pub and hostel near the monastery.

Dívčí Kámen

Dívčí Kámen means "maiden's rock" and you can see fantastic extensive ruins of a castle overlooking the Vltava here. The nearest village is Třísov, a former Celtic settlement, 1½ km walk away (red markers). Buses and trains in this area are infrequent. Hitchhiking may be possible, but there is little traffic. From the railway station in Holubov, Dívčí Kámen is 3km along the yellow marked track, or from Zlatá Koruna, 7km on the red marked track (opposite direction to Kleť). One can also walk the 12km along the red marked route beside the Vltava to Dívčí Kámen from Boršov n. Vltava on the main České Budějovice-Český Krumlov road. Unfortunately the Vltava stinks here of pollution. A lot of the problem comes from a pulp mill above Český Krumlov. The effluent is piped to an outlet below the town so you don't smell it in Český Krumlov itself.

ŠUMAVA

The Šumava are forested mountains stretching along the Czechoslovak-German border in southwestern Bohemia. They include glacial lakes and lots of peat bogs, some of which are completely closed nature reserves. With their beautiful tranquil nature the Šumava are a popular holiday area for Czechs. From the Czech side the Šumava seem deceptively low because they incline gradually into the interior. Lynx have been reintroduced to the area, and there are now about 20. Human settlement is sparse. The area includes Lipno hydro lake. For the last 15 years there have been plans to make the area a national park, but a problem is the industry already in the area.

Before the Velvet Revolution the military were taking over more and more of Šumava and closing it to the public. Large areas were reopened in 1990, attracting swarms of Czech trampers who had never been able to visit these areas before. About 230km of new tramping routes have been marked, mostly following routes that existed before World War Two. Pedestrian border crossings to Germany and Austria have opened, but as yet are open only for citizens of Czechoslovakia and the respective neighbouring country, though there is talk of opening them to all. But you can still hear the military firing sometimes, and you should check locally as to exactly where you may walk and what areas the military still occupy, especially if you plan other walks than those I describe.

Accommodation

Accommodation is difficult to get, even in the off season when there are many children's groups and workers on company paid breaks. All dormitory accommodation etc is full in summer. Campsites could possibly be used even when closed. People are beginning to rent rooms to tourists, but no list of addresses exists, and when you find them they are usually full.

Eating

If there is no pub in the village, chalets owned by factories etc will have some hours when they are open to the public.

Maps

New maps were under preparation at the time of writing, covering both sides of the border. The pre-Velvet Revolution maps which cover the Šumava area are occasionally available. Most of what is described below is on the maps

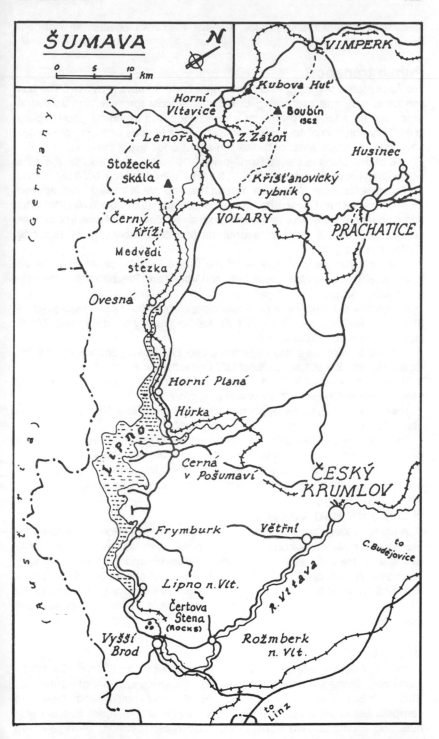

Šumava Prachaticko and *Lipno*. *Šumava Klatovsko* covers the northern Šumava.

Public transport

The main means of getting to and getting around Šumava is by train. The bus service is bad, and hitchhiking is difficult, at least for men. Ann Johnston writes that for a lone woman with a rucksack it was extremely good. Volary is the transport hub of southern Šumava, where various different train routes have their terminus. Most of these run about once every three hours.

One of them runs to České Budějovice (3½ hours) via Horní Planá, Černa v Pošumavi and Český Krumlov. Use this train for Medvědi stezka and Stožecká skála. From Volary be careful that you get in the right carriage, as most trains split at Cerný Kříž with one part going on to Nové Údolí. But some trains run via Stožec anyway. The train to Nové Údolí runs in the peak season, and then at weekends until the end of October. Trains as far as Stožec run every day.

Another train runs to Čičenice on the České Budějovice – Plzeň line via Prachatice. There are also buses between Volary and Prachatice, but the train runs more frequently.

A third line is from Volary to Strakonice, also on the České Budějovice – Plzeň line, via Vimperk. Use this train for Soumarský Most, Lenora, Zátoň, Horní Vltavice and Kubova Huť.

There is a bus once a day between České Budějovice and Volary, leaving České Budějovice at 1.40pm, and taking nearly two hours.

The bus to Prachatice from České Budějovice takes one hour, while by train it takes two hours and involves changing.

There is a train as far as Lipno nad Vltavou from České Budějovice, taking about 2½ hours, and stopping in Vyšší Brod.

There are long distance buses connections to Lipno and Frymburk, and a direct bus from Prague (Praha-Smichov) to Volary and Nová Pec.

From Volary to Plzeň take the train to Strakonice or Čičenice depending on which is more convenient in terms of time and connections.

Rožmberk nad Vltavou

Approaching from Český Krumlov, it's a beautiful drive through the forest by the Vltava between Zátoň and Rožmberk. With its remarkable castle overlooking the old village, Rožmberk is an idyllic spot, and worth visiting. The castle itself is open from April to October, but closed Mondays, and in April and October open at the weekends only. Its history goes back to the 13th Century, but it was rebuilt in Renaissance style. There is a campsite just downstream of the castle.

Vyšší Brod

Higher up the river Vltava lies Vyšší Brod, with its 13th Century Cistercian monastery. Someone here advertises riding lessons and hire of horses; tel. (0337) 92 301. The town has a couple of cheap hotels, and there is a campsite below the dam. The hostel "Na Myslivně" (TU A, tel. 924 52) with huts and rooms is 1km from Vyšší Brod Klášťor station. There are two stations in Vyšší Brod. Use Vyšší Brod Kláštor station for the camp, hostel, or if visiting the monastery. From this station it is a 6.5km walk along a little country road the direct way to Rožmberk, or following the railway and Vltava up to Lipno is a 12.5km walk on the green marked route . There are two nearby road border crossings. Note that if you cross at the Horní Dvořiště-Summerau rail border crossing you must change trains.

Čertova stěna

Čertova stěna is a much visited formation of rocks, but personally I didn't find it very interesting. It is a short walk from the Vyšší Brod-Lipno road, or a 3km walk following the red markers from Vyšší Brod.

Lipno

Lipno Hydro Lake (726m) on the upper reaches of the river Vltava is about 43km long, with many resorts on its shores. The dam itself, above Lipno railway station, is surprisingly small considering the size of the lake it holds. Lipno is particularly popular for boating and fishing.

In July and August there is a boat service on the lake four times daily between Lipno, Frymburk, Černá v Pošumaví and Horní Planá. In June and September it operates twice a day on Sundays only.

Rowboats and cycleboats (not yachts) can be hired at Lipno.

The causeway at Černá v Pošumaví is particularly popular with fishermen (men only), especially around the bridge. In season rowing boats can be hired by the south end of the causeway. Look for the sign "Půjčovna Lodí". Note that Černá v Pošumaví railway station lies on the other side of the causeway at Hůrka.

In Horní Planá the Austrian writer Adalbert Stifter's house is preserved as a museum.

The blue marked track on the east side of the lake is not very interesting, and the other side of the lake was the last I heard still closed by the military. There is a green marked track from Lipno following the river Vltava and railway to the monastery at Vyšší Brod, though the paper mills you pass at Loučovice aren't a pleasant sight.

Accommodation

There are lots of camps in and between Lipno and Frymburk, some with chalets. At Lipno itself there are camps and chalets, plus a simple hotel at one of the camps and another in the village, and at both Kobylnice (on the point between Lipno and Frymburk) and Frymburk are both a motor camp and a campsite, all of which are in the trees between the road and lake. At Frymburk there are also chalets.

At Hůrka there is Turistická ubytovna (A) opposite Černa v Pošumaví Railway Station. On the Hůrka side of the causeway is a campsite open in season only. It is situated between the road, railway and lake, and trees give some shelter.

In Černa v Pošumaví itself there is autocamping near the causeway, and there are three campsites on the road to Jestřábí. All open seasonally only.

Not far along this road is Hotel Racek (B, tel. 961 03) where you are unlikely to be able to get a bed.

Trails

Medvědi stezka (the Bear Trail)

Medvědi stezka (the Bear Trail) is the yellow marked track from Ovesná at the top of Lipno Lake to Černy Kříž. Both ends were accessible only by train, but maybe the roads are open now? The walk is 15km long, and takes about 6 hours including time to sightsee. The first part of the route winds up through large intriguing boulders, good to shelter under if it rains. There are no more bears in the Šumava, the last one was shot at the monument you pass later on the trip. Now there are bears only in Slovakia. At the sign "kaple" (chapel) you can get right inside the rocks. If you look uphill from the sign to the top of a rock, you might be forgiven for imagining that the builders of Stonehenge had been here. About 100 metres past here is Viklan, a clever balancing trick.

From the boulders the track drops to the beautiful little lake, Jelení jezírko. Then you come to the village of Jeleni, where the ditch coming out of the tunnel is part of the 44km Švarcenberský kanál which connected the Vltava with the Danube to transport timber. It was built from 1789 to 1822 and part of it was in use until 1962. 2km further on from Jeleni is a short side track to Medvědí kámen, a stone with the inscription in German "Bären Stein" marking the place where the last bear in the Šumava was killed in 1856. The actual bear is in the hunting museum in Hluboka (see section on České Budějovice). From here the track winds slowly down to the railway station at Černy Kříž.

Třístoličník and Plechý

The whole of this area was opened to the public in 1990 for the first time since World War Two.

Třístoličník (Dreisesselberg in German) is a 1302m high peak on the German border. There is now a path open from Nové Údolí, from where it's about 8km to walk. The new pedestrian border crossing at Nové Údolí is open only for citizens of Czechoslovakia and Germany. Plechý is a 1378m high peak on the Austrian border. From Černý Kříž walk towards Jelení, but turn right before you get there. Plešné jezero is a nice lake below the peak. On the way up you pass a monument to Adalbert Stifter.

Stožecká skála

Stožecká skála is a two hour return trip from Černy Kříž railway station following the blue marked track westwards. From the top one can see Germany.

Prachatice

Prachatice is one of the Šumava towns well worth visiting. Founded in the early 14th Century as a trading post between Bavaria and Bohemia, Wenceslas IV gave Prachatice a monopoly on the supply of salt at the end of the 14th Century, resulting in prosperity for the town. Some of the fortifications built in 1323 survive. The oldest and best preserved building is St James Church, with its striking roof timbers and beautifully carved wooden decoration. The exteriors of both town halls on the square are worth seeing. The new town hall is the one with the tower, the old town hall stands to its left. They are decorated with biblical and legendary scenes.

I found Prachatice a very pleasant place, and the people friendly and helpful, even if no-one spoke English.

Husinec

Nearby Husinec was the birthplace of Jan Hus. In the house on the square where he was born is a museum devoted to his life and work. One can see the lime tree under which he preached. He preached under lime trees in other villages too. There is a baker's school in Husinec, explaining why the area has such good bread.

Information

Information on Šumava can be obtained from *odbor cestovního ruchu* (travel department) of *Okresní národní Výbor* (District National Committee) on the square.

Accommodation

There are three hotels, the first two both on the main square. **Národní dům**, (B); tel. 35 61, 25 64. Doubles only, Kčs 120 without bath, 180 with bath. Individuals must pay for two beds. **Zlatá stezka**, (B); tel: 38 41. Newly renovated. Doubles Kčs 249. Comfortable with lively bar. **Hotel ČSVTS** is a new hotel. There is also a new *turistická ubytovna*. If that's full you could try asking if you could sleep at the workers' hostel Ubytovna OSP.

Eating

Prachatice's nice local bread is baked in big round loaves. The restaurant opposite the town halls is a rather ordinary smoky place, but I found the waitress friendly and the cooking better than normal.

Tramping

From Prachatice you can climb Libín (1,086m) on the red marked track heading south. The 6km walk takes about 1½ hours. The track is good, but sometimes the markers disappear in newly felled areas. On top is a tall lookout tower, open all the time. From Libín you can drop down to the Prachatice-Volary road at Libínské Sedlo (½ hour, 2km), from where you can follow the green marked track back to Prachatice, or walk, hitch, or hope for a bus on the road. You can also continue to Volary (22km from Prachatice).

Following the red marked track in a northerly direction from Prachatice brings you after a 6km walk to Husinec.

Kříšťanovický Rybník

This is a nice lake off the Prachatice-Volary road, 8km from Prachatice, and 1.5km walk from the nearest bus stop. You can see it from Libín, from where it is a 6km walk. The campsite is open June to August.

Volary
Volary is a useful centre for the Šumava, with houses in alpine style.

Accommodation
It is difficult to get accommodation at any time of the year. Both hotels, **Bobík** (B*, tel. 923 51-4, on the square), and **Turistická chata** (B, tel. 922 60, near the railway station) are usually full, as is the *ubytovací hostinec* **Sport**, down a side road near the station (tel. 923 12). Hotel Turistická chata is usually booked up by schools.

Your best bet may be the **Turistická chata** (TU A, tel. 921 67) in one of the nice old wooden buildings on the right if you head toward the square from the station. Open all year (but when I was there closed for painting!). Some chance of private accommodation.

Soumarský Most
Soumarský Most is 5km from Volary towards Lenora, and popular with canoeists who use the Vltava above Lipno lake. Campsite by the station open mid June to mid September.

Lenora
Lenora is the last of the former glassmaking places in the area. Accessible by bus or train. Accommodation: Ubytovací Hostinec U Hynků, 384 42 Lenora; tel. 988 43.

Horní Vltavice
Horní Vltavice has the best camping ground in the Šumava, as well as a good pub. There is tent camping and cabins, open in the summer only. From here one can make a roundtrip over Boubín (see below). Horní Vltavice Railway Station is up above the village. Trains stop here in summer only. From Horní Vltavice it is 13km to the Strážný-Philippsreut road border crossing, open 24 hours. Winter sports are practised at Strážný.

Boubín
There is some interesting walking in the area of Boubín. The following is described as a one way walk from Kubova Huť to z. Zátoň (railway station), but as a longer walk you could make it a round trip from Horní Vltavice. Horní Vltavice to Kubova Huť is a 4km walk. From Kubova Huť it is 5.5km on the blue marked track to Boubín, at 1362m, the highest point in the publicly accessible part of the Šumava. This part of the trip is neither very interesting nor very steep, taking 1¼ hours up through the forest. There is not much view from the top, as it is covered in trees. The monument Johnův kámen and the monument on top of Boubín have the altitude written in feet.

Following the blue markers again brings one to a deer park. In the park you must walk on the marked paths only. The park may be closed to the public in the months of June, September and October. The blue markers do not enter the park, but lead down to Boubínský prales, a small area of virgin forest. You can't enter it, but you can walk around its perimeter. There is a little lake at the bottom, Boubínské Jezírko, with refreshments for sale in season. From here it is 3km following the green markers to z. Zátoň. On the way you pass a campsite, accessible by road, and open from mid May to mid September. The entire trip from Kubova Huť to z. Zátoň is 14.5km and takes four hours with stops, if you neither enter the deer park nor circumnavigate Boubínský prales. To Horní Vltavice, instead of following the green markers from the lake, continue following the blue markers to the village of Zátoň, then the green markers to Horní Vltavice.

Vimperk

Vimperk (760m) was a German town before the war and still has a German flavour. It has a not very interesting old castle. A miniature Koran used to be produced here and sold only in Saudi Arabia for $600 per copy. The man who made them is now dead, and no-one knows how he did it. From Vimperk you can walk to Máŕský Vrch (907m) with an open lookout tower on top, but you can't see all around. There is a nature reserve here. One can also climb Boubín from Vimperk, but it is 12km, a much longer walk than from Kubova Huť.

Churánov

Churánov is a good winter sports area, accessible by bus from Vimperk. Hotels only; no dormitories or camping.

Antigl

Antigl is another pleasant area.

Rejštejn to Sušice

A red-marked path follows the Otava river from Rejštejn to Sušice, a walk which Ann Johnston writes is "extremely pleasant". It is also possible to travel this stretch by canoe when the water is high enough, but you need your own; there is nowhere to hire them.

There are several campsites for overnighting, of which Autokemp Annín (B) has been recommended by many. As well as tent sites there are cabins, and Ann recommends the food. The camp is open from mid-May to mid-September, postal address: Autokemp Jednoty Annín, 341 91 Dlouhá Ves; tel. (0187) 88 21.

The Otava can also be followed upstream from Rejštejn, but the red markers follow the road a lot.

Železná Ruda

Železná Ruda and nearby Špičák are winter sports resorts. The hotels will undoubtedly be full, though there are some private rooms.

There are two nice glacial lakes nearby, Černé (Black) jezero and Čertovo (Devil's) jezero, accessible by marked path from Špičácké sedlo, the saddle on the road north of Špičák. There is actually also a road up to Čertovo jezero from lower Špičák village (signposted to Bumbálka). 2km from Želzná Ruda is the road border crossing to Bayer. Eisenstein (open 24 hours). There is now a red-marked path from Železná Ruda to Alžbětín, by the border, that continues up to the lakes.

The area to the east of the Železná Ruda-Javorna road was still being used by the military at the time of writing. Hojsova Stráž, 12km north of here, is another winter resort.

TŘEBOŇ

Třeboň epitomises a certain type of South Bohemian landscape, with its forest, meadows, peatbogs and fish lakes. This peaceful South Bohemian town and spa is the centre of a large area of fish lakes, created centuries ago for breeding fish and connected by an ingenious system of canals created in the 16th Century. The lakes are surrounded by centuries old oak and linden trees and the whole district is a major sanctuary for water birds.

Visit Třeboň in the autumn if you want to see the fish harvested. The town is especially famed for the carp from these fish dams that are eaten for Christmas dinner in Czechoslovakia. They are bought living and kept alive in the bath. But because the fish come from this area, here it is possible to get them all year.

Třeboň was founded in 1220. Many Late Gothic, Renaissance and Baroque buildings remain today. Today's castle buildings were erected on the site of the original 13th Century castle from the 16th to 18th Centuries. The Town Hall and remnants of the town walls, ramparts and gates date from the 16th Century. There are many old houses, and a Baroque brewery from the 18th Century.

One of the fish lakes is right by the town, attractive with its trees and boats. Walking around it to the left brings one to the imposing neo-Gothic mausoleum of the Schwarzenberg family (1874-77).

North of Třeboň is the Velký a Malý Tisý nature reserve where captive-bred white-tailed sea eagles, *Haliaeetus albicilla*, from Germany have been released and have begun breeding. These birds had not bred in Czechoslovakia since the 1850s, although a few continued to spend the winter in the Třeboň area.

For walking in the surrounds of Třeboň, buy the map *Táborsko*.

A 40km cycle track (you can also walk it) connects the lakes and points of interest in the area.

Getting there and accommodation

Třeboň lies on the Vienna-Prague express train route. Bus service from České Budějovice and Brno. The bus station is a little out of the centre of town towards České Budějovice. The road frontier crossing to Austria, Halámky-Neu Nagelberg, is 30km away, and open around the clock.

There are hotels and a campsite (which can get full), but the town is also within easy day-tripping distance of České Budějovice.

ČERVENÁ LHOTA

Known for its castle, Červená Lhota lies out in the country and can be reached by bus from Tábor or Soběslav. Some buses on the Praha-Florenc to Jindřichův Hradec route stop here. For marked tramping routes in the area see the map *Táborsko*.

Access to the small, originally Gothic, Červena Lhota Castle is gained by a stone bridge over the water which surrounds it. The castle has been restored several times, first in Renaissance and then Baroque style, with the latest restoration taking place in recent times. Today it houses a collection of furniture and paintings and is open to the public.

BECHYNĚ

The town of Bechyně lies on the Lužnice river and has a population of 5,000. Bechyně's school of ceramics was founded in 1884, and the former brewery and granary house an exhibition of ceramics and pottery. The Renaissance chateau, formerly a Gothic castle, is not open to the public. Bechyně spa, based on its springs, treats muscle problems.

Bechyně is accessible via Czechoslovakia's first electric railway from Tábor (see Tábor section). The river Lužnice is popular for canoeing, and there are campsites provided along its banks. One can walk along the river Lužnice all the way to Tábor, or in the opposite direction to Týn n. Vltava, using the campsites provided for overnighting.

TÁBOR

A Celtic settlement may have existed on the site of Tábor as early as the 1st Century BC. In the 13th Century a community called Hradiště existed here and a castle was built in the 14th Century. Tábor is best known as being one of the focal points of the Hussite movement. The Hussites lived in nearby Sezimovo Ústí, but while they were fighting in Prague in the winter of 1420, those remaining, mostly the elderly, women and children, were driven out by Oldřich Z Ústí. While Oldřich was drinking at Carnival, the Hussites killed his fighters, took off his clothes, and set him on his horse, which they then frightened so it bolted. They burnt Sezimovo Ústí, and founded the Hussite town of Tábor, as its site was much easier to defend. They gave the town the name Hradiště Hory Tábor (Castle of Mt Tábor) after the biblical mountain Tábor. The streets were purposely made crooked, to help the town withstand enemy attacks. The military commander of the Hussites, Jan Žižka, was one of the chief leaders. He died in 1424, and the head on the Kčs 20 note comes from a statue of him. The community was formed on the basis of everything being communally owned, but communal life in its true form didn't last very long. Whenever fire destroyed the town, most of the new houses respected the original plan of the town.

The **castle** was already here when the Hussites arrived, but it was burnt out. The Rosenburgs expanded it, but left it after a fire. It was later converted into a brewery, and today only the castle tower, Kotnov, remains, though its Gothic roof is missing.

In 1903 the first electric railway in what was then Austro-Hungary was constructed between Tábor and Bechyně. The original wooden carriages were used until about 25 years ago, but the line is now modernised.

Construction of the **Town Hall** began about 1440 and was completed in 1521. Its concert chamber is the second largest in Czechoslovakia and in summer concerts of medieval music are held in it. Today the Town Hall is a museum and open from April to October from 8.30am to 5.00pm. It shows the history of the Hussite movement. Historians are not sure when Jan Hus was born. He was important for Czech nationalism as well as the religious Hussite movement and he became an important symbol because he died as a martyr. After his death people gave up thinking they could change things through the power of words, and took to arms. Sigismund, the Czech king and Roman Emperor, didn't like the Hussites. 452 Czech and Moravian nobility signed a petition to Sigismund complaining about Hus's death. A copy of it is in the museum; the original is in Edinburgh. The three bells were made in the 16th Century in memory of Hus.

From the Town Hall access is gained to the underground passages built in the 1430s as protection from catastrophe. There were 12 to 15 km of tunnels under Tábor, but most of the network has been destroyed because of lack of money for reconstruction. The 650 metres open to the public today have only been open since 1968. The temperature in the tunnels is 7 to 8°C, good for storing beer and food. The tunnels must be visited with a guide.

Both the Town Hall and the **church** are on the main square, Žižkovo náměstí. The church was originally built of wood in 1521 in Gothic style, and is called The Church of the Transfiguration of Our Lord on Mount Tábor. Later Renaissance alterations include the dragons who spit the rainwater out. The tower was shot at by the Swedes in the Thirty Years War, and was rebuilt in Baroque style in its distinct "three onion" form. The Renaissance fountain in the square with a warrior in armour dates from 1567, the date Tábor received its town rights.

A couple of bastions, and one gate, **Bechyně**, which houses an archaeological museum, remain. Although vibration from traffic is damaging the old houses today, some of them, including the remaining Gothic houses, are well worth seeing. Restoration work began at the Augustine abbey, but had to move to nearby Bechyně gate, as the houses there were falling down. The setting of the old town is in itself beautiful, high above the river Lužnice. Jordán Lake (also a biblical name) on the River Tismenice was created in 1492 by the oldest dam in Czechoslovakia to supply the town with water. The fall of the water powered a pumping system that pumped water through wooden pipes to the water tower, from where water flowed to the tanks where people collected their water. Some of these tanks remain today.

In the park in front of the station is a 1928 Jugenstil sculpture by František Bilek (1872-1941) of Hus at the stake and the events leading up to this.

Just west of the old town is **Klokoty Abbey**. There was a small church here in the 12th and 13th Centuries. After the Thirty Years War the Catholics were powerful, and they rebuilt Klokoty in Baroque style in 1703-4, and added a convent in 1728-9. The Catholics gave the abbey up at the end of the 19th Century, but the beautiful church is still in use, as is the Catholic cemetery. You can walk there on the green marked track from town, or if you don't feel like the grunt up the hill, bus 11 runs nearby. If walking, the tiny bridge at the bottom of the hill is the oldest in Tábor, and you pass the stations of the cross on the way up to the church. Another abbey, the **Augustine Abbey**, was built in the town after the re-Catholicisation.

In my own experience (and others have agreed) the people working in shops, hotels, etc in Tábor all seemed more friendly and helpful than normal in Czechoslovakia. There are mosquitoes around the river and in the green areas.

To and from Tábor

Prague: *Osobní* 3 hours, *rychlík* 2 and frequent buses about 1½ hours.
Brno: One direct train a day takes 4 hours, otherwise you must change trains, making it better to take the bus.
České Budějovice: Trains: *rychlík* 1 hour, *osobní* 2 hours. Reasonably regular. Regular buses take 1 hour or 1 hour 20 minutes, depending on the route.
Vienna: Trains twice daily.

Sleeping & eating
Hotels
The best hotel in town is **Hotel Palcát**, ★★★, and it is easy to get a room. It has a nice interior, class II restaurant, kavárna with a band playing sometimes, and night club called "P Club" (open 8.00pm to 3.00am, closed Sunday and Monday). It is in the centre of the new town, at tř. 9 května 2, tel. 229 01-5. Doubles Kčs 225, singles Kčs 150.

Second best hotel is by the railway station. **Hotel Slávia**, ★★, Valdenská 591, tel. 235 74. About 75 beds. Often difficult to get a room in the summer. With bathroom: doubles Kčs 198, singles Kčs 132. Without bathroom: doubles Kčs 165, single (there is only one) Kčs 110, plus Kčs 30 if you want to take a bath.

Hotel Jordán, C, ul. Ant. Zápotockého, tel. 234 02 is cheaper, but is expected to close for renovation from 1992 to 1994, and may be upgraded to B category upon reopening.

Hotel Slovan is B class, in the main street, and was renovated in 1988.

Hostel
OT TJ Vodní Stavby, Turistická ubytovna B, Pintova ul. 2101, tel. 241 28 is good but primitive. Out of town by the river. 2.5km from the railway station on the red marked track west, or take bus no. 3 or 4 (make sure it's going in the right direction). Leave the markers or the bus at the Kotnova stop from where you follow the signs for 1km.

There is a new hostel, **Turistická ubytovna Luznice**, more expensive than the above, but also of a higher standard. It is in the new suburb, sidliště Lužnice, about 3km from the station. Take bus 11, 12 or 10 towards Sezimovo Ustí I. There are singles, doubles and triples with a kitchen·and fridge, and a bathroom to every three rooms. There is no catering, but the restaurant **Na Slovač** is 400m away and "Centrum" *vinárna* has a disco.

Camping and Cabins

Autokemp Knížecí rybník, Tábor 4-Zárybnična Lhota, PSČ 391 54, tel. 224 80. Camping, accommodation in cabins (both A & B class), plus rooms (UH accommodation from Kčs 50 per night) and restaurant. By a lake with swimming and boating. 6km from centre. Driving take highway 19 towards Jihlava. 700m walk from Smyslov railway station. Bus no. 3. Restaurant open all year. Cabins only from 15/5 to 15/9.

Autokemp Malý Jordán, Tábor-Náchod, tel. 321 03. Camping and class B cabins. Just north of Tábor on the E55, the road to Prague. 2.5km walk on the red marked track northwards from Tábor railway station. Bus no. 2. Open 15/6 to 15/6.

There is a camp site down the river, **U Harachovky**, open 15/6 to 15/9. Follow the red markers or take bus number 3 or 4 from the station to Most Sokolovska, then follow the red markers for 3km.

There are eateries around the square in the old town, otherwise try the hotels.

Information

There is a Čedok office next door to Hotel Palcát.

Information in English on Tábor and a map of the old town is found in the series *Getting to Know Czechoslovakia* No. 10, "Česko-Moravská Vrchovina". (Kčs 24). For a detailed map of the area, but not the town, see *Táborsko* (Kčs 8). There is a bookshop opposite Palcát.

Change money at Státní banka Československá or Hotel Palcát.

The railway station and bus station are together. They are a little way out from the old town, but within walking distance, via the area where today's hotels, shops etc are situated.

Emergency breakdown service for E55, tel 8428.

Luggage may be left at the railway station. They don't seem to complain about weights of packs.

The post office by the station is Pošta 2, and has post code 390 02.

The local bus routes all meet at the station, but when catching a bus here, make sure you get it in the right direction.

Excursions and tramping from Tábor

It is possible to follow the red marked tramping route along the river Lužnice to Bechyně, a 32km walk from the station, or 30km from the bridge Most Sokolovska. Or if you just want to walk the first part of the trip, the footbridge at U Harrachovka is 5.5km from the station. The river is also used for canoeing. In the other direction it is a 4.5km walk following the yellow markers along the river to Sezimovo Ústí I.

Near Tábor are the limestone caves, Chýnovská Jeskyně. They are not as interesting as the caves of the Moravian Karst or those in Slovakia, and there is no information in English. Communism hasn't got rid of the Czechs' religious superstitions, as you'll notice when you see all the coins in the pools in the caves. Open to the public since the end of the last century, the caves are now open May 1 to September 30, 8.00am to 5.00pm. The caves are signposted from Chýnov, on the Tábor-Jihlava road. From Chýnov railway station they are a 3km walk following the blue markers. Otherwise a bus from Tábor stops 1½ km away.

The high priests forced Hus to leave Prague, so he went to Kozí Hrad, because a friend of his worked there, and stayed from 1412 to 1414. He said that it was not right for the priests to exploit the people the way they did. When the news of his whereabouts spread, people started coming in their tens of thousands. The high priests called him to Constance, to his death, and today Tábor and Constance are twin towns. Kozí Hrádek is 5km southeast of Tábor. There is not so much to see now, but it is interesting from an historical point of view, and they even have a pamphlet in English. The tiny hostinec is open in the afternoons and early evenings in the summer only. To get there by road, head towards Jihlava and turn right in Měšice. By bus it is a 1km walk (green markers) from a bus stop on the infrequent route 28060 from Tábor. You can also follow the green markers 2.5km from the camp Autokemp Knížecí rybník, accessible by bus number 3 from Tábor. To return another way, the red markers from the castle ruins lead after 3km to Sezimovo Ústí II, from where there are buses and trains to Tábor. The semi-detached houses in Sezimovo Ústí near the railway station were built by Baťa. The machinery for shoe-making was built here.

(Poland)

(Germany)

ČESKÉ
ŠVÝCARSKO

LIBEREC

Děčín

Ústí n. Labem

Česka
Lípa

Teplice

Litoměřice

Terezín

Mladá
Boleslav

Mělník

Louny

KLADNO

PRAGUE
(PRAHA)

N

NORTH of PRAGUE

North of Prague

MĚLNÍK

Not far north of Prague, Mělník, with its 20,000 inhabitants, is the centre of Bohemian wine production. The historical part of the town is located in a beautiful spot overlooking the confluence of the rivers Elbe and Vltava. The new suburbs are pretty terrible, but the centre is most attractive. Some of the 15th Century fortifications survive.

In the **castle** is a museum with an exhibition of wine making, open summer only from 8.00am to 5.00pm. The vineyards on the slope between the castle and the Elbe are named after St Ludmila, the patron saint of Czech vineyards. Beside the castle is the **Church of St Peter and Paul** with its imposing 60 metre high tower. If you walk up between the castle and the church there is a beautiful view out over the vineyards and the confluence of Vltava and Elbe below.

Nám. Miru is the large and beautiful square in the centre of the old part of Mělník. Between it and nám. R. Armady (the small square where Čedok is found) is the 15th Century **Pražská brána** (Prague Gate), one of the original entrances to the town.

To and from Mělník
There are frequent buses to Mělník from the Holešovice bus station in Prague. Mělník's bus station is on the edge of town, but it takes only five minutes or so to walk up the hill to the centre. From the railway station the centre is 10 minutes. Luggage can be left at the bus station office until 6.00pm when it closes, or at the railway station until about 10.00pm.

Accommodation
There is a camp with bungalows open all year about 1km from the centre. Four bed bungalows cost Kčs 132.

Hotel Ludmila has singles for Kčs 194 and doubles for Kčs 292.

Information
Čedok is on the small square, nám. R. Armady, and you can change money here. None of their staff speaks English. Between the castle and the church is a map of the town on a board — a bit dated, but useful — and a map of walking routes in the area. Mělník's post code is 276 01.

Out of Mělník

North of Mělník and also on the Elbe is **Liběchov**, where there is a really good museum of Asian art, and nearby, an Asian restaurant.

In the hilly interior of Mělník is the 14th Century Gothic castle **Kokořín**, which gave its name to the surrounding area. There are numerous legends concerning the local robbers who took refuge in the fortifications, and the castle's history and glorious setting have inspired many, including Goethe. Restoration work in this century has respected the original Gothic features. The surrounds of Kokořín, including the lovely Kokořínský Důl, are noted for their forest and nature. For exploring, buy the map *Mělnicko*.

Eating

There is a restaurant (Zamecka vinárna) in the castle where you can eat overlooking the castle's vineyards and the Elbe — open 11.00am to 11.00pm daily, except Monday when it is closed, and Saturday when it is open longer. There are cheaper places to eat around the castle entrance.

TEREZÍN

The fortress and town of Terezín was founded in 1780 by Joseph II. In the 19th Century the fortress was a political prison. In 1942 the Nazis converted the town of Terezín, known to many by its German name Theresienstadt, into a ghetto, a concentration camp where 150,000 Jews were sent from various countries in Europe. The so called "Small Fortress", the best fortified section, became a prison of the Prague Gestapo. Some 35,000 people lost their lives in Terezín during the Second World War, and 84,000 died in the concentration camps they were taken to from Terezín.

Today there is a cemetery as a memorial. The Small Fortress is open to the public all year, its underground passages having been converted to a museum of the resistance against fascism.

Terezín lies on the E55, the main road to Berlin from Prague. There is a map of the town on the back of the map *Severní Čechy* in the *Poznáváme Československo* series, which also includes information on Terezín in English.

Accommodation

The following have post code 411 55 Terezín, and are on Litoměřice telephone exchange (area code 416). **Parkhotel**, C, Máchova 1, tel. 922 60, doubles and trebles only. **Sokolovna**, TU A, U hřiště 4, tel. 9924 73. **Autokemp Terezín**, A, tel. 922 78, open 1/4 to 31/10.

ÚSTÍ NAD LABEM

Ústí nad Labem is the main town of northern Bohemia, and the relics of its long history can be seen in its castle and other old buildings. Today the town is infamous as being one of the most polluted in Czechoslovakia. Three chemical plants combined with the high sulphur coal mined and burnt around here, create conditions where its inhabitants can no longer play sport outdoors in winter. The surrounding forest is either dead or dying.

It is often necessary to change trains here if travelling between western and northern Bohemia. If it proves impossible to get accommodation in České Švýcarsko, Ústí nad Labem could be used as a base for the area.

ČESKÉ ŠVÝCARSKO

České Švýcarsko (Bohemian Switzerland) is an amazing area of extraordinary sandstone rock formations, described in 1717 as forgotten by God and mankind, and fit only for thieves and robbing knights. In 1726 two Swiss painters were so overawed by the beauty of the countryside that they decided not to return home, saying they had discovered Switzerland here. Hence the name, but the area is also known as Českosaské Švýcarsko (Czech-Saxon Switzerland), Labské Pískovce (Elbe Sandstones) and Děčínské stěny (the Děčín Rocks).

In the Tertiary period the calcareous sandstone of the Děčín Uplands was penetrated by volcanic activity. In later periods as the upper sandstone layers were weathered away, volcanic outcrops were left rising above the surrounding terrain, giving today's striking landscape. The plain was unevenly raised during movements in the Tertiary, creating fissures which were widened by weathering.

České Švýcarsko is mostly forested, and is lovely in autumn when the leaves are changing colour. In spring and summer there are beautiful flowers around Tisa. I noticed lots of birds, which seem to be lacking in some parts of Czechoslovakia. The Elbe with its barge traffic flows through the area.

Before the 1989 revolution the area's proximity to the East German border meant that foreigners were checked. The police are hopefully a little more relaxed now.

Some of the most interesting places to visit are Pravčická brána, the Kamenice River canyons and Tisa.

Děčín

The main centre of the area is the town of Děčín, situated on the Elbe. The main railway station and the bus station are both across the river (three stops by bus) from the centre of town. Be careful when you ask for directions in Děčín as, seeing a foreigner with luggage, people assume that you are homeward bound to Germany, and will send you to the railway station or the road to Dresden.

There are two chateaux in Děčín. The one to the true right of the river is an impressive complex developed from the original castle built in 1128. Chopin was a guest here in 1835. For many years it was occupied by the Russian army, but now that they are pulling out, maybe it will open to the public. On the side of the castle entrance ramp closest to the square is a falling down church with beautiful frescoes and other ornamentation inside. Watch your head for falling debris on the way in. On the other side of the river is a small chateau perched on top of a high bluff (Pastýřská stěna) directly above the river, where there are also large gardens. It is a pleasant

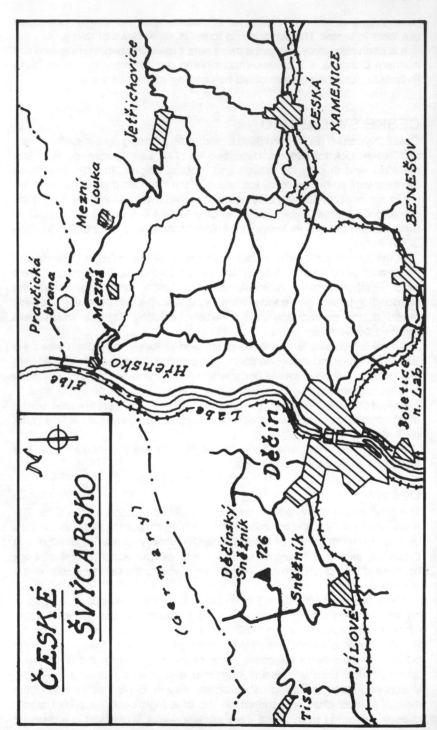

walk up through a park on the red marked track from the bridge, or an elevator (výtah) operates up inside the hill from 10.00am to 7.00pm in season, (afternoons only off season). It costs two local bus tickets each way; buy them in advance; there is a vending machine at the entrance.

There is a 28°C thermal pool at the camping ground.

The drive along the road from Děčín to Hřensko follows the Elbe and is beautiful. One can also walk the 18km to Hřensko via bluffs and woods along the red marked route which starts in Děčín. This walk could be shortened by making use of the country bus to Labská Stráň, Arnoltice and Janov.

To and from Děčín

Děčín lies on the main Prague-Berlin railway and is the customs post on the Czech side. There is an exchange office on the platform. There are a few buses each day between Prague and Děčín via Melník and Benešov, taking about 2½ hours.

Between Děčín and Karlovy Vary and Cheb there is one direct train a day (rychlík), which leaves Děčín early in the morning. The ticket is valid two days. Otherwise take a train towards Prague and change at Ústí nad Labem.

There is a bus service to Krkonoše. The bus station is on the west side of the river. If you're on the east side, buses to Hřensko stop near the town square, while other buses stop by a pond about 5 to 10 minutes walk from the square. To hitch to Germany or Hřensko walk to the edge of town to find a good spot.

There is a boat service between Děčín and Dresden.

Getting around

The local buses are same as normal, except that you can't use the front door which is reserved for the driver.

Accommodation

Everything gets full in the summer holiday period. Two hotels are:

Grand Hotel, B*, 405 02 Děčín IV, Rybalkovo nám. 97/18, tel. 270 41, opposite the railway station.

Sport, C, 405 02 Děčín IV, Prokopa Holého 36/55, tel. 22405, 22166. Alterations in 1990 may lead to upgrading to B.

Other places to stay are:

Hotel Pošta, TU B, Děčín I, Leninovo nám. 82, tel. 228 31. On the main square. A run down old hotel used as TU. May refuse to take western travellers. May be closed for renovation for a period.

Ubytovna TJ Spartak Děčín, TU B, Děčín II, Riegrova 8, tel. 235 85. Kitchen. Central.

U Kaple, TU B & CHO B, Děčín VI, U kaple 554, tel. 235 41. Open 1/4 to 31/10.

Ubytovna TJ Sokol Bělá, TU B, Děčín X-Bělá, Tělocvičná 9, tel. 238 35.

U koupaliště, A-kemp & TU A, Děčín I, tel. 227 55. Centrally located camping ground, with hot pools, open 1/5 to 30/9.

Eating

The Asia is Chinese and is the best restaurant in town. Find it on the main road below Pastýřská stěna. The next best place is the *kavárna* in the chateau itself.

On Leninovo nám. there is a local pub (sk.III) in Hotel Pošta with unexciting food (closed Wednesday). Koruna restaurant is just along from Pošta, sk.II, but closed for reconstruction until about 1993. There is also a cheap sk.IV *bufet* on the upstream end of the square, open daytime only (till 7.00pm).

Evenings

The best nightlife is probably not in the hotels, but in youth clubs, or at the trade union premises at Labská 691/23 where there may be something on at the weekend. (From the town square head towards Germany in a straight line and you'll walk into it.)

Between Leninovo and the bridge are a cinema, video café and an outdoor café.

Astra is a new *kavárna* on ul. Prokop Holy, the same street as the railway station. Open midday to midnight, except Sunday and Monday. There is a *vinárna* with music every day in the Grand Hotel.

Národní Kavárna is on the main square by the pedestrian underpass. Open Monday to Saturday 8.00pm to 2.00am.

Hřensko

Hřensko is a beautiful village, nestled under cliffs in the Kamenice River valley where it meets the Elbe. At 116 metres above sea level, it is the lowest village in Bohemia. The other side of the Elbe here is already Germany. The inhabitants were fishermen and forestry workers. In 1567 a customs post was established here. The tourist boom began last century.

The buses to Hřensko from Děčín stop also on the east side of the bridge in Děčín.

In the summer there is a regular boat service on the Elbe between Děčín and Hřensko. From the beginning of May till the end of August it sails from Děčín at 8.00am, 11.00am and 3.00pm, and from Hřensko at 9.15am, 1.00pm and 4.15pm. In the last half of April and the first half of September it departs Děčín at 9.00am and 1.00pm, and Hřensko at 11.00am and 2.30pm. Tel. 23410.

The post office is at the bottom of the valley, and open from 8.00am to 3.00pm.

Accommodation

Hotel Labe, hotel C, tel. 981 88. At the bottom of the valley.
Restaurant Praha, TU B, tel. 981 04, in the valley.
Klepáč, TU A, 407 17 Hřensko, tel. (412) 982 83. With a waterwheel outside. Just up the road from the entrance to Soutěska. Booked up by CKM during the holidays, otherwise open to the public. Nice sk.III restaurant.
Jitřenka, TU A, 407 17 Hřensko, tel. 981 27, open in season only.

Note that Národní dům and Beseda Hřensko are closed for reconstruction, and are expected to reopen in 1995.

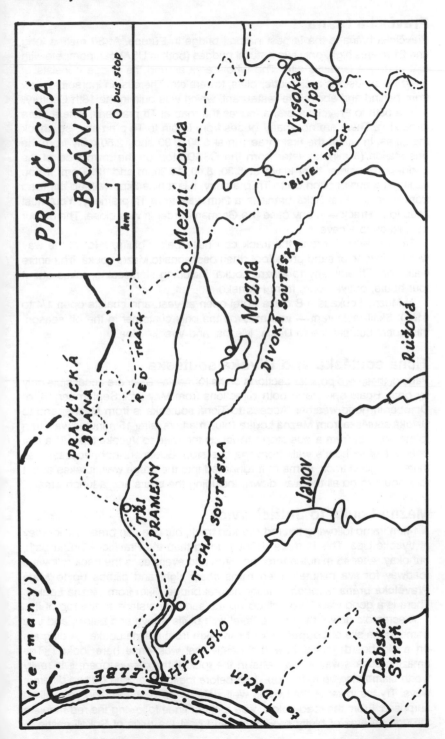

Pravčická brána

Pravčická brána is the largest natural bridge in Europe. At 30 metres long and 21 metres high, only two natural bridges (both in USA) can compete with it. It is truly a fantastic site. The whole area around the bridge consists of amazing sandstone rock bluffs, cliffs, towers etc. There is an incredible view from behind and above the restaurant, which was built in the 18th Century.

The path to Pravčická brána leaves the road at Tři prameny, where there is parking. There are not many buses from Děčín to Tři prameny, so check the times. In winter the first three run at 5.30, 9.30 and 12.50 daily from the bus station (3 minutes later from the ČSAD stop on the town side of the bridge). In summer they leave at 5.30, 8.40, 10.30am and 12.50pm. If you can't get a bus or hitch up to Tři prameny, it is a nice 3km walk up the road from Hřensko. Pravčická brána is a 2km walk from Tři prameny. You must keep to the track — in any case the German border is very close. The detour path leads to a cave.

From Pravčická brána the track continues below bluffs, a lot of the way with sandstone or sand underfoot, then descends to Mezní Louka. The entire walk from Tři prameny to Mezní Louka, including sightseeing, takes about four hours, or five hours from Hřensko.

At Mezná Louka is a B class hotel open all year, and chalets open 1/4 to 31/10. Sk.III restaurant — you may be the only customer in the off season. Infrequent bus service to Děčín, Mezná, and Vysoké Lipa.

Tichá soutěska and Divoká soutěska

Parts of these two popular sections of the Kamenice River are accessible only by boat. Boats operate in both directions from May until September 15, or October in good weather. Access to Tichá soutěska is from Mezná, and to Divoká soutěska from Mezná Louka (blue markers, after 15 minutes walk turn to the right) or from a bus stop further up the road to Vysoké Lipa. The first boat is half an hour's walk from the bus stop. Boots are not necessary, as there is a good track, some of it tunnelled into the gorge wall. It takes about four hours to go all the way down, including the boats and a lunch break.

Mezná Louka to Jetřichovice

A 14km tramp following the red marked track, but one can break the journey at Vysoké Lipa. This is more difficult going than the Pravčická brána path, but okay. After 45 minutes through birch and evergreens the track follows a roadway for five minutes, then turns *sharp* right and climbs up to **Malá Pravčická brána**, a *much* smaller natural bridge (3km from Mezná Louka). There is a good view if you climb up the sandstone steps to the top of it.

A scramble down, then more level with bluffs above and below, and you come to the site of **Loupežnický hrad** (4km from Mezná Louka). A diagram on a signboard shows how the castle that was once here looked. The amazing access way is via clefts in the rock. If the gate is open, it is really worth clambering up to the top. Just before the top, you can go two different ways. Try the lower of the two as well, right to the very end, and you will be surprised. From the road below, you can continue following the red markers through an area of bluffy mountains and past the ruins of Sokoli castle to

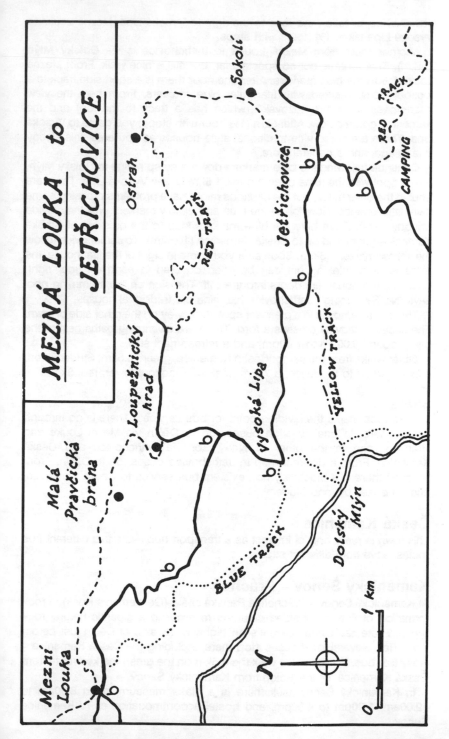

Jetřichovice, or follow the road to the right to Vysoké Lipa. Mezná Louka to Vysoké Lipa takes 1¾ hours with stops.

Another route from Mezná Louka to Jetřichovice is via **Dolský Mlýn** (14km). This route is not so spectacular, but still a nice walk. From Mezná Louka follow the blue markers. After one hour there is a short side track to a lookout point, marked with triangular blue markers. From here the view encompasses the hill Růžovský (which has a track to the top) and the Kamenice gorge below. After 5km (1½ hour with stops) you come to Vysoké Lipa. There are some nice traditional style houses as you enter this sleepy little village, and a general store.

Continue following the blue markers down a steep ravine to Dolský Mlýn, a nice spot with the ruins of an old mill 1.5km below Vysoká Lipa. There are trout in the clear rivers, but the cautious might have problems crossing some hairy little bridges. Now follow the blue and yellow markers until they divide (muddy here). From here the blue markers lead to the outskirts of Srbská Kamenice (3km) and on to Česká Kamenice (10.5km). To Jetřichovice follow the yellow markers (3km). Soon after you come in sight of the first house, the remains of a little log hut can be seen covered in earth on your right. Opposite the house are doors into the cliff. The sign on the swimming pool says "No Swimming"! Jetřichovice has nice old traditional houses.

There is a campsite in a pleasant spot 1km away on the other side of town. The access roadway crosses a ford. There are swimming baths next to the camp open 10.00am to 7.00pm, and a refreshment stall.

Other walks from the camp: Česká Kamenice, green, 6.5km; Studený, red, 4.5km; turnoff to Studenec, a 736m peak with lookout tower, red, 9km.

Buses

Vysoká Lipa marks the dividing point for bus services. There is no through service here. In one direction buses run to Děčín via Mezní Louka and Hřensko, and in the other to Nový Bor via Jetřichovice and Česká Kamenice. From a different stop in Jetřichovice buses run to Děčín. From Studený there is a practically non-existent bus service to Česká Kamenice, and no buses beyond Studený.

Česká Kamenice

This town is really only of interest as a transport hub. Note that different bus routes leave from different streets.

Kamenický Šenov – Prácheň

At Kamenický Šenov – Prácheň is Panská skála (Gentleman's Rock), a rock formation of five to six sided columns resembling a gigantic natural rock organ. Protected since 1895, it's on highway 13 east of Děčín just before Nový Bor. Several local buses stop there, including the Česká Kamenice – Nový Bor bus. You can also walk the 8.5km on the green marked route from Česká Kamenice, or the 1.5km from Kamenický Šenov.

In Kamenický Šenov itself there is a glass museum, open 8.00am to 12.00am, 1.00pm to 4.00pm, and hostel accommodation at TJ Kamenice Šenov.

Benešov nad Ploučnicí

Benešov used to be part of the domain of Ostrý Castle. In the mid 14th Century many German settlers arrived, eventually outnumbering the Slavs. In 1407 the estate was taken over by the Lords of Dubá. They were enemies of the Hussite movement, and there was fighting here. An invasion in 1445 put an end to the fighting. Ostrý was ransacked and eventually destroyed, never to be rebuilt. The ruins of Ostrý Castle are outside Benešov on a bluff across the river from the road to Česka Lipa. By bus get off at the Ostrý stop.

In Benešov itself is a chateau just up from the square, where there is a museum of porcelain and china in the lower chateau, open from May to September (tel. 943 75). The compulsory guided tours are in Czech only, but notes in German can be borrowed, or there is a booklet you can buy which includes the history of the chateau in English. The upper chateau will open in 1992, partly as a hotel for foreigners. They both date from the 1500s. The Gothic parish church is open only on Sundays. Historical buildings include 15th and 16th Century noblemen's houses in the vicinity of the chateau.

Benešov is 14km south-east of Děčín. There are trains and buses from Děčín, but all buses stop in the square, which is much handier than the railway station. The Prague-Děčín bus stops in Benešov. Hotel Jelen on the square has a restaurant and a stand-up eating place. There is a post office on the square.

Tiské stěny

The natural rock formation, Tiské stěny, at Tisá, is described as a "rock town". The rocks have been weathered to form huge towers.

An infrequent bus service from Děčín bus station to Tisá takes ¾ hour. If you are staying on the town side of the bridge, you can catch the bus from the ČSAD bus stop across the bridge and a few metres along to the right. Hitching is not bad. Another way to get there is to take the bus or train to Libouchec, and walk or change to a bus to Tisá there (these run more often than those from Děčín). Or you can walk the 18.5km from Děčín on the red marked track starting by the bridge. The rocks are 500 metres up from the town of Tisá. Kčs 2 entry in season, otherwise free. A marked route leads around, over and under the rocks. It begins with a circular route to the left, then leads out to the road east of Tisá via the rocks to the right. You can return to Tisá via the red marked track which cuts back over the top of the rocks giving a good view. Allow about two hours to explore.

There is a campsite just west of the rocks, and *turistická ubytovna* with kitchen. Tel. Ústí nad Labem 902 47. Open all year. Where the route around the rocks exits to the road, there is a *turistická chata* (Ve skalách), with rooms and dorms and a restaurant. Tel. 902 75. Open Monday noon to 5pm, Tuesday 10am to 8pm, Friday and Saturday 10am to 10pm, Sunday 9am to 4.30pm. Closed Wednesday and Thursday. You can't start seeing the rocks from this end. The track is not marked in that direction.

Sněžník

Buses to Tisá from Děčín stop here. At the crossroads is Hraniční bouda, with a nice little sk.III restaurant open 7.00am to 7.00pm, and TU B accommodation in season. Tel. Děčín 933 49.

From Sněžník you can walk up Děčínský Sněžník (726m), also known as Vysoký Sněžník, a strange mountain with bluffs all around and a big plateau on top (2km, ½ hour). The road up is closed. The chata on top was wrecked in 1985, but there is a lookout tower. There is an interesting area of dwarfed forest on top, but acid rain has just about finished it off.

Děčínský Sněžník to Děčín

Apart from returning to Sněžník village three other possible ways of continuing to Děčín are as follows. One is to follow the green markers down to Jílové (6km) and catch the train from there. Another is to follow the red marked track back to Děčín (9.5km). The third is to follow the red markers until the junction with the green marked track to the left (40 minutes). Then follow the green markers 13km to Děčín. After the village of Maxičky this route drops down to the Elbe valley at Čertova Voda and follows it upstream past holiday cottages and houses. A shorter alternative from Maxičky is to follow the yellow markers to the right to Děčín (5.5km). An alternative from Čertova Voda is to follow the yellow markers downstream 3km to Dolní Žleb, where there is a car ferry across the Elbe (operates until 8.00pm in summer).

Information

Map: *Českosaské Švýcarsko*, published by Kartografie, n. p., Praha & Veb Tourist Verlag, East Berlin is a detailed map with walking tracks. Sometimes not very accurate, but a good guide.

Accommodation: A lot of the accommodation in the area is controlled by Centrální ubytovaci služba Grand Děčín. Tel. 270 41.

Hitchhiking: Generally not so easy. No traffic out of season.

The town of Litoměřice, near Terezín

N

(Poland)

Krkonoše

Trutnov

Kuks

Jablonec
n. Nisou

LIBEREC

HRADEC
~ KRÁLOVE

Český Raj

Česka
Lípa

Mladá Boleslav

Poděbrady

KOLÍN

Brandýs
n. Labem
-Stará Boleslav

Mělník

PRAGUE
(PRAHA)

NORTHEAST of PRAGUE

Northeast of Prague

BRANDÝS NAD LABEM AND STARÁ BOLESLAV

Not far northeast of Prague, the twin towns of Brandýs nad Labem and Stará Boleslav lie each on their own side of the river Elbe. Stará Boleslav's history can be traced back to the 10th Century, when legend has it that Boleslav, jealous of his brother Wenceslas' popularity with the Czech people, ordered him murdered. Brandýs was founded in the 14th Century.

You can only visit the courtyard of the **castle** in Brandýs — the building itself is closed to the public. There is a new **local history museum** in Arnoldinovský dům on the square in Brandýs, open all year from 9.00am to 12.00am, 1.30pm to 4.30pm, closed Mondays. Down towards the river from the square is **Klatovna Muzeum** with an exhibitions of art and torture. Open daily from mid-April to the end of October from 10.00am to 12.00am and 2.00pm to 5.00pm. Neither museum has any information in any foreign language.

Between the two towns you will cross a marked walking route along the Elbe, and a kayak course in the canal beside the river.

On my visit in 1989 I had the surprise of my life when, walking in to Stará Boleslav I found that they were digging up skeletons in the main street! During excavations to lay gas mains, old graves were found underneath the street. Although the dig continued for some time, it was eventually stopped because of the traffic disruption it caused. The graves continue under the surrounding houses.

Entering Stará Boleslav from Brandýs you'll come to **St Wenceslas Church** before the tower. St Wenceslas was murdered at the doors of an earlier church. The original doors are not preserved, but the site is marked. In the 17th Century the church was destroyed by the Swedish army, but was repaired again after the Thirty Years War. There is information in English about the church.

Stará Boleslav has a summer outdoor cinema.

To and from Prague

By car use motorway E65 (or highway 10) from Prague. Bus is by far the best form of public transport from Prague and Mladá Boleslav. There is a railcar service from Neratovice to Čelákovice via Brandýs. There is also a bus service to Čelákovice, and both Neratovice and Čelákovice lie on rail lines to

Prague. Local town buses (buy ticket in advance) operate infrequently between Brandýs nad Labem and Stará Boleslav.

Accommodation
Hotel Praha, C, by the tower in Stará Boleslav was in my experience unfriendly and unhelpful. **Hotel Černý kůň**, C, is on the square in Brandýs. There is a **summer hostel** at KU-LDT Houštka, koleje UK, 250 01 Houštka u Staré Boleslavi, tel. (0202) 2302, but it was under reconstruction in 1991 for an indefinite period.

MLADÁ BOLESLAV
Mladá Boleslav lies on the E65, northeast of Prague, and is best known for its Škoda car works. It all started in 1895 when Laurin and Klement began producing bicycles here. Their production of cars began in 1905. In 1989 the news that a lot of the workers were prisoners leaked out, and some countries refused to import more Škodas. The amnesty after the revolution interrupted production since so many of the workers had been prisoners. Under the previous regime many English experts worked at Škoda for short periods. After the Velvet Revolution foreign car manufacturers were queuing up to get involved in Škoda, and the "Favorit" turned out to be the VW concern which, if all goes according to plan, will own 70% of the Škoda car company by 1995. Škoda cars will continue to be sold under their own name.

To and from Mladá Boleslav
By car take the E65 (highway 10) motorway from Prague. There are many buses from Prague, and they are much quicker than the train.

Accommodation
Hotel Věnec, B, is centrally situated at Staroměstské nám. 89, tel. (0326) 21991. Doubles Kčs 186, singles Kčs 120, 3 beds Kčs 241, one apartment for Kčs 385 for 2 persons, Kčs 418 for 3, an 8 bed dorm Kčs 458 and a 12 bed dorm Kčs 687 — with the dorms you must pay for all beds.
Hotel Hvězda, C, Rudé armády 445, tel 23859, is near the bus and trains stations.
Hotel Autoškoda, B, Neubrandenburská 794, tel 61 2201, is further out.
Autokemp Kosmonosy, AC B, 293 06 Mladá Boleslav, tel. 242 02, is a few kilometres out at Kosmonosy, open mid-May to mid-September.

Information and orientation
The bus and train stations are beside each other, a little way out of the centre. The Škoda works are just past the bus station, heading out from town. Čedok is on the edge of the old town on tř. Lidových milici. Judging by the problems I had, I guess I was the first person to cash a traveller's cheque there. I recommend trying the bank instead if it is open. The telephone area code is (0326). Pošta 1, the main post office, has a separate entrance for phone and telegram, open weekdays 7.30am to 9.00pm, Saturdays 7.30am

to 2.00pm and Sundays 8.00am to 12.00am. Tusex and another post office (Pošta 3) are opposite the bus station.

What to see
A small museum in the castle is open May to October 9.00am to 5.00pm and the rest of the year 8.00am to 4.00pm, closed 12.00am to 1.00pm all year. The rest of the castle is under repair until about 1997-9. The Renaissance town hall can be seen only from the outside, as it is used for offices. In the former Church of the Bohemian Brothers on Českobratrské nám. there is an art gallery open June to August 10.00am to 5.00pm.

In nearby Kosmonosy is a Baroque castle and a 17th Century monastery, but both are closed to the public.

ČESKÝ RÁJ (BOHEMIAN PARADISE)
Český Ráj is a region of castles, towering rock outcrops and bizarre rock formations, created by the erosion of the soft sandstone lying between Turnov, Jičín and Mnichovo Hradiště. There is some argument as to exactly what area Český Ráj covers — some say it stretches as far as Mladá Boleslav — so it is a subjective area you define in your own head. Some of the best places to see are as follows: Valdstejn Castle; the Hrubá Skála rock formations; the ruins of Trosky Castle; the Prachovské skaly rock formations; and Kost Castle. All of these are most easily accessible from Turnov, except Prachovské skaly which is handier to Jičín. The area is best enjoyed by foot. Český Ráj is not such a well-known tourist area, so here you will meet mostly Czechs.

Trosky
In my opinion, Trosky is one of the most spectacular ruins in Czechoslovakia, even in the rain when it is covered in mist. Perched upon two adjoining hill tops, the castle ruins can be seen from afar and are a Český Ráj landmark. Founded at the end of the 14th Century, it has lain desolate since the end of the Thirty Years' War. Trosky is closed on Mondays. It is not possible to walk right to the top, as the towers are crumbling.

There is a car park below the castle, and about five times a day a bus from Turnov to the junction below Trosky Hotel — don't rely on finding legible timetables at the stops.

Prachovské skály
Prachovské skály are the most popular and most fascinating of the rock formations of Český Ráj, and cover a large area. There are three marked round trips (*okruh*), the longest being 3.5km. I recommend number 3 if you have the time and energy. It climbs up and down a lot of steps, and leads through nooks and crannies amongst the rocks. Keep to the paths marked with colour — the others are for rock climbers.

The main road and bus access is from Jičín. One can also enter from the bus stop at Maršov, but the track is not marked (presumably because you avoid paying the entrance fee if you enter here). You simply walk up the drive

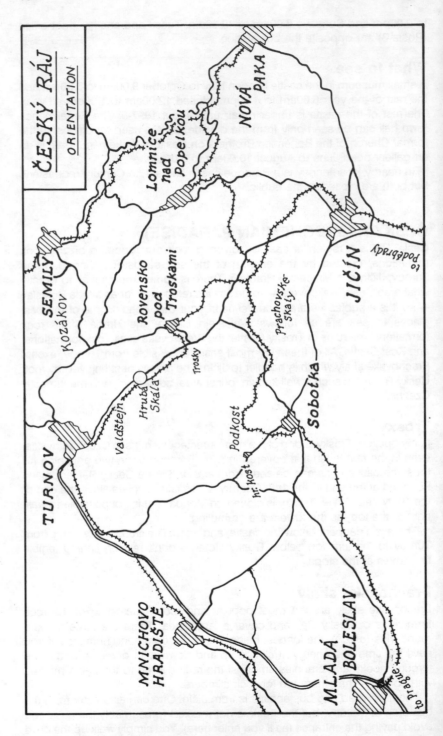

opposite the bus shelter, then up a track that leads a little to the left, until you come to the green marked track (only 50m altogether). If exiting here, turn down the track by the sign "Maršov".

Kost

Kost is one of the best preserved castles in Bohemia. The original Gothic castle was built in the 14th Century, with extensions being added later. In the 16th Century part of it burnt down. This century has seen its restoration, and it now houses a collection of Gothic art and graphics. The castle is interesting because it should be possible to see three sides from whatever angle you look at it. In fact, I found it more interesting from the outside than from the inside. There are tours, but they are not so worthwhile if you don't understand Czech, although they do have a leaflet in English on the castle's history. In the summer it is open every day except Monday, while in April, May, September and October it is open only at the weekends. The rest of the year it is closed. (Tel. 71 44).

Tramping

Český Ráj is ideal for tramping, and here you will meet mostly Czechs. But in hot weather in grassy areas they will be far outnumbered by the vicious horseflies! Don't forget insect repellent. You can tramp through the whole area from Turnov to Jičín, a 30km trip along the *Zlatá stezka Čes. ráje* (Golden Trail of the Bohemian Paradise), which could be broken by staying in the camp sites on the way. Drinking water sources are rare, so fill up at the camps.

Turnov–Valdštejn–Hrubá, Skála–Trosky–Prachovské, Skály–Jičín

It is, of course, not necessary to walk the whole way, and all of the places mentioned here are accessible as shorter walks. I have included walking distances to other places, especially nearby bus stops and railway stations.

Valdštejn Castle was built in the 13th Century on three rocky outcrops and has been the setting for many films. The best preserved part is the stone access bridge, lined with Baroque statues. The castle (tel. 21 384) is open from May 1 to September 30 from 9.00am to 4.00pm (closed Monday). One can buy refreshments. There is no public road access. From Turnov station it is 3km on the red or green marked track, or 4km on the yellow from Sedmihorky station.

The **Hrubá Skála** rock formations are said to resemble a ghost city, and the 200 or so rocks rising vertically skywards are popular with climbers. It is 3km from Valdštejn to **Hrubá Skála castle** the most direct way, following the red markers along the top of a bluff, but it can take five hours as there are various side tracks to lookouts, and lots to explore in the area around Hrubá Skála. This route leads you along at the same height as the top of the outcrops, with views out across them. You can also walk along the bottom of the rocks by following the yellow markers and later the green markers to the right leading up to Hrubá Skála castle through the cleft in the rocks, Myši díra. If the heat is getting you down, you can make a detour via Autocamping

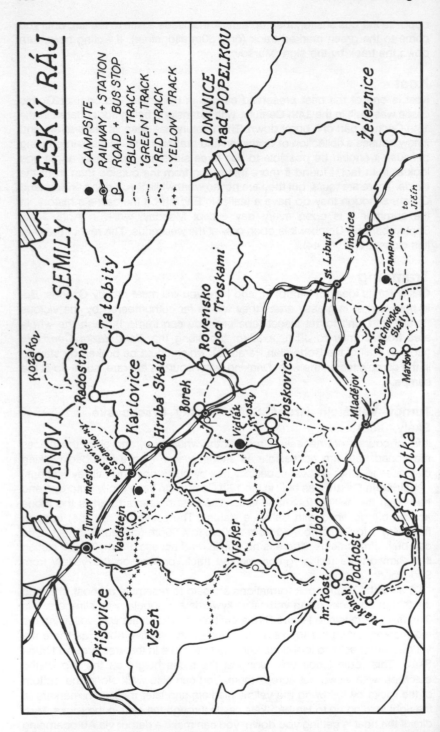

ČESKÝ RÁJ

CAMPSITE
RAILWAY + STATION
ROAD + BUS STOP
'BLUE' TRACK
'GREEN' TRACK
'RED' TRACK
'YELLOW' TRACK

SEMILY

LOMNICE nad POPELKOU

Železnice

to Jičín

Tatobity

Kozákov

Radostná

Karlovice

Hrubá Skála

Borek

Rovensko pod Troskami

st. Libuň

Jinolice

CAMPING

Prachovské Skály

Maršov

TURNOV

Sedmihorky

z. Turnov město

Valdštejn

Vidlák

Troskovice

Mladějov

Sobotka

Vyskeř

Libošovice

Příšovice

Všeň

hr. Kost

Podkost

Prakařeň

Sedmihorky (a 45 minute walk) where you can swim in the small lake. From here it is 2.5km to Hrubá Skála castle via Myši díra. Boots are unnecessary in this part of Český Ráj. The castle at Hrubá Skála is not open to the public. Refreshments are available outside the entrance and there is a restaurant with better than average meals open from 11.00am to 10.00pm. Some walking distances from Hrubá Skála: Turnov 7km via Valdštejn, red markers; Kost Castle 10.5km, blue; Hrubá Skála railway station 2.5km, blue; Prachovské skály 18km, red.

From Hrubá Skála the red marked route leads by road to **Vidlák**, a 4km or 1½ hour walk. If you want to avoid "road bashing", take the green marked track south from Hrubá Skála, then follow the yellow markers left to Vidlák, a 5km walk altogether. At Vidlák is a camp site, restaurant and lake.

From Vidlák the red markers ascend 2.5km through forest and orchards to **Trosky** (see my description earlier). From Trosky the red marked route leads to Dolní Mlýn, an interesting and pleasant 3km walk, first down through sandstone bluffs and crannies, then through forest. Other walking distances from Trosky are: Borek p. Tr. railway station and bus stop 3km, blue markers; Ktová station 3km, green; Malechovice station 6.5km, blue; Dolní Mlýn via the green marked route 3km.

Dolní Mlýn is a mill pond. A few yards along the track towards Mladějov is a drinking water source (Pitná Voda). The red marked route continues 2km to the village of **Mladějov** as a level track along the bottom of a little gorge. Other walking distances from Dolní Mlýn are: Kost 10km, red; Prachovské skály 8.5km, red.

From Mladějov the red marked route continues to Prachovské skály, then on to Jičín, or there is an occasional bus from Mladějov to Jičín (get off at the Maršov stop for Prachovské skály). Occasional buses on the Lomnice-Libuň-Sobotka route also stop in Mladějov. Buses generally run on weekdays only. There is also a railway station.

Borek–Vidlák–Kost–Sobotka

This route starts from Borek where there is a bus stop and a railway station on the line between Jičín and Turnov. Follow the yellow markers along a road, then through forest and meadows and past lakes to Vidlák (3km, watch out for nettles on this stretch), where you cross the previous route I describe.

From Vidlák to Kost is 9km, whichever of the following routes you take. The yellow markers continue on a level route along a valley and past a lake. When you meet a roadway you follow it to the left, either following the green markers all the way to Kost, or taking the red marked route through the fields to the village of Libošovice, where there is a store. From Libošovice to Kost the red markers are hard to find, but the route is level and straightforward, so just stay in the flat bottomed valley when you can't see any markers.

Kost to Turnov is 18km on the green marked route via Valdštejn. Our route follows the red markers through the scenic valley of Plakánek and then by road to Sobotka. Karel Čapek called Sobotka "a town of poets, schoolmasters and shoemakers". This small town had its origins in the late 13th Century. Above the town stands Humprecht hunting manor. Sobotka is on the railway line which crosses Český Ráj, meeting the Turnov-Hradec Králové line at Libuň.

Kozákov

The blue marked route northeast from Sedmihorky leads to the 744m high mountain of Kosákov. People find semiprecious stones here. Kozákov is 8km from Sedmihorky or 9km from Sedmihorky Camping.

Climbing

To climb here you must be a member of a climbing club and the climbing is, of course, on sandstone. Hrubá Skála is popular for rock climbing. There are books on the top of each rock for you to sign if you make it. Prachovské skály is another good climbing area.

Getting there

Mnichovo Hradiště and Turnov are on the E65, north-east of Prague. Trains on the Turnov-Hradec Králové line stop at Jičín and at the small stations that are useful for access to Český Ráj, such as Borek and Sedmihorky. The trains run roughly hourly, though not all trains stop at every station. More trains stop at Borek than at Sedmihorky. The Mladá Boleslav-Stará Paka railway line passes through Český Ráj, crossing the Turnov-Hradec Králové line at Libuň.

Maps

Český Ráj a Poděbradsko is a detailed map covering the whole area, but for Prachovské skály the detail in inadequate.

Prachovské skály is a detailed map of those rock formations, but if you don't have one just follow your nose around them, or look at the plan outside the chata.

Accommodation

Autocamp Karlovice-Sedmihorky is perhaps the most convenient place to stay. An A class camp with tent camping, huts and a swimming hole, its problem is that is gets full, in which case you get turned away at the entrance. Open April 1 to October 31. Situated near Hrubá Skála and Valdštejn, and convenient for a round trip. One kilometre from highway 35 (Turnov-Jičín) at Sedmihorky, where there is also a bus stop and railway station.

Tabořiště U Vidláku is a primitive camp site which gets much fuller than Sedmihorky, though there is no-one to turn you away. By car or bike turn off at Borek. There is no public transport, so try hitching or follow the yellow marked track, which is more direct than by road, 3km from Borek railway station or bus stop. The bus stop at Trosky is actually nearer, but that bus is very infrequent. The camp site is sheltered in a clearing in the forest, but that also means the sun comes late and leaves early. The water in the middle of the site is for drinking only, while the water outside the toilets is for washing only. Someone comes around to collect the fees: Kčs 8 per person; Kčs 11 per tent. The restaurant is across the road.

Hotel Trosky, below the castle, has UH accommodation for 12 people for Kčs 100 per person per night. Note that it is closed on Mondays all year, and also on Tuesdays in winter. There is usually room, but it's best to phone first on (0436) 91290. Restaurant and buffet. From the terrace you can look up through the trees to Trosky.

At **Mladějov** there is a motel.

At the end of the bus route from Jičín to Prachovské skály there is a *turistická chata* with TU B and UH accommodation. (See *Useful information* if you are having trouble understanding the various accommodation categories.)

There is a large campsite by the lakes at **Jinolice**, but it gets full and they turn people away. There is an occasional bus in the daytime, otherwise it is about a 2km walk from Jinolice station or the bus stop on the main Jičín-Turnov road. From the camp it is not far, but wet underfoot, on the blue marked route to Prachovské skály.

Under Kost Castle is the unfriendly C category **Hotel Podkost**, with a sk.III restaurant.

Other accommodation is found in the towns.

KRKONOŠE (GIANT MOUNTAINS)

The Krkonoše (Giant Mountains) cover an area of about 40km by 20km along the Polish border in northern Bohemia. The highest peak, Sněžka (1602m.), is the highest mountain in Bohemia. The Krkonoše tend to be shaped as rolling hills with rounded tops, but there can be near vertical dropoffs into the valleys. Typical for the mountains are the dwarf pines which grow on the slopes above 1300 metres. The source of the Elbe (Labe in Czech) lies in the Krkonoše and the largest resort, Špindlerův Mlýn, lies on the Elbe.

In the Middle Ages people told their children there was a figure called Krakonoš who lived in the mountains and came down and visited them occasionally, punishing the bad and rewarding the good. The mountains were the frontier between the Austro-Hungarian Empire and Germany (Silesia, which was then German, but is now Polish).

Because of their proximity to Prague, 139km away, the Krkonoše can be very crowded, especially on Sundays. In 1988 there were 8 million tourists. The main centre of the region is Vrchlabí. It lies outside the mountains, but is a centre for transport and accommodation booking. The main centres in the mountains are Harrachov (especially for skiing, 704m), Špindlerův Mlýn (780m) and Pec pod Sněžkou (756m).

The Krkonoše are famed for their weather. There is some form of precipitation on 200 days of the year. This leads to good snow conditions in winter, but to many cancelled or miserable trips in summer. The Krkonoše are deceptively low. Lying about 800km north of the Alps, you can expect the same weather at 1000m here as you would receive at a height of 1800 to 2000m in the Alps. The average temperature around Špindlerův Mlýn is 4°C and at the top of Sněžka 1.1°C.

Krkonoše was declared a national park in 1963. But the trees are dying since it is one of the areas in Europe worst hit by acid rain. Over 10,000 ha of mainly pine forests are slowly losing all their needles as insects are attacking the weakened trees. There is a lot of milling in an attempt to stop these insects spreading to the more healthy trees.

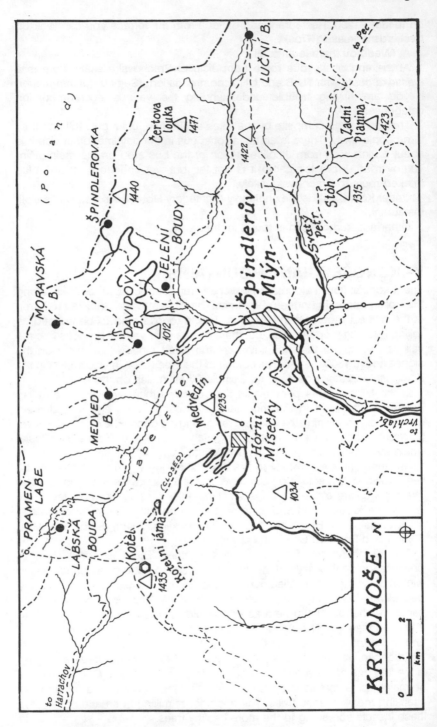

Goats and cows have grazed the mountain meadows through the years. The herdsmen built wooden huts called *boudy* (singular *bouda*) to protect themselves from the weather. The original huts developed into farmsteads, and later into chalets where visitors could spend the night. Today the name *bouda* has been preserved, but a *bouda* may be anything from a simple hut to a big hotel. The term *bouda* is known only in the Krkonoše.

To and from Krkonoše

There are direct buses from Prague to Vrchlabi, Špindlerův Mlýn, Janské Lázně, etc, and it is best to have a booking in holiday periods and weekends. Trains from Prague to Vrchlabi or Svoboda nad Úpou. Buses to Vrchlabí are better than the train. They also stop centrally, while the station is 2km south of the centre. Buses to Špindlerův Mlýn and Prague leave from the square in Vrchlabí, while all other buses leave from the bus station, on the left a little way down the main road from the square. To Děčín take the Ustí n. L. bus from Vrchlabi, which runs three times a day and takes about four hours to Děčín.

The only open crossing to Poland is the road from Harrachov. Those who require a Czechoslovak visa cannot re-enter Czechoslovakia without first obtaining another visa.

Getting around

There are many buses between Vrchlabi and Špindlerův Mlýn, but even so they can get full in season. There are buses between the various resorts in summer only. Otherwise travelling between resorts by bus requires many changes. Buses as far as the Polish border above Špindlerův Mlýn. This road is open only to buses in winter. Buses to Vítlovice-Krkonoš above Horní Místečky in summer only. Most bus routes in the area don't operate in the evening.

At Špindlerův Mlýn there is a big parking area at the bottom of the town. Parking is otherwise prohibited in the town, and all side roads, including the road to Svatý Petr, are closed to cars. There are queues to park in season and a hefty parking fee to discourage motorists.

Information

In Vrchlabí there is a national park information office up the main road from the square, open 9.00am to 12.00am and 1.00pm to 4.00pm daily except Sunday (from November 1 to April 30 also closed Saturday). At the top end of Špindlerův Mlýn, on the Špinderovka road is another national park information office. No one speaks English, but they are very helpful, and it is amazing how much you can communicate with your hands and a map and a few words of Czech and English. Open seven days a week from April to September inclusive, rest of year Monday to Friday. There are also information offices in Pec and Harrochov. At the top of the road above Horní Mísečky there may be an information office open in season.

The main Čedok office for the area is in Vrchlabí at Leninova ul. 148, 543 01 Vrchlabí; tel. 21131, 21191, 22571, 21632. Telex 194431. Other offices are in Špindlerův Mlýn, Pec pod Sněžkou and Janské Lázně.

Most of what you'll need in Vrchlabí is on the main street. Nearly everything closes from 12.00am to 2.00pm. Čedok and the post office are next door to each other, down the road from the bus station. Vrchlabí's post office (including telephone and telegram) is open every day, although weekend opening hours are limited.

Telephone area codes are: Vrchlabí and Špindlerův Mlýn 438; Harrachov 432; Pec 439.

In Špindlerův Mlýn you can change money at Čedok or Montana Hotel.

There is a good walking map *Krkonoše* costing Kčs 8.50. It may be difficult to find, so grab it in another part of the country if you see it. There is also a winter version of this map with skiing routes marked.

Accommodation

It is difficult to get accommodation in the Krkonoše. In season it is booked out, and out of season most accommodation is closed. Čedok have a near monopoly on accommodation in the area. Čedok Vrchlabi make bookings for the whole Krkonoše. The local office at Špindlerův Mlýn can't make bookings directly. So if you have planned ahead, you can write direct to Čedok Vrchlabi to book, or book through another Čedok office or a travel agent in your home country. Čedok prefer bookings by the week, but it may be possible to make a shorter booking. It is difficult to get bookings if you want to walk from *bouda* to *bouda*, as Čedok don't like this, but it is possible. Otherwise you could use one *bouda* as a base instead.

Neither Sport-hotels nor camping can be booked through Čedok. Except in Pec pod Sněžkou Čedok don't book private accommodation. As far as staying in mountain *boudy* is concerned, you'll be lucky to get in any of the smaller ones without prior reservation.

Many of the hotels are small cosy wooden buildings.

Harrachov

Accommodation open in season only. Hotels in B*, B and C grades, hostels (*turistická ubytovna*) in TU A and TU B grades. The new **Juniorhotel Harrochov** has rooms and dorms: Rýžoviště, 512 46 Harrochov v Krkonoších, tel. (0432) 92 94 51-5. Camping ground (B) open 1 May to 30 October: **Autokemp Jiskra**, 512 46 Harrachov, tel. (0432) 92 93 89.

Horní Mísečky

C class hotel and good cheap hostel (TU A) accommodation. There is one reception for all the hotels and hostels. With 220 beds here it shouldn't be difficult to get a bed. Open all year except May and November.

Špindlerův Mlýn

A wide range of accommodation here, from camping to an A* hotel, but it still is not easy to find somewhere to stay. New hotels are planned. Postcode is 543 51.

Autokemping B next door to the national park information office at the top end of Špindlerův Mlýn. Open in season for tents and caravans. Some refreshments available. Just below here on the other side of the road on-site 2 man tents are available from about June to September. Everything is provided.

Book hotel and hostel accommodation through Čedok Vrchlabi.

Montana, A*, modern, large, sk.I restaurant, tel. 935 51. Double Kčs 454.

Hotel Savoy, B*, opened in 1891, recently renovated, nice looking, 300m up from bus stop and parking area, don't cross the river. Tel. 93521-3.

Praha, B, nice old building, central, tel. 933 15.

Hotel Hvězda, hotel C & TU B, central by the bridge, tel. 934 59.

Hotel Start, hotel C & TU A, sk.II* restaurant, old building, open 8.00am to 2.00pm & 6.00pm to 10.00pm, closed Thursday.

Lomnice, TU A, nice building, tel. 932 20.

Vrchlabi

Hotel Labuť, C, on the square, double Kčs 189, triple Kčs 284. In the winter it gets completely booked up, but in the summer there is some chance of getting a room.

TU accommodation 2km from the centre towards Turnov.

Private accommodation is not available through Čedok, but through CIS by the square. Their office is open Monday to Thursday 7.30am to 4.30pm and Friday 7.30am to 3.00pm, tel. 22 721.

Vejsplachy is a large camping ground in the town, open from mid June to mid September.

Autocamping Čistá v Krkonoších is a smaller camp in more pleasant surroundings 8km east of Vrchlabí, and open during the same period. The only problem is the noise from a nearby aerial cableway. There are outdoor cold showers, cooking elements, and a little shop with limited supplies open limited hours. Buses towards Turnov stop outside.

Pec pod Sněžkou

Hotel Horizont, B*, a huge hotel which is anything but horizontal, tel. 963 13, 963 22, 963 78.

Hotel Hořec, B, hotel on a more human scale, tel. 962 04.

Both are open in season only. Čedok's local office will book private accommodation here.

Janské Lázně

All accommodation booked through Čedok. B & C class hotels, and hostel accommodation.

Rokytnice nad Jizerou

15km from Harrachov, the local Čedok office can book accommodation here.

Huts (Boudy)

Labská bouda. The mountain hut to end all mountain huts! A huge modern weird looking place. B class hotel. Access by foot or ski only (the roadway is not open to the public). The shortest way to walk in in summer is the 2.5km trip from the top of the road above Horní Mísečky. Buses run to the top of this road in summer only. In winter the shortest way in is the 5.5km trip from Horní Mísečky. Open all year except May and November. A reservation should not be necessary. Doubles Kčs 203, and a few singles at Kčs 182. Pleasant sk.III restaurant, but a little expensive. Sk.IV *bufet* in season. Tel. Špindlerův Mlýn 932 25 or 935 80.

Luční bouda is very large with a restaurant and coffee bar. Hotel rooms cost Kčs 84 per person, while dormitory accommodation costs Kčs 51. Open mid December to mid April and mid May to late October, otherwise closed. In winter it's booked up, but in summer you could just turn up, though to be sure it's best to book four to five days in advance. Access by foot only (see section below, *Tramping*), it is very close to the Polish border.

What to see (without tramping or skiing to it)

The road from Špindlerův Mlýn to Špindlerovka on the Polish border is open to foreigners, but foreigners may not walk along the border track. In summer cars may drive up, but in winter it is open to buses only.

In Vrchlabi there is the **Krkonoše Museum**. The 16th Century chateau on the square once looked more like a castle, but now houses the national park headquarters and the local council.

The drive through Jizerský důl is very nice.

Janské Lázně is a holiday and spa resort. The springs are said to have been found by a man called Jan who was sent to find the hideout of robbers, hence the name "Janské". Most of today's spa buildings were built in 1868.

Trutnov is an historical town, with a Gothic layout and houses from the 16th and 17th Centuries.

Lifts

Most lifts are open for both summer and winter seasons, but closed in October, November and May.

There is a chairlift up Sněžka from 1.5km north of Pec pod Sněžkou. The waiting time is usually about 1 hour, and the 4km long trip has a mid-station at Růžová hora. It is an open lift, which some find a bit frightening at first — remember warm clothing. There is a *hospoda* at the top, open while the lift is operating, but one cannot sleep there. A new lift on the Polish side leads to within ¾ hour of the top.

The Špindlerův Mlýn-Medvedín lift leaves almost opposite the camp at Špindlerův Mlýn. But the bridge across the river here is private, so to reach it walk up the blue marked track on the west side of the river from the town.

There is a cableway up Čierná Hora (1299m, Black Mountain) from Janské Lázně.

Tramping

The Krkonoše seem deceptively safe. Sudden weather changes can occur at any time of year, so it is wise to take precautions. Don't be on the tops in fog or during storms. Tell someone where you are going and when you expect to return. Avoid areas where there is a danger of avalanche.

Foreigners may walk to the border, but not along the track along the border. In winter one may walk in the valleys only; one may not walk on the mountain tops. Many tracks have been closed, either temporarily or permanently, to give nature a chance to recover as the Krkonoše are over-utilised. So even if you have a map, check which tracks are open before planning your trip.

Walking times from Harrachov
–Vosecká bouda, red markers, 2¼ hours.
–Dvoračky, green markers, 2¼ hours.
–Labská Bouda, 3 hours.
–Špindlerův Mlýn via Dvoračky, 4 hours.

Špindlerův Mlýn (780m) to Svatý Petr (853m)
The oldest part of Špindlerův Mlýn is the mining village of Svatý Petr (St Peter's), a 20 minute walk from Špindlerův Mlýn.

Špindlerův Mlýn to the source of the Elbe
Walking up the Elbe from Špindlerův Mlýn is a nice trip. From Špindlerův Mlýn the 9.5km to Labská Bouda takes 2¾ hours. It is a good track, but partly over boulders, so it's best to have boots. The walk up the valley is long but pleasant. In the upper reaches there are big bluffs above you. At the top of the valley, the track zig-zags up beside the first Elbe waterfalls to Labská Bouda. It is not hard going, though you climb a long way up. The tops around Labská Bouda are open and flat, and it can be *cold*. From Labská Bouda it is only a short 1 km walk to Pramen Labe, the source of the Elbe. There are coats of arms of the towns down the Elbe, all the way to Hamburg. From Labská Bouda it is a further 10.5km following the blue markers to Harrachov. A possible round-trip from Špindlerův Mlýn is to follow the Elbe up as described, then return via Horní Mísečky. This whole round trip, including a visit to Pramen Labe, other stops and lunch takes about 7½ hours. From Pramen Labe the way leads over open tops, past army pill boxes to Vrbatova bouda. Don't follow the poles if they are up — they mark ski tracks, not walking tracks.

Špindlerův Mlýn to Luční bouda (1410m)
The walk from Špindlerův Mlýn to Luční bouda is 6km and takes 3 hours. After climbing out of Špindlerův Mlýn on the red marked track for 20 minutes, you reach the second yellow marked track leading to the left. This is an alternative route, the same length as the main route, but leading higher above the developed area of Sv. Petr and meeting the red marked route again after an hour's walk. From here it is 3km to Luční bouda. From this upper junction continue climbing until the junction with the blue marked track, where a 200m detour to the left will bring you to a 1422m peak with a view, a 50 minute walk altogether. The blue marked track to the right was closed in 1989. From here the track continues across open tops to Luční bouda (Luční means meadow), which has a room where you can eat your sandwiches and buy drinks. For more information on Luční bouda see *Accommodation* above.

Foreigners may not approach Sněžka from here, as only the blue marked track to the Polish-Czechoslovak border is open to them, and not the red marked track along the border. You could continue to Pec from Luční bouda. Otherwise an alternative route back to Špindlerův Mlýn is as follows. Head back in the direction you came, but following the blue markers this time. After 4km and 1¼ hours you come to another *bouda*. From here it is 3.5km further to the road above Špindlerův Mlýn. But if you instead turn left and follow the yellow markers, they will lead you after 5.5km back to the centre of Špindlerův Mlýn (1¾ hours).

Other walks from Špindlerův Mlýn post office:
–Špindlerovka, 8.5km, 2 hours.
–Horní Mísečky, red markers, 4km.
–Pec pod Sněžkou, green markers, 12km, 3½ hours.
–Vrchlabí, 15.5km.
–Davidovy boudy, yellow markers, 4½ km. A new Davidovy bouda is under construction. From here it is a further 2km to Moravská bouda, or 1½ km to Medvědí boudy (blue).

From Pec pod Sněžkou
Remember that the track along the border may not be used by foreigners, so you cannot use it to climb Sněžka. Walking up from Pec involves walking under the chairlift for a large part of the way.
–Špindlerův Mlýn via Výrovka, green markers, 3½ hours.
–Lučiny, 1 hour.
–Černý důl, blue markers, 2½ hours.
–Růžová hora, 1 hour.

From Janské Lázně
Černá hora (Black Mountain 1299m) is accessible by lift or the red marked track from Janské Lázně. Half an hour's walk from the top of the lift is a botanic reserve where there are Arctic plants left here from the Ice Age.

Skiing
The Krkonoše get a lot of snow, being the first and last mountains in Czechoslovakia to receive snow, and so having the longest season. There is snow on the ground from about November to April. The ski season is from about the end of December to the end of March. It is a good area for cross country skiing, but it is very crowded. Facilities are not up to West European standards, but then neither are the prices. Most foreign skiers are German. There are long waits for lifts (eg one to two hours at the weekend). Ski gear can be hired in Špindlerův Mlýn, but it is difficult to hire good quality gear. Cross country skiers must follow the marked routes. For example there are marked routes from Horní Mísečky, and an 8km long route along Labský důl. Ski tracks on the tops are marked with poles.

Rokytnice is the best centre for downhill skiing, with longer pistes than Špindlerův Mlýn. There are two main skiing areas at Špindlerův Mlýn: from the top of Pláň; or the chairlift link to Horní Mísečky. At Pec the lifts have a joint ticket system. As well as the main resorts, there is a ski centre at Janské Lázně.

Climbing

The Krkonoše is not a good area for climbing. The climbing season is winter, and permission is needed from the park office.

Discos in Spindlerův Mlýn

Disco Labužník (sk.II*) is just up from Savoy Hotel. Open 8.00pm to 3.00am, closed Tuesday. "Entry in formal attire only". In season there is another disco at Vinárna Bernardýn up the valley opposite the campsite in Špindlerův Mlýn. Closed Thursday.

Krkonoše

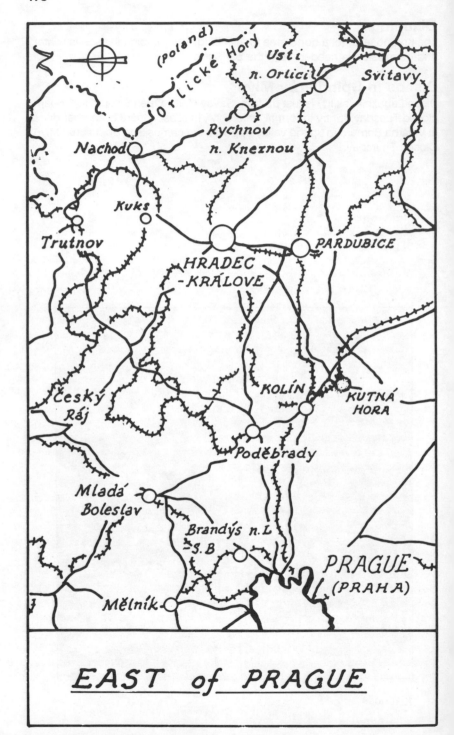

EAST of PRAGUE

East of Prague

PODĚBRADY

Poděbrady is a pleasant relaxed spa town, specialising in the treatment of cardio-vascular diseases. Jiří z Poděbrad (George of Poděbrady), known as the Hussites' king, was born in the castle here in 1420. After the country had been ruled by foreign monarchs, King George mounted the throne in 1458 as the first Czech king since 1306. He envisaged the establishment of an alliance of European states, partly in the cause of peace, partly to ward off the Turks, and partly to weaken the influence of the church on European politics. In the 16th Century the castle was converted into a Renaissance mansion, and used as a hunting lodge by Ferdinand I, Rudolph II and Maria Theresa. Parts of the castle are open to the public from May to October (closed Monday). Behind the castle you can watch the barges on the Elbe.

The rail and bus station are next door to each other. Poděbrady is on the bus routes Prague-Špindlerův Mlýn and Prague-Pec pod Sněžkou, both in Krkonoše. Across the road from the station is a Bohemian glass exhibition with cut crystal glass. From opposite the station a nice constitutional walkway leads to the town square. You may find music being played for the spa's patients along the way. The castle is across the square on your left.

There are two B* hotels in the centre, and a *turistická ubytovna*. The good campsite is open May to September, and can be reached on foot by a pleasant walk along the banks of the Elbe from the middle of town.

KOLÍN

Kolín was founded in 1261 and the town's centre is an historical reserve. St Bartholomew's Church is a magnificent sight. This Gothic structure was partly rebuilt by the architect of St Vitus' Cathedral in Prague, Peter Parler. The museum next to the church is open daily except Monday. Kolín had the second largest Jewish community in Bohemia. The Jewish Synagogue is in a bad state of repair. If the door at Na Hrabách 12 is open, you can walk to the end of the hall and get a glimpse of the synagogue through the windows. The castle is now a brewery and is closed to the public. The town hall (*radnice*) on the square was being restored when I visited in 1989.

Hotel Savoy, B, on Rubešova is centrally situated. Some trains on the Prague-Brno-Bratislava route stop in Kolín. To get to the centre turn to the

The Gothic church of sv. Barbara, Kutná Hora

right from the station and it's a 10 minute walk. The bus station is outside the railway station.

KUTNÁ HORA

Kutná Hora was an important silver mining centre as far back as the 10th Century. The town was once the wealthiest in Bohemia and the second largest after Prague. But conditions were bad for the miners, who were forced to work for little pay. There have been various attempts to reopen the silver mines on a commercial basis through the centuries, but they have never reached their former grandeur. Nazi Germany was interested in the area as a source of lead and zinc.

Sv. Barbara is the most famous church in Kutná Hora. Some of the builders of Prague's famous edifices had a hand in it. Open from 8.00am to 12.00am and 1.00pm to 5.00pm (closed Monday), a sign on the door tells you where to find the key. You go around with a guide — ask for the information sheet in English.

The museum Hrádek will be opening in about 1992, but in the meantime meet here if you would like to tour a **silver mine**. This mine was only rediscovered in recent times, and has been open to the public since 1968. Before you go on the tour, you can hear a tape in real English (rather than "Czech English"). You are provided with a coat, helmet and lamp, and the tour is very interesting. But make the visit before you get a liking for Czech beer, or you won't get your beerpot through the narrow tunnels! The mine is open from the beginning of May till the end of October.

Vlašský dvůr (The Italian Court), was built in 1300 by Wenceslas II as a mint where experts from Florence (hence the building's name) began minting the Prague Groschen. Copies of the oldest Prague Groschen are minted here and sold as souvenirs. Vlašský dvůr is open to the public every day from April 1 to September 30 from 8.00am to 5.00pm, and the rest of the year closing at 4.00pm. You go around with a guide — ask for the info sheet in English again. The counsellors' plate of 1595 is a Latin exhortation to counsellors to always be just. There is a copy of it in the United Nations in New York. To me, the highlight of the tour was the large painting (1888) by Adolf Liebscher of the Hussites led by Jan Žižka near Kutná Hora.

There are other sights and museums in the old town, all well signposted, but I consider the above to be the most interesting. Some of the other sights are: Sv Jakub church, which is closed; the Ursuline Convent (klaštor voršilek) with a not particularly interesting exhibition of porcelain, glass and clocks, with information in English; and Kamenný dům with an exhibition of Gothic sculpture, open daily except Monday.

To, from and around Kutná Hora

Many trains between Prague and Brno or Bratislava stop at Kutná Hora hlavní nádraží, the main railway station, which is several kilometres outside the centre. Local bus number 1 takes you from it to the centre, but they are not very regular. Buy a ticket from the PNS kiosk at the station. Or try a local train to Kutná Hora mešto station. Kutná Hora's bus station is more central. There are both trains and buses to Kolín. To get to Pardubice by public transport, you must travel via Kolín, from where there are direct trains.

Accommodation

There is a camp at Malešov, out of town, open mid-May to mid-October. A *turistická ubytovna* and the only hotel, **Hotel Medínek** (B*, double Kčs 300) are both centrally situated. The hotel is full in season, otherwise it should be possible to get a bed.

Information

For information try Čedok on the square or Tourgast in the hotel. Kutná Hora is well prepared for tourists, with all the sights well signposted and English information available everywhere. The post office in the old centre is Pošta 6. The main post office, Pošta 1, is in a new area between the old centre and the main railway station.

PARDUBICE

Back in the 13th Century there was already quite a settlement at Pardubice, which became a town in 1340. Both the fire of 1507 and the siege of the Swedish armies in 1645 during the Thirty Years War caused great damage to the town, but there are enough surviving buildings to give some idea of Pardubice's long history. The **castle** is open as a museum. To many the name Pardubice is synonymous with the steeplechase held here in October. More information and a map of the old town centre are to be found in the map *Východní Čechy*, number 5 in the *Poznáváme Československo* series.

Interhotel Labe Pardubice, a new flash hotel, has good food in the sk.II restaurant on the first floor. There are several other hotels, a hostel and a camp. The phone code is 40. Pardubice lies on the main railway line from Prague to Košice. The train trip from Prague takes about 1½ hours.

HRADEC KRÁLOVÉ

Hradec Králové is an important town today, and one of the oldest towns in Bohemia, founded in the beginning of the 13th Century. See the brick Gothic cathedral, the town hall and the Gothic and Renaissance houses. There are several hotels in the town and a summer hostel at Pedagogická fakulta UK, 502 96 Hradec Králové, Koleje UK — Na kotli 1447, tel. (049) 24668.

KUKS

Kuks lies on the Elbe, north of Hradec Králové. A spa was founded here between 1695 and 1724. Originally there was a complex of buildings on both sides of the Elbe, and although many have disappeared over time, Kuks is still a worthy example of Bohemian Baroque art. Today Kuks is best known for the sculpture of M. B. Braun.

ORLICKÉ HORY

The Orlické Hory are a mountain range extending for 40km along the Polish border in northeastern Bohemia. The highest mountain is Velká Deštná at 1,115 metres above sea level, while the main ridge is generally 800 to 900 metres. The area and its forests offer many walks and rambles, with the usual Czechoslovak delicacies of mushrooms, blueberries and raspberries tempting you along the way. For a longer trip, a red marked track leads along the main ridge. Acid rain is only just starting to show signs of its damage here. In the winter Orlické Hory are a good area for cross-country skiing. By car take the E67 from Prague via Hradec Králové.

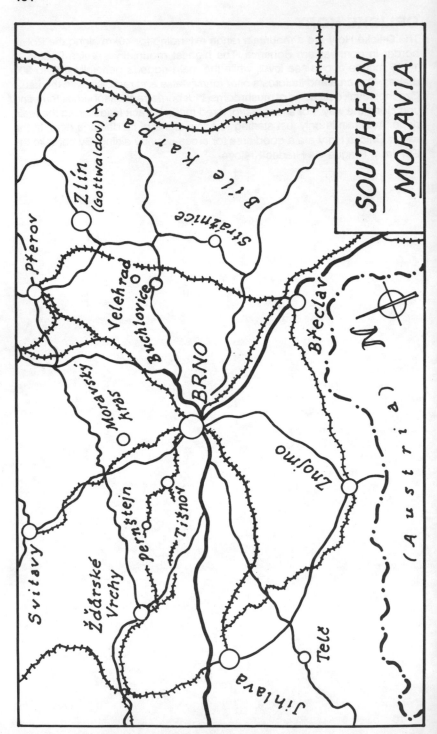

SOUTHERN MORAVIA

Southern Moravia

BRNO
Brno, with a population of 372,000, is the third largest city in Czechoslovakia, and was the ancient capital of Moravia. It was the home of Mendel, and the modern composer Leoš Janáček (1854-1928). Today Brno is an important industrial centre, particularly for the machine industry. It is also an important university town, and the student influence is strong.

To and from Brno
There is now a motorway from Prague to Brno and on to Bratislava, with an express bus service. There are no longer flights to Brno, except during exhibitions. Regular trains from Prague. *Rychlík* train to Bratislava takes about 2 hours and *osobní* about 3 hours. For transport to the Moravian Karst see the *Moravský kras* section. Best way to Tábor is by bus, which takes 2½ to 3½ hours. By train to Tábor takes about 7 hours, except the once a day direct *rychlík* service which takes 4 hours.

July 1989 saw the celebration of 150 years of rail traffic between Brno and Vienna, which began as the first steam railway in Czechoslovakia. There is also a bus service to Vienna, and seasonal buses to Italy via Austria.

The railway station is centrally located, but the bus station has recently moved a little outside the centre of town.

Getting around
Brno's public transport system differs from the rest of the country in the following ways. Single trip tickets are narrower than the normal Czechoslovak tickets. Day tickets are bought from the red machines, which print the day and time on the ticket. Some routes operate rather strange hours, and some finish for the day between about 5.00pm and 7.00pm. The red colour means night service. Night buses run once an hour and they all meet outside the railway station. In Brno slang trams are called *šalina*.

Accommodation
Hotels
Continental, ****, Leninova 20, 657 64 Brno; tel. 75 05 01, 75 07 27. Central. Up to US$40 per person.
International, A*, Husova 16, 656 67 Brno; tel. 2134111. Central. Modern.

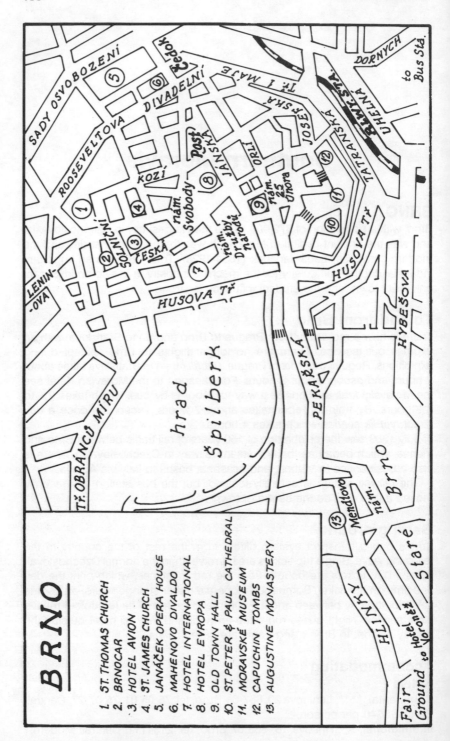

BRNO

1. ST. THOMAS CHURCH
2. BRNOCAR
3. HOTEL AVION
4. ST. JAMES CHURCH
5. JANÁČEK OPERA HOUSE
6. MAHENOVO DIVADLO
7. HOTEL INTERNATIONAL
8. HOTEL EVROPA
9. OLD TOWN HALL
10. ST. PETER & PAUL CATHEDRAL
11. MORAVSKÉ MUSEUM
12. CAPUCHIN TOMBS
13. AUGUSTINE MONASTERY

Voroněž I, A*, Křížkovského 47, 603 73 Brno; tel. 33 63 43, 33 31 35. A
little out of the centre. Brno's best hotel, especially popular with visitors to the
trade fairs, because of its vicinity to the fairground. Built by Polish workers.
About US$30 to US$40 per person per night.
Voroněž II, B*, next door to the above at no. 49.
Avion, B*, Česká 20, 602 00 Brno; tel. 276 06, 277 97, 266 75. Smaller than
any of the above which all sleep hundreds. Central.
Evropa, B, nám. Svobody 13, 602 00 Brno; tel. 266 21, 278 51. On the corner
of Jánská. Central.
Grandhotel, tř. 1. máje 18-20, 657 83 Brno, and **Slavia**, Solniční 15/17,
662 16 Brno have both recently been reconstructed.

Private accommodation
Private accommodation is cheaper than hotels, but you must be staying for
three days or longer. Book through Čedok. Singles Kčs 100, doubles Kčs
150. Those who must register with the police must do so themselves.

Hostels
In July and August CKM operate temporary hostels in student halls of
residence. As the hostels they use tend to vary from year to year, it is best
to check first with their office at Česká 11. The price for YHA members is Kčs
45, non-members Kčs 83. Booked from abroad, price is about £10 full board.
Some beds at one of the hostels are reserved for foreign travellers who turn
up after 5.00pm, so there should be a bed, but may not be. The other hostels
are for CKM groups only, but if there is space the door-keeper has discretion
to allow you to sleep there.
  If you have the International Youth Hostel Handbook, you may notice a
hostel listed at Brněnská Přehrada. In practice, if there is a group there you
can't stay there, and if there is not a group it is closed. In exceptional
circumstances you may be able to sleep there when there is a group there,
provided it is not a children's group. Cost, if you haven't given up already,
Kčs 50 per night.
  Other hostels in Brno send you to Sport-Turist first to get a voucher. But
Sport-Turist will only issue vouchers for groups, and will send you on to
Čedok to be booked into an expensive hotel. During the September trade fair
only, Čedok arrange accommodation in student hostels.

Camping
Camping Bobrava, A, 664 42 Modřice; tel. Brno 32 01 10. South of Brno.
Open about June to September, sometimes longer. Take a local train to
Popovice U Rajhradu station, five minutes from the camp. You can also take
tram 2 to last stop (Modřice), then walk 1km, but it's much easier by train.
Also motel and cabins.
Obora, A, 635 00 Brno; tel. 49 42 84. At Brněnská přehrada. Camping and
cabins. Open all year. Accessible by bus (roughly hourly), or in summer only
by bus and boat.

Other

Trains stop in Brno at various strange hours of the night, so many people sleep in the station. If you follow suit, sleep in the waiting room, or you may be awoken by a friendly policeman's foot.

Information

Maps: Detailed map of Brno with public transport available for Kčs 9. Map of *Brněnská přehrada* Kčs 3.

Police: For registration or visa extensions, Leninova 46, morning only.

Changing money: At Státní banka československa at nám Svobody 21 or Rooseweltova 18; at Hotels Voroněž, International, Continental, Grand, Slavia and Slovan; at Čedok, Divadelní 3 or nám. Svobody 4.

Left luggage at the railway station, where the weight limit of 15kg is strictly enforced.

Čedok: The Čedok office for foreigners is at Divadelní 3, open 9.00am to 5.00pm (summer to 6.00pm), 9.00am to 12.00am Saturday. The phone numbers for their accommodation service are 23 166, 23 179 and 23 178. Telex 62257. Guides may he hired through Čedok.

Sport-Turist They are hopeless and send foreign visitors to Čedok.

Rekrea: At Radnická 11.

Autoturist: Are on Pekařská.

CKM: At Česká 11, 657 04 Brno; tel. 236 41-3. Can issue ISIC's.

Rental cars: From Brnocar; office on Solniční open Monday to Friday 7.00am to 7.00pm, Saturday 7.00am to 6.00pm, Sunday 8.00am to 8.00pm, all year. Their garage is under Hotel Intercontinental. For Czechs the price is Kčs 98 per day, but for you it is around US$4.50 per hour or US$26 per day, US$145 per week, plus 26c. per kilometre. Unlimited mileage costs US$62 per day, US$290 per week. 15% tax is charged on top of these prices. Only the person who signs the contract can drive. The car is insured, but you are not unless you pay US$1.60 per day extra for that. The car can be used in Czechoslovakia and Austria only. If you want to pick it up or drop it off outside Brno there are delivery and collection fees. To rent a car you need your passport, visa (if you have one) and driving licence. You cannot pay in Czechoslovak Kčs, (except for the odd times when Brnocar cannot bank your dollars). During holiday periods reservation is necessary.

Late night shopping: There is a shop open until 9.00pm on weekdays and 6.00pm on Saturdays on the corner of Poštovská and Gagarinova. Other shops close at 12.00am on Saturday.

Film processing: Western colour print film using the C41 process can be developed and printed in 24 hours at Gagarinova 17, open Monday to Friday.

Showers: Cheap showers in the railway station.

Post Office: The post office at the main railway station (Pošta 2) is open around the clock. The main post office is on Poštovská. Post code 602 00.

What to see

Overlooking Brno is its castle, **Špilberk**. Built in the second half of the 13th Century, as an early Gothic stronghold, it was later rebuilt as a Baroque fortress. Špilberk successfully resisted assaults by the Mongols, Hussites,

Swedes, Turks and the Prussian King Frederick, but Napoleon succeeded in capturing it. Under the Habsburgs the castle became a notorious prison, and the horrors of this were revived during the Nazi occupation, when an estimated 80,000 prisoners suffered here. From 1984 to 1994 Špilberk is under reconstruction, and while parts of it were still open to the public before, on my last visit it was completely closed.

Between the castle and the railway station is **Petrov Hill**. Brno's original castle stood here. Premysl II recognized the strategic importance of Špilberk Hill, and moved his residence there. Today **St Peter and Paul's Cathedral** stands on Petrov Hill, on the site of a former Romanesque basilica. The cathedral is huge, and its two towers with their distinctive spires are a Brno landmark, especially noticeable if you enter Brno by train. The cathedral suffered severe damage during the siege of Brno by the Swedes from 1643-45. Late last century and early this century it was "re-Gothicised". It has recently been restored and is worth a look inside if you find it open.

Connected with the cathedral is the story of the bell-toller who saved Brno from the Swedes. On Ascension Day 1645, General Tortensson decided to launch the last attack, declaring that if the town did not surrender by midday he would raise the siege. The bell-ringer could see that Brno was on the point of yielding, when, moved by a sudden inspiration, he rang the bells of the cathedral, announcing midday, while it was in fact only 11 o'clock in the morning. The general halted the attack, and the Swedish troops withdrew. Since that time midday has been rung from the bells of the cathedral at 11 o'clock, one hour early.

The railway station itself has a nice exterior. Today's town centre lies north of the station and east of Špilberk. Here you will find the **Old Town Hall** (Stará radnice) with the Brno Dragon hanging from the roof inside the entrance and the Brno Wheel. The foundations of the Old Town Hall date from the 13th Century, while its present Gothic appearance dates from the beginning of the 16th Century. The "dragon" is actually a crocodile received by Archduke Matthias as a gift from the Turks in 1608. Matthias presented it to the town of Brno. There are many legends attached to the Brno Dragon. The Brno Wheel is said to have been made by the Lednice cartwright Jiří Birk in 1636. He made a bet that he could fell a tree, make a cartwheel from it, and roll it to Brno, all before the evening bells (that is within 12 hours). He won the bet even though Lednice is 33 miles south of Brno. But people began to suspect him of being in league with the devil, and orders for his work dwindled, leaving him to die in poverty. Another legend concerns the Portal with the Crooked Pinnacle which you can see on the front of the Old Town Hall. The Aldermen promised much for the work of Master Pilgram, but gave little. So Master Pilgram got the City Fathers' wrath up by carving a crooked pinnacle over the statue of justice as a symbol of their breach of promise. A new straight pinnacle was fixed there by another master sculptor, but it curved by itself overnight! The tower of the Old Town Hall is open from April to September from 9.00am to 5.00pm, closed Mondays.

Next door to the Old Town Hall is an **aquarium**, open all year except Mondays and public holidays from 9.30am to 5.30pm.

The **New Town Hall** (Nová radnice) on náměstí Družby národů is today the seat of the Municipal National Committee. It has a nice courtyard, open from 8.00am to 5.00pm, 9.00am to 3.00pm Sundays and holidays. Only the courtyard is open to the public. On the same square is the Gothic **St Michael's Church** founded in the 1330s. It was the church of the Dominican Monastery. In the second half of the 17th Century it was reconstructed in Baroque style. There are carved figures of saints.

The main art gallery, the **Moravian Gallery**, is on Husova near Hotel International. There are also other smaller galleries around the town.

Náměstí 25. února (Square of the 25th February), the old vegetable market, might well have received its old name **Zelný trh** (Vegetable or Cabbage Market) back by the time you read this. The square was in any case commonly known as Zelný trh, even under the communists. The old fountain, designed as a cave of immense unhewn boulders, has been reconstructed. Carp used to be sold out of the fountain's waters before Christmas every year. It is said to be good luck to kiss the statue of the god Amphitrites on top of it. The whole area around here, including Stará radnice, had to be reconstructed. There are tunnels everywhere underneath the area from old sewers. There are different levels of sewers from different ages. The buildings started sinking into them, necessitating reconstruction. In slang the sewer system is known as "ementál", because of its similarity with the cheese with the holes in it. Mozart performed in the **Reduta Theatre**, also on nám. 25 února, in 1767. Built in neo-Classicist style, Reduta is the oldest theatre in Brno, and is now used for operetta.

In the **Capuchin tombs** (Kapucínská Hrobka) on Kapucínské nám. near the railway station are housed the mummified bodies of Capuchin monks and local dignitaries. An air passage was specially designed to keep the bodies in a dry state. Open Tuesday to Saturday 9.00am to 4.30pm, Sunday 11.00am to 4.30pm. Closed lunchtime. Up the steps from here is Moravské Muzeum v Brno (the **Moravian Museum**). Open 9.00am to 6.00pm, closed Mondays. Exhibitions include coins, geology, zoology, Ciril and Metoděj (the two Greeks who helped unify Moravia), and Uherské Hradiště in the 8th and 9th Century (where gold was produced, and much of interest from the days of the Great Moravian Empire was found). The **Kapucínské gardens** lie behind the tombs and museum and are open the same hours as the museum. The Moravian Gallery on ul. Husova houses old furniture etc. through different periods, as well as other exhibitions.

St James's Church at Jakubské nám. is distinguishable by its very tall slender spire. The church was completed in the beginning of the 16th Century and reconstructed in neo-Gothic style in the late 19th Century. It is not too ornate in decoration, but it is impressive. On the outside, on the right hand side of the tower above the Gothic window, is a grotesque little man with his buttocks pointing at you. There are legends associated with it, but it seemed to have been the usual sculptor's joke of the time.

The university is scattered around the central area, and you can mark the strong student influence. **St Thomas's Church** at náměstí Rudé armady is the former convent church of the Augustinian Monastery founded in 1350. Earlier Gothic, now Baroque, it is open only for mass, but you can see a little bit through the glass doors. The ex-monastery is attached.

One modern building in Brno worth seeing is the **Leoš Janáček Opera House**, built from 1960 to 1965 and named after the composer Leoš Janáček

(1854 — 1928) who lived in Brno from 1881. He based his works on Moravian folk-music. The original opera house, **Mahenovo Theatre**, is close by. Dating from the 1880s, it was the first theatre in Europe to use Edison lamps, and has recently been renovated. Baťa shoes, now known throughout the world, originally came from Czechoslovakia. (See section on Zlín for more details). The Centrum store near the national theatre was one of Baťa's shops. The architecture was far ahead of its pre-war time.

Staré Brno was where Mendel lived. Mendel was a poor student. After joining the Augustine order he moved to the monastery in Staré Brno where he began botanical experiments in the monastery garden and produced his report on the fundamentals of genetics. It was some years before his work was appreciated. The monastery building remains, and the brick-built Church of the Ascension of Our Lady, from 1322, is one of the best preserved original Gothic buildings in Brno. A memorial was built to Mendel in 1965 and there is a **museum** in the monastery on Mendlovo nám.

On the outskirts of Brno is **Brněnská přehrada** (Brno Dam) where there is a boat service and walks. Moravský kras begins on the outskirts of Brno, but has its own section in this book.

Out of Brno
Austerlitz battleground
Slavkov, better known by its German name Austerlitz, is not far to the east of Brno. In the famous Battle of Austerlitz in December 1805 Napoleon defeated the Russian Tzar and the Austrian Emperor. Napoleon was a guest at the chateau in Slavkov after the battle, and concluded an armistice there. The Baroque chateau contains mementoes of the Napoleonic wars.

About halfway between Brno and Slavkov is the hill Žuráň, from which Napoleon directed the first part of the battle. A plaque marks the place.

South of Žuráň and just south of the village of Prace is Pracký kopec. By conquering this hill, Napoleon gained victory. A monument to the soldiers who fell, called Tumulus of Peace, was erected on the battlefield in 1911. Bones of the soldiers have been found, and in 1976 a skeleton was found. There is a museum with an exhibition of the battle and of the Napoleonic wars.

The map *Okolí Brna, východ* covers this area in detail. Marked walking routes connect Žuráň and Pracký kopec.

Organised tours
Čedok arrange a half day tour of the Moravian Karst (see separate section) every Tuesday from mid-May to mid-September for about US$15, and a walking tour of Brno every Thursday in the same period for about US$7. You can book through hotel receptions or Čedok (tel. 24651). There is no longer a tour to Slavkov.

Events
Recurring events in Brno include several international trade fairs. SALIMA (foodstuffs) is held in February in uneven numbered years. In April there is a consumer goods fair, primarily aimed at business, but open to the public. The

Grand Prix takes place every August. The International Engineering Trade Fair and International music festival are both held in September, the music festival beginning immediately after the trade fair.

Eating and evenings

The centre of Brno is very alive by Czechoslovak standards, with theatre, concerts, opera, pubs, wine bars etc. The booking office for modern concerts, student clubs etc is on Dvořakovo. The booking office for classical concerts, theatre, opera etc is between Maheno and Janaček theatres.

There are various places to eat or spend an evening on the street Česká. At **Na České Gril Bar** on the corner of Česká and Jakubská there tend to be foreign students. The **Sputnik** food complex covers two storeys with everything from quick eats to a sk.I *vinárna* open till the wee small hours.

The sk.II restaurant at the railway station is a very pleasant oasis, open until 10.00pm, but the food is nothing special. If you eat in the restaurant you can use their coat check, and so leave luggage over 15kg there to get around the left luggage weight limit problem. There is also a bufet at the station. **Transit** is a stand-up place for quick eats opposite the station and open all night.

At the **Hotel International** restaurant you should have a tie and suit on, but you may get away without. Clean toilets. "Interclub" open 9.00pm to 3.00am, closed Sunday & Monday.

Černohorská pivnice is a raucous pub on the corner of třida Vítězství and Kapucínské náměstí, ie just up the street opposite the station. Open weekdays 9.00am to 11.00pm, Saturdays till 3.00pm, and closed Sundays.

Vinárna Baroko (sk.II) is a nice wine cellar at Orlí 17. Open 7.00pm to 2.00am, closed Sundays. **Apetit Gril** on Kozi is a popular place for a drink. Wine and spirits in modern surroundings. **Hotel Evropa** (nám. Svobody 13) has a *kávarná* with dancing to live music Monday to Saturday 8.00pm to 3.00am.

The *vinárna* **U Královny Elišky** (At the Queen Eliska) is an interesting looking place in the historical wine cellars of the monastery at Mendel Square. Sk.II. Open 7.00pm to 2.00am, closed Sunday. Live music.

Every hotel has some sort of restaurant and place to spend the evening.

Student clubs

"V" Club, ul. Gorkého, open every day.
"Topas" club, Tanferovy kolej, open every day.
Two clubs at Leninovy kolej, Leninova 88.
Club of Kaunicovy kolej.   •
Club of Purkyňovy kolej, Purkyňova ulica.

JIHLAVA

Jihlava is the largest town on the Bohemian-Moravian Highlands, and is situated on the historic border between Bohemia and Moravia. The Czech community originated in the 12th Century. In the 13th Century a royal town of the same name, populated mainly by Germans, originated to the south of the Czech community. At this time rich silver deposits were found in the area and the town underwent rapid development. The Royal Mint was situated here until the early 14th Century. The composer Gustav Mahler spent his childhood here.

The town is an historic reserve. Many of Jihlava's old churches have survived, as has much of the interesting town walls. Jihlava's town square is the second largest in Czechoslovakia and one of the largest in Europe. Part of the town's underground passages are accessible.

Accommodation

Grandhotel, Husova 1 takes DM70 for a double. Robert Broughton writes that **Hotel Jihlava** (***, Semilucká 7, double DM30) was the worst place he stayed in, and recommends trying **Zlatá hvězda**, ***, nám. Miru 32, which also has a good restaurant.

There are exchange offices in both Jihlava and Zlatá hvězka hotels.

TELČ

29km south of Jihlava is one of the best preserved ancient towns in Czechoslovakia, Telč. Originating in the 13th Century, it became an historical town reserve in 1970, and today has a population of 6000. A 49m high Romanesque church tower still remains from the early 13th Century. The houses on the square were built of wood until a fire in 1387. After a devastating fire in 1530 the Gothic houses were rebuilt in Renaissance style. The square has a Baroque fountain in its centre, but still essentially retains its Renaissance atmosphere. The chateau, which you can visit by guided tour, was originally a Gothic castle from the 14th Century, but was converted into its present day Renaissance style in the second half of the 16th Century. There are two hotels, **Černý orel** on the main square and **U nádraží** by the station, and a hostel.

ŽĎÁRSKÉ VRCHY

Žďárské Vrchy (Žďár Hills) are a "protected landscape region" in the highest part of the Bohemian-Moravian Highlands. Apart from small remnants, the original pine and beech forests have been replaced with spruce forests. The watershed between the North and Black Seas passes through here. It is a good area for cross-country skiing.

The main centre is Nové Město na Moravě where the Horácké Museum includes an exhibition on skiing. Near Hlinsko is a skansen.

There are many nice small *ubytovací hostinec* in the area, but they are always booked up.

PERNŠTEJN

The medieval castle of Pernštejn was regarded as unassailable during the Middle Ages. The castle was modified from a fortress to a palatial residence over time. In 1645 the Swedes besieged it, but in vain. Today it is one of the best preserved castles in Bohemia and Moravia. The oldest parts of the castle are the round tower and the ramparts which rise straight from the rocks on which the building stands. On a tour one can see amongst other things period furniture, Rococo wall paintings, collections of armour and the dungeons. Open April to September, closed Mondays.

Pernštejn is northwest of Brno and within daytripping distance of Brno, Tišnov or Žďárké vrchy. Get there by train, or it's about 50 minutes from Brno by car.

TIŠNOV

At Předklášteří, once an independent community but today a part of Tišnov, you'll find the Cistercian convent of **Porta Coeli**, Latin for "gate of heaven". The convent church was adapted in Baroque style in the 18th Century, but its famous beautifully carved portal dates from the period just after the founding of the convent in 1233. The church contains valuable paintings and furnishings. The convent buildings today house the Podhorárcko Museum.

Tišnov lies between Pernštejn and Brno and is accessible by train from both. You could visit both Pernštejn and Tišnov on the same day trip from Brno. Hotel Květnice, **, is at nám. Miru 12, tel. 362. Or by the station you can sleep at U nádraží, UH, Janáčkova 287. The post code for Tišnov is 666 00 and the phone code 504.

MORAVSKÝ KRAS (MORAVIAN KARST)

Moravský kras (the Moravian Karst) is a real wonderland, the most interesting part of which lies about 30km north of Brno. With its many limestone caves, the huge Macocha Abyss and boat trips on the underground Punkva River, it is well worth a visit.

Macocha is a 138 metre deep vertical sided abyss caused by the collapse of a cave roof. You can drive to the top. Macocha means stepmother (who in Czech tales is usually evil). The most popular cave is Punkevní. Via this system of caves you walk to the bottom of Macocha Abyss, and so take a boat for nearly half a kilometre down the underground Punkva River, a breathtakingly beautiful trip. Open all year: April to September 7.00am to last tour at 3.15pm (2.45pm at weekends); October to March 7.30am to last tour at 1.45pm (2.45pm at weekends). Tour takes about one hour.

Balcarka Cave lies on the eastern edge of Moravský kras and has stalactites and stalagmites and underground pools. Open April to September 7.00am to last tour 3.30pm, October to March 7.30am to last tour 2.00pm.

Kateřinská Cave is where the Punkva River surfaces. Here you can see a huge underground "cathedral", 100m long, 20m high and 40m wide, and interesting stalactite and stalagmite formations. Open April to September 7.00am to last tour 3.45pm; October to March 7.30am to last tour 2.45pm.

North of this area is the **Sloupsko-Šošůvské** cave system, forming an extensive maze on two levels connected by holes, and including a famous stalagmite known as the "Candelabrum". One of the stories the guide tells is about the wooden beams in the Beamed Gallery. It is said that unfaithful wives were hanged here. As there were too many unfaithful husbands to hang, they were thrown down the chasm. The tour takes one hour, and the temperature is 7°C. During the tourist season concerts are held in Eliščina Cave, which has excellent acoustics.

Tours of the caves are conducted in Czech and maybe German, but at the entrance to each cave you can borrow a description of the cave in English, which you take with you on the tour and return when you come out again. The caves are very popular, so expect queues and crowds in summertime. There are lots of other caves which are not open to the public. Navigating "untamed" caves is completely different, involving crawling, climbing and even swimming, in very muddy conditions.

In **Rájec-Jestřebí** is a well-preserved chateau furnished as it was left by its owners, the Salm family, after World War Two. It was built on the site of an old fort, part of which has survived, but today's appearance dates mostly from the 18th Century, while the interior was adapted in the 19th Century. The Salm family came from Vienna in the 17th Century and created an iron industry in the region and generally developed the area a lot. This was not a rich farming area, so the men took up work in the iron industry. Some of the avenues leading to different parts of the estate still exist. The people liked the Salms as they helped the area so much. The Salms didn't cooperate with the Germans during the war, and hoped to return afterwards, but having left everything, they couldn't return under the communists.

In Blansko castle, worth a look at in itself, is **Blansko museum**, with an exhibition of the iron industry and products, open April to October, Tuesday to Sunday 9.00am to 5.00pm, and the rest of the year Tuesday to Friday 8.00am to 4.00pm. Near Blansko station is a deep lake in an old quarry pit, where people swim and fish (and camp illegally).

Tramping

There are walking tracks around Moravský kras and interesting karst landscape with dolines etc to explore.

Sloup to Macocha is about a 6km walk. The road from Sloup to Punkevní is for most of the way closed to traffic and makes a beautiful walk down a gorge. The alternative red marked route takes you through the forest above the gorge, while the yellow marked route follows the border of the forest and the fields. Some walking distances from Punkevní following the red markers are Macocha 1.5km uphill, Sloup 7.5km via Macocha and Skalní Mlýn 1.5km down the road.

Just up the road from the entrance to Punkevní a green marked track climbs up to the ruins of Blansek castle. Follow the track for 500m, then a side track to the left for 300m. From the ruins you can see that it was quite an extensive castle. No-one knows why it was built; it has been deserted since the 15th Century. (There is an unmarked track from the ruins down to the Punkevní caves car park.) It is possible to continue following the green markers, later meeting the blue, all the way to Blansko town and Blansko mešto station.

The same blue markers from Blansko lead to Sloup via Vavřinec.

If you are staying at Jedovnice you can use the yellow marked route from the village to the main cave area.

Maps
A good detailed map of the area is available sometimes (*Moravský kras*, Kčs 3). Grab it if you see it. If you can't get hold of this, the map *Okolí Brna, východ* is some help.

Accommodation
Camping
Camping at **Autokemp Olžovec**, 679 06 Jedovnice; tel. Blansko 931 34. Open 15/5 to 15/10. On a lake. Can drive to, or walk about 2km from the bus stop in Jedovnice.
   There is camping at Sloup, and a new camp at Vavřinec near Sloup. The camp at Sloup is better, with swimming, cottages and a shop. Vavřinec is more an overflow if Sloup becomes full.

Hotels
Hotel Dukla, ***, Budovatelů 1928, 678 01 Blansko; tel. 50 00-2. Doubles only.
Hotel Riviera, C, 679 06 Jedovnice; tel. 932 09. Sk.III restaurant.

To and from Blansko
From Brno and Prague there are both trains and buses to Blansko. To Olomouc the bus is best. There are two buses every morning from Monday to Friday from Blansko Bus Station to Prostějov, from where there are many buses to Olomouc. There are buses to Jedovnice from Blansko and Brno.
   There are two railway stations in Blansko. For the caves use Blansko station, which is adjacent to the bus station. For the centre of Blansko and the castle use Blansko mesto station.

Getting around
From May to September (in September only if there are enough passengers) there is a bus leaving from Blansko Bus Station at 8.00am and 11.00am which takes you to Punkevní, Kateřinská and Balcarka Caves as well as the top of Macocha Abyss, waiting for you at each place. Tickets cost Kčs 25 for the caves (students half price), plus Kčs 16 for the bus. Apart from the summer bus, public transport is not particularly good in the area of the caves, but walking is pleasant.
   Sloup, Vavřinec and Jedovnice are accessible by bus from Blansko. Sloup is 15km from Blansko station.
   Macocha and all of the caves are accessible by road. The road from Punkevní to Sloup is closed to cars. For walking around the area see *Tramping* section, above.

ZNOJMO
Znojmo is an ancient South Moravian town. In the 11th Century it was a Přemyslid stronghold. The Romanesque Rotunda of St Catherine, containing valuable wall paintings, is the only remnant to have been preserved from this period. The original Romanesque castle gave way to a Gothic castle, which

laid the foundations for today's less fortified Baroque descendant. The town boasts many old churches and beautiful Baroque and Renaissance houses. Underground passages under 15th to 17th Century houses are open to the public. The South Moravian museum at Přemyslovců ul. 6 is open Tuesday to Sunday 9.00am to 4.00pm.

The river Dyje and its environs between Znojmo and Vranov have been left in a relatively natural state, and have been made a reserve. The closing of the border region during Iron Curtain days benefited the environment here. At Vranov is a castle and a preserved Baroque water mill.

There are buses from, amongst other places, Prague, Vienna, České Budějovice and Bratislava, plus local buses to the Austrian border.

Hotels: **Dukla**, ***, A. Zápotockého, tel. 763 22; **Družba**, ***, sídliště Pražká. There is also hostel type accommodation (TU) signposted from the station.

A map of the old town and more information is included on the back of the map *Českomoravská vrchovina* in the *Poznáváme Československo* series.

The emergency breakdown service for motorists is at Přímětice 156; tel. 752 37.

Znojmo's post code is 669 00, and the area code for phoning is 624. Pošta 2 is by the station.

BŘECLAV DISTRICT

South of Brno, between the river Dyje and the Austrian border, is a pleasant rural district with castles, lakes and old hunting estates. In Lednice there is one of the most visited chateaux in Czechoslovakia. This area was in the hands of the Lichtenstein family from the 13th Century until the end of the Second World War. Hunting lodges and various follies were built on the estate. The little map *Pavlovské vrchy* (Kčs 3) is excellent for those wanting to explore this area.

Břeclav

The town of Břeclav itself is an important railway junction. Prague-Bratislava and Brno-Vienna trains stop here. The exchange office at the railway station is open 24 hours. The rail service between Břeclav and Lednice runs only on weekdays, but there are lots of buses to Lednice and Valtice, plus a few to Bratislava.

Just off the road towards Lednice is a castle which was restored in the 19th Century. It is now used for offices etc. Its tower is in ruins. There is a camping ground beside the castle open mid April to the end of September. From Břeclav one can walk to Lednice by following the green marked track through the wet lowland forests of the river Dyje.

In Poštorná, just out of Břeclav on the road to Lednice there is a late 19th Century octagonal church built by the Lichtenstein family.

Lednické rybníky

Lednické rybníky are lakes created for fishing in the 15th Century. The road from Břeclav to Lednice passes by one of them. From here it is a short walk

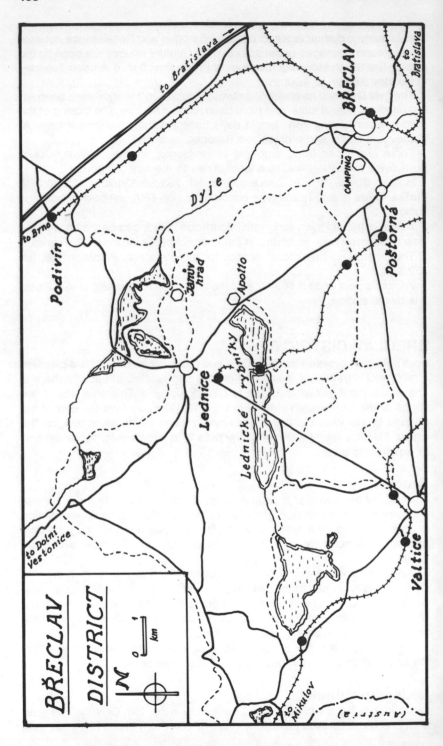

to the pseudo "Temple of Apollo", a folly, and a nice spot for picnics. The area is a nature reserve for nesting birds, so some of it is closed. One may swim in the area marked by buoys but not to the island which is a nature reserve. Windsurfing is prohibited. There is a sk.III self service restaurant and accommodation in season, and camping on the other side of the road. The road from Lednice to Valtice also passes the lakes.

Lednice

The castle in Lednice is open from the May 1 to October 31, weekends only in October. The **medieval castle** was modified over time to its present form. The rooms, with their beautiful wooden interiors, may be seen with a guide. The other part of the castle houses a museum. The original Church of St James was demolished and replaced with living quarters and the present St James Chapel. Down the lake from the castle you can see the 60 metre high minaret built between 1798 and 1802.

From Lednice it is a 3km walk (follow the green or yellow markers) to **Janův hrad**, a castle built as a ruin. One can continue from here following the green markers to Břeclav, 10.5km altogether. From Lednice the red marked route takes walkers to Valtice via Apollo, the lake and woods (13.5km). In a westerly direction the red markers lead to Mikulov (16km).

Across the road from the castle is **Zámecký Hotel** (tel. 98220). In season it's booked out by Čedok; out of season you may be able to get a room, but the castle is closed. Better than average sk.III restaurant. Sk.II snackbar, sometimes with live music, and *cukráreň* for those with a sweet tooth.

There is a *turistická ubytovna* 1km towards Mikulov with 200 beds and owned by a sports club. In summer it is full with student brigades and seasonal fruit factory workers. In Lednice is the "Fruta" factory, which makes salads, *kompot* (stewed fruit) etc.

Valtice

Valtice is a wine producing centre. Its originally Gothic castle is now a chateau with early Baroque style throughout, and is open from April to October (in April and October at weekends only).

Hotel Hubertus (B*) is at the castle (tel. 945 37). UH & TU B at Besední dům, Mikulovská 173 (tel. 941 20). Train service to Břeclav. There are two railway stations in Valtice.

Dolní Věstonice

South Moravia was populated by mammoth hunters 30,000 years ago. Mammoth bones and other artifacts have been found in Dolní Vestonice. The museum here is open May to September 8.00am to noon, 1.00pm to 4.00pm, closed Monday, rest of year open weekends only, same hours. Děvín (550m) is a nice mountain to climb. One can follow the same track along the length of Pavlovské vrchy (Pavlov Hills) to Mikulov. West of Dolní Věstonice at Pasohlávky on the other side of the lake is a rather exposed camp with a good view across the lake to Pavlovské vrchy, popular with windsurfers.

Mikulov

Mikulov is an old town with a chateau dating from the 13th Century when Mikulov was an important strongpoint on the South Moravian border. There is a Jewish ghetto and an old Jewish cemetery. Mikulov is a border crossing point on the E461 from Brno to Vienna.

STRÁŽNICE

Strážnice is best known for its folk-lore festival, the biggest in Bohemia and Moravia, where folk traditions are not as well preserved as in Slovakia. This is a festival of living folk tradition, with costumes, dances, songs and customs from the Moravian Slovácko area. It is usually held in the last weekend of June, but the timing can vary.

In the 17th Century Strážnice was the third largest town in Moravia. The towers of the town gates remain, but the walls are gone. The town's late Gothic castle was changed to Baroque in the 19th Century. It is in its grounds that the folk festival is held. The museum in the castle includes a display of mostly home-made folk instruments. Open May 1 to October 31: Tuesday to Saturday 8.00am to 12.00am, 1.00pm to 5.00pm; Sunday 9.00am to 12.00am, 2.00pm to 5.00pm; last entry 4.00pm. Also at the castle is the Zámecká vinárna, a wine restaurant open Tuesday to Thursday 5.00pm to midnight, Friday and Saturday 5.00pm to 1.00am, with live music on Friday & Saturday.

Muzeum Vesnice Jihovýchodní Moravy is a Skansen museum covering a large area. Open Tuesday to Saturday 8.00am to 5.00pm, Sunday 10.00am to 6.00pm.

The railway station is painted with folk art.

To and from Strážnice

From Brno by train or bus. To Bratislava by train, change at Kúty. Strážnice to Kúty is railcar.

Accommodation

Strážnice Autokemping is behind the castle in the castle grounds. Nice surroundings. Motel, *chata* and tent camping. *Chata* and motel open all year. The camping area is open 1/5 to 31/10, but you can camp in the *chata* area in winter. *Chata* are 2, 3 or 4 person. Motel: all twin rooms. In holiday periods beds are booked up, but some beds are reserved for one night people. Outside holiday periods there should be beds available. Restaurant open meal times, but not always in winter. Beside the camping ground is a swimming pool and mini golf.

The town's two hotels are across the square from each other. **Černý orel** (B) is the older of the two. Normally full Thursday to Saturday, but one or two rooms free. Tel. 94 26 55. **Hotel Strážnice**, *** (B*), tel. 94 22 06. In the high season it is a problem to get a room without a reservation. The town's turistická ubytovna is available only for footballers, so try Hotel Černý orel which has a six-bed dormitory.

Brno

BÍLÉ (BIELE) KARPATY (WHITE CARPATHIANS)

The border between Moravia and Slovakia runs along the crest of these mountains, called Bílé Karpaty in Czech, and Biele Karpaty in Slovak, which translated to English means the White Carpathians.

The highest point in this part of the Carpathian mountain chain is Velká Javořina (Veľká Javorina in Slovak) at 970 metres. The road up on the Moravian side is closed in winter, but the road up from Cetuna on the Slovak side is open all year round. On Javorina there is a TV transmitter, ski field, and Holubyho chata.

In the village of Velká nad Veličkou there is a three day long traditional folk festival about the third week of July. Vápenky is a nice small village below Velká Javořina on the Moravian side. Stráni-květná has a factory producing striking glass.

Strážnice on the Moravian side, or Nové Mesto nad Váhom, between Bratislava and Žilina on the Slovakian side, are convenient access points to the places described above. Trenčín gives access to the northern part of the hills. The road map *Jižní Moravia* in the *Poznávme Československo* series covers Strážnice and the part of Bílé Karpaty I describe, while Trenčín and the northern part are found on the map *Považie* in the same series. *Auto Atlas ČSSR* is not detailed enough for you to find the little villages. For tramping I recommend you buy the map *Biele Karpaty*.

BUCHLOVICE AND VELEHRAD

Buchlovice lies east of Brno on highway 50, just before Uherské Hradiště. It has a very nice Baroque chateau and gardens. The chateau was built in Italian style from the beginning of the 17th Century and is adorned with sculptures. The park was originally laid out in formal Italian style, but later transformed into a French garden, and finally an English park. In 1908 Buchlovice Chateau played host to the Austrian and Russian foreign ministers who were negotiating the Austrian annexation of Bosnia and Herzegovina. It's possible to swim here.

Velehrad lies a few kilometres to the east of Buchlovice, off the main road. Archaeologists think it may be a centre of the Great Moravian Empire. In the nearby town of Uherské Hradiště is a museum with artifacts from the Great Moravian Empire.

There is an *ubytovací hostinec* and camping ground (open summer only) in Buchlovice, and hotels in Uherské Hradiště.

ZLÍN (GOTTWALDOV)

Zlín is the home of Baťa shoes, and was a small village when Baťa built a shoe factory there, one of a series he set up in places where people were poor. Another was in Svit, was once called Baťovany and now called Partizanske. He built housing and schools for the workers, as well as other factories, using progressive architecture for his time, and built large shops in the centre of each town in the country. But he was a bit of a tyrant although he treated his workers well by the standards of the time. He banned the

Communist Party at his factory. In 1938, he was flying to Dresden on business. The pilot said there was too much fog; Baťa said "I'm the employer, do as I say". The plane crashed and they were both killed. His brother took over Baťa's empire until it was nationalised after the Second World War. Baťa left Czechoslovakia, but Baťa factories had been set up all over the world before the war, and still trade under the Baťa name.

During communist rule Zlín was renamed Gottwaldov after the first communist president, but took its original name back after the Velvet Revolution in 1989. The town is still the centre of Czechoslovakia's shoe making industry, but the make is called Svit instead of Baťa. The factory is like a town within a town. There is a museum of shoe making.

The largest hotel in Zlín is **Hotel Moskva**, nám. Práce, 762 70 Zlín. There is also another hotel, and chalet (summer only) and hostel type accommodation. By rail you can get a train to Zlín itself, or to Otrokovice from where there are town buses to Zlín.

Slušovice

Slušovice is a very go-ahead agricultural cooperative and one of the most successful in Czechoslovakia. It is based on shares, so everyone gets a share of the profits. Their methods are very advanced for Czechoslovakia. In Slušovice you can buy all sorts of things unavailable elsewhere in the country — they produce muesli and some health foods for example. The cooperative has branched out into other areas now, including computer software. Slušovice was allowed to import and export without going through the normal channels. They employ headhunters to get them the best brains.

Slušovice's success is maybe nothing spectacular by western standards, but what is surprising is that all this happened under the communists, before the Velvet Revolution. Some say that connections in high places meant that they had favourable treatment.

Slušovice is about 6km from Zlín, and there is a bus service. Many visit for the steeplechase, but if it's really the horses you've come to see, be warned that all the viewing stands are reserved for those with a special invitation.

Kroměříž

Kroměříž is an old town 38km northwest of Zlín. In the time of the Great Moravian Empire a fort and a Slavic settlement arose here. The town later became the property of the Bishop of Olomouc and in 1777 the Archbishop of Olomouc. In the 13th Century the town had a Gothic layout, later coming under Renaissance influence. Under the siege by General Tortenson and the Swedish army at the end of the Thirty Years War in 1643, Kroměříž was almost completely destroyed. Rebuilding was done in Baroque style. A Baroque chateau replaced the original Gothic castle, and is today a museum, including an art gallery containing works of Dutch, German and Italian painters of the 15th to 19th Centuries.

Hotel Haná, B, is on Velké nám., tel. (0634) 228 04.

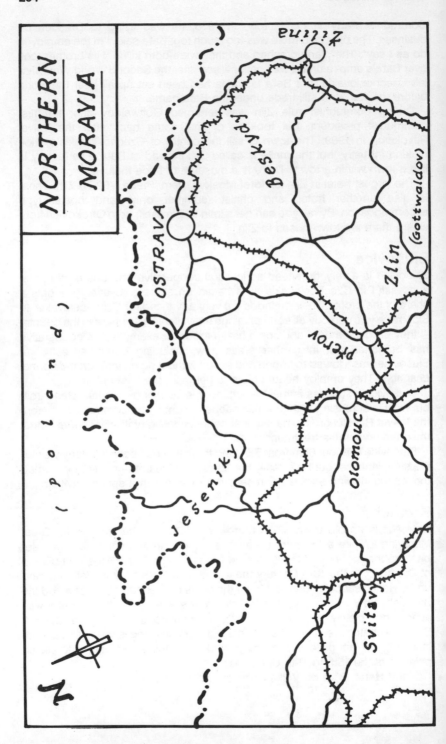

Northern Moravia

A lot of Northern Moravia is a polluted industrial agglomerate. Ostrava is the centre of Czechoslovakia's iron and steel industry, where coal and iron ore are extracted and utilised. There has been rapid industrial expansion here since the Second World War. But there is natural beauty in the area around its periphery, in the Jeseníky and Beskedy mountains. And Olomouc is one of the most important historical towns in Czechoslovakia. Another town not covered here that you might find worth visiting is **Opava**. If you do find yourself in **Ostrava**, which is a transport hub for northern Moravia, note that the bus station is *not* near the railway station.

OLOMOUC

The first historical mention of Olomouc is from 1055, though the origins of the town must go back much earlier. From 1187 to 1641 it was the capital of Moravia, as well as being an important trade and religious centre. The bishopric was founded in 1063. The town was seriously damaged during the Thirty Years War, after which 90% of its dwellings were uninhabitable, and in 1642 it lost its position as Moravia's capital to Brno. The town's many large Baroque ecclesiastical buildings date from the period after this war. On the other hand Olomouc was not badly damaged during the Second World War: most of the damage occurred during the last days of liberation, and was from guns, not bombs. The historical town centre is the second largest in Czechoslovakia, and has been protected as an historical reserve.

Today Olomouc has a population of about 107,000 and is an important centre in the Haná agricultural district. Its main industries are water pumps production, iron works and food processing. A large part of the (at the time of writing rapidly withdrawing) Soviet troops in Czechoslovakia were stationed around Olomouc. The amount of environmental devastation they have caused has shocked many, and a lot of groundwater in the area is polluted from used diesel that was just drained into the ground. The recreation area Lipava was taken over by the Soviet army, and the villages in this area were used as target practice for their tanks. A furore developed when the Soviets were accused of also ruining Baroque churches for this purpose.

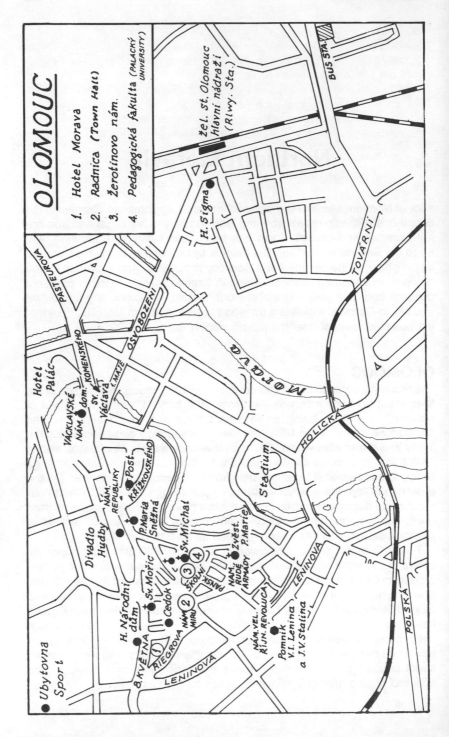

OLOMOUC

1. Hotel Morava
2. Radnica (Town Hall)
3. Žerotínovo nám.
4. Pedagogická fakulta (PALACKÝ UNIVERSITY)

To, from and around Olomouc

Olomouc lies on the main Prague-Košice railway line. Heading north, there are both trains and buses to Bruntál, but the train trip is more interesting. There are a few direct buses to Bratislava. The bus station and main railway station are both outside the centre. Any tram from either leads you to the centre. Heading out to the bus station, it is one stop further out than the railway station, on tram 4 or 5 only. There is left luggage at the bus station. For local transport you pay on the bus or tram (no change given) and get your ticket from the driver.

Accommodation

Hotels

Interhotel Flora ***, Krapkova 34, tel. 232 41, is the best hotel in town, with doubles only, with shower.

Hotel Národní dům, B*, ul. 8. května 21, tel. 251 79, has singles and doubles with extra beds available. Some rooms have bath or shower. Situated in the centre, this hotel is about 100 years old. It was a centre for Czechs, as in Austro-Hungarian times there were many Germans in Olomouc.

Hotel Palác, B*, třída 1. máje 27, 770 00 Olomouc, tel. 2384, 240 96, or 25 508, is also in the centre, with singles and doubles, some with shower.

Hotel Sigma, B*, tel. 289 62 or 289 83, is situated opposite the main railway station, and has doubles only, all with shower.

Hotel Morava, B, is in the centre at Riegrova 16, tel. 296 71 or 289 64.

Hotelový dům, C, at Volgogradská 8, tel. 267 61 is one of the cheapest hotels in town, with doubles only and one shower per two rooms.

Note: Hotels in Olomouc are usually full.

Other

There is a **motel** at the bus station, with about 40 beds in double rooms with shower.

Ubytovna Sport, TU A, Plavecký stadión, U Husova sboru, tel. 273 85-6, at the town swimming baths, not far from the centre, is the best hostel.

During July and August there is accommodation in **student hostels** through CKM or Čedok, but it's cheaper through CKM if you have a student or youth hostel card.

The nearest **camping** is 18km away at Dolní Žleb, Šternberk.

Information

Čedok is at Nám. Míru 2, 771 03 Olomouc, tel. 28831; Rekrea is at Ztracená 9, tel. 227 30, 263 29; and CKM are at Denisova 4, tel. 290 09. There is a town map costing Kčs 10. A motorway is under construction between Brno and Olomouc, parts of which are open. Pošta 1 is on nám. Republiky.

What to see

The following is arranged so that you can use it as a walking tour of the historical part of Olomouc, starting at the town hall and finishing at the cathedral.

The oldest remaining buildings date from the 13th Century. The **town hall**, in the centre of Nám. Míru, was constructed between 1378 and 1607. Not always used as a town hall, it was bought back by the town at the end of the 19th Century. A festival hall was found, which had been divided into rooms. It is now used for weddings and baptisms, and is the second largest after the one in Prague Castle.

The original performing **astronomical clock** on the town hall was built by the end of the 15th Century, the exact date is uncertain. It was destroyed one day before the end of the Second World War by the Germans. The rebuilt modern clock was designed by Karel Svolinský and finished on May 9 1955, in a "socialist" style with ceramic mosaic. The yellow colour symbolises the riches of the fertile plains of Haná from which Olomouc lives. The two large figures represent manual work and intellectual work, while the 12 figures around represent the 12 months of the year and the work done in the villages in these months. The clock performs to Moravian folk melodies. The whole performance is only at 12.00am every day, and ends with the rooster flapping its wings. At other times there is a short performance only. The original clock had religious motifs and was made by Pohl of Nürnberg. There is a legend that he was blinded after he built it, so that he couldn't build another, but this is untrue. You can see the old clock in pictures in the windows to the left of the modern clock.

The square around the town hall has had many names, depending on the political power at the time. From being named after Hitler, then Stalin, it is now named **Nám. Miru** (Peace Square), although it is commonly known as the Upper Square. It is surrounded by noblemen's houses. On this square is the **Trinity Column**. The Olomouc sculptor who started this in 1726 died before he finished it, so others continued with it until it was finally finished in 1856. Maria Theresa was at the unveiling ceremony. The statues are of patrons of Olomouc and Moravia, including the patrons of churches that are now destroyed. It was designed to look even bigger than it is, and to dominate the view from the streets leading to the square. At the top are the Father, Son and Holy Ghost. The Virgin Mary is supported by two angels. Oděvy, opposite Čedok, was one of Baťa's shops. What is now the pharmacy (*lékárna*) at number 10 is the only building in Empire style. The only bishop actually born in Olomouc was born in this house. The old main entrance to the town hall, opposite the pharmacy, was by an Italian artist. The emblems are of the different parts of the Austro-Hungarian Empire.

The **Fountain of Caesar** (1725) is also on nám. Miru, and was made from one stone. Caesar was said to be the founder of the town at the time, but that couldn't have been possible. It is one of a series of six fountains built in the 17th Century to provide the town with drinking water. The others are the Hecules, Neptune, Jupiter, Triton and Mercury fountains. The house behind this has a black dog on the wall. Before houses had numbers, they had signs, and this was the "House of the black dog". Also on the square is the theatre **Divadlo Oldřicha Stibora**, while just off the square on ulice 28. řijna is Dejmal's who made famous cakes, and the name was kept after nationalisation.

Of the many other churches around the town, many are closed. Of those that are open, perhaps the most notable is sv. Mǒric **(Church of St**

Maurice), which stands just north of nám. Miru, and dates from the 15th Century. The exterior is original Gothic, while the interior was burnt by fire and reconstructed in Baroque or neo-Gothic style. There are beautiful stained-glass windows. The outstanding Baroque organ by Breslau organ builder M. Engler in 1740-45 has 10,400 pipes, and is one of the largest organs in the world allowing two organists to play together. An organ festival is held around the end of August, beginning of September.

Just south of nám. Miru (or the Upper Square) is nám. Rudé Armády (Red Army square) also known by its old name, **Lower Square**. Here you'll find the **Neptune and Jupiter Fountains**, and in the centre of the square is a plague column. The Capuchin church, Kostel Zvěstování P. Marie, was completed in 1661. The house with the black horse has a legend attached to it. When the Swedes were here, a girl fell in love with one of the soldiers. She made an aphrodisiac drink, but the horse drank it and chased her everywhere until she jumped out of the window of this house — the horse couldn't fit through! One of the buildings worth seeing is number 38, the Renaissance **Haunschildůr palac**. It stands on the corner of Ulice Lafayettova, named after the French General Lafayet who was kept as a political prisoner here for seven years.

If you follow Lafayettova you will come to the broad street Třida Leninova, which is where the old **walls of the town** stood. There were two parallel walls, and the gates in them were not opposite each other, to make it harder for the enemy to get in. Remains of the town walls are visible in some places around the town. On the other side of Třida Leninova is nám. Velké říjové revoluce (which may have a new name by now), where there is (or was in 1990) a **statue of Lenin and Stalin**, one of the last statues of Stalin in Czechoslovakia.

Returning to the Lower Square, follow Panská to the narrow lane Školní ulice where all the houses have been reconstructed. The square **Žerotínovo nám**. is named after Žerotín who was executed in 1621 in Prague after the Battle of White Mountain. **Palacký University** in Olomouc is older than Brno's, and in fact the second oldest in Czechoslovakia. It opened in 1573 and today includes a medical faculty with its own hospital. It was originally a Jesuit school, then becoming a Jesuit university. From the mid 19th Century only the Faculty of Theology remained, until after World War Two, when the university was reopened. The part of the university on Žerotínovo nám. was the theology faculty. The formerly Gothic Kostel sv. Michala (the **Church of St Michael**) on the same square was reconstructed in baroque style and has recently been renovated. The gold is typical for the Counter Reformation when the church wanted to show that it had power and money. The church stands atop one of the three hills of Olomouc, and its three domes are one of the dominating features of Olomouc's skyline.

Nearby is a chapel in memory of Jan Sarkander, built on the site of the town prison where he was tortured and died in 1620. The street Mahlerova is named after Gustav Mahler who conducted here for one year. Mendel, the founder of modern genetics, studied here just below the chapel.

The Jugenstil **Divadlo Hudby** at Denisova 47 is now a theatre and shops, but from the 13th to 18th Centuries there was a hospital here. The **district museum** (open 9.00am to 5.00pm) is on nám. Republiky in a former convent.

The Baroque Kostel P. Marie Sněžné (the **Church of the Virgin Mary of the Snow**) across the square was the university church. It has good acoustics, and in summer there are organ concerts here every Saturday. The **Triton Fountain** is also on this square. The street Křížkovského turns off at nám. Republiky and leads to the palaces of the high clergymen. Franz Josef I was enthroned as emperor of the Austro-Hungarian Empire at the **Bishop's Palace** on nám. J. V. Friče. At the end of Komenského by the bridge over the river Morava is a Russian church from 1937-39. The Czech Orthodox churches were all closed during World War Two.

The **Cathedral of St Wenceslas** (dóm sv. Václava) stands on top of one of the three hills Olomouc was founded on, at Václavské náměstí. Originally a Romance basilica, it was rebuilt in first Renaissance, then Baroque and finally last century in neo-Gothic style. The three statues high over the entrance are of St Wenceslas, and Cyril and Methodius, who brought christianity to Czechoslovakia. The round tower behind the chapel beside the church was part of the fortifications. Mozart was here when he had smallpox, and there is a plaque to him opposite the cathedral. Adjacent to the cathedral was the Romance **palace of the Premyslids**. A small part remains, with original Romance windows, and has recently been opened to the public.

Out of Olomouc

Atop a hill outside Olomouc, dominating the surrounding countryside, is **Kopeček**, a former pilgrims' centre. The church, dating from the second half of the 17th Century, is open to the public, and there is a good view of Olomouc from here.

Šternberk is an historical town with a castle from the 13th Century open from April 1 to October 31. The first production of clocks in Czechoslovakia took place in Šternberk. The present factory specialises in alarm clocks. The clock museum is found below the castle and is associated with the factory.

Events

EXOTA is an international exhibition of exotic birds, held at the beginning of October every year. Flora, an international exhibition of flowers, is held in Olomouc every odd numbered year. It is divided into two parts, the first at the end of April and beginning of May, and the second in mid August. In even numbered years, when Flora is held in Bratislava, a small rose exhibition is held in Olomouc.

Eating

For eating try the hotels or there are many places around the main square. I had a very good meal at Pipi Gril on Nám. Míru. It is a small pleasant sk.III place with some different dishes to the usual fare available in Czechoslovakia. It's open Monday to Friday only from 11.00am to 6.30pm. Hanácká restaurant at number 38 on the Lower Square is sk.III and has good food.

Olomouc is famous for its small cheeses called *tvarůžky syrečky*.

JESENÍKY

The Jeseníky contain the highest mountain in Moravia, Praděd (1492m). These mountains are covered by coniferous woods, mostly spruce, with some larch, which at higher altitudes give way to dwarf pines. Red deer, roe deer and chamois are found here. The chamois are not the same type as those found in the Tatras, but come from the Austrian alps. There are only about five lynx. Wolves are very rare — they are sighted about once in 10 years when they cross from Poland. In 1989 there was a bear here, which had made its way from Slovakia. The authorities, worried because of the many tourists, so shot it with a tranquillising dart. Unfortunately the marksman shot it in the wrong place, and the bear eventually died.

There are about 50 black grouse in Jeseníky. Twenty years ago capercaillie, a very large type of grouse, were hunted here. Now there are only five or ten left. The peregrine that lived here 10 to 15 years ago have suffered a worse fate. There are now none left in Bohemia and Moravia, and possibly it's the same in Slovakia.

Acid rain is affecting the higher parts and the valleys in which the wind blows a lot. Many roads are closed to private vehicles, including the road up Praděd, which is crowned by a television transmitter. The northern part of the Jeseníky, apart from Rejvíz, is not as developed as the south. The Jeseníky, a protected area since 1969, comprise 740km², within which there are smaller nature reserves. The park headquarters are in **Malá Morávka**. Dlouhé stráně is a hydroelectric power scheme where the water is pumped up at night and let down during the day. Situated in the middle of the protected area, it is an ecological disaster.

The Jeseníky were part of the Sudetenland Hitler took, and there were Germans living here before the war. There was once lots of gold in the Jeseníky, but there is no longer much to be found. The main centres are Šumperk, Bruntál and Jeseník.

Bruntál was a mining town, with a recorded history going back to 1213. It is not so interesting, although in 1992 the castle is expected to reopen. You can walk up the extinct volcano Uhlířský v. (672m), by following the green marked route south from Bruntál. The derelict Catholic church at the top was vandalised by Russians hoping to find treasures. The border between Silesia and Moravia ran below this hill, which is why the village of Kočov is divided into Slezký Kočov and Mor. Kočov.

Jeseník (432m), a spa town, lies in the north. What was once its castle is now a museum.

Karlova Studánka is a spa for the treatment of the respiratory problems of people from polluted Ostrava. Just a small village, it has beautiful old wooden spa buildings and mineral water free for drinking. There is no asphalt on the road through the spa, so that the vapour asphalt gives off is avoided. The waterfall behind Hubertus is from a channel from a defunct power station. There were once many small hydroelectric power stations in the area, but the communists closed them, as they felt one must think big. Some are now being restored.

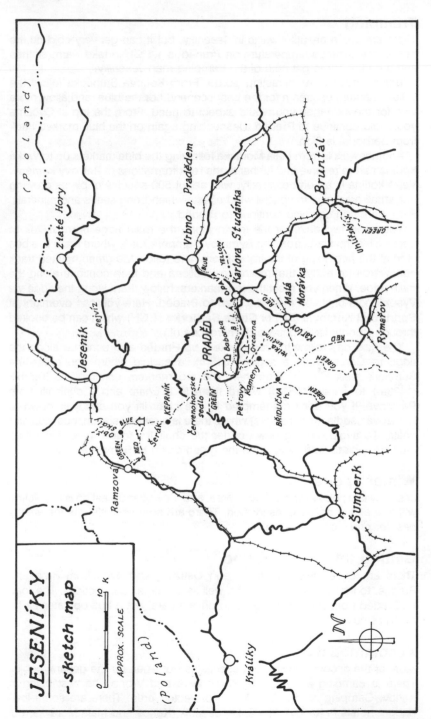

Tramping

There are some beautiful walks in Jeseníky, but it can get very cold on the peaks (the average temperature on Praděd is 1.1°C) so take warm clothes and a parka. Try to get hold of the tramping map *Jeseníky*.

Bílá Opava is an interesting gorge. From Karlova Studánka follow the yellow markers upstream for the best scenery, not the blue, and allow more time for the 4km than you would expect to need. From the top at Ovčárna you could continue to **Praděd**. Descending again on the blue marked track from Barborka is 6km.

Another walk is from Malá Morávka following the blue markers up to **Velká kotlina** nature reserve and further to the rock formations of **Petrovy kameny**. Velká kotlina is a European rarity, with about 500 species of plants growing in a small area, due to special wind effects which bring seeds and minerals. From here you can also continue to Praděd.

You need two days for the tramp along the main ridge from Skřítek to Šerák. This trip starts from the Rýmařov-Šumperk road, where there is a bus stop at the beginning of the track. From here follow the green marked track northwards up above the treeline to Břidličná and then continue along the main ridge. When you meet the red markers, follow them along the ridge via Vysoká hole until you meet the road to Praděd. Here you can overnight at **Sporthotel Kursovní** (SH) or **Chata Barborka** (T CH) which can be booked through Sportturist in Ostrava (Dimitrovova ul.).

The next day follow the red markers up Praděd and continue along the ridge to Červenohorské sedlo (1013m), a saddle where you cross the Šumperk-Jeseník road. From here the red markers continue via Keprník (1423m) to Šerák (1351m) where there is a *chata* and a chair lift from Ramzová. If you don't get tempted by the chair lift you can walk down to Ramzová saddle, (red markers) where there is a railway station, bus stop and chata. To avoid walking down under the chair lift, follow instead the blue marked track to Obří skály, then the green down to Ramzová.

Winter sports

Jeseníky is a popular winter sports area, and their over-utilisation is conflicting with the aim of nature conservation. There are some ski lifts, but the area is best for cross-county skiing.

Getting there and around

There are buses from Olomouc and Ostrava, and even from Brno and Prague, to the Jeseníky centres, as well as some rail connections. The road up Praděd from Hvězda is closed to private cars, but a bus operates as far as Ovčárna.

Accommodation

Most of the accommodation in Jeseníky is not open for the general public. There is camping at Karlov, Malá Morávka and Vrbno, the best being in Karlov. Camping is forbidden in the protected area. There are some low-budget hotels in Karlova Studánka, Jeseník, Karlov and Malá Morávka, but most accommodation available to the public lies in the surrounding main centres. For example **Hotel Společenský Dům**, 792 01 Bruntál (tel. 3100) has doubles at Kčs 168, triples at Kčs 206 and rooms for four for Kčs 310. But even here it gets booked up in the summer.

Eating and drinking

Praděd has a liqueur named after it. The food I had at Hotel Karlov's sk.III restaurant was good, even if the service was slow. The television tower on Praděd is not open to the public, but there is a public restaurant in its base.

BESKYDY

The steep sided but round ridged Beskydy mountains lie in northeastern Moravia. You'll cross them if travelling between Olomouc or Jeseníky and the mountains of Slovakia. It was not so long ago that the Beskydy had their original forest cover. But the demand for wood led to its destruction and the planting of spruce. Much of this happened in the 1820s, when industry began to develop in the region. Some small areas of original forest cover remain. But now acid rain is taking its toll. The highest peak is Lysá Hora (1324m).

At **Rožnov pod Radhoštěm**, the most interesting town in the area, there is an open air museum, which took its inspiration from the skansen (an open air museum portraying life of in the past) in Stockholm. It is divided into two parts, a wooden town, established in 1925, and Valašská dědina, a Wallachian village. The first part is open from May 1 to November 15 from 8.30am to 5.00pm, but in July and August from 8.00am to 7.00pm. The second part is open 9.00am to 5.00pm, but from mid December to the end of March only on Monday, Wednesday, Saturday and Sunday.

Pustevny (1018m) is named after the hermits who lived here in caves in the 18th and 19th Centuries. Radhošť (1129m) can be climbed from here or Rožnov pod Radhoštěm. Pustevny is also the best known of the winter resorts. Although there are some tows, the area is more favourable for cross country skiing.

There are lakes and many marked hiking routes in the Beskydy, and even a few traditional Wallachian houses and shepherds' huts. For detailed exploring buy the map *Beskydy*, number 42 in the *Soubor turistický* map series.

Accommodation

Hotel Tanečnice at Pustevny was rebuilt in 1987. There is camping and a hotel at the reservoir at Bystřička, and accommodation in Rožnov pod Radhoštěm. In fact there are various types of accommodation scattered all around the Beskydy and in the surrounding towns.

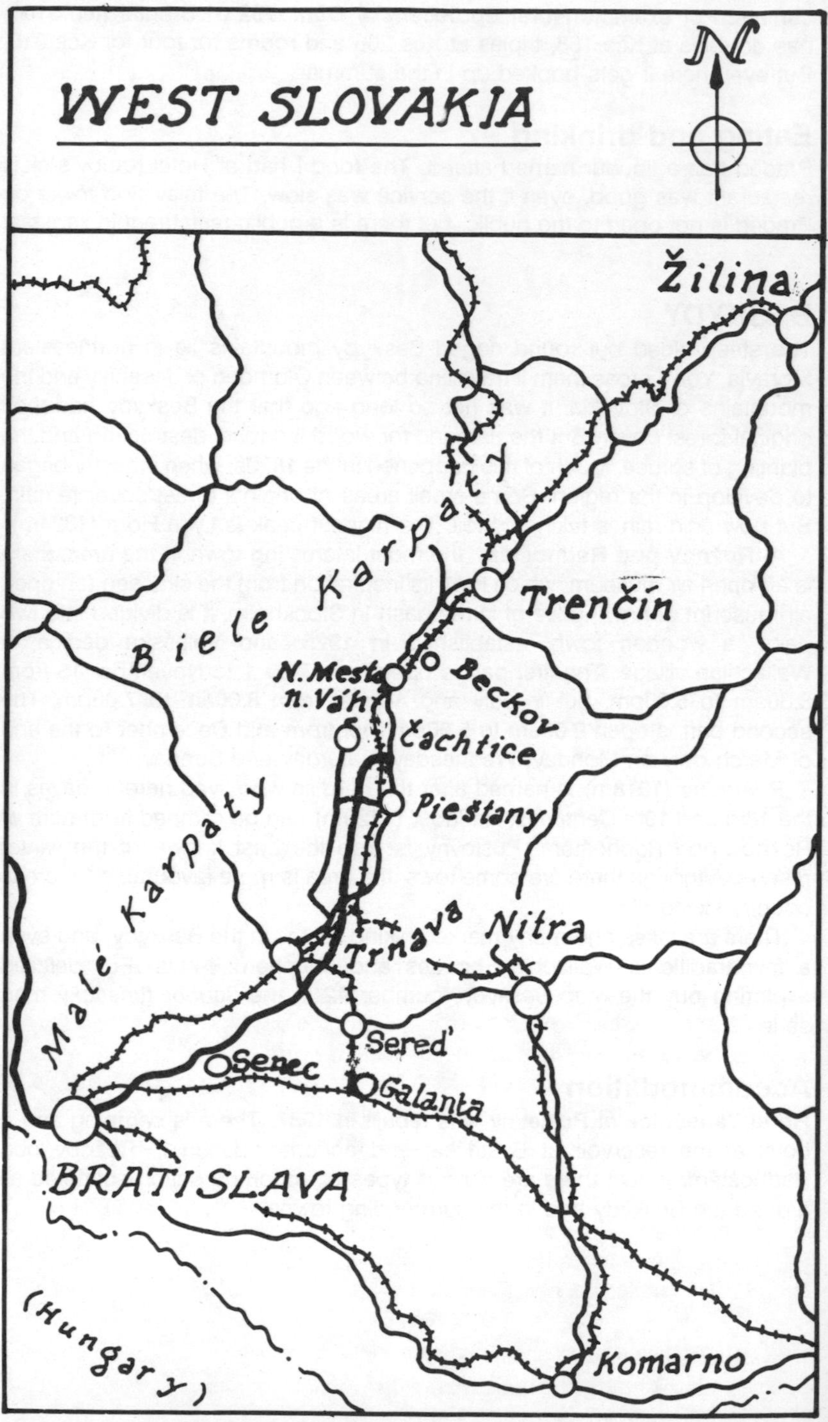

WEST SLOVAKIA

N

Žilina

Biele Karpaty

Trenčín

N. Mesto
n. Váh

Beckov

Čachtice

Piešťany

Malé Karpaty

Trnava

Nitra

Sereď

Senec

Galanta

BRATISLAVA

(Hungary)

Komárno

West Slovakia

BRATISLAVA

Bratislava, with a population of 440,000, is the second largest city in Czechoslovakia and, since 1969, the capital of Slovakia. It lies on the River Danube, at the western extremity of the long arch of the Carpathian mountain chain. Its suburbs approach the Austrian border, and it is only a few short kilometres north of the Hungarian border. In fact there used to be a tram to Vienna, and older people may have memories of riding there by bicycle. For many years this border was very difficult for Czechoslovaks to cross, and many refugees lived on the other side of it. Now it is at last open for them again.

Bratislava lies rather out on a limb in the southwest corner of Slovakia, so with all the beautiful old towns and wonders of nature in other parts of Czechoslovakia, it may not seem worth a special trip. But if you are passing that way anyway, or have enough time, there is a lot to see, and it is interesting to feel the effects of the proximity of Austria and Hungary, and to meet the people, in whose veins are mixed Slovak, German, Hungarian and Gypsy blood.

History

The first human traces here date from the late Stone Age. In the 1st Century BC a Celtic tribe built a settlement here. Later it became a part of the Roman Empire. The first Slavs arrived here in the 5th and 6th Centuries AD. In the 9th Century Bratislava was part of the Great Moravian Empire. In the 11th and 12th Centuries Bratislava castle was a frontier bastion of the Magyar State. In 1241 the Tatars plundered the settlement, but failed to take the castle. Budapest was under threat by the Turks, so in 1536 Bratislava became the capital of Hungary. The Turks never occupied Bratislava. In 1773 the census showed that 26,845 people lived in the city, making it the largest in Hungary. In 1811 the castle was burnt down owing to the carelessness of soldiers. After Slovakia was granted autonomy in 1938, Czechs were forced to leave. On April 4 1945 Bratislava was liberated from the Germans by the Soviets.

Bratislava today

Bratislava has undergone rapid expansion, and is very much a mixture of old and new. The town is overlooked by its castle, which has undergone extensive reconstruction, and below it lies the old town, which is definitely worth exploring. On the hill above the castle lived the affluent citizens. But many of the new suburbs, Petržalka on the other side of the Danube in particular, look like architectural and sociological disaster areas.

It can be beautiful along the Danube, which is fast flowing here. You'll probably either like or detest Most SNP, the modern bridge built in 1972, obviously designed as a showpiece, which connects the two sides of the river. The old bridge was re-built by Soviet sappers after the Germans damaged the original in 1945. After reconstruction in the eighties it is now open only for motorists and pedestrians, not for cyclists. A fourth bridge, Most Mládeže (Bridge of Youth), west of the castle may be completed in 1991, so the main road will cross to Petržalka and bypass the centre of Bratislava before crossing back over most Hrdinov Dukly, which opened in 1985.

The Malé Karpaty foothills begin right in the town, so peaceful woods are only a walk from the centre, and vineyards on their slopes stretch right down into the town.

Today Bratislava has 8% of Slovakia's population, and 10% of its industry, the most important of which is chemical industry.

Radio and television can be received from three countries. It is popular to listen to Austrian radio, mainly for its music. The Hungarian minority can watch television from Budapest. You'll see a lot of jeans in Bratislava, in contrast to the more conservative eastern part of the country. There are a lot of expensive things in the shops that you don't see in the rest of Slovakia.

Mosquitoes are *very bad* in Bratislava, particularly in Petržalka, but also generally by the Danube where they breed in pools caused by its rise and fall.

To and from Bratislava
By car
Bratislava is connected with Prague by motorway via Brno, and has main road connections to Vienna and Budapest.

By bus and train
Prague: By *rychlík* train 5 hours. Often late as many of them are international trains which don't begin from Bratislava. Trains on the same route stop at Brno, and many travel on to Berlin. Bus is more expensive and takes 4 hours.
Žilina: By *rýchlik* train or by bus.
Banská Bystrica: Best by bus, which is much faster than by train.
Budapest: There are several trains daily.
Vienna: The bus leaves from Mlynské Nivy Bus Station in Bratislava and takes about 2 hours. The train takes about 3 hours. Buy your ticket at the station or Čedok. Both train and bus cost ÖS74 and must be paid for in foreign currency.

By boat
The boat services on the Danube may change a bit from year to year, but the Vienna service is pretty stable, and there is normally a service to Budapest.

At the time of writing there was a boat service to **Budapest** on Wednesdays from the end of April to early September. US$10 one way, US$20 return, must be paid in western currency. The boat leaves Bratislava early in the morning, and takes 3½ hours to reach Budapest. From Budapest it leaves late afternoon, taking 4¼ hours for the return trip upstream.

The boat service to **Vienna** gets filled up by people on day package tours to Bratislava, for which you can get a special visa on the boat. The boat leaves Bratislava Thursday to Sunday at 5.00pm. The only way you can get on it if you are not on the package tour is to ask the captain if he can take you. If he does, it may be on the understanding that you will have to stand. Fare (Ös115) must be paid in western money. There are some interesting views along the river. The Czechoslovak side used to be horrible with its barbed wire, guards etc, but by the time you read this they might be removed. You get a superb view of the ruins of Devín.

By air
There are international flights to Moscow, Leningrad, Sofia and Berlin. There are several direct flights a day to Prague, two per day to Košice, and one per day to Poprad. ČSA's international office is at Mostová 3 (tel. 31 12 17, 31 12 03), while their domestic office is at Gorkého 5 (tel. 33 07 88, 33 07 90). Their airport bus leaves Mostová one hour before domestic flights and two hours before international flights. To the airport from Hlavná stanica (the main railway station) take bus no. 24.

Hitchhiking
Difficult on the Bratislava-Brno-Prague route. Try from somewhere along Viedenská cesta for Vienna. Hitching to Hungary is difficult.

Getting around
Bratislava has an efficient public transport service using tram, bus and trolley bus. There is an information and ticket office for local transport underneath Mierové nám., where you can get a free route map. The regular street map (see below) also shows all local transport routes. But there are lots of public works all the time, so the streets, and bus and tram routes are always changing. The tunnel under the castle is open only for trams. Buy tickets beforehand from kiosks, and punch them yourself as you enter the bus. For buses to the airport see above. Tram number 4's route has been extended to Zlaté piesky (see Camping section below for more information). Night buses run from nám. SNP roughly hourly from 12.40am until the last bus at about 3.30am to most parts of the city. The night bus to Zlaté piesky is no. 132 which leaves at 12.40, 1.40 and 2.35am. "ZZ" at bus stops means night bus, and the numbers for night buses are written in red at bus stops instead of the normal black.

There is a ferry service across the river. It operates from about early April to early October from 10.00am to 8.00pm Tuesday to Friday, 10.00am to 9.00pm Saturday and 9.00am to 8.00pm Sunday. From early September, until it stops operating for the season, it finishes at 6.00pm every day, and starts at 10.00am on Sundays. The open boat crosses every half an hour, with a lunch break from 12.00am to 12.30am.

Bratislava is not terribly friendly to cyclists with its traffic and tram lines. Although the old bridge is closed to bicycles, you can walk your bike over on the footpath. **Most Hrdinov Dukly** has what is maybe Czechoslovakia's first cycle track, but owing to lack of signposting even the locals have trouble finding it. It is now regretted that cycle tracks were not included in the plans for Petržalka. Bicycles can be hired at the recreation area Kormorán by the lake Veľký Dražiak in Petržalka.

Maps and guidebooks

Bratislava, Town Plan is a detailed map of Bratislava including suburbs, public transport and index, Kčs 12. *Bratislava, Town-Monuments* is a map of the town centre with information on historic buildings, museums etc in various languages, including English. *Bratislava* is a map in book form, but the first map is kept more up to date.

Bratislava Guide, by O. Došek, D. Učníková & M. Murín, Šport, Bratislava, 1978, is a thorough guide to Bratislava in English, but as well as being a bit dated, it's unfortunately out of print. *Bratislava, Stadtführer*, published by Šport, Bratislava, 1989, is the German edition of a Slovak guide.

Accommodation
Camping and bungalows

There are two camping grounds out at **Zlaté piesky** (which means Golden Sands). Hotel Flora's camp is the largest, and is on the lake. Bungalows for four people, if fewer than four people, you still pay same price. Open for tents May to September, bungalows all year. From June to mid September there is a *disco club*, restaurant and many *bufets*. From May to the end of September Golf Club (sk.III + 10%) is open 11.00am to 10.00pm, with drinks and some food. Mini golf. Nice surroundings, noisy if near the main road. Facilities in a bad state of repair, but it has hot water and cooking elements. You can hire rowing boats, windsurfers and water bicycles from May to September.

The other camp is a little further down the same road. It has the same facilities in the same state of disrepair. It is smaller, but not as nice as Flora and has no direct access to the lake. The three-bed bungalows have hot and cold water, toilet, communal shower; best to book them through Čedok. For tents open 1 June to 15 September, for bungalows 15 January to 20 December. Tel. 651 70.

Zlaté piesky is a long way out, but there are fast buses. From Monday to Friday during rush hours only take bus 110 to the last stop. Otherwise take bus 32 from nám. Fr. Zupku at the beginning of Trnavská cesta, and get off just past a petrol station. Or tram 4 has recently been extended to Zlaté piesky, and also stops at nám. Fr. Zupku. From the railway station to nám. Fr. Zupku you can take bus 22, 23 or 24. Time from the centre of town to Zlaté piesky including changing bus is about 40 minutes.

The camps at Zrkadlový háj listed "1983 Camping" book closed down about 15 years ago. New camps are planned.

Hostels

CKM have some sort of arrangement for YHA members and others that their own staff don't seem to understand. The following is a rough guide to this chaotic system.

CKM have summer hostels from about early July to late August. If possible check with the local CKM office first, and find out what is open where (if they know themselves, which they didn't when I asked them). There may be a notice in their window when they are closed. The hostels are in student dorms, and CKM really intend them for their package tourists, but you can stay there if you can find out where there is a spare bed. Some of the addresses they use are: Studentský domov J Hronca, Bernolákova 1, 800 00 Bratislava, tel. 42612, (tram 11); Šd L. Štúra, Asmolovova ulica, 800 00 Bratislava — Mlynská Dolina (bus 39); Študentský domov DRUŽBA, University Komenského, nábř. Svobody 33, 810 00 Bratislava, tel. 580 41; and Ul Prokopa Velikého 41, 817 07 Bratislava, tel. 37 25 18. Booked from abroad the hostels are more expensive, at £8.60 per night full board.

There is also a YHA member price of Kčs 50 at CKM's **Juniorhotel Sputnik**, Drieňova ul, 801 00 Bratislava; tel. 227883, 222604, but it is usually full. Sk.III restaurant. Disco.

T J Vinohrady, Nabr. L. Svobodu 17, 841 01; tel. 239661 have accommodation in four bed rooms for about Kčs 60 per person. Preference is given to sportsmen, but if it is not full others may stay there. Communal toilets, showers and kitchen. No restaurant. Open all year. Heated in winter. There are also T J Vinohrady dorms (TU A) near Juniorhotel Sputnik at Presovská ul., 801 00 Bratislava, tel. 671 405. Slovakoturist use them for groups, but you can go there in person and try and get a bed.

Motel

Motel Zlaté piesky (Interhotel), Cat. A, tel. 651 70. At the end of the road to the camping grounds. 30 doubles with shower etc. Open 1/3 to 30/10. See *Camping* for more on Zlaté piesky.

Hotels

The majority of hotels in Bratislava are B* category. There are no cheap hotels (C class). New hotels are under construction or planned.

Hotel Devín, *****, Riečna 4, 811 02 Bratislava; tel. 330 851-4. Singles Kčs 591, doubles Kčs 790 including breakfast. Advanced bookings necessary all year. French, Slovak and Asian restaurants. Across the road from the Danube, near the SNP bridge.

Hotel Kyjev, A*, Rajská ul.; tel. 520 41, 563 41. A few singles at Kčs 420, doubles Kčs 630, including breakfast. By the department store Prior.

Hotel Forum, ****, Mierové námestie 2, 816 25 Bratislava; tel. 348 111, telex 92189 ihbfo c; fax 314645. Built by a French company with Yugoslav workers and opened in 1989. Because of their foreign debt they prefer payment in foreign currency. Singles Kčs 690, doubles Kčs 1,086. Flash, modern and central. ČSA and Pragocar have counters in the hotel for guests. Booked up in summer.

Hotel Flora, B*, Zlaté piesky; tel. 672 841. Doubles and apartments (sleep 3). Sk.II + 10% restaurant. Best to reserve through Čedok. See Camping for more information on Zlaté piesky.
Hotel Carlton, B*, Interhotel, Hviezdoslavovo nám. 7, 816 09 Bratislava; tel. 582 09, 331 851. Very central. Singles Kčs 324, doubles Kčs 627. Oldest hotel in Bratislava. Closing for renovation for a period in 1991 or 1992.
Tatra, B*, nám. 1. mája 7, 811 06 Bratislava; tel. 512 78. Expensive sk.II restaurant, *kaviareň* & bar. Recently renovated.
Hotel Bratislava, B*, Urxova 9, 821 03 Bratislava; tel. 295641 or 293523, telex 092336. Outside the centre. Largest hotel in Bratislava.
Juniorhotel Sputnik, B*, (see Hostels), singles and doubles with shower or bath. Best to book through CKM in Prague. Usually full of package tourists.
Hotel Palace, Poštová 1; tel. 333 656-7. In the centre. Doubles Kčs 292, doubles with bath Kčs 418, singles Kčs 188, must pay in crowns, no exchange office. Booked up all year; postal reservations held till 5.00pm.

Private
Accommodation in private homes through Čedok, nám. SNP 14, but they'll usually only arrange it for Czechoslovak citizens.

Travel agents
Čedok have a special office for foreigners at Štúrova 13 (tel. 520 02, 558 34). Someone speaks English. Helpful. Open 9.00am to 6.00pm Monday to Friday, 9.00am to 12.00am on Saturday. Currency exchange. Guides can be hired through them. I was quoted Kčs 150 for 3 hours.
CKM, Hviezdoslavovo nám. 16, 814 16 Bratislava; tel. 331 607. Open Monday to Friday, afternoon only. Student cards are issued Tuesday and Thursday 1.00pm to 4.00pm only.
Tatratour, Dibrovovo námestie 7, 815 09 Bratislava; tel. 335 852. In the old town. Can help with information on Bratislava. Open Monday, Wednesday, Thursday and Friday 8.30am to 4.30pm, Tuesday 9.00am to 6.00pm, Saturdays from 15/5 to 15/9 only 9.00am to 12.00am.
Autoturist, Štúrovo nám 1; tel. 337 381. Entrance from alleyway. Open Monday, Tuesday and Thursday 9.00am to 12.00am and 1.00pm to 4.00pm; Wednesday 10.00am to 12.00am, 1.00pm to 4.00pm; Friday 9.00am to 12.00am, 1.00pm to 2.30pm. The exchange office is open Monday to Friday 9.00am to 12.00am (from 10.00am Wednesdays).
Slovakoturist, Nálepkova 13, tel. 333 466. Open Monday 9.00am to 5.30pm, Tuesday to Friday 9.00am to 4.00pm. Currency exchange.

Other practical information and addresses
Bratislava Informačná a Propagačná Služba (BIPS), the **Bratislava information and publicity service**, is at Leningradská 1, (tel. 333 715, 334 370). Information on Bratislava, cultural programmes, events, guides, tours. Open weekdays 8.00am to 4.30pm, extended to 6.00pm from July to September, and Saturdays all year from 8.00am to 1.00pm.

For registering at the police or extending visas, the office you need is at Legerského 1. Take tram no. 3, 5, 7 or 11 towards Rača. Open 8.00am to 1.00pm. Tel. 663 51. The **main post office**, *hlavná pošta*, is at nám. SNP 34. Poste Restante is open every day. Weekdays open 7.00am to 9.00pm, Saturday 7.00am to 5.00pm, Sunday 9.00am to 4.00pm. The telephone and telegram office is on Kolárska. The area code when phoning Bratislava is 7.

The branches of Štátna banka československá at Dunajská 24 or Gorkého 7, Čedok Štúrova, or Slovakoturist will change money. The exchange office on the road to Vienna is open 24 hours. There is an exchange office in the harbour building. After the exchange offices close, try the big hotels.

If transferring money to Czechoslovakia, transfer it to Československá obchodní banka, Ul. Lehotského 3. A bit out of the centre. Look for the upside-down triangle.

The following countries have **consulates** in Bratislava.

Austria Rakúsky generálny koonzulát, Červeňova 17, tel. 311 103.

Bulgaria Generálny konzulát Bulharskej ľudovej republiky, Kuzmányho 1/a, tel. 315 308, 315 683.

Cuba Generálny konzulát Kubánskej republiky, Somolického ul., tel. 427 77, 446 82.

Finland Fínske veľvyslanectvo, Gorkého 15, tel. 330 829.

Hungary Generálny konzulát Maďarskej ľudovej republiky, Palisády 60, tel. 335 601.

Poland Generálny konzulát Poľskej ľudovej republiky, Hummelova 4, tel. 315 222.

Romania Generálny konzulát Rumunskej socialistickej republiky, Ul. Fraňa Kráľa 11, tel. 311 440.

USSR Generálny konzulát Zväzu sovietskych socialistických republík, tel. 313 468.

Cars may be rented from Pragocar on Hviezdoslavovo nám., Čedok, or Slovakoturist. Price example from Slovakoturist for Škoda Favorit: US$28 per day, US$171 per week, plus 26c. per km. Insurance US$5 per day, US$30 per week. With unlimited mileage: US$77 per day, US$306 per week, extra days US$45, including insurance. 15% is added to all charges. A car can be picked up at any branch office; from towns with no branch office there is an extra charge of 20c per km. One way rentals within 200km (eg Vienna) do not incur extra charges. Must be paid in foreign currency or by credit card. Book through Slovakoturist, 816 15 Bratislava, Volgogradská 1; tel. 523 13, 558 82; telex 92321.

Emergency breakdown service phone (07) 24 40 13.

What to see
A walking tour of Bratislava
I have described the following in the form of a walking tour which you may or may not choose to follow. The tour is by no means comprehensive, but does take in many of the main sights, and gives you a look at the various sides to the city. The tour is set out in a continuous form, but it is not necessarily intended as a one-day tour. I would recommend at least two

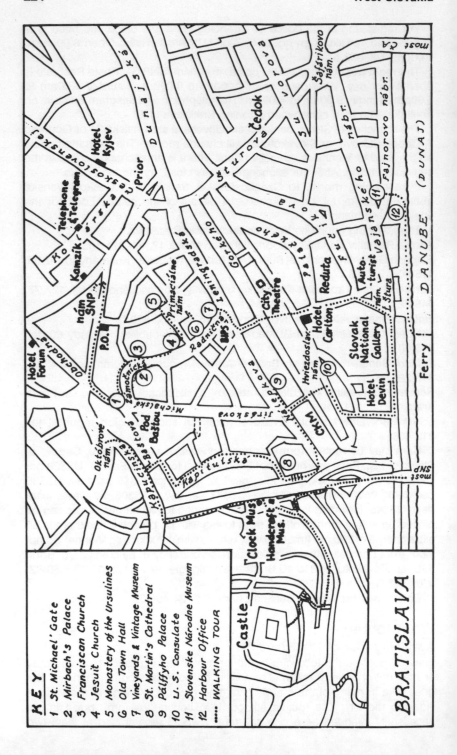

KEY
1 St. Michael' Gate
2 Mirbach's Palace
3 Franciscan Church
4 Jesuit Church
5 Monastery of the Ursulines
6 Old Town Hall
7 Vineyards & Vintage Museum
8 St. Martin's Cathedral
9 Pálffyho Palace
10 U.S. Consulate
11 Slovenske Národne Museum
12 Harbour Office
..... WALKING TOUR

BRATISLAVA

days; longer if you like to browse in museums etc.

The main square in the centre of town is **námestie SNP**, the square of the Slovak national uprising. A group of statues erected to commemorate the 30th anniversary of the uprising dominates the square, and there are flames to keep "ever alive the message of the Slovak national uprising". Using the immediate area around the statues and flames for relaxing is likely to be frowned upon by the police. The square was previously called Stalin Square. Across the road from the square is the main post office. Following this street uphill, then taking the first turning left (Michalská) leads one into the old town. Michalská crosses a bridge, under which the city moat ran. Travelling actors' companies gave performances here in the 18th Century. At Michalská 26, in what was one of the oldest pharmacies in Bratislava, is the **Pharmacy Múzeum**, open Tuesday to Sunday 10.00am to 5.00pm. St Michael's Gate, originally built in the 14th Century, is the only gate left today. In the gate itself is the Armament and **City Fortification Museum**, open daily except Tuesday from 10.00am to 5.00pm, extended to 8.00pm in July and August. From the lookout at the top is a view over the rooftops of the old town and up to the castle.

Turning left into Zámočnícka and continuing on into Dibrovovo nám. brings you to the Rococo style Mirbach's Palace (1770), which houses the municipal gallery. It is open Tuesday to Friday from 10.00am to 6.00pm (to 8.00pm in July and August) and weekends from 10.00am to 5.00pm. Don't miss the beautiful sculpture in the courtyard. On the opposite side of the street is the 13th Century Franciscan church, today a mixture of Gothic, Renaissance and baroque styles. There is access through the church to the **Chapel of St John the Evangelist**, the most important Gothic legacy in Slovakia.

Continuing down Dibrovovo nám. brings you to the **Jesuit Church** on the left side, which was a Protestant church before the Counter-Reformation. It has no tower, because the emperor ordered that it must blend in with the surrounding houses. The rich interior decoration came after the Jesuit takeover.

Just across Kostolná from here is the **Old Town Hall**, like many other buildings in Bratislava a mixture of Gothic, Renaissance and Baroque. It is a lovely building, especially the courtyard where there are concerts in summer. On the first floor is the **town museum**, and in the cellar in the former cells the **Museum of Feudal Justice**. Open Tuesday to Sunday, 10.00am to 5.00pm. Behind the Old Town Hall is Primaciálne nám., with Primaciálny Palác **(Primate's Palace)** at no. 2. Built in 1781 as the archbishop's palace, from 1903 the building was used as the town hall. Recent reconstruction should be completed as this edition comes to print. At Uršulínska 5, by Primaciálne nám. is the **Monastery of the Ursulines**, erected in 1687 together with a school. The well in the square was re-discovered in 1977. Walk back through the town hall courtyard and the square in front of you, surrounded by mansions, is nám. 4. aprila. After the archaeological excavations are finished, there are plans to restore the square to its former medieval style. Next to the town hall at Radničná 1 you'll find the **Vineyards and Vintage Museum** in the Palace of the Apponyi Family (1762), open daily except Tuesday, 10.00am to 5.00pm.

At the end of Radničná, turn right into Leningradská and first left into Rybárska brána. Across the road at the bottom of this street is the **City Theatre** built in 1888 in Neo-Renaissance style. Today it is the opera and ballet scene of the Slovak National Theatre. From here you can see the US consulate (see map), which was closed from 1948 until after the Velvet Revolution. Near the other side of the theatre is a turning, Mostová. A little way down here, on the corner of Palačkého, is **Reduta**, the concert hall of the Slovak Philharmonic Orchestra. This Neo-Baroque building from 1914 is very ornate, and worth a look inside if possible.

Continuing down Mostová brings you to the Danube waterfront. If you haven't seen it before, you can now see **Most SNP**, the bridge that the city sacrificed much of its heritage to build. The oldest part of the town, including the Jewish Synagogue, was demolished to build the access road and remains of the old town walls were found while excavating for the road. Turning to the right brings one to the **Slovak National Gallery** (Slovenská Národná Galeria). This is in the restored building of the former Water Barracks, built 1759-66. Judge for yourself what you think of what has been done to the building. Open 10.00am to 5.00pm, closed Mondays.

Continue past Hotel Devín, then turn up the street to the right to Hviedzdoslavovo nám. Cross this square and follow the street Strakova to Nálepkova where you turn right. At number 19 is Pálffyho Palác (**Pálffy's Palace**), today an art gallery (open daily except Monday 10.00am to 5.00pm, weekdays till 8.00pm in July and August). During work on this building graves were discovered from the Great Moravian period, as well as evidence of Celtic settlement.

Turn back along Nálepkova, follow it to its end, then walk up the stairs to the right to **St Martin's Cathedral**. Originally built in the 14th and 15th Century on the site of an older church, it underwent various additions and reconstructions. The tower was built in the moat of the castle, and had a defensive function until the end of the 15th Century. From 1563 to 1830 the cathedral was the coronation church of 10 Hungarian kings and eight queens. Vibration from the new road to Most SNP was weakening the building, so strengthening work was necessary. The cathedral is open every day from 6.00am to 12.00am, and from Monday to Thursday also from 1.00pm to 4.00pm. From here follow Kapitulská, where some of the Gothic and Baroque houses have been restored.

Turn right at the end of Kapitulská, left into Klariská, and right again at the top of the stairs. This brings you to Októbrové námestie. On this square is the **Church of the Trinities**, built from 1717-27. The interior is decorated by the Italian painter Galli Bibiena. The monastery was rebuilt to become the county hall in 1844. Today it houses offices of the Slovak National Council. The column in the middle of Októbrové námestie dates from 1723 and is of the Madonna. It commemorates the plague epidemic the town suffered from in 1712-13. Behind the column lies the little **Capuchin church**, modest in decoration, and small and quiet with people coming in to pray. Built 1708-11.

From Októbrové námestie head back along Kapucinska towards the castle. After crossing the access road to Most SNP, turn left and follow Židovská along above it. At the bottom end of the street, at Židovská 1, is the House of the Good Shepherd, built in 1760. Today it is the **Clock Museum**, the only museum in Bratislava to have any written material available in English. Open daily except Monday 10.00am to 5.00pm. Across the road from here is the **Handcraft Museum**, which is open 10.00am to 5.00pm, closed Tuesday. From here one can climb up the hill to **Bratislava Castle**. Various castles have existed on this site over the centuries. It was an important site for the Great Moravian Empire, when a castle built of clay and wood existed here. After the fall of the empire, Hungarian kings continued to fortify the site. In 1526 Hungary became part of the Habsburg empire, and the castle began to be used as the governor's residence and to protect the empire against the Turks and disgruntled Transylvanian princes. The castle was rebuilt several times during the Habsburg rule. Later reconstruction was to make it more a place to live in than a fortress. In 1802 the castle became soldiers' barracks, and in 1811 it was destroyed by fire. In 1954 reconstruction work began, and stretched over the next decade. Today the castle houses Slovak Government offices and a museum, which is open 9.00am to 4.00pm, while the castle grounds are open from 9.00am to 8.00pm from April 1 to September 30, and from 9.00am to 6.00pm during the rest of the year.

Dropping down from the castle the same way you came up, walk across the Danube over Most SNP. On the other side you can pay Kčs 3 to go up in the lift to the café **Bystrica**, with excellent views and high prices. If it is clear you should be able to see Austria and Hungary. There is only the *kaviareň* up there; there is no viewing deck as such (though there is a good view of Petržalka from the toilets!). Open May 1 to August 31 10.00am to 11.00pm; rest of year closes at 10.00pm; Mondays open from 1.00pm. Just past here on the upstream side of Viedenská cesta the closed border area began. Walking downstream from here brings you to a ferry back across the river – see the Getting Around section for operating schedule. If the ferry is not operating, continue to the old bridge.

On the town side of the river again are the water transport offices. From early April to late October there are cruises on the Danube hourly from 9.00am to 6.00pm every day. Opposite the harbour offices, on the corner of Vajanského nábrežie and Fajnorovo nábr. is Slovenske Národne Múzeum (the **Slovak National Museum**), open 9.00am to 5.00pm, closed Mondays. And so ends our tour.

Still within walking distance

The street Obrancov mieru has many old buildings and palaces along it. At no. 25 is Múzeum V. I. Lenin, open Tuesday to Friday 8.00am to 6.00pm, weekends 9.00am to 3.00pm, closed Mondays. On Tolstého ul., a side street to Obrancov mieru, the buildings have nice facades and statuary. On the hill above here is the impressive Slavín War Memorial, built in honour of the Soviet soldiers who lost their lives when they drove the Nazis out of Slovakia. It shows the dates different towns were liberated.

It is a nice walk out along Banskobystrická, with gardens and buildings including the Government Building of the Slovak Socialist Republic, but most of the grounds and buildings are closed to the public. This leads one to nám. Slobody on the right, not bad for a modern square. It has a fountain, memorial, grass and seats, and even toilets. On the other side of Banskobystrická is a smaller shadier park. In Sovietske nám. there is a column erected in 1732 in honour of St Florian to move him to protect the city from fires.

On the outskirts of Bratislava

Zlaté piesky is a lake with swimming and boating. The mosquitoes are not as bad here as in the rest of Bratislava. Entrance to the lake costs Kčs 3. In 1976 a plane crashed into the lake in summer and many people were killed. Kamzík: A peak (440m) in the Malé Karpaty mountains above Bratislava, with a television tower on top. One can drive to the top, walk from the main railway station by following the red markers (¾ hour), or take trolley bus no. 213 to the last stop and then walk (½ hour). The buses run late, and when they finish night bus 143 runs down from the same stop. There is no bus to the top. At the top there are restaurants open in the evening, and a *bufet* open daytime only. One of the restaurants is the sk.l Expo Koliba. In the television tower is a coffee bar which is supposed to revolve hourly. There are also ski tows.

Železná studnička: The valley behind Kamzík. There are four natural lakes, one of which you can hire boats on, but they are no good for swimming. There is a chairlift up to Kamzík which operates at weekends, or every day in winter if the snow is good. Železná studnička is also a starting point for hikes. Accessible by bus no. 33.

The Zoo: The zoo in Mlynská dolina has recently been moved a bit, as the access road to the new bridge took part of it.

Devín. The impressive ruins of Devín Castle sit upon a promontory overlooking the point where the river Morava enters the Danube. Take bus 29 from underneath Most SNP to the last stop and then follow the signs. The castle closes at 6.00pm, and is closed Monday. Until recently it was still a strategic point. The bus trip out follows the old "Iron Curtain", a high fence to stop people approaching the Danube and Austria. When I tried to visit the castle in 1985 I was stopped and taken away for questioning for a couple of hours. These days the border police are more relaxed, and crowds of tourists visit Devín. If you do travel along the Danube by boat between Bratislava and Vienna, you get a good view of Devín Castle.

Rusovce: The village of Rusovce lies south of Bratislava near the Austrian and Hungarian borders. Its attractions are a château, a Roman Museum, and an unofficial nudist swimming lake. The château was built in the English neo-Gothic style and is surrounded by an English style park. The building is now used by the Slovak Folk Ensemble and is closed to the public, but you are free to wander in the grounds. The small Roman Museum is open from May to September, 10.00am to 5.00pm, closed Mondays. Nude swimming is practised in a nearby lake formed in an old gravel pit. Rusovce is accessible by car or bus no. 116.

Outside Bratislava

The Danube: There were some nice spots downstream on the Danube, but work on the two huge dams that Czechoslovakia and Hungary began building has been very destructive. The old regimes ignored protests about the devastating ecological consequences. Hungary's economy found the cost too much to bear, so Austria came to the rescue with US$500 million in credits in exchange for the total estimated electricity output of one of the dams over a 20 year period. Then Hungary began having second thoughts, to the fury of the Czechoslovakia communist government. At the time of writing the fate of the project had not been decided. Hungary had stopped work completely, but Czechoslovakia felt they had gone too far to give up. The dam at Gabčikovo is almost ready to generate power, but only at half capacity because the Hungarians stopped work.

Malé Karpaty: The Little Carpathian Mountains stretch north from Bratislava, and are a popular destination for trampers at weekends. There are caves, Driny jaskyňa, open to the public near the top end of the hills. The cave is of tectonic origin and was not formed by underground water flow. Tours from 1/4 to 15/5 and 16/9 to 31/10 at 9.00am, 11.00am and 2.00pm. 16/5 to 15/9 hourly from 9.00am until the last tour at 4.00pm. Rest of year closed.

The area to the east of Bratislava is not very interesting, with lots of towns and industry.

Organised tours

BIPS arrange sightseeing tours in the summer using the trams. Otherwise they can organise tours if you book in advance.

The following three tours can be booked at Čedok and operate every Wednesday from May 15 to September 15, and in July and August on Saturday also. Pickup from some hotels and Čedok.

Sightseeing Tour of Bratislava: Afternoon tour, 3 hours, Kčs 60.

Malé Karpaty (Little Carpathians), evening tour, finishing with dinner at Zochova chalet with Gypsy music. Return to Bratislava about 10.00pm. Kčs 161.

Sightseeing Tour of Bratislava with Malé Karpaty. From early afternoon till about 10.00pm, Kčs 178, including dinner.

Events

Bratislava received city rights in 1291, so this will be celebrated in 1991, if you read this in time. A lot of reconstruction work has been underway in the old town in preparation.

The Bratislava lyre: International pop song festival held in May.

INCHEBA: This is an International chemical fair held in June every year. Hotels are all booked up six months in advance.

Kultúrne leto: (Cultural summer): Held every year in July and August. Galleries are open longer hours than normal, and there are concerts, theatre and many outdoor activities around the town.

Grape Harvest: The foothills of Malé Karpaty are covered with vines. The grapes are harvested in early autumn. Shortly afterwards, for a period of only about two to three weeks in early autumn, the delicious young wine *burčiak* is available in Bratislava.

Biennials of Illustrations Bratislava (BIB): This international exhibition of illustrations for children's books, with entries from all over the world, is held in September and October every odd numbered year (ie 1991, 1993, etc).

This is really worth seeing if you are in Bratislava at the right time. In the House of Culture, just down from nám. SNP towards Prior.

The Bratislava Music Festival: An international music festival lasting two weeks and starting about the end of September.

Sport

Sporting complexes are not normally open for the general public in Czechoslovakia, but they can be hired by groups. Here are some exceptions which are open to the public some of the time:

Swimming

Outdoor swimming pools are open from June to mid September, or they sometimes open in May if the weather is good. On Vajnorská ulica there is a heated indoor swimming pool. At 50m it is the largest in Bratislava. Open 7.30am to 10.00pm, closed Mondays. In daytime available for schools only, and sometimes open only for professionals. Can hire bathing clothes. Centrál on Miletičova near nám. Fr. Zupka has swimming, sauna and massage and is open 6.00am to 10.00pm.

Ice skating

There are two ice skating stadiums next door to each other on Trnavská cesta. Sometimes closed for training. Another stadium on Bajkalská ulica.

Tennis

One can play tennis and hire rackets at Zlaté piesky.

Boating

Rowing boats, windsurfers and water bicycles can be hired at Zlaté piesky.

It is possible, but only for experienced sportsmen, to borrow canoes, seven man dinghies or kayaks from T J Vinohrady at Nabr. L. Svobodu 17, 841 01 Bratislava (tel. 329661). The boats may be used on the small branch of the Danube by the club-house. The Danube itself is dangerous because of its swift flow and barge traffic. The club is open all year round. Boats may only be taken away to other areas if arranged beforehand. Groups wanting to use boats must ask in advance, in which case the club's committee must decide whether or not to lend the boats.

Every year TID, an international Danube trip from West Germany to Bulgaria is held. See the general section on Water Sports for details.

Eating and evenings

There are eateries everywhere in the centre. The many wine cellars evoke memories of Vienna, but they are maybe classier in Bratislava. They usually close at midnight. *Vináreň* with Gypsy music are a Bratislava trademark. In the summer there are a lot of places to take a drink outdoors.

Vináreň, sk.III, downstairs in **Kamzík**, nám SNP. Nice. Open midday to midnight. Closed Monday. Cover charge after 5.30pm. On street level in the same building is a large stand up place with many counters with different food. Sk.III. Open Monday to Friday 6.30am to 8.30pm; Saturday till 2.00pm.

Buchlovice Chateau

Malá Fatra, Vrátna dolina

Chapel of Calvary, Banská Štiavnica   (Photo by John Skelton)

There is a **burger bar**(!) in the ground floor of Hotel Palace in Poštova, with entrance from the street.

There is a collection of various types of eateries opposite Štatna banka čs on Štúrova.

For those on special diets there is a special dining room (**Diétna jedáleň**) catering for you, open lunchtimes Monday to Saturday. The problem is I can't remember exactly where it is! But it is number 8 on either Leningradská, Gorkého or Jesenského, three parallel streets.

Vináreň pod Baštou (Under the Bastion), Bastova ulica, is signposted from inside Michael's Gate. Quite nice wine cellar, but non-smokers might find the air a bit thick. Open Monday to Saturday 11.00am to midnight. Cover charge from 6.30pm to 11.00pm. Sk.II.

There are various evening hangouts on Zámočnícka ulice.

Cukráreň next to Čedok for those with sweet tooth. Jukebox. Monday to Sat. 8.00am to 8.00pm, Sunday 10.00am to 6.00pm. **Umelecká Záhrada** (Garden of Artists) is what the beer garden on the east side of the old bridge and the town side of the Danube is known as.

There is a *kaviareň* in the tower of Most SNP (see Walking tour section above). **Kaviareň Danubius**, sk.II, on the first floor in the harbour building, with a balcony over the Danube.

On **Mount Kamzík** there is a revolving *kaviareň* in the TV tower; **Koliba**, a nice sk.I restaurant; and another restaurant where it is possible to sit outdoors.

Stará Sladovňa (the Old Malt House), seating 1500 people, is the second biggest restaurant in Europe. Find it at Cintoriska 32. From 1872 to 1976 this was a malt-house, where malt barley used to ripen in dark malt rooms. Now it has become a large capacity restaurant complex, so large that the locals have dubbed it "The Mammoth". A beer restaurant, while most others in Bratislava are wine restaurants. Nice place, despite its size. Various restaurants and beer garden. Sk.II + 10%. Cover charge sometimes. Traditional jazz on Thursday evening.

Smíchovský dvor on the corner of Heydukova and Markušova is a quite okay restaurant (sk.II + 10%). Open 9.30am to 10.00pm daily except Sunday, there is an upstairs too if it looks full. **Veľký Františkáni** is a *vináreň* at 10 Dibrovo nám., sk.I, foreigners and young people, often speak English.

Čarda Kormorán is a Hungarian restaurant with Hungarian Gypsy music, sk.II + 10%, open 11.00am to 11.00pm. A very nice restaurant in the recreation area Kormorán by the lake Veľký Draždiak in Petržalka. The mosquitoes like it too.

Other evening hangouts: Kyjev Klub in Kjev Hotel, sk.I open till 3.00am; Kláštorná vináreň, 1 Pugačevova; there are not many discos, Hotel Carlton has one from 9.00pm to 3.00am. Mierové nám. is an evening meeting place of the young.

There is an indoor market (and a supermarket in the basement) at nám. Fr. Zupka on Malinovského, open Tuesday to Friday 5.30am to 6.00pm and Saturday 5.30am to 2.00pm. On Duajská is a smaller market and the open markets (*centrálne trhovisko*) are on Miletičova.

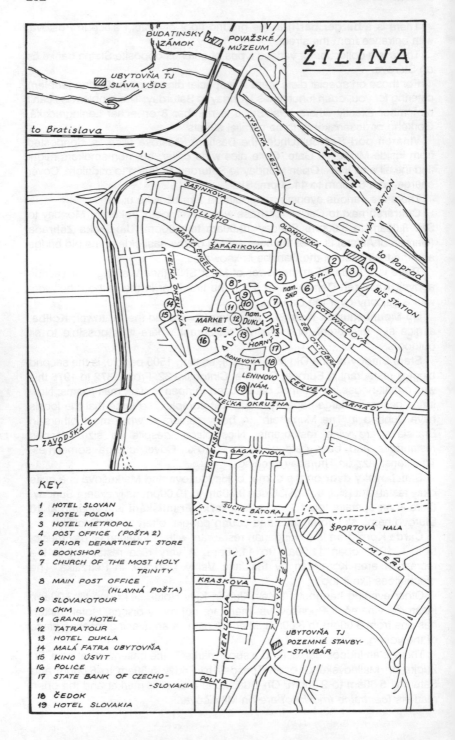

ŽILINA

KEY

1 HOTEL SLOVAN
2 HOTEL POLOM
3 HOTEL METROPOL
4 POST OFFICE (POŠTA 2)
5 PRIOR DEPARTMENT STORE
6 BOOKSHOP
7 CHURCH OF THE MOST HOLY
                    TRINITY
8 MAIN POST OFFICE
                (HLAVNÁ POŠTA)
9 SLOVAKOTOUR
10 CKM
11 GRAND HOTEL
12 TATRATOUR
13 HOTEL DUKLA
14 MALÁ FATRA UBYTOVŇA
15 KINO ÚSVIT
16 POLICE
17 STATE BANK OF CZECHO-
                    -SLOVAKIA
18 ČEDOK
19 HOTEL SLOVAKIA

BRATISLAVA TO ŽILINA

Except for the first part of the journey, both the railway and the E75 (highway 61) from Bratislava to Žilina follow the valley of the river Váh. There are lots of legends associated with the castles of the valley.

Senec

25km by road out of Bratislava is Senec, with a lake with swimming and water sports. (The Bratislava-Žilina railway does not pass through Senec.)

Piešťany

Piešťany is a popular tourist resort and Slovakia's most famous spa. The springs here were known to the Romans. There is kayaking in the river, and boating on the dam lake Sľňava. Marked paths run from the spa itself. Guidebook in German. Bus or train from Bratislava. Air service from Prague. Bus service from Vienna. Camping and chalets on Sľňava open May to September. Hotels from cheap to luxury.

Čachtice

Lying near the town of Nové Mesto nad Váhom, Čachtice is a little off the main road and railway. The ruins of Čachtice Castle are accessible from here. In the 13th Century this castle was an important strong-point on the Hungarian border. At the turn of the 16th-17th Centuries there lived here "the cruel lady of Čachtice", the Hungarian Alžbeta Nádasdy-Báthory, who tortured and murdered no fewer than 651 peasant girls to bathe in their warm blood, believing this would bring her eternal youth. It was said to have started when her maid was clumsy with her hairbrush. Báthory hit her in the face and blood spurted out. A lesbian, Báthory was the source of inspiration for the vampire idea. In Victorian times allusion to vampires was the only way one could talk about some sides of female sexuality.

The castle has been uninhabited since a fire of 1708. There is interesting limestone country with caves and springs, and the area around the castle is a nature reserve with some rare species of lime-tolerating plants.

Biele Karpaty (White Carpathians)

See the section on Bilé Karpaty, under Southern Moravia.

Beckov

Beckov is also near Nové Mesto nad Váhom, but on the opposite side of the river Váh. The ruins of Beckov Castle lie on chalky rocks. The first fortified castle replaced an earlier building here in 1208. It is said that before the castle was built a nobleman and his wife lived in a mansion near the site. After the woman gave birth to twins, she decided to employ a wet nurse. But she couldn't find anyone she wanted, until a giantess appeared at the gate. The giantess was very good with the children, and there were no problems until the woman felt that the children were becoming too close to the giantess. She persuaded her husband to sack her. But the nobleman had dreams of a castle. The giantess wagered that if she could build a castle within a year, she could keep the children. The nobleman laughingly agreed. Every night more of the castle appeared, until, before the year was up, it was finished and the giantess claimed the children. The nobleman said he would give her all the money he had and the servants too, instead. But on returning to the house, he found the giantess and children were gone. Before the year was up, the noblewoman poisoned her husband in revenge for the grief he had caused her.

The best known owner was "the lord of the Váh valley and the Tatras", Matúš Čák, who rebuilt the castle in the 14th Century.

It is said that Beckov was given to the Fool. But the owner threw the Fool from the castle. As the Fool fell he said: "to the year, to the day". Exactly a year later the owner went crazy and jumped from the castle.

The castle was destroyed in 1729, and never rebuilt. The ruins of the Renaissance palace, chapel and parts of the fortifications are all that survive, apart from the good view.

In the village of Beckov are a former monastery and 14th Century Gothic church. Walking in the Považský Inovec Hills. Chalets and *ubytovací hostinec*.

Trenčín

The town of Trenčín is overlooked by its castle, which originated as an 11th Century fortress. This castle was also owned by Matúš Čáks, who had a residential palace built in it. In the 16th Century it played an important defensive role against the Turks. The castle had no water, and a legend associated with this concerns the period when the Turks were here. The castle owner got rather attached to the Turk Fatimah, whom he had imprisoned. The owner was told that he would have to dig a well to get her back. A look at the position of the castle, high on a rock, shows how difficult a demand this was to meet. The castle was severely damaged by fire in 1790. Reconstruction began in 1954.

Today a town of 48,000 inhabitants, Trenčín was at one time on the border of the Roman Empire. The rock on which the castle stands bears one of the oldest Roman inscriptions in Czechoslovakia (from 179 A.D.), recording the victory of the Second Roman Legion over the Quadi. In the town are remains of its fortifications and several Gothic and Baroque buildings. Walking in the Bielé Karpaty. Hotels, hostels, camping.

Trenčianske Teplice

One of Slovakia's better known spas, Trenčianske Teplice is situated in a valley surrounded by forest covered hills, a little way off the main Váh valley. On the southern outskirts of the town is an area known as Zelená žaba (the Green Frog), with a natural warm water pool.

By train change to the narrow gauge electric railway at Trenčianska Teplá. Buses from Vienna and Bratislava. By road, 5km off the E75, turn off at Trenčianska Teplá. Two category C hotels, and one B*.

Bratislava (Photo by John Skelton)

MOUNTAIN REGIONS
of SLOVAKIA

Mountain regions of Slovakia

MALÁ FATRA AND ŽILINA

Malá Fatra (the Little Fatras) are a mountain range in Central Slovakia. They encompass Vrátna dolina, said to be the most beautiful valley in Slovakia. The entrance to the valley from Terchová passes between spectacular rocky crags. Malá Fatra cover a small area, so the views tend to be out over villages farms and towns. But a lot of variety is to be found in this area. Some of the tops are open and flattish; others steep and craggy. Lower down one can find anything from pleasant forest to precipitous little ravines. It's an excellent tramping area. The main town in the area is Žilina.

Malá Fatra are very popular with German tourists, but the further you get away from Vrátna dolina the more peace and quiet you are likely to be able to find, and the more likely you are to meet the native Slovaks. '

Terchová is the birthplace of the Slovak folk hero, Juro Jánošík, the local Robin Hood. Jánošík studied to be a priest. When he came home, he found that his father had been beaten by a rich man, so he became a highwayman, taking only from the rich, and giving to the poor. He was eventually captured and hung by his ribs. He refused to say where his hiding places were, and Slovaks believe his treasures are still to be found.

To and from Žilina

Žilina is a main north-south east-west crossroads. The most convenient public transport is train. Žilina is a major railway station. There are regular *rýchlik* trains to Bratislava except between about 7.15pm and 2.00am when there are no trains at all. Travel time about 3¼ hours. Buses are faster. There is a good train service on to Poprad and Košice. From Prague by train takes about 8 hours. There are buses to Ostrava. For Orava and Roháče take the Dolný Kubín, Námestovo or Trstená bus from platform 3. To Banská Bystrica one can go by bus or train, but the bus is quicker.

Getting around

To Vrátna in Malá Fatra there are buses from platform 9 or 10 at Žilina bus station roughly hourly from 6.00am to about 6.00pm. Hitchhiking is reasonable. The bus station is close to the railway station. To Rajecké Teplice by bus or train, but bus is faster. There is a local bus service around Žilina, but it is possible to walk around the central part of the town.

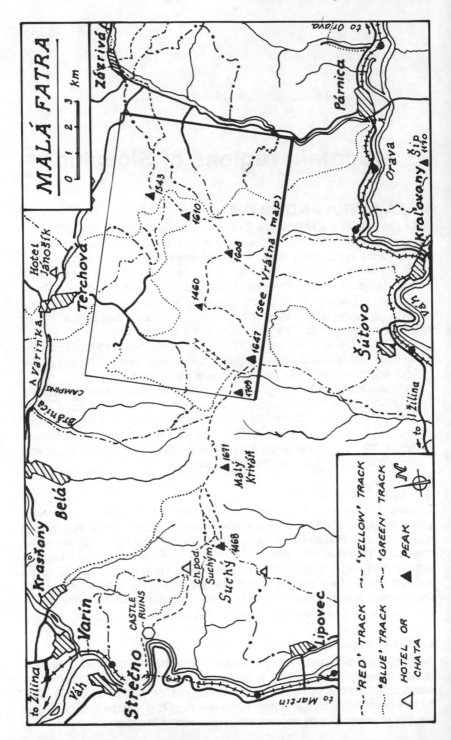

MALÁ FATRA

0 1 2 3 km

to Orava

Zázrivá

Párnica

Orava

Šíp
1170

Kraľovany

Hotel
Jánošík

Terchová

1343

1610

1608

1460

(see 'Vrátna' map)

1647

1709

Šútovo

Váh

Varínka

CAMPING

Brtnica

to Žilina

Belá

Malý
Kriváň
1671

Krasňany

ch.pod
Suchým

Suchý
1468

Lipovec

Varín

CASTLE
RUINS

Strečno

Váh

to Žilina

to Martin

'RED' TRACK ·-· 'YELLOW' TRACK

'BLUE' TRACK ···· 'GREEN' TRACK

△ HOTEL OR   ▲ PEAK
   CHATA

N

Maps and guides

Žilina can be a bit confusing to find one's way around, but it isn't so bad if you stick to the station and central areas. A street map of Žilina is available sometimes. The map *Malá Fatra*, number 11 in the *Letná turistická mapa* series, covers Žilina and the whole Malá Fatra. Another map, *Malá Fatra Vrátna*, number 12 in the same series, doesn't extend as far as Žilina, but covers the area I describe under tramping in much more detail than the first map. A map of *Javorníky Kysuce* (Kčs 7) covers area to the west of Žilina and is occasionally available. The bookshop on the corner of ulica SNP and nám. SNP has a better selection of maps than normal. There is a book on Malá Fatra available in Slovak and German only (*Malá Fatra*, Josef Gargulák – Vladimír Križo, Šport).

Accommodation

Žilina

Hostels

The cheapest place to stay is **T J Slovan Malá Fatra ubytovňa**, ul. Veľká okružná 26, 010 01 Žilina; tel. 206 92. TU B (12 bed dorm), TU A (5 bed dorm) and Hotel C (doubles). Check in from 2.00pm to 8.00pm. It's just a place to crash — nothing there, but it has the basics one needs. Often full, especially at weekends.

Better than the above, but outside the centre, is the new **Ubytovna TJ Pozemné stavby — Stavbár**, Tajovkého 5, tel. 456 10. It is owned by a volleyball club, and is next to a summer cinema. Take bus 3 from the railway station.

In the summer there is accommodation in student hostels (*internát*) of the school VŠDS. The old hostels are on Wolkrova, while the new are off cesta Mieru.

Ubytovna TJ Slavia VŠDS (tel. 217 24) is accommodation owned by the school's sports club available in summer. Nice and quiet on the Váh river, but no public transport, unless you walk from the bus from Považský Chlmec.

Motel

Motel Šibenice is a new motel about 5km towards Strečno from Zilina. The restaurant is open 8.00am to 10.00pm, while the *bufet* is open all night.

Hotels

All the following hotels have post code 010 01.

Hotel Slovakia, B*, nám. V. I. Lenina, tel. 46572-3, telex 75606, is the best and largest hotel. Horizont-Club on the 7th floor with a view. Swimming pool & sauna in basement.

Hotel Polom, B*, Volgogradské nám. tel. 211 51, 211 52, is just across the road from the railway station. All rooms have shower and toilet. Singles Kčs 202, doubles Kčs 302. Gets more booked up during the week than at weekends. Exchange office. Accepts credit cards.

Hotel Metropol, B, is also opposite the station. Kčs 152 double without bath,

Kčs 27 per person to use the shower. But I don't recommend it for its noise if nothing else.
Grand Hotel, B, Sládkovičova ulice 1, (by nám. Dukla, the Town Square); tel. 210 56. Sk.II restaurant and *kaviareň*.
Hotel Slovan, B, Šafárikova ul. 16, (behind Prior).
Hotel Dukla, C, Dimitrovova ul. 3; tel. 202 34.

Rajecké Teplice
Velká Fatra is a newly renovated hotel. Restaurant open 10.00am to 10.00pm.
Private accommodation here can be booked through the local tourist office (CIK).

Súľovské skaly
Chata Súľov (*Turistická ubytovňa* A) has about 80 beds. Post code 646 70. Tel. Bytča 84 14.

Rajec
There is a new hostel in Rajec with beds for 80 people. In the summer there are open swimming pools here.

Camping
There is no camping in Žilina. **Autokemping Stop**, 013 24 Strečno; tel. Žilina 925 84, has camping and cabins, but only a little space for tents. Open all year. Footbridge access from Strečno to Malá Fatra.
ATC Varín is a motor camp with bungalows at Varín by the bridge on the Žilina-Terchová road. Open all year. Book at Slovakotour, Žilina. Also walking access into Malá Fatra from here.
There is a campsite near Branica also on the road from Žilina to Vrátna, between Belá and Terchová. Not all buses stop here. First bus stop after Branica is the closest to reception. Only facilities are pit toilets and drinking water taps. Strung out along the road, between the road and the river. Noise from road, but not too much traffic. Open 15 June to 15 September.
There is a Čedok camp in Vrátna dolina itself. **Autokemping Vrátna**, 013 26 Terchová; tel. Žilina 952 20. Open 15 May to 30 September. Also bungalows.
There is camping on the road between Žilina and Rajecké Teplice about 10-12km from Žilina. A nice spot, it is open only in summer, though you could camp there all year.
Note that Verejné táborisko Staryhrad near Nezbudská Lúčka and the campsite at the bottom of Dolné diery have been closed down.

Mountain hotels and chalets
Hotel Jánošík in Terchová is named after the hero of the legend. C grade. Tel. Žilina 951 85. Address 016 06 Terchová.
Hotel Diery, B, is 5km by bus from Terchova at Biely Potok.
Hotel Boboty, B*, 013 06 Terchová-Vrátna; tel. Žilina 952 27 is on a turning off the road to Štefanová. Sauna. Singles US$23, doubles US$38.

Chata pod Sokolím, hotel C & TU A, 013 06 Terchová-Vrátna; tel. Žilina 953 26. Cold water only. Central heating. Access for cars, or 5 minutes walk from the bus. Also restaurant nearby and bungalows.
Ch. na Grúni is small and can sleep about 20.
Chata Vrátna, Hotel B & TU A, 013 06 Terchová-Vrátna; tel. Žilina 952 23, is at the top of Vrátna dolina. Singles Kčs 125, doubles Kčs 187-234, no bath. Use of shower Kčs 32! Posh sk.II restaurant. TU and cheaper eatery underneath. Closed October-November.
Chata pod Suchým, 013 13 Varín, no telephone, is accessible by foot only: about 2½ hours from Varín or Strečno. Closed April and November, rest of year open. Nice. Friendly people. 1075m. Dorm Kčs 46, double Kčs 144. There is bedding. Sk.III eatery with nice wooden tables and chairs, decorated with deer antlers.
   Note that chata pod Chlebom and chata pod Rozcutcom have both burnt down.
   Private accommodation in Vrátna can be booked through Slovakotour in Terchova.

Information
Many shops in Žilina are closed at lunchtime.
   The main post office holds mail for only two weeks. Pošta 2 is by the station.
   Čedok are at Leninovo nám., phone 485 11 for accommodation enquiries. Open Monday to Friday 9.00am to 6.00pm, Sat. 9.00am to 12. CKM are at nám. Dukla 10; tel. 235 21.
   There is a new information and accommodation booking office for tourists at Hodzova 5 (post address: CIK Slovakotour Zilina, 010 28 Zilina). Also open weekends during winter and summer seasons. They can book for the whole area, but only cheaper accommodation; for hotels use Čedok.
   Information in Rajecké Teplice can be had from the Cestovná informačná kancelária (CIK).
   Left luggage at the railway station, usually only if it weighs less than 15kg (depends on who is working there at the time).

Eating
See also *Accommodation.*

Žilina
There are a lot of possibilities around the railway station and nám. Dukla areas.
   The restaurant in Žilina railway station (sk.II) is open till 10.00pm. A stand-up *bufet* is open all the time, except from 7.00am to 8.00am and from 7.00pm to 8.00pm. Hot food, salad, drinks, etc. No alcohol served in the evening.
   Ponorka, Zápotockého ul. 29, near the bus station is a pleasant enough little grill and drink bar, but lots of smokers, as one can smoke anytime, unlike most catering establishments in Czechoslovakia. Next door at no. 31 is a *piváreň.*

There are restaurants in all the hotels open till about 10.00pm, the best and most expensive one being in Hotel Slovakia.

Evenings
Žilina has two cinemas and one summer cinema showing films outdoors from May to the end of August every two or three days, daily in July and August. Otherwise try the hotels, or Restaurant Junior, which is outside the centre. Grand Hotel has a night bar, entrance Kčs 20. There are also night bars in Hotel Metropol and Hotel Slovakia. After the restaurants close, night bars take over until about 3.00am or 4.00am.

Events
There is a folk festival in Terchová called Janošíkove Dni (Janošík Days), usually held at the end of August, but it may be held a different time. It is not touristic, but involves the local community. Get someone to translate the bawdy lyrics.

What to see
Žilina
Between nám. SNP and nám. Dukla (often called just námestie) is the Farský Kostel, the **Parish Church of the Most Holy Trinity**. Its history can be read in English. On the square nám. **Dukla** is the Catholic church, and beside it an **art gallery** open daily except Monday.

In the suburb of Závodie (take bus no. 21 or 30) is the church of **St Stephen** (Sv. Štefan), with fresco decoration that was uncovered in the 1950s and restored. The oldest part of the church (the round part with the frescoes inside) dates from the 11th to 12th Century when Christianity was first introduced to Slovakia, which was then a part of the Great Moravian Empire. The frescoes in front of the altar are the oldest ones dating from the 11th Century, while those behind the altar are of Hungarian kings and are from the 14th to 15th Centuries. Under the sanctuary is a 200 year old tomb, but it was robbed during World War One. The churchyard wall was built as defence against Turkish invasion, with the local population taking refuge here. Archaeological research will continue until about 1992-3, after which there will be a notice at the gate, which is normally locked, with the address of the person with the key. Until that time you'll have to ask around to find out who can let you in.

In the suburb of **Budatín**, at the confluence of the Kysuca and Váh rivers, is a chateau dating from the 14th Century. It guarded the road leading from Hungary to Silesia near a ford where a toll was levied. Partly ruined by fire in the mid-19th Century, it was reconstructed in its present form in 1920-22. It now serves as a regional museum of the Váh region.

Terchová
The main sight is the entrance to Vrátna dolina, with its spectacular rocky crags, but you could also visit the Jánošík Museum. There is some traditional terrace farming around Terchova, for example on the road towards Dolný Kubín or in Šípková where the farming was never collectivised.

Vrátna
From Chata Vrátna, at the top of the road up Vrátna dolina, a chairlift takes you to within easy walking distance of the peaks Chleb (1647m) and Veľký Kriváň (1709m). Expect queues. Open all year except October-November.

Strečno
The ruins of Strečno Castle stand high atop a steep craggy peak at the entrance to the Strečno Gorge. Founded in 1321, it held an important position on the trade route leading through the Váh Valley. Often in the hands of anti-royalists, the castle was destroyed in 1678. Today a major reconstruction project is underway, so the castle is covered with scaffolding and only partly open. The idea is to maintain the skyline as it is, but to build a museum inside, showing the castle's development, and especially to house an exhibition of the Slovak National Uprising.

Near Strečno is a monument to French partisans who fought here in World War Two.

Bytča
In Bytča is a Renaissance manor house (1571-74).

Súľovské Skaly
Southwest of Žilina is Súľovské Skaly, a nature reserve of beautiful rock outcrops, including the ruins of various castles, such as the medieval Súľov Castle. Access via Bytča.

Tramping
Tracks are well marked.

From chata Vrátna (750m):
• To top of chairlift (green markers): 1¾ hours
• Chata na Grúni (yellow). 45 minutes. Food available here.
• Chata pod Chlebom (burnt down, green): 2¼ hours.
• Šutovo railway station (green): 4¾ hours.
• Poludňový Grúň, 1460m. (yellow): 2 hours.

But most people come to Vrátna to ride up in the chairlift. At the top it can be very cold compared to Vrátna. There is a sk.IV *bufet* at very inflated prices. From here it is a 5 minute walk to the Snilovské saddle on the main ridge or a 3 hour walk on the blue marked track along a side ridge finishing up at Starý Dvor bus stop in Vrátna dolina.

The ridge track at Snilovské sedlo is part of *Mezinárodna Horská Cesta Priateľstva* from Eisenach to Budapest, but this route is more symbolic than anything else, and not many people seem to have heard of it. From Snilovské sedlo (1520m) it is 25 minutes to the top of Chleb or 35 minutes to the top of Veľký Kriváň. Other walking times along the main ridge: to the left: Medziholie 3¾ hours, Zázrivá 7¾ hours; to the right: Suchy 3½ hours, Strečno railway station 6½ hours.

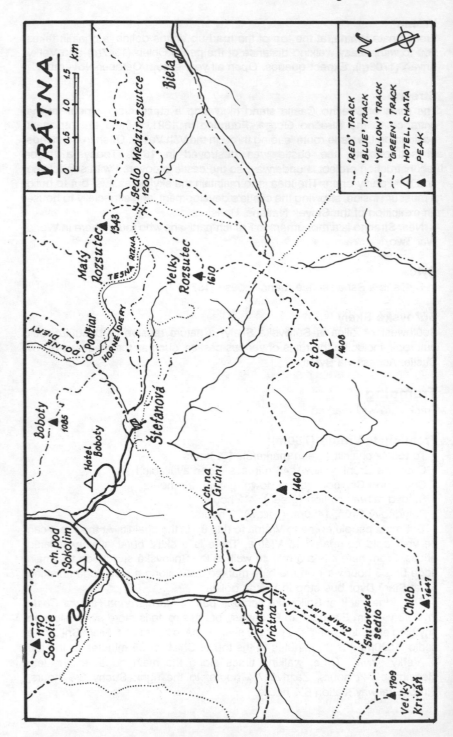

VRÁTNA

0   0,5   1,0   1,5   km

'RED' TRACK
'BLUE' TRACK
'YELLOW' TRACK
'GREEN' TRACK
HOTEL, CHATA
PEAK

Biela

Sedlo Medzirozsutce
1200

Malý Rozsutec
1343

TESNÁ RIZNA

Velký Rozsutec
1610

Podžiar

HORNÉ DIERY

DOLNÉ DIERY

Boboty
1085

Hotel Boboty

Štefanová

Stoh
1408

ch.na Grúni

1460

ch.pod Sokolím

1170 Sokolie

Chata Vrátna

CHLADNÝ LIST

Snilovské sedlo

Chleb
1647

Velký Krivaň
1709

Snilovské sedlo to Strečno (and adjoining tracks)

This is a nice walk, beginning on an open rounded ridge, then becoming more craggy until it drops into the forest after Suchý. The descent passes interesting castle ruins.

Taking the track to the right from Snilovské sedlo brings one to Bublen (1605m) after 1¼ hours. From here it is 5¼ hours on to Strečno, or 2¾ hours down the green track to Branica, by the campsite. (Uphill this track takes 3¼ hours.) About 15 minutes on the Strečno side of Bublen there are some small springs, which you may be able to drink out of if there is enough water and not too many people churning them up. Continuing on the red marked track towards Strečno, the next peak you cross is Priehyb (1462m). From here one can cut out to Krašnany on the blue track (2 hours to the bus stop), and it is now 2¼ hours back to the chairlift. The next fork brings a choice of following the red track over Suchý (1468m), or cutting under it on the yellow track. The first choice takes 1 hour 5 minutes to where the tracks meet again, the second 25 minutes. The route now begins to descend to chata pod Suchým, the last 5 minutes steeply. The chalet is a welcome little retreat (see *Accommodation*).

From chata pod Suchým it is 2¼ hours down the green marked track to Varín, or 2 hours on the red marked track to Strečno. By now you are in a more friendly area, with fewer tourists and more local people. The red marked track follows a ridge a little way from the chalet, then drops steeply down, past a crucifix where you'll probably see fresh as well as plastic flowers, to Starý Hrad. This castle was built in the 13th Century to guard a ford over the river Váh. Its ruins are a fantastic sight, high above the river and surrounded by trees. From the castle it is only 50 minutes to Strečno railway station. Five minutes after the castle the track hits a roadway. There are nice picnic spots on the way down. Down in the main valley the track leaves the roadway again, and cuts across above the railway. From the station there are trains back to Žilina stopping at Varín on the way — check the train timetable before you set out. Otherwise the main road is just across the footbridge in Strečno.

Štefanová–Veľký Rozsutec–Horné diery–Dolné diery

This is a really good trip, taking about 7 hours. You can drive to Šefanová (625m), hitchhike or catch the Vrátna bus. Follow the green marked track from Štefanová to Medziholie (1½ hours). This part is a real "highway", a wide track with lots of people. Steep as far as Šlahorka, then not so steep. Nice scenery. From Medziholie (1185m) the red track to the right leads to the top of Stoh after 1¼ hours. Our route is the red track to the left, a STEEP, popular, but satisfying climb to the top of Veľký Rozsutec (1610m), from where there is a good view (1¼ hour, 1 hour if you are very fast). Veľký Rozsutec is a craggy peak, unlike most Malá Fatra peaks which are rounded. The descent to Medzirozsutce saddle (1200m) takes just under an hour. There is a water source just below the saddle. Other walking times from here: Malý Rozsutec, green, 25 minutes; Zázrivá, red, 2 hours; back to Medziholie on the blue track behind Veľký Rozsutec, 1 hour.

Our route leads down Tesná rizna and Horné diery to Podžiar (1½ hours, blue). Horné diery is beautiful, like the valleys in Slovenský Raj. Now you are in the part of Malá Fatra where Jánošík is thought to have hidden his booty.

Podžiar is an open grassy area 715 metres above sea level. From here our route leads down Dolné diery and out to the road at Biely Potok in 40 minutes, but it is possible to cut back to Štefanová from Podžiar in 25 minutes. Another alternative is to walk down Dolné diery to the bottom of Nové diery (25 minutes), then follow the yellow marked track up Nové diery and back to Podžiar (35 minutes) before returning to Štefanová. From the bottom of Dolné diery at Biely Potok it is a 20 minute walk to Hotel Jánošík, or 30 minutes to Terchová.

You might prefer to walk this trip in the opposite direction. In some ways it is nicer walking up the little ravines, but if you walk in this direction it is a very steep downhill drop off Veľký Rozsutec. Times in this direction: Biely Potok–Podžiar 40 minutes; Podžiar–Medzirozsutce 1¾ hours; Medzirozsutce–Veľký Rozsutec 1¾ hours; Veľký Rozsutec–Medziholie 1 hour; Medziholie–Štefanová 1¼ hours.

Súľovské skaly
You can walk from Žilina to Súľovské skaly on an easy route via the ruined castle Lietavský hrad. Or if you want a shorter walk, there is a bus to Lietava. From Lietavský hrad there is also a green marked route south to Rajecké Teplice, so you could return this way and bathe in the thermal pool after an exhausting day.

From Súľovské skaly there is a green marked route south to Rajec.

Skiing
There are ski lifts and tows in Vrátna dolina for downhill skiing, eg by the camping ground. The area around Ch. na Grúni has good skiing, also for beginners. The chairlift from Vrátna to Snilovské sedlo leads one to another downhill skiing area. Cross country ski tracks are also marked from here. In ideal weather and snow conditions it is possible to ski from the top of the chairlift via the peaks along the main ridge to Medziholie in about 4 hours.

Thermal swimming
There are thermal swimming pools at Rajecké Teplice, about ½ an hour south of Žilina by bus.

ČIČMANY
Čičmany is a quiet little mountain village south of Žilina where beautifully decorated wooden houses are still preserved in the lower part of the town. Some of the best houses burnt down in 1923, but they were later restored by the Institute of Ethnography. There is a museum, but it is not always open. Čičmany is quite high up, and can be cool even in summer.

Buses to Čičmany leave from Žilina bus station from platform 17, but there are not very many, and the timetable differs on different days of the week, so check the timetable carefully. Access from other directions is difficult without your own transport.

High Tatras (Vysoké Tatry)

Suchá Belá, Slovenský Raj (Photo by S. Hayman)

Two faces of Slovakia (Photo by John Skelton)

Accommodation

Hotel (B) and dormitory accommodation at **Kaštieľ** (tel. Rajec 9297). Double with shower Kčs 195, without shower Kčs 156. Single without shower Kčs 104. Dormitory bed Kčs 39 to Kčs 47. Use of shower Kčs 21. Restaurant and bar. Private accommodation is also available.

Tramping

Čičmany is on the *Strážovské vrchy* map, or on the edge of the *old* Malá Fatra map (pre 1988). From Čičmany it is 5 hours to Fačkovské sedlo, 3¼ hours to Tužina or 3 hours to Pružina. There are buses from all three, but best check the timetable first.

From the village of Fačkov, below Čičmany on the road to Žilina, you can climb Kľak by following the blue marked track to the southeast (2¾ hours one way).

Following the blue markers to the northwest from Fačkov takes you through forest, a lot of which is being milled, to Domaniža, which has some nice old wooden houses in its centre. The walk doesn't have anything particular to recommend it. Keep an eye out for markers, which can be hard to find in places. From Domaniža there are buses to Rajec and Pov. Bystrica, both of which have public transport connections with Žilina.

Skiing

There are four ski lifts in Čičmany. The runs are not long nor are the mountains very high, but there are good conditions and the ski field is not as frequented as Vrátna.

VEĽKÁ FATRA

The Veľká Fatra mountains lie to the southeast of Malá Fatra, between Malá Fatra and Nízke Tatry, and offer pleasant ridge and valley walks. There are not so many tourists here. The highest point is the relatively inconspicuous Ostredok (1592m). Bears still live here.

Useful bases for Veľká Fatra with accommodation are Martin, Ružomberok (on the main Žilina – Poprad rail and road route), Donovaly (see Nízke Tatry) and Banská Bystrica (see Banská Bystrica). Try and buy the map *Veľká Fatra* if you are interested in tramping in this area.

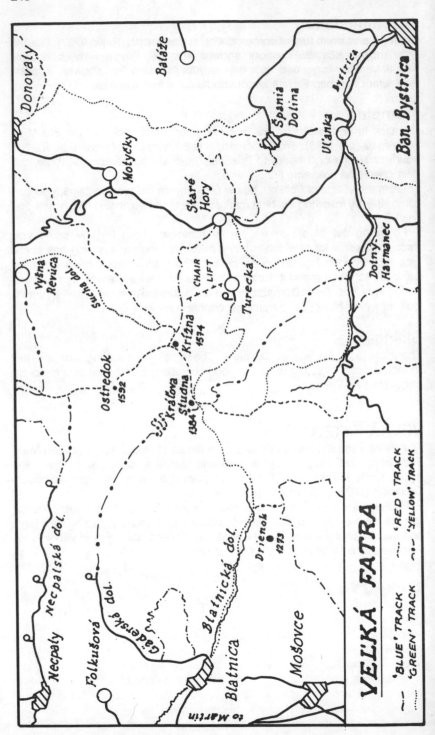

Tramping in the southern Veľká Fatra

There is a chair lift from Turecká (657m) to the top of the ridge to the north (1387m) operating at intervals from 8.00am to 4.00pm every day from June to September, but weekends only in May and October. Dress in warm clothes. For information phone (088) 992 73 or 992 78. There are only a few buses to Turecká. The bus leaving at about 8.20am from Banská Bystrica bus station (it stops also in nám. 1. majá) gets you to the chair lift in time for the 9.00am departure. Ask the driver to stop at the *lanovka* in Turecká. If there is no bus to Turecká, take one to Staré Hory, from where it is a 40 minute walk up a picturesque valley to the chair lift. Or forget the lift, and take the blue marked track out of Staré Hory up over Majerova skala to the top of the lift.

From the top of the chair lift it is a 1¾ hour walk down to Staré Hory. Turning instead to the left it is a 45 minute walk along a rounded ridge to Krížna (1574m). Though the walk is easy, take warm clothes as it is very exposed to the weather. From Krížna you could follow the red marked track to the right out to Donovaly (6½ hours), or only as far as Veľký Šturec (3¼ hours). Heading north instead (red markers also) it is 1½ hours walk to Ostredok, 3¼ to Plaská (1535m) or 3¾ to the chata Borišov.

Heading instead west from Krížna the red markers follow the ridge down to the springs at Kráľova Studňa (1 hour). 15 minutes further is the mountain hotel Kraľová Studňa, (category C & TU-A, tel. 258 80). Other walking times from the springs are: Malý Šturec, on the main Martin-Banská Bystrica road, 3 hours, red; Blatnice via Blatnická dolina 3½ hours, green; and Blatnica via Gaderská dolina 4½ hours, yellow.

Taking the last named route, the steep descent to Gaderská dolina takes 1 hour and is slippery when wet. The walk down the valley is on a road. There is a bus up the lower part of it twice a day on weekends only in late July and August only. It is supposed to be a beautiful walk, but it rained so hard as I walked down, that I couldn't see anything.

From Blatnica there is a local bus to Martin. To get to Banská Bystrica from here by public transport you must travel via Martin, even though this requires doubling back, because the express buses from Martin to Banská Bystrica don't stop anywhere before Turč. Teplice.

Using Blatnica as a base, you could do the following round trip: Blatnica dolina — Kráľova studňa — Gaderská dolina.

ORAVA, INCLUDING CHOČSKÉ VRCHY AND ROHÁČE (ZÁPADNÉ TATRY)

The Orava region lies in northern Slovakia. Near the Polish border is a huge man-made dam, under which five villages drowned. From here the Orava River flows down through the hills and past the spectacular Orava Castle to the Váh at Kraľovany. The area is surrounded by hills and mountains, including Chočské vrchy and Západné Tatry (the Western Tatras).

Orava was until relatively recently rather poor and underdeveloped. When the army passed through on the way to help Vienna defend itself from the Turks in the 17th Century, they were so angry that they could find nothing to eat in the villages that they burnt them down. Many people left to take seasonal work elsewhere or to emigrate to America. Modern developments have swept aside much of the culture of the past, but there are still many traditional wooden houses surviving in the villages. An open-air museum preserves some of the history.

I will be organising and leading trips to Orava and Roháče, so if you are interested please write, enclosing an international postal reply coupon.

Chočské vrchy

These hills provide an interesting tramping area, with forest, bluffs etc.

Veľký Choč

One side of the Kčs 10 note shows the mountain Choč (1611m) which is up behind Dolný Kubín. Tracks lead up it from Vyšný Kubín, Jasenová and Valaská Dubová on the Dolný Kubín — Ružomberok road.

Podšíp

Podšíp was a deserted village. Today people are rebuilding the old wooden houses in their original style. From Kraľovany on the main Žilina-Poprad railway line take the train up the branch line to Kraľovany zastávka railway station. The trains run about once every two hours, so it may be quicker to walk the 3km. From Kraľovany zastávka (accessible by car) a yellow marked track leads you up to Podšíp. It is a nice walk, and you can continue on to the summit of Šíp (1169m), an impressive craggy mountain.

Kvačianska and Prosiecka dolina

These two karst valleys lie at the other end of Chočské vrchy. A nice round trip can be made by walking up Prosiecka dolina then down Kvačianska dolina. The round trip is best in this direction. An old mill has been reconstructed here.

Oravský Hrad

Oravský Hrad (Orava Castle) is a dramatic sight, and really worth visiting if you like castles. It sits imposingly at various levels on a rock which rises spectacularly 112 metres up from the Orava river at the village of Oravský Podzámok. It was built in about 1267 and rebuilt and extended at various times over the centuries. In 1800 the entire complex was destroyed by fire, leaving only walls standing. It was roofed over again and in 1895 reconstruction began, but was interrupted by the First World War. Reconstruction began again in 1953, resulting in the present state of the castle.

Orava Castle is again being restored over the next eight years, and will be only partly open and for shorter than normal hours. You must go around with a group, which takes 90 minutes, and requires a minimum of 15 people. Hopefully there will be enough people around·— otherwise find out when a bus load is expected. There is no leaflet available in English, only in German, Russian and Hungarian. Part of the castle is devoted to a museum of the area.

The statue in the town is of the Slovak poet, writer and playwright Pavel Országh Hviezdoslav (1841-1921), who came from this area, and whom you will find on the other side of the Kčs 10 note.

Orava Lake

The dam creating the 35sq. km Orava Lake was completed in 1954, completely drowning five villages and partly covering two more, Námestovo and Bobrovo. Of the villages that were submerged, the church of one of them, Slanice, remains above water level on an island which can be reached by boat from Slanická Osada or Camping Goral from May to September if there is a minimum of 10 passengers. The **Baroque church** (1766-69) was restored in the 19th Century, but remained empty after 1953 and was damaged. Since 1965 it has been owned by the Orava Gallery, and now houses an exhibition of traditional Slovak sculpture. In the summer classical concerts make use of its good acoustics. Slanice was founded in 1564. There is an exhibition of photos of the drowned villages and a model of the lake showing the villages and roads underneath in the Klinovský family burial chapel. Anton Bernolák, the first person to try to codify the Slovak language, was born here. There was no written Slovak language, and Hungarian was the official language. He died in 1813, and a plaque was laid in his memory in 1913.

The lake is used for swimming, fishing and water sports, and boats and windsurfers can be hired from the camping grounds. The main recreation area lies between Námestovo and the river outlet. In 1989 Orava Lake was emptied so the dam could be repaired, but it should be full again in 1991.

Oravské Beskydy

These mountains lie to the northwest of Orava lake. The highest peak in the area is **Babia hora** (1725m), on the Polish border, which you climb from Oravská Polhora. This was a pilgrimage trip because Lenin has been there.

Pilsko (1557m) is 2¼ hours tramping from the top of the village of Oravské Veselé. The track begins in the forest, which becomes more stunted as you rise in altitude, eventually emerging above the tree line in the area around the top. Not many people come here, so it is a good area for berries. But the track is not well marked, so keep a lookout for markers. One alternative route down again is to follow the same route back a little way to where the blue marked track leads off to the left, then follow this to Oravská Polhora, from where there is a bus. Another is to continue from Pilsko the short way to the Polish border, from where you turn right (the track is not clear) and follow the border to Hliny, a closed road border crossing. Follow this road down to Oravská Polhora.

To make a longer trip in this area, you could start further west from Novoť, following the green marked route from here to the Polish border, then following the border all the way to Hliny via Pilsko, an 8 hour trip.

Roháče (Západné Tatry)

Known as Roháče by the people of Orava and Západné Tatry by the Liptov people on the other side of the mountains, the West Tatras form a chain from

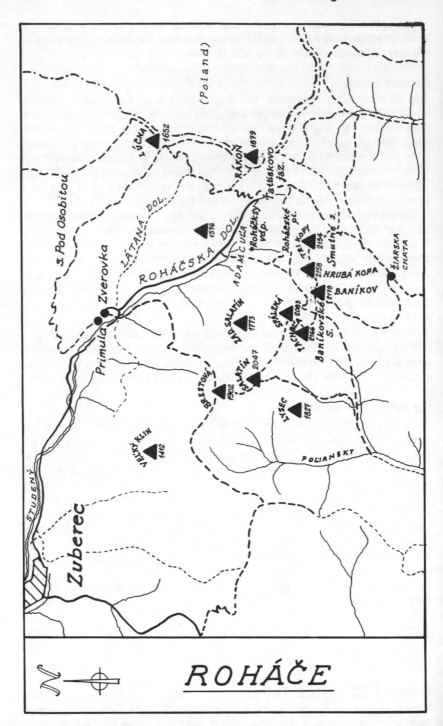

ROHÁČE

Orava to the High Tatras. They have recently become a part of Tatra National Park. There is not so much development or people in the West Tatras as in the High Tatras. Glacial lakes are common. The most popular area is Roháčska dolina and the surrounding peaks and ranges. This area was once glaciated. Roháče Glacier, which no longer exists, was 12km long and over 100 metres thick.

There is an open air **museum** at Zuberec-Brestová, open daily except Monday from 8.00am to 4.00pm (last entry 3.30pm), but in November and December only open if you book in advance.

At Oravice in the north are **hot springs** (27.5°C). At the moment there are two very small pools, but there are plans to build large pools and a hotel and bungalows.

Tramping routes

When planning your trip, note that the yellow marked track over Osobitá and the blue marked track between Roháčske pl. and Tri kopy are both permanently closed, and all tracks in Roháče are closed during the November to June snow season. Within the national park you must keep to the marked tracks, which are well trodden and signed. If starting from the Liptov (south) side of the mountains, note that there are normally long walks up valleys to the ascents. Tramping in Roháče requires the correct gear, ie knickerbockers or wool trousers and shorts, waterproof parka and over-trousers, jersey, woollen mittens, balaclava, boots, wool socks, map, food, first aid kit and a waterbottle if you're going onto the tops.

Roháčske plesá (Roháče tarns)

Turn off the Roháče valley road at Adamcuľa and follow the blue marked track up Spálená dolina to a mountain tarn. On the way there is a short side track to the waterfall Roháčsky vodopád. From the first tarn, follow the green marked track past three more tarns before dropping back down to the end of the road.

Ťatliakovo jazlerko — Smutné sedlo — Tri kopy — Hrubá kopa — Baníkov — Adamcuľa

The peaks Tri kopy, Hrubá kopa and Baníkov are difficult to climb but popular. This is a gruelling high altitude trip, (nearly all of it above the tree line), which should only be attempted in good weather and led by someone with tramping experience. Take water, high energy snacks, and lunch.

At the top of the road up Roháčske dolina is the delightful tarn, Ťatliakovo jazierko. From here a good track (blue markers) leads up a boulder ridden valley with views up to the surrounding peaks. After half an hour you come to a fork where the track from the above tarn trip comes down. From here there is a grind up a good track for another 1½ hours to Smutné sedlo (1965m, blue markers). From this saddle there is a view to the north to the mountain Rákoň and to the south down Žiarska dolina to Žiarska chata and all the way across to Nízke Tatry.

Walking times in other directions from Smutné sedlo are: Volovec 3¾ hours (red), Žiarska chata 1½ hours (blue) and Žiar 3 hours (blue).

From Smutné sedlo follow the red markers to the right. The 45 minute stiff climb up Tri kopy (2154m) is steeper and more difficult than the climb to the saddle, but you'll be rewarded by a fantastic view over Poland, Nízke Tatry and all the way along Roháče to the snow capped peaks of Vysoké Tatry, where the sharp peak you can see to the right is Krivaň. The track from Tri kopy down to the tarns is closed.

The route from Tri kopy over the peaks of Hrubá kopa to Baníkov (2178m) takes about 1½ hours, is even more difficult, and involves rock climbing with the aid of fixed chains. From Baníkov you descend to Baníkovské sedlo (2045m).

Other walking times from this saddle are: Jalovec 3 hours (blue); Roháčske plesa 2 hours (green); Ťatliakové pleso via the other tarns 3 hours (green); continuing along the main ridge to Brestová 2½ hours (red); Žiarska chata via Baníkov and Príslop 2½ hours (green).

From Baníkovské sedlo turn to the right and follow the yellow markers down to Adamcuľa (2¼ hours). After 2 hours you come to the waterfall mentioned in the Roháčske plesa route guide.

Other tramping times from Ťatliakovo jazierko are:
– Sedlo Zábratu, 45 minutes, green.
– Rákoň, 1¼ hours, via sedlo Zábratu.
– Roháčské plesá, 1 hour, green.
– Baníkovské sedlo, 3½ hours, green.

Brestová
From Chata Zverovka or the road bridge below it follow the blue marked route for 3½ hours to the top of Brestová (1902m). The track follows up Roháčské dolina on the opposite side of the river to the road, then swings to the right for a steep climb straight up to the ridge. If descending this way, watch for the track where it swings sharply to the right and disappears into dwarf pines. The track is not as good as the ascents higher up the valley. The going becomes easier once you come up on the ridge, which you follow up to Brestová.

If you want to make a round trip of this route, it takes 3½ hours from Brestová to Baníkovské sedlo from where it's another 2¼ hours down to the road at Adamcuľa — a long day.

Primula — sedlo pod Osobitou — Lúčna — Rákoň — Látaná dolina
Head up behind Chata Primula till you find the green markers which you follow to the left. If starting from Zverovka the markers start outside the chata. The track heads down the valley a bit, before the steep climb up to sedlo pod Osobitou (1540m, 1½ hours). Remember that the track up Osobitá is closed. From here the green markers follow the ridge to the right for 2 hours to Lúčna, a 1652m peak on the Polish border. The craggy mountain you can see in front of you as you walk along the ridge is Kominiarski Wierch (1829m) in Poland. At Lúčna you are likely to meet Poles who have climbed it from the other side, before the Velvet Revolution this was a good way to hear news of what was really happening in Czechoslovakia.

The blue markers to the left lead to Bobrovecké sedlo (45 minutes) and on to Oravice (3 hours). If you want to shorten the trip, there is a green marked track leading directly down to Látaná dolina, bypassing Rákoň. Otherwise our route leads from Lúčna to the right following the blue markers along the border to Rákoň (1879m, 1 hour). I can't tell you what the view is like from there, because the cloud closed in on me.

From Rákoň it is 45 minutes further to Volovec (2063m), or 1 hour down to Ťatliakovo pleso. Our route follows the yellow markers to the right down to Sedlo Zábratu (30 minutes), then the green markers to the right down into Látaná dolina (45 minutes). From the next junction follow the yellow markers down Látaná dolina to Zverovka and Primula (1¼ hours).

Other
To the west the limestone bluffs of Sivý Vrch can be climbed by taking the track up from the village of Myšičková.

Juráňova dolina: one can walk up through the gorge from Oravice.

Skiing
There is a 3km long poma at Kubínska hoľa, and six or seven other tows around Dolný Kubín.

Maps
For Roháče get hold of the map *Západné Tatry Roháče*. For Orava lake and the area north of it, and the whole Orava valley you may be lucky enough to find the map *Orava, vodná nádrž Orava*. There is a map of *Chočské vrchy*.

Access
Public transport services are not as good here as is usual in Czechoslovakia. Kraľovany is on the main Žilina-Poprad railway line and road. From here there is a highway right up the Orava valley, and on into Poland via the Trstená-Chyzne crossing, which may be used by foreigners. The highway, on which buses run, is parallelled by a railway as far as Trstená, with slow local trains about every couple of hours.

Dolný Kubín is the main town of the area. There are several buses from Žilina, some of which run via Martin while others run via Terchova, a few even driving right up the Vrátna valley on the way. They take from 1¼ to 2¼ hours, and there is good scenery whichever way you travel. There is one direct bus connection between Dolný Kubín and Liptovský Mikuláš per day. From Liptovský Mikuláš this leaves at 8.30am. If you come in on this bus, you must then wait over an hour in Dolný Kubín for the next train up the valley, which leaves at 10.29am. There is a lot of buses between Dolný Kubín and Ružomberok, but not at weekends. For this route the Alej Slobody stop is closer to the centre and the camp than the bus station. There is at least one bus a day to Banská Bystrica. In the tourist season there are some direct buses from main centres.

Access to Roháče is from a side road turning off the main valley road at Podbiel, and requires changing buses or changing from train to bus here. There are six buses daily from Podbiel as far as Chata Zverovka. From June

1 to August 31 there is one bus a day in the morning to Adamcuľa. The upper part of Roháčska dolina is closed to cars above the car park about half way between the lodges and Adamcuľa. For Oravice turn off at Trstená if travelling by bus, but it is shorter to turn off at Podbiel if you have your own transport.

Access to Kvačianska and Prosiecka valleys is easiest from the other side of the mountains, from Liptovský Mikuláš for example.

Before planning trips find out when buses you intend catching run, as there are not very many of them.

Sleeping and eating

Accommodation at the cheaper end of the spectrum (camping, rooms, chata) can be booked through Slovakotour, Hviezdoslavovo námestie 34, 026 01 Dolný Kubín; tel. (0845) 3531. They have branch offices at Roháče and Orava lake. Čedok have an office in Dolný Kubín. Everything in Roháče and the Orava lake camps gets full in the summer, even for tents. The chaty in Roháče and Západné Tatry get full all year.

Dolný Kubín

Tilia Camp, Gäceľ, 026 01 Dolný Kubín, tel (0845) 3445 is open all year. Autokemping A and bungalows. There is usually tent space, though the bungalows get full in winter. It is 2km from the town. There is no bus, but the route is signposted. Canoes can be hired. There is a very pleasant restaurant, **Pod lipami**, by the camp. The camp's name, "Tilia", is the Latin word for the Slovak "lipa", which means lime tree. "Pod lipami" means under the lime tree. There are also hotels in Dolný Kubín.

Dolný Kubín has good bread.

Oravské Podzámok

Hotel Odboj: C class hotel and turistická ubytovňa B. Tel. Dolný Kubín 931 15. Various places to eat and drink in hotel.

Orava Lake

Both of the following camps are category B and are open from June 15 to September 15; both have water bicycles, rowing boats, windsurfers and bicycles to rent: **Stara hora**, tel. (0846) 2223, by Hotel Goral. **Slanická osada**, tel. (0846) 2205.

Betula, tel. (0846) 2869 has bungalows and tent sites.

"Roháče" is a restaurant on a high and dry boat in Námestovo.

Salaš are restaurants, usually in wooden buildings, specialising in such delicacies as *bryndzové halušky*. They are named after the huts where the shepherds spent the summer with the sheep.

Roháče

Camping is not allowed within the national park. The camp at Roháče has closed down (much to the dismay of some local people I met who had just tramped across from the Liptov side, expecting to be able to overnight in their tent), but there is a camp at Oravice (Krokus Camp, ATC B).

The *chata* at Oravice can be booked through Čedok, while some small huts can be booked through Slovakotour.

Slovakotour, Zuberec can get you private accommodation in Zuberec. There are many traditional wooden houses in this village. **Chata Primula**, Tur. chata, tel. (0847) 951 79, is a new mountain lodge on the site of the previous camp, just before Chata Zverovka. Open all year apart from a couple of weeks. Kčs 78, bath Kčs 16. Gets full. Book Slovakotour. **Chata Zverovka**, TU A, 027 32 Zuberec; tel. (0847) 951 06 is an old mountain lodge, also cabins. Book Čedok, Dolný Kubín.

If you are planning crossing to the other side of the mountains, there is camping at the bottom of Račková dolina, but the camp sites at the bottom of Žiarska dolina have closed down.

Traditional wooden houses

At Bobrová raľa, a part of Podbiel, typical wooden houses have been renovated and refurnished to be used as tourist accommodation. Bookings through Slovakotour, Dolný Kubín. During the summer reception is manned so you could ask on-site if there is room.

BANSKÁ BYSTRICA

Banská Bystrica is a convenient centre for visiting Nízke Tatry and Veľká Fatra (see those sections for more details). It was an old German town, and in medieval times it prospered owing to its silver and copper mines. In the following centuries the town declined, until 1918 when new industry began to grow here. On the 29 August, 1944, the town's freed radio station declared the beginning of the Slovak uprising against the Nazis. Today Banská Bystrica has a population of 84,000, and is Central Slovakia's political, economic and cultural centre.

The oldest buildings are found on námestie Červenej Armády, (nám. ČA for short, or **Red Army Square** in English). Part of the old castle has been preserved. The main town gate is one of the few relics of the fortifications that remain. The **Church of the Virgin Mary** on nám. ČA is worth a look inside if it is open. There is information in English on the wall. The 15th Century town hall is now an art gallery, open daily except Monday.

In one of the restored houses on nám. SNP (Square of the Slovak National Uprising) is an **art gallery**, and in another a museum open daily except Saturday. The church on the same square has information in English inside the entrance.

A modern landmark is the **monument** to the Slovak National Uprising, a colossal feature containing a museum.

East of Banská Bystrica is the Poľana protected landscape area, with a geological structure and geomorphology created by volcanic activity in the Tertiary period. 90% of it is covered in forest, and it is a good area for nature lovers.

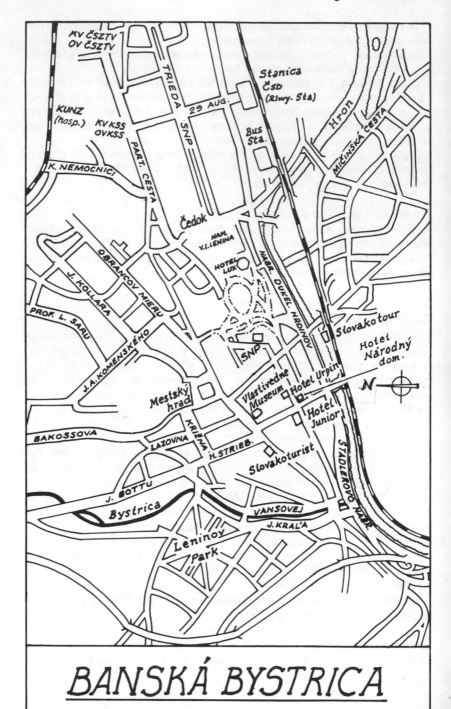

BANSKÁ BYSTRICA

To and from Banská Bystrica

Bus is the main means of transport, and from Bratislava it is much faster than the train. There are regular buses to Bratislava from early in the morning, but none in the evening. Starohorská dolina is a beautiful valley on the road between Banská Bystrica and Donovaly. Buses travel this route and continue to Ružomberok.

The railway and bus stations are beside each other, about 1½ km from the centre. Some buses also stop in the centre.

Getting around

Nám. SNP is the central place for the local town buses.

Accommodation

Camping

There's an A class Interhotel camp on Tajovského cesta open 15 May to 15 September. Tel. 355 90. Tent sites and hotel (see Hotel Turist below). Not far out, you can take bus 3, 7, 19 or 23.

YHA Hostel

YHA members can stay at CKM's Junior Hotel for the special hosteller's rate of Kčs 50. Address: ul Februárového víťazstva 12, 947 58 Banská Bystrica; tel. 233 67. But they cater mainly for groups, and individuals will only be told in the evening one night at a time if they may sleep there. Full in the summer holiday and winter ski seasons. Don't trust them to honour phone bookings. Restaurant with good service, stale bread and flies.

Hotels:

Hotel Lux, B* (***), nám. Lenina 6, 975 92 Banská Bystrica; tel. 241 40-41. 200 beds. Singles & doubles. Very comfortable and expensive. Closest hotel to bus and train stations. For the town's jet set.
Národný Dom, B*, ul. Februárového víťazstva 7, 974 00 Banská Bystrica; tel. 237 37. 48 beds. Opposite Juniorhotel.
Urpín, B*, Nejedlého ul. 5, 974 00 Banská Bystrica; tel. 245 56. 72 beds.
    Prices for the last two hotels, which may be booked through Čedok: singles with shower US$23, without shower US$21; doubles with shower US$38, without US$34; in Národný dom only, doubles with bath US$42. These two and the following hotel are within a few yards of each other.
CKM Junior Hotel, B, see under YHA hostel. "Normal" price single Kčs 134, twin Kčs 202 and three bed room Kčs 252.
Hotel Turist, B*, Tajovského cesta; tel. 355 90. At the camp.

Motels:

Motel Uľanka, tel. 53657. A motel open 24 hours, a few kilometres out on the road towards Donovaly and Martin, before these routes fork.

Travel agents

Slovakotour, Hronské predmestie 12; tel. 249 29. Open 7.30am to 4.00pm.

Čedok, Nám. Lenina, 974 01 Banská Bystrica; tel. 425 75. Open 9.00am to 5.00pm, but closing 6.00pm on Thursday and 12.00am Saturday.
CKM, Horná 65, 974 58 Banská Bystrica; tel. 258 46. Open weekdays 10.00am to 12.00am and 1.00pm to 4.00pm. For ISIC Tuesday and Thursday only from 1.00pm to 3.00pm.
Tatratour and **Slovakoturist** are both in Malinovského, while **Autoturist** is at Partizánska cesta 65.

Other information
Pošta 1, the main post office, is on nám. ČA, and the post code is 974 01. The telephone area code is 088.
Changing money. The bank is at nám. Lenina, otherwise you can change at Čedok, Hotel Lux at any time or Hotel Národný dom from 7.00am to 10.00pm.
ČSA, Partizánska cesta 6 (opposite Horná ulica).
There is a street map of the town.

Evenings
Even if you don't find the town very interesting, it's hard to deny that the girls are gorgeous (I'm no judge of guys). There is a disco at nám. SNP 6. Národný Dom has a Disco Club open every night from 8.00pm to 2.00am. Hotel Lux has a night bar.

BANSKÁ ŠTIAVNICA
Banská Štiavnica is an old gold mining town situated in the Štiavnica hills and there is still mining activity taking place very close to the town. Follow the main road from Bratislava to Banská Bystrica and turn left 22km before Zvolen just after Krupina.

Many say it is one of the musts when visiting Czechoslovakia. Most of the town was built at the time of the big silver finds in the 15th and 16th Centuries and it is rich with historical buildings. An ambitious fortification scheme was undertaken after 1541 when the Turks took Buda, the Magyar's capital. Even the church was altered as a last line of defence. The peak of Banská Štiavnica's glory was in the 18th Century, at the end of which it was the second largest town in Slovakia. In 1735 the first mining college in the world opened here. See the old and new castle, the latter housing the Slovak Mining Museum.

John Skelton writes: "The monument on top of the hill is called **Calvary** and is a baroque group of sacred chapels. It was constructed between the years 1744-1751 on the initiative of a Jesuit priest called Frantisek Pergber. Each of the chapls contain woodcarvings of biblical scenes from the Last Supper etc. They were restored in 1894 by the architect V Grossman and wood carver J Karuse. The path up to Calvary can be located by following a steep road which turns sharp left after passing the only antique shop on the main road, down the relatively steep hill going out of town from the town square. It takes about 15 minutes to walk up the road but is worth the effort. The view is superb from the top of the monument."

The surrounding hills are a protected landscape region, and include reservoirs originally created for mining purposes. In nearby Antol is a fine chateau housing a forestry and hunting museum. Čedok and Slovakotour have offices, and there is a hotel. The telephone area code is 0859.

NÍZKE TATRY (LOW TATRAS)

Nízke Tatry lie south of the Západné and Vysoké Tatry mountain range, and are the highest mountains in Czechoslovakia outside that range. But Nízke Tatry cover a much greater area than Vysoké Tatry: the main range alone is about 80 km long. The characters of the two mountain ranges are also different. Nízke Tatry are more rounded in shape than the jagged peaks of Vysoké Tatry, but sometimes end in steep limestone valleys in their lower reaches. The highest peaks are Ďumbier (2043m) and Chopok (2024m). The upper mountains are granite, while the Demänovská Wall is limestone. There were valley glaciers on the northern side. One can see moraine and glacial lakes, but these are more marked in the Vysoké Tatry. There has been a lot of tourist development in Nízke Tatry in recent years, with hotels, chair lifts and ski runs. But in spite of this, some of the quietest and most unspoilt areas in Czechoslovakia lie in the Nízke Tatry, especially in the eastern part. Bears and lynx still live here.

Nízke Tatry offer all sorts of possibilities for walking and tramping. Tramping is easier than in Vysoké Tatry as the environment is not as harsh. There is a track all the way along the main ridge. The mountain chalets here don't get as full as those in the High Tatras. I was told it was possible to find somewhere to sleep if you just turn up. The summer season for walking in the mountains is from the end of May until October, while the skiing season runs from the end of November until April. Jasná is the pride of Czechoslovak ski resorts. There is angling in the river Čierny Váh, especially for trout, and fishing also in Liptovská Mara, the large hydro lake by Liptovský Mikuláš. Like Vysoké Tatry, the Nízke Tatry are expensive by Czechoslovak standards.

The main towns in the area are Liptovský Mikuláš in the north and Banská Bystrica in the southwest. The main resort areas are Demänovská dolina and Jasná near Liptovský Mikuláš, Bystria dolina on the opposite side of the main range to Jasná, Donovaly on the saddle on the Ružomberok – Banská Bystrica road at the western end of Nízke Tatry, and Čertovica mountain station again on the main divide but half way along Nízke Tatry between the eastern and western parts.

A detailed map of the area, *Nízke Tatry*, is available for Kčs 11. There is a guidebook in German, *Niedere Tatra*, costing Kčs 21.

Liptovský Mikuláš

Liptovský Mikuláš is a good centre for access to Nízke Tatry. A town of 24,000 people, it lies on the main road and railway between Žilina and Poprad. The town played a role in Slovakia's political and cultural life in the 19th Century.

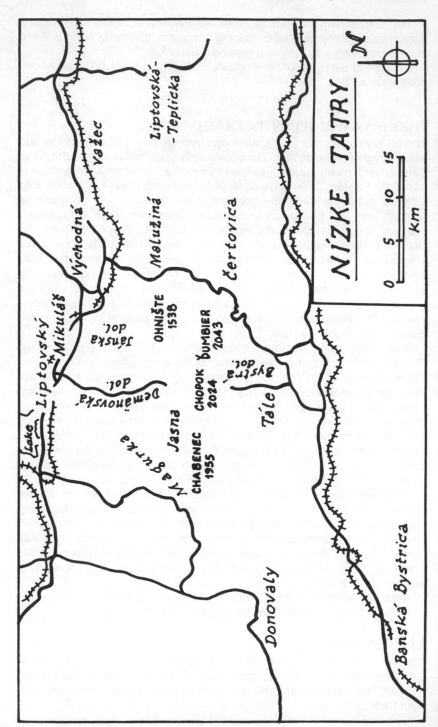

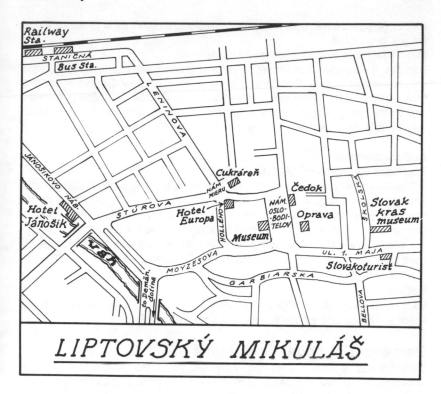

LIPTOVSKÝ MIKULÁŠ

There is a museum of the Slovak Kras, Múzeum Slovneského Krasu, on ulica Školská No. 4 (the road turning off opposite Slovakoturist). It has exhibits on cave mapping and exploration, and samples from caves. What's more, it has a clean toilet with hot water, toilet paper etc! Open 1/4 to 31/10 Monday to Friday 8.00am to 4.00pm, weekends 9.00am to 12 noon. Rest of year Monday to Friday only 8.00am to 4.00pm. In the Literárnohistorické múzeum Janka Kráľa, nám. Osloboditeľov 30, are exhibits on the literary and revolutionary traditions of Slovakia, and on local history. Open Tuesday to Friday 9.00am to 4.00pm, weekends 9.00am to 12 noon, entry Kčs 2.

There is fishing in Liptovská Mara and a windsurfing school.

To and from Liptovský Mikuláš
Liptovský Mikuláš lies on the main Žilina-Košice railway line, with regular trains. There is also one bus a day to Žilina, leaving at 9.35am. Bus service up Demänovská dolina to Jasná; last bus 10.30pm. One bus a day to Dolný Kubín on the river Orava at 8.30am.

Information
Čedok: Námestie Osloboditeľov 7.
Slovakoturist: Ulica 1 maja 34.

Left Luggage: At the railway station. Weight shouldn't be a problem if you carry it in yourself.

Map: There is a map of *Liptovský Mikuláš*.

Repairs: If your gear is the worst for wear you can have sports clothing, tents etc repaired at Oprava Športových odevov, and bags at Oprava koženého tavaru, both on the same side of the square as Čedok (go through an alley and up the stairs). Explain that you are a tourist and can't wait the usual three weeks, months or whatever. They were very helpful to me.

Accommodation

Post code for Liptovský Mikuláš is 031 01.

The flashiest hotel in town is **Hotel Jánošík**, B class, a multi-storey hotel and the town's largest, on Jánošíkovo nábrežie (tel. 227 26). Nearer the central square, at Šturova 13, is **Hotel Europa**, C class. There are 12 double rooms, one 3 bed room, four 4 bed rooms and one 5 bed room.

Hostels are: **Hotel Lodenica**, tel. 223 49, *turistická ubytovňa* A & B; **Partizán**, Vajanskeho 23, tel. 222 20. TU B; **Dynamo**, Palúdzka, tel. 240 61-2.

Eating

Sk.II restaurant, plus stand-up self-service food and grog *bufet* in Hotel Europa. Opposite the hotel is a very comfy *cukráreň*.

Demänovská dolina and Jasná

Demänovská dolina is overrun with German and other tourists, but notwithstanding that, it is beautiful and has many attractions. Čedok arrange day trips here from the High Tatras (see *Vysoké Tatry*). But if you have more time it is worth spending a few days in the area.

The whole Demänová cave system has over 20km of passages, but only two limestone caves in Demänovská dolina are open to the public. Demänovská ľadová jaskyňa (**Demänová Ice Cave**) is situated in the limestone massif under the rock Bašta and is the oldest known cave in Slovakia. 700 metres are open to the public here. The cave was created when the Demänovka River flowed underground. The higher parts of the cave have normal limestone formations, while the lower parts are permanently ice covered. The best time to visit is in spring, when new ice and icicles are formed by water getting in through cracks. Worth seeing. Open 16/5 to 15/9, rest of year and Mondays closed. First tour 9.00am, then hourly till last tour at 4.00pm. Kčs 6, Kčs 3 children under 15 and students. The entrance is 15 minutes strolling pace up the hill from the car park and bus stop on the road.

Higher up the valley is Demänovská Jaskyňa Slobody (**Demänová Cave of Liberty**) with its beautiful limestone formations and lakelets. During the Slovak National Uprising partisans had their arms and food stored in this cave. From 16/5 to 15/9 there are hourly tours from 8.00am to the last tour at 4.00pm. Rest of the year tours at 9.00am, 11.00am, and 2.00pm. Closed Mondays. Kčs 8, Kčs 4 children under 15 and students. Accessible from car park and bus stop by walking or by chairlift.

From Jasná one can travel by chairlift right across the mountains, via Chopok, the second highest peak in Nízke Tatry. If the weather is good

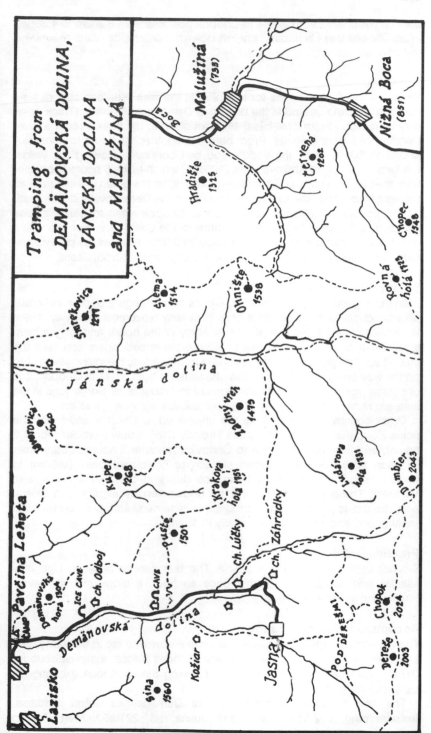

Tramping from DEMÄNOVSKÁ DOLINA, JÁNSKA DOLINA and MALUŽINÁ

enough the chairlift from Jasná to Chopok operates from 8.30am to 4.30pm. From Chopok there is another chairlift down the other side of the mountains to Srdiečko Hotel.

Tramping

There are many possibilities for tramping in the area. You can start directly from the camping ground at the bottom of Demänovská dolina. (Track open only in season.) From here it is a 1¾ hour climb to the peak directly above, Demänovská Hora (1304m). From here it is another 1½ hours to Ľanovské saddle (1253m). From the saddle you can continue following the yellow markers to the top of Krakova Hoľa (1751m), which takes 5 hours altogether from the camping ground. Alternatively drop down the green marked track to the right from Ľanovské sedlo, finishing up on the Demänovská dolina road.

It is popular to take the chairlift up to Chopok, then to tramp in one direction or the other along the main ridge of the Low Tatras. For example it is 2 to 3 hour tramp along the main ridge track (red markers) to ch. Hrdinov SNP, a mountain chalet. One can also walk to Chopok from Jasná.

Skiing

Jasná is a good winter sports area. Čedok can arrange group or individual ski instruction. Skiing is possible here from early November until May. There is no avalanche danger around Jasná. Many of the hotels and lodges have small ski runs right next to them. More experienced skiers can take the chairlift up. The greatest choice of runs is from Luková, the intermediate stop on the way up to Chopok. With the chair-lifts up both sides of Chopok, it is of course possible to ski on both sides of the mountains. Some runs in the area are rather difficult; others are more suitable for average skiers.

Cross-country skiers can take the chairlift up to Chopok and follow the poles along the main ridge to chata Hrdinov SNP, below Ďumbier (about 3 hours), and from here continue to Čertovica (another 3 hours). In the other direction from Chopok one can ski across Chabenec peak (1955m) to Ďurková saddle (5 to 6 hours), and so descend down to the village of Magurka. These trips should only be undertaken by experienced skiers, accustomed to cross-country mountainous terrain, and only under ideal weather and snow conditions, usually in spring.

Practical information

Slovakoturist has an office in Jasná. The bus service between Liptovský Mikuláš and Jasná runs roughly once an hour. It stops at both caves. Hitchhiking in the valley is difficult.

Accommodation and eating

There are many hotels, bungalows, *turistické ubytovne* etc in the valley, and especially up at Jasná. If writing to any of these places, the post code for Demänovská dolina is 032 51, and if phoning the telephone exchange is Liptovský Mikuláš.

The only camp is at the bottom of Demänovská dolina. Address: **Autokemping**, 032 51 Demänovská dolina; tel. 221 85. Open May to

September. A few minutes walk from the bus stop. Overpriced. Fee for one person alone Kčs 44. Except for the occasional short period with hot water, the only facilities are cold water showers, hand basins and toilets. One can shower at the adjacent hotel for Kčs 21. The hotel is class B, open all year, and has doubles for Kčs 187. Address: **Hotel Bystrina**, 032 51 Demänovská dolina; tel. Liptovský Mikuláš 221 83. Unhelpful staff. There is a sk.II restaurant on the grounds, open from 7.00am to 9.00pm daily, but don't bother going there within an hour or two of closing time, or you'll be ignored. Sk.IV outdoors hostinec, open 8.00am to 8.00pm, sells mainly beer, but also a few odds and ends such as biscuits and salami. To buy groceries, follow the turnoff opposite the camp entrance to the nearby village of Pavčina Lehota. Turn right at the "T" junction in the village, and you'll find a small shop. If you follow the main valley road just a little way up from the camp entrance, you'll come to Tri Studničky which has a nice little restaurant (sk.III + 10%) open 10.00am to 8.00pm, but often reserved by groups.

Horský Hotel Jaskyňa Slobody, C + TU A, 51 beds, sk.III restaurant, tel. 916 71.

At Jasná CKM have a "C" grade hotel, that also has dormitories, **Juniorhotel B. Bjørnson**, named after the Norwegian writer who lived here for a few years. From the bus stop, the hotel is on the way to the Chopok chairlift. Usually full. Dorms: 3 bed room Kčs 72 per bed, 6 or 8 bed room Kčs 46 per bed. Also annex used for YHA members. Quite nice sk.III restaurant. Can hire winter sports equipment. **Hotel Družba**, B*, sk.II restaurant, tel. 915 55; **Hotel Liptov**, B*, sk.II restaurant, tel. 915 06; **Mikulášska chata**, C plus TU A, sk.II restaurant, nice building, tel. 916 72; **Chata na Záhradkách**, with dormitory accommodation, sk.III restaurant. There are various places to eat in Jasná.

Jánska dolina

Jánska dolina is the next main valley to the east of Demänovská dolina. From the valley bottom at Liptovský Ján one can walk all the way up the valley and so to the top of Ďumbier in 5 hours. Another trip is to follow the blue marked track up the valley as far as Pred Bystrou. From here branch left up Púchalka valley (yellow). The green marked track to the left from the saddle leads up to the karst tableland, Ohnište. Good view from the summit. The plateau is a nature reserve with interesting rock formations and beautiful flowers in summer. Continuing along the track takes one to the peak Slemä via Michalské saddle. From Slemä keep following the track down to a junction, from where various possibilities are open, including going back to Liptovský Ján over the peak Smrekovica. This roundtrip takes 9 hours.

Malužina

Malužina is a village on Highway 72, the road crossing between the eastern and western part of Nízke Tatry, and it is worth mentioning because it has a nice campsite, and is a convenient access point for those interested in walking up to Ohnište. The campsite's address is Verejné táborisko Zväzarmu, 032 34 Malužina. Open 15 June to 15 September. Access by bus from Kráľova Lehota railway station.

Čertovica

Čertovica (1238m) is on the road saddle between the eastern and western Nízke Tatry. Access: see Malužina section above. Tramping in summer offers good access to the central part of Nízke Tatry, especially the highest mountain, Ďumbier. There are two ski tows, but skiing here is best suited for beginners, or for those experienced with long distance ski touring. To ski up to Chata Hrdinov SNP takes about 4 hours. Accommodation in Chata Čertovica, (C class hotel and TU A). Address: 032 34 Malužina; tel. Malužina 92 59. Other accommodation and small ski fields in Vyšná Boca and Nižná Boca, between Čertovica and Malužina.

Východná

Východná is on the main road between Liptovský Mikuláš and Poprad. The largest folk festival in Slovakia is held here about the first weekend of July, with amateur groups from villages dressed in their costumes and demonstrating such events as wedding rituals, the welcoming of spring, etc. People sleep in sleeping bags in hay-sheds. Ask the owners first.

Važec

Važec is a small village between Východná and Poprad. In 1931 fire completely destroyed the pretty village which attracted writers, artists and photographers. Today its main attraction is **Važecká jaskyňa**, a cave formed by the underground flow of the river Biely Váh, and especially interesting for its stalactites and stalagmites. Only recently opened to the public. From 16/5 to 15/9 the first hourly tour leaves at 9.00am and the last at 4.00pm. From 1/4 to 15/5 and 16/9 to 31/10 there are tours at 9.00am, 11.00am and 2.00pm. Rest of the year and Mondays: closed. Hotel and *turistická ubytovňa*.

Liptovská-Teplička

This village in northeast Nízke Tatry used to be very isolated: access was by track or bush railway up the Čierny Váh. The villagers speak their own dialect. There was terraced farming here. Collectivisation led to erosion through the destruction of the terraces. There are now new houses here too and roads. Today the village is accessible by bus from Štrba, Svit and Poprad. Accommodation: **Turistická Ubytovňa a Váh**, 059 40 Liptovská Teplička, tel. Poprad 925 30. 27 beds, hot & cold water, central heating. One can climb Kráľova hoľa (1948m) from here (green marked track southwards).

Švermovo

Švermovo's lies at an altitude of 901m at the eastern end of the main range of Nízke Tatry. The village was burnt down by the Nazis in 1944 because the partisans in the mountains got food here. A couple of the original wooden houses are left.

Two tracks lead up into the mountains, meeting at the top of Králova hoľa. Access is by train or bus. The railway spirals over itself here.

Hotel Telgart, B.

Bystrá dolina and Tále

Bystrá dolina is the valley opposite Jasná on the south side of the mountains. Near the bottom of the valley is Bystrianska jaskyňa, a cave created by the river Bystrá. It is used to treat children with respiratory and allergy problems, and can only be toured by special request. On the way up the valley is Tále, an accommodation centre with a little ski field, suitable for beginners or cross country, and a toboggan course.

The road up the valley ends at Hotel Srdiečko, at which point it is considerably colder than at Tále. From here the chairlift rises via the mid-way stop at Kosodrevina to Chopok, giving access across to Jasná and Demänovská dolina and to the ski fields on both sides of Chopok. The chairlift is closed for maintenance from mid October to mid December and for a period after the winter season. The southern slopes of Chopok are for experienced skiers, with the season lasting from December to April or the beginning of May. From Kosodrevina it is possible to ski cross country to ch. Hrdinov SNP in about 1½ hours. See the section Demänovská dolina and Jasná above, for other possibilities.

Access

By car turn off Highway 66 at Podbrezová. Public transport: train to Podbrezová station, then bus service up to Hotel Srdiečko. There is one bus per day direct from Bratislava to Tále. By chairlift from Jasná.

Accommodation

If you don't have a prior booking Slovakotour or Čedok in Banská Bystrica may be able to help you.

Hotel Srdiečko, B, (1330m). At the top of the road and bottom of the chairlift. Singles US$12 to 15, doubles US$18 to 22. Lowest prices only out of season. Address: Mýto pod Ďumbierom — Chopok Juh, 977 01 Brezno; tel. Brezno 951 21.

Hotel Kosodrevina, B*, (1690 m). At the mid-way stop on the chairlift from Srdiečko to Chopok. Singles US$9 to 14, doubles US$16 to 26. Lowest prices only out of season. Access by chairlift. Postal address same as Hotel Srdiečko. Tel. Brezno 951 05.

Chata Hrdinov SNP pod Ďumbierom, TU A, (1740 m). Access by foot or skiing only. 2 hour from top of chairlift, or follow the green marked track turning off the road a bit below Hotel Srdiečko. Tel. Brezno 951 20.

Motel Tále: B grade motel, A grade camping ground, and B grade chalets. Chalets and motel open all year round, camping open in summer season only. Motel doubles with shower US$28. Tel. Brezno 951 91.

Hotel Partizán, B*, also at Tále. Singles without bath US$9 low season, US$13 high season. Real doubles, not twins, US$16 to US$26 depending on washing facilities and season. Heated indoor pool and sauna. Tel. Brezno 951 31.

A new hotel is planned at Tále. Private accommodation in Bystrá can be booked through Slovakotour in Bystrá or travel agents in Banská Bystrica.

Nemecká

At Nemecká is a monument to the 900 people who were burnt in the limekiln here by the Germans in January 1945. The name of the village means German, but it dates from a much earlier period when Germans settled here. There is tramping access to the western end of Nízke Tatry from here.

Banská Bystrica

This has been described.

Donovaly

Donovaly (960 m) lies between Nízke Tatry and Veľká Fatra on Highway 59 between Ružomberok and Banská Bystrica. Bus service from Banská Bystrica. Donovaly is a summer and winter holiday resort. Ski season from December to April. A couple of chair-lifts and some shorter ski tows. Cross country skiing. Sledging. Donovaly is at the westerly end of the marked route along the crest of the Low Tatras.

Accommodation

Športhotel Donovaly, B, 976 39 Donovaly; tel. Banská Bystrica 997 20. Doubles US$21 in season. Autokemping, tel. Banská Bystrica 991 35, camping & chalets. Open January to March, and June 15 to September 15.

Magurka

Magurka lies just below the main ridge of Nízke Tatry on the north side between Donovaly and Chopok. Accommodation in Chata Magurka (TU B) or in chalets. Chalets open only in season. Access by train to Ružomberok, then bus to Železného, from where it is about a half hour walk to Magurka. In summer it may be possible to drive in. From Chopok it is about a 4 to 5 hour tramp along the main ridge, dropping down the green marked track from Ďurkovej saddle to Magurka. Small ski lift.

VYSOKÉ TATRY (HIGH TATRAS)

The highlight of Slovakia for most people are the towering majestic Vysoké Tatry (High Tatras), the highest mountains in Czechoslovakia. This alpine area, with its jagged rocky peaks and beautiful mountain lakes, offers excellent tramping in summer and skiing in winter, but it can get rather crowded.

The Vysoké Tatry are the northernmost part of the 1200km long arch formed by the Carpathian Mountains. They lie in the north of Slovakia, on the Polish border. In fact a smaller part of them lies in Poland. You are not allowed to cross the border. The area is protected as a national park.

Gerlachovský štít (2655m) and Lomnický štít (2632m) are the highest mountains in Czechoslovakia. Other important peaks are Vysoká (2560m), Končistá (2535m) and Kriváň (2494m).

In the Quaternary era the Vysoké Tatry were covered for the most part by alpine glaciers. The present landscape is a result of glacial erosion.

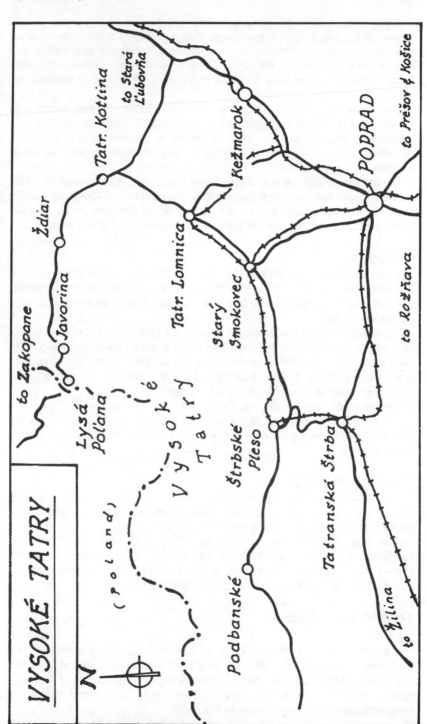

Coniferous trees predominate, by far the most common being the spruce. Higher up the dwarf pine predominates. Picking flowers is forbidden. Berries abound. Roe deer are found at lower altitudes, and red deer higher up. Among the wildlife, if you are lucky, you may see marmot or chamois. The type of chamois found here is unique to Vysoké Tatry. It is endangered by the overabundance of tourists.

One of the first and most prominent scientists to devote their attention to the Tatras was Robert Townson, an Edinburgh physician, geographer and traveller. He studied the area, and was the first to ascend some of its peaks, publishing his experiences and impressions in a work entitled *Travels in Hungary in the year 1793*.

The oldest tourist centre, Starý Smokovec, was established in 1793. Tourism began to flourish in the late 1800s. It is now one of Czechoslovakia's main tourist areas, and prices are higher than in the rest of the country. Poprad lies outside the national park, and is the normal arrival point.

Seasons
In winter the temperatures are below zero, but there is not much precipitation. The first snow usually comes in November, and the last in April. The first signs of spring arrive in April, and the snow thaws on the southern slopes by the middle of May.

In the Tatra resorts the temperature is about 12°C to 15°C in summer, but higher up it averages only 4°C. Summer is the wettest time of year, and it can even snow. On a typical summer day it will be clear in the morning, then clouds will gradually gather resulting in thunderstorms in the middle of the day. By the late afternoon it will be clear again.

Early autumn can be the most pleasant time in the Vysoké Tatry. The weather tends to be more settled, it is not as hot and crowded as in summer, and apart from late night frosts it is warmer than in spring. Late autumn is typically rainy.

Books and maps
For those who read German: *Hohe Tatra*, by Július Andráši and Ivan Bohuš, Šport, 1986. There was an excellent guide in English, but it has been out of print for many years and there are no plans to reprint it.

The first detailed map of Vysoké Tatry was produced by army cartographers in 1870, but if you would like something more up to date, *Vysoké Tatry, Letná Turistická Mapa* is an indispensable map for hiking. Kčs 8. There is also a skiing map of Vysoké Tatry for Kčs 4.50.

To and from Poprad
By Air
There is a ČSA flight about twice a day from Prague to Tatry/Poprad via Bratislava. There are also flights to "East" Berlin (Schönefeld) and Dresden, and charter flights from various places including London (Britannia Airways). Poprad Airport is open all year. ČSA's office is on the corner of Hviezdoslavova and Jagorovova in Poprad.

By rail

Regular trains on the main line between Žilina and Košice stop at Poprad. If you're heading for Štrbské-Pleso, get off at Tatranská-Štrba. Connections or direct trains from Prague and Bratislava.

By road

Buses are the main means of transport when travelling in a north-south direction (eg between Vysoké Tatry and Banská Bystrica or Rožňava) and between Vysoké Tatry, Levoča and Prešov. There is a bus from Poprad to Podlesok in Slovenský Raj. The main bus station is in Poprad, but there are also some long distance buses from Starý Smokovec (eg Prešov).

To cross to the Polish part of the Tatras, take a bus to Lysa Poľana, walk over the bridge to customs, and catch a Polish bus to Zakopane. You must have first obtained a Polish visa from a Polish consulate. There is an exchange office there where you can change your compulsory minimum exchange for Poland, but there is no Czechoslovak bank at the border. On Wednesday only there is a Hungarian bus to Zakopane in Poland which stops in Poprad, Starý Smokovec, Tatr. Lomnice and Ždiar on its way from Budapest. But check the current situation.

For drivers

Poprad is accessible by main highways, including the E50.

There are often people hitchhiking out of Poprad, and hitchhiking to Ždiar is possible.

Getting around

The main means of transport is by electric train. From Tatranský Štrba there is a rack railway which climbs the 425 m to Štrnské Pleso in 4.8km. From Poprad there are rail services to Starý Smokovec and Tatranská Lomnica. Direct trains to Tatranská Lomnica are the fastest, otherwise change at either Studený Potok or Starý Smokovec. All of the main resorts are connected by rail. There are ski racks on the Tatran Railway. At Poprad you can avoid the queues by buying local tickets from the automats, but instructions are in Slovak only. If boarding at an unmanned station, buy your ticket from the conductor.

There are some buses also, and when these run they are usually quicker than the trains (eg Stary Smokovec to Poprad 20 minutes as against 40 minutes by train). Travelling north of Tatranská Lomnica to Tatranská Kotlina, Ždiar and Javorina one must use buses. The last buses from the Polish border at Ľysa Poľana leave at 18.25 and 19.40 (but check if these times have changed), and from Javorina post office 5 minutes later. There are more buses from Ždiar. Most public transport runs about once an hour.

From Poprad there are good roads up towards the mountain resorts, but the road between the resorts is closed to cars from July 1 to August 31 unless you can prove you have booked accommodation there. So leave your car in one of the parking areas and use public transport or continue by foot. There are plans to close the park to cars in winter as well, and maybe to introduce trolley buses. All of this is to protect the environment.

Information

Čedok in Starý Smokovec (tel. 2415 or 2497) is the best source of information. The office is open Monday to Friday from 8.00am to 6.00pm, and from 8.00am to 12.00am on Saturdays. They have a leaflet in English entitled *With Čedok in the High Tatras in Summer*, describing some of the attractions and walks in the area. The exchange office is open slightly shorter hours. There is someone who speaks English, and my impression was that the staff were helpful. The Čedok office in Poprad is open from 9.00am to 5.00pm (6.00pm on Wednesdays, and 12.00am on Saturdays). The exchange office closes half and hour earlier, and is closed between 1.00pm and 1.30pm. Čedok's Poprad address is nám. Dukelských hrdinov 60, 058 01 Poprad, (tel. 23 262 or 23 651). Čedok in Kežmarok are at Dulkianska 41, near Hotel Lipa.

The new travel agency **Intertour** has an office in Hotel Gerlach, and their staff speak foreign languages.

Mail sent to Poprad's main **post office** should be addressed to Poste Restante, Pošta 1, 058 01 Poprad and collected from the telephone and telegraph office just outside the post office at Marxova ul. 11. Pošta 2 is by the station.

The **telephone** area code for Poprad is (092) and for Vysoké Tatry (0969).

Money can be changed at either Čedok office, or at the bank in Poprad at Marxova ul. 9, open M-F 7.15am-12.00am, and 12.30pm to 3.15pm.

There are **luggage lockers** at the railway station in Poprad, but if they are full or not large enough there is a left luggage service with a 15kg maximum. One can eat at both the railway and bus stations, but there are long queues at the bus station.

Horska Služba, the **mountain rescue service**, is next door to Čedok in Starý Smokovec. They can give you advice, provide guides and hopefully rescue you should the need arise.

Skiing gear in winter and **bicycles** in summer can be hired from Švajčiarsky dom near Grand Hotel in Starý Smokovec. Ski instructors are also available. Open 8.00am to 4.00pm.

Accommodation

It probably won't be very easy to find anywhere to stay, and many places are much of a muchness, so just find *somewhere*, then get out of it and into the mountains. A tent is your best bet if it is warm enough, otherwise it may be easiest to ask Čedok in Starý Smokovec to find you somewhere to stay. Try not to let them hoodwink you into something more expensive than you intended. The aim seems to be to herd western travellers into the more expensive hotels.

Camping

Poprad: There are no camps in Poprad; the one you may see on maps is closed.

Tatranská Štrba: a camp within walking distance of the Tatranská Štrba — Štrbské Pleso rack railway. Dirty and no hot water. Open May to September. Postal address: Autokemping, 059 41 Tatranská Štrba. Tel. 921 61.

Dolný Smokovec: "Tatracamp pod Lesom", 059 81 Dolný Smokovec, tel. Starý Smokovec 24 06. A new camp 2.5km before Starý Smokovec on the road up from Poprad (get off at Pod lesom stop on the Poprad – Starý Smokovec railway line). Camping. Bungalows. Sk.III restaurant. Open 15 May to 15 September.

Stará Lesná: Stanový tábor Stará Lesná, 059 60 Tatranská Lomnica. Cheaper but crowded camp. Open 15 June to 15 September. 3km from Tatranská Lomnica, 1km from Stará Lesná station. Tel. (0969) 96 74 93.

Tatranská Lomnica: (1) Eurocamp FICC, 059 60 Tatranská Lomnica, tel. Starý Smokovec 96 77 41-5. A huge expensive camp, open all year round. Camping or bungalows. About 3km down from Tatranská Lomnica (bus service, or Tatranská Lomnica – Eurocamp stop on the train). (2) Autokemping Tatranec, 059 60 Tatranská Lomnica, tel. (0969) 96 77 04. Up the road from Eurocamp. Friendly. Cheaper than Eurocamp. Bungalows. The showers are sometimes hot! Open for tents 15 May to 15 September, bungalows all year.

Kežmarok: There is a camp with cabins and tent sites about 2km on the Poprad side of Kežmarok, open summer only.

Turistická Ubytovňa

Poprad: There is a pub with dorms in Poprad near the station: Ubytovňa Slávia, Wolkrova, 058 11 Poprad. It costs 43 Kčs a night, but is booked up by Čedok for three months in both the summer and winter seasons.

Horný Smokovec: *turistická ubytovňa* in Juniorhotel (see below)

Tatranská Lomnica: Alpínka (TU B), 059 60 Tatranská Lomnica, tel. 96376.

Ždiar: Protežka (TU B), 059 55 Ždiar. Tel. (0969) 9891. Sleeps 47 in 3 to 7 bed rooms. Hot and cold water. Central heating.

Kežmarok: Ubytovací hostinec, Kčs 60 per person, small, by the castle, enquiries through Hotel Lipa (see below).

YHA hostel

YHA members can get a special price at CKM's Juniorhotel, 06201 Horný Smokovec (tel. 2661-3), if there is any space, which there rarely is. Bus and train stop nearby. If booked from abroad the price leaps up.

Hotels

Poprad: (1) Hotel Europa, B*, Wolkrova ul., by the railway station. Tel. 327 44. (2) Hotel Gerlach, Hviezdoslavovo nám, tel. 337 59. B*. 270 beds. Snack bar on the 8th floor with a view.

Svit: Spoločensky Dom, ***, 150 beds.

Spišská Belá: Hotel with bungalows and TU on same site.

Štrbské Pleso: (1) Hotel Patria A*, 059 85 Štrbské Pleso, tel. Starý Smokovec 925 91, telex 078255. US$14 to 20 per person in double rooms with bath. (2) Hotel Panoráma B*, 059 85 Štrbské Pleso, tel. 921 11. A reverse pyramid, a rather strange example of Czechoslovak modern architecture. By the railway. US$10 to 20 per person. (3) Hotel Fis, B*, 059 85 Štrbské Pleso, tel. Starý Smokovec 922 21. 15 minutes walk from the railway station. Used by Czechoslovak sportsmen.

Nový Smokovec (post code 062 01): (1) Park Hotel B*, tel. 2342-5. Interesting shape. Close to railway station. US$17 to 30 per person. Used by English package tours. (2) Hotel Tokajík B*, tel. 2061-2. Small traditional style building. US$15 to 30 per person. (3) Hotel Bystrina C, tel. 2618. 300m from station. Double rooms with shower. Only breakfast and light refreshments served. (4) MS Hotel, B, tel 2976, 2972. 300m from station. 2 & 4 bed rooms. Sk.III restaurant.

Starý Smokovec (post code 062 01): (1) Grandhotel, A*, tel. 2154-6, telex 078270. Central. Nice exterior. US$20 to 40 per person half board. (2) Hotel Úderník, B, tel. 2741.

Horný Smokovec (post code 062 01): (1) Bellevue Hotel, A* B*, tel. 2941-5, telex 078269. 500m from station. US$17 to 40 per person half board. (2) Hotel Šport, B, tel. 2361. 500m from station. (3) Juniorhotel Vysoké Tatry, B, tel 2661-3. Singles, doubles, 3 bed rooms and 4 bunk rooms. Allow two months if booking by letter.

Tatranská Lomnica (post code 059 60): (1) Grandhotel Praha, B* (some rooms upgraded to A*), tel. 967941-6, telex 78271. 1km from station. (2) Hotel Slovan, B*, tel. 967 851. (3) Hotel Lomnica, B, tel. 967251. 100m from station. Older style. Outdoor cafe in summer. (4) Hotel Mier, C, tel. Starý Smokovec 967 936.

Kežmarok: (1) Hotel Lipa, B***, 060 01 Kežmarok, tel. 2037-9, central, apartments Kčs 688 (2 people), doubles Kčs 370, singles Kčs 246, extra bed Kčs 89, nice restaurant, very comfortable rooms, on one side of the hotel with a view of Vysoké Tatry from the balcony but also traffic noise, the other side quieter. (2) Hotel Štart, B, tel. (0968) 2915-6, up behind the castle, less central if using public transport, doubles with hand-basin Kčs 211, showers in corridor.

Private Accommodation

Private accommodation can be booked through Slovakotour in Nová Lesná, tel. (0969) 2224, but you must register with the police yourself. There are cheap guest houses that weren't allowed to take visitors from the "capitalist" countries — the situation has undoubtedly changed now.

Mountain huts

One can't just walk into the mountain huts in the Vysoké Tatry and expect to be able to sleep there. They tend to be bases for climbers who must book one year in advance. Others may be able to stay there if they book long in advance through Slovakoturist. Their local office is in Hotel MS in Novy Smokovec, behind the circular Park Hotel. Some of the huts are named after the first climbers in the Tatry.

Some of the huts are in fact hotels (Popradské pleso and Sliezký dom) where ordinary tourists can stay.

Eating and drinking

Alfonz in the centre of Poprad has cheap pub meals. Astoria has self service and a sk.II restaurant, with speciality pizza. Tatranka is a good piváreň.

The following restaurants in the mountain resorts have been recommended to me: Zbojnicka Koliba (Highwaymen's Den) in Tatranská Lomnica, a sk. 1 wine restaurant in a log cabin, a few minutes walk from Grandhotel Praha, where reservations may be made; Hotel Lomnica in Tatranská Lomnica; and both the Grandhotels. Park Hotel has a Czechoslovakian rarity: a menu in English! The local beer is Pivo Tatran and packs a punch.

In Kežmarok Hradná Vináreň at the castle (but with access from the outside) has Slovak specialities and is open from 12.00am to 10.00pm. Slovak specialities are also on the menu at the *salaš* at the hotel and bungalows at Veľký Slavkov.

Evenings
Try the hotels. Hotel Gerlach in Poprad has a night club in the basement, a pleasant place for dancing and popular with teenagers.

The settlements and their attractions
Poprad
The main centre in the area, but not very interesting. Most people arrive by train. Hotel Europa is just outside the station to the right. A little further along in the same direction is the bus station.

There was a trial season with sightseeing tours by plane – ask around to see if it is being repeated if you interested. There is an archaeological museum in Poprad.

Spišska Sobota, one of the four medieval towns that merged to form Poprad, is a 15 minute walk from the centre, or take bus 4. The old buildings in its centre have been protected.

Štrbské Pleso, Starý Smokovec, and Tatranská Lomnica
These resorts are pleasant, nicely laid out towns with a lot of greenery and parks. Štrbské Pleso is situated on the lake of the same name, and above the town is a ski jump. Starý Smokovec is the main tourist centre, and forms one entity together with Nový Smokovec and Horný Smokovec which are within walking distance. From Tatranská Lomnica there is an aerial cableway to Lomnický štít (2632), with a change at Skalnaté pleso, but expect long queues. One can be on the summit until the next car arrives. In 1993 a new cableway to Skalnaté pleso is expected to open with large cars. In Tatranská Lomnica is the **Tatra National Park (TANAP) Museum**. It's open Monday to Friday 8.00am to 12 noon and 1.00pm to 5.00pm; Saturdays and Sundays 8.00am to 12 noon.

Tatranská Kotlina
This settlement's attraction is Belianská jaskyňa, a cave 15 to 20 minutes walk uphill from the road, which was first explored in 1881. From mid-May to mid-September there are tours every 1½ hours from 9.30am until the last tour which leaves at 3.30pm. For the rest of the year there are tours at 9.30am, 11.00am and 2.30pm. Like everything else in Czechoslovakia it is closed on Mondays, but unlike the others it is open all year. Take enough clothing as it may be rather cold inside (15°C in summer and -4°C in winter).

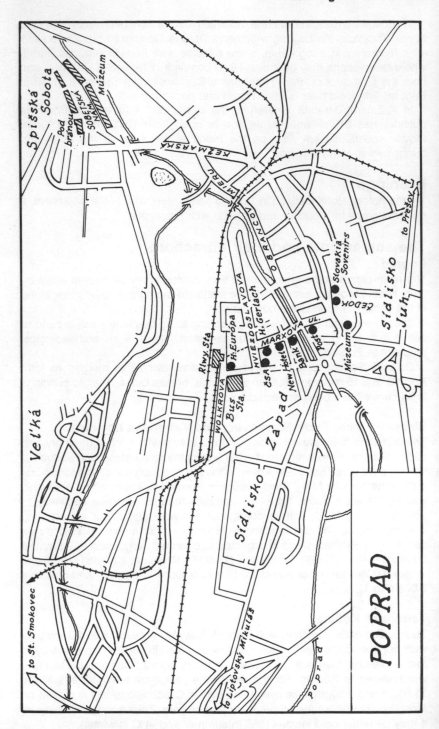

POPRAD

Ždiar

A fair way away from the main resorts, and sprawls several kilometres along the valley between the Belianské Tatry and the Spišská Magura range. The village was founded by Walachian colonists in the 15th Century. It is notable for its architecture and folklore, but unfortunately both are dying out. It has beautiful wooden houses with finely painted facades. The traditional style house was built around a courtyard, which is typical of highland communities in the Carpathians. More recently houses were built in the style found in the Zakopane area in Poland. Until recently the villagers used to wear their local costume, but today you'd be lucky to see them.

The Spis Towns: Kežmarok

In the Middle Ages the Spis towns were inhabited mostly be Germans as can be seen in the architecture. Many people and especially the elderly can speak a German dialect, and until the Second World War schools taught in both Slovak and German. One of these towns worth visiting is **Kežmarok**, which is about 700 years old. The main sights are the castle and Kostel sv. Križa, the church in the centre of the old town. Everything is within walking distance. In the castle is a museum, which is open all year with hourly tours in summer, less often in winter, as long as there are a minimum of five people. The tour is a bit boring if you don't understand Slovak, but there is an information sheet in German, and the tour does give you a chance to see the inside walls. Kostel sv. Križa is open weekdays from June to September from 9.00am to 12.00am and 2.00pm to 5.00pm. The rest of the time it is open only for services (daily). It is a magnificent church. The wooden pews at the back are from 1518 and there is work by Master Pavol of Levoča. Beside the church is a beautiful Renaissance bell-tower — the bells work. The plainness of Nový Evanjelický kostel (the New Evangelical Church) is an interesting contrast to all the Catholic churches. For Kčs 2 you can see a mausoleum containing the tomb of Imre Tököly, once the lord of the castle. The church is open from May 1 to October 15, closed Monday. Nearby is Kežmarok's wooden church, built entirely without nails and iron. Today it is in a state of disrepair and is closed. Other sights are the old town hall and the smaller Kostel P. Márie (Church of the Virgin).

Tramping

Within the Tatra National Park, one is obliged keep to routes well marked and trodden, and can be fined for leaving them. Many tracks are closed from November 1 to June 30 every year and are marked on the map as such, while other tracks may be temporarily closed. This is because of danger of avalanches, because the chamois arrive at that time of year, and as a nature protection measure. But they are still open for climbers (see *Climbing* below). The Belianske Tatry, between the main part of Vysoké Tatry and Ždiar are completely closed to everyone, including climbers.

See the introductory *Tramping* chapter for advice on hiking in the mountains. Most tracks are not marked with poles, though there may be painted markers on rocks to help you find the way. Horska Sluzba (the mountain rescue service) in Starý Smokovec can help you plan trips, and advise you about weather conditions. Before the fall of the iron curtain, Vysoké Tatry was packed with thousands of people, mainly from East Germany, so that it was the people in front of you on the tracks that held you up, not exhaustion. How the situation will develop now remains to be seen. Insects can get unbearable to those who are troubled by them but are not common above the bushline.

There are a multitude of possible trips and variations on them. For longer trips it's important to make an early start. It's best to sleep in Štrbské Pleso, Starý Smokovec, Tatranská Lomnice or other settlements along the road between them so that you can get straight up into the mountains if the weather is good in the morning. Here are some ideas, some route guides and some walking times. "Gun trampers" who don't stop for rests or taking photos will not take as long as these times.

From Štrbské Pleso

Štrbské Pleso, at 1355m above sea level is the highest of the Tatran resorts. Among other tramps, it is possible to ascend two of the Tatran peaks from here.

It is a one hour walk to **Jamské pleso** (1447m), on a red marked track leading to the west from Štrbské Pleso. From here a blue marked track leads to the top of **Kriváň** (2494m). The complete trip to Kriváň and back to Štrbské Pleso takes about 7 hours. The track above Jamské pleso is closed in winter.

There is a chairlift from Štrbské Pleso to **Solisko**, where refreshments are available. From here one can ascend **Predné Solisko** (2093). Alternatively, follow the blue marked track to the left from the top of the chairlift to **Furkotská dolina**. Heading up the valley (yellow markers) takes you past some beautiful lakes, then up a steep climb to the saddle, **Bystré sedlo**, at the top of the valley. From here there is a side track to the top of a hill, where the view includes frozen lakes. The descent to **Mlynicka dolina** on the other side is again steep. Following the valley down brings you back to Štrbské Pleso, passing a waterfall on the way. A whole day is required to enjoy this round trip. One can walk to Furkotska dolina from Štrbské Pleso by two different routes, instead of taking the chairlift up. In winter most of this trip is closed. The ridge between the two valleys forms the watershed between the Váh and Poprad river systems, and thus of the Black and Baltic Seas.

One of the best views in the Tatras is from the summit of **Rysy** (2499) on the Polish border. From Štrbské Pleso follow the red marked track to **Popradské pleso** (you don't have time to pick the raspberries!), the blue track from here up **Mengusovská dolina**, then branch to the right and follow the red markers to the summit. The track passes **Chata pod Rysmi**, the highest chalet in Czechoslovakia, and crosses a snowfield. The return trip from Štrbské Pleso takes 8½ hours, from Popradské pleso 6½ hours, and from Chata pod Rysmi 2 hours. Rysy may also be climbed from Poland, but if you ascend from the Slovak side you must descend the same way. The track above Popradské pleso is closed in winter.

Another possible trip is to follow the red track to Popradské pleso as above, but from Popradské pleso, keep following the red markers. They lead

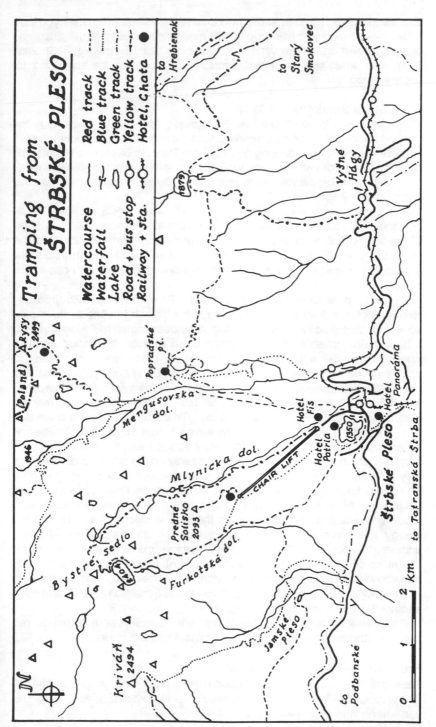

Tramping from
ŠTRBSKÉ PLESO

Red track
Blue track
Green track
Yellow track
Hotel, Chata

Watercourse
Waterfall
Lake
Road + bus stop
Railway + sta.

up a steep zig-zag climb to **sedlo pod Ostrvou** (1959m). From here you can follow the red marked track around the mountain slopes near the bushline, dropping down one of the various tracks to the Starý Smokovec – Štrbské Pleso road when you have had enough, and catching the train back to Štrbské Pleso.

From Starý Smokovec (1010)
Starý Smokovec is overlooked by **Slavkovský štít** (2452), which may be climbed by following the blue marked track from the town. 9 hours return.

There is a cable car with long queues from Starý Smokovec to **Hrebienok** (1263m, 2 km) from where many walks are possible. Alternatively it takes ¾ hour to walk to Hrebienok. From Hrebienok you save half an hour on the climb up Slavkovský štít.

From Starý Smokovec it takes 10½ hours to walk right across the Tatras to **Lysá poľana** via **Veľká Studená** dolina, **Prielom** (2288m) and **Bielovodská dolina**, or 9½ hours to **Javorina** via **Téryho chata** (see the round trip below for description of the first part of this trip). Both tracks are open only in the summer season. These are one way times. You can return by bus.

A round trip **Hrebienok – Téryho chata – Priečne sedlo – Zbojnícka – Hrebienok** takes 8 hours, and crossing of the difficult Priečne sedlo is *only allowed in this direction*. The track begins by descending to Studený potok, a beautiful mountain stream cascading down through the rocks, which it follow to Kamzík, a big clearing. The blue marked track continues to Zbojnícka chata (2 hours), Prielom (2288m, 3¾ hours) and Lysá Poľana (8½ hours). The round trip takes the red marked track from Kamzík via Obrovský waterfall to Nálepkova chata, 1 hour from Hrebienok, then the green marked track up Malá Studená dolina. Other walking times from Nálepkova chata are: Skalnaté pleso 1 hour, red; Starý Smokovec 1 hour 15 minutes; Hrebienok 45 minutes. You climb a lot in the 1¾ hours it takes from Nálepkova to Téryho chata, but the track is graded all the way and is not difficult. At the hut they sell simple food and drink. If you meet the guys who cart the supplies up on their backs you'll forgive the marked up prices. One I spoke with had 60kg on his back. At Téryho you're already in a high alpine landscape with mountain tarns near the hut. Now is the time to decide if you have time, energy and the right weather to continue. The track continues climbing another 1½ hours to Priečne saddle (yellow markers) and you reach Zbojnícka chata after 3 hours. There are chains to assist you on this track, and above Téryho chata it is closed from November 1 to June 30. If you're heading for Javorina (green markers) you cross Sedielko (2372m) and have another 5½ hours to walk.

Other walking times from Hrebienok are: Sliezsky dom 2 hours, red markers; Zbojnícka chata 2¾ hours; Skalnaté pleso 2 hours.

From Tatranská Lomnica (860)
Tatranská Lomnica is not such a good starting point for high altitude tramps, unless you take the overhead cableway up to Skalnaté pleso. (See *The settlements and their attractions*).

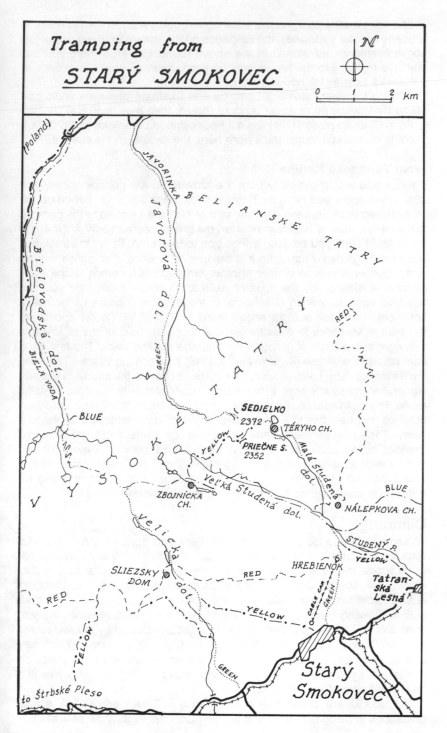

Tramping from
STARÝ SMOKOVEC

N

0 1 2 km

(Poland)

JAVORINKA

Javorová dol.

BELIANSKE TATRY

Bielovodská dol.

BIELA VODA

GREEN

RED

TATRY

BLUE

SEDIELKO
2372

TÉRYHO CH.

YELLOW

PRIEČNE S.
2352

Malá Studená dol.

VYSOKÉ

Veľká Studená dol.

ZBOJNÍCKA
CH.

BLUE

NÁLEPKOVA CH.

Velícka dol.

STUDENÝ P.

YELLOW

SLIEZSKY
DOM

RED

HREBIENOK

CABLE CAR

GREEN

Tatranská
Lesná

RED

YELLOW

YELLOW

GREEN

Starý
Smokovec

to Štrbské Pleso

You can take the blue marked track up through the forest for 1¾ hours to **Studenovodské vodopády**, the cascades on the stream **Studený potok** just above Hrebienok mentioned in the above round trip. From here you can continue higher into the mountains, or drop down to Starý Smokovec or **Tatranská Lesná** (1½ hours, yellow).

Walking between Tatranská Lomnica and **Skalnaté pleso** via sedlo pod Malou Svišťovkou takes about 3 hours (green, then blue, markers).

From Skalnaté pleso (1751) it is a 2 hour climb to **Lomnické sedlo** (2190). There is no marked tourist track from here, the saddle, to the summit.

From Tatranská Kotlina

If you would like to get away from the crowds on the popular tracks, and don't mind going less high, try Tatranská Kotlina to Javorina. Set off on the blue marked track from the opposite end of Tatranská Kotlina to the track up to the caves. After ½ hour turn right on the green marked track. Another 1½ hours (3/4 hour if you are fast) brings you to Hviezdoň. So far the track has been nicely graded. From here it is steeper for a while, then sidles around with mountain views, until after another small climb it comes to the track junction at Biele pl. by the ruins of Kežmarska chata. From here you can descend again to the left (2½ hours to the road, or 3 hours to Tatranská Lomnica). The track straight ahead leads to Zelené pl. (½ hr) and on to Skalnaté pl. via Veľka Svišťovska (another 2 hours). To continue to Javorina turn right at the Biele pl. junction on the blue marked track. The last grind from here to the saddle (Kopské sedlo, 1749) between the Vysoké Tatry and the Belianske Tatry takes ½ hour. The ridge just before the saddle is actually higher than the saddle itself. In these upper parts of the trip there are beautiful alpine flowers in season. After another hour, the track arrives at a collection of tables and benches at a bridge over the river in the bottom of a pleasant valley. Then a "supertrack" leads down, through bluffs, and turns right into Javorina dolina. Look back up the valley for good mountain views. The last ¾ hour is on a roadway, and is not so interesting. From Javorina the last bus leaves about 7.45pm (the exact time changes a bit from year to year) for Poprad via Starý Smokovec. Hitchhiking may be possible.

Climbing

To climb without a guide in the Vysoké Tatry you must be a member of a climbing club and have a membership card. You can climb anywhere except in the special nature reserves where climbing is forbidden; ie Slavkovska dol., Kolová dol., Mlynár, Čierna Javorova dolina and Nefcerka dolina. Climbing is also forbidden on any walls off Slavkovska and Kolová dolinas. Nefcerka dolina is closed only up to the bushline. You may climb its walls, but you must enter it another way. Climbing walls must be reached by marked tourist track and then the shortest way to the wall. Anything from stage 2 difficulty and up may be climbed. Stage 1 climbs, which are easy, may not be climbed, but you can descend by a stage one route. The climbing area is a fairly small area of the mountains.

Guidebooks are all old, and available only in Slovak and Polish. A new guidebook is being prepared and will be published in German as well.

People who are not members of a climbing club may climb only with a guide. A guide to climb Gerlach, the highest peak, costs Kčs 400 and can take a maximum of five people. The more difficult the climb, the higher the price of the guide. When climbing leave your intentions at the nearest mountain hut. Write the time you are leaving, when you expect to be back, what route you plan to take, and its difficulty. When you get back sign in again. If you don't arrive back the Mountain Rescue Service will be notified. Some of the most popular climbs are:

- west wall of Lomnicky štít
- south wall of Kežmardký štít
- north wall of Malý Kežmarský štít (at 900m, this is the largest wall in the Vysoké Tatry)
- Siroka věza
- yellow wall of Prostredy hrot
- north wall of Javorový štít (mainly in winter)
- Batizovsky štít.

Climbing in the Vysoké Tatry started at the end of the 19th Century. Now the 7th and 8th stages of difficulty are starting to be climbed.

Climbing is possible all year round. There is ice climbing as well as rock climbing, skiing off peaks, and the new sport, ski rally, is popular with climbers.

Skiing

The skiing season is from December to May, the best period being from Christmas to the end of March. In April skiing is possible only at higher altitudes, specifically at Skalnaté Pleso and on Predné Solisko mountain slopes. The weather tends to be clearer in winter than in summer.

It is best to have your own gear with you, otherwise see *Information* section for ski hire. Some hotels have a limited amount of skiing gear available usually only for their own guests.

Cesta uzavretá – nebezpečenstvo lavín means "Path Closed – Avalanche Danger".

Štrbské Pleso is the most important skiing centre, with downhill skiing, cross country and two ski jumps. Other important ski centres are Hrebienok above Starý Smokovec, and Skalnaté pleso above Tatranská Lomnica. Ždiar is a good place for learners and families. The snow conditions in Ždiar are good each year; not much snow is needed as there is grass underneath. At Štrbské Pleso you will have the longest waits for lifts (typically 30-40 minutes). At Lomnické sedlo and Ždiar the waiting time is more like 5-10 minutes. A new centre has opened at Jezersko, close by in the Spišská Magura mountains, with new lifts and good skiing. It is connected by lift to Bachledova dolina. See *Skiing* in the introductory part of the book for summer skiing.

Tours

Čedok in Starý Smokovec arrange the following bus tours:

Jasná: A day trip for skiers to Jasná in the Low Tatras. Every Tuesday from January 15 to March 31. Cost about US$16, including lunch.

Demänovské Jaskyne – Jasná: A day trip every Tuesday from early June to late September, including tour of cave, lunch, and return chairlift up Chopok. All inclusive price about US$22.

Dunajec – Červený Kláštor: Every Tuesday, Wednesday, Thursday and Friday from June 1 to September 30. Cost about US$28. See Pieniny section under *East Slovakia*.

"The Last Supper" in the chapel of Banská Štiavnica
(Photo by John Skelton)

In the High Tatras

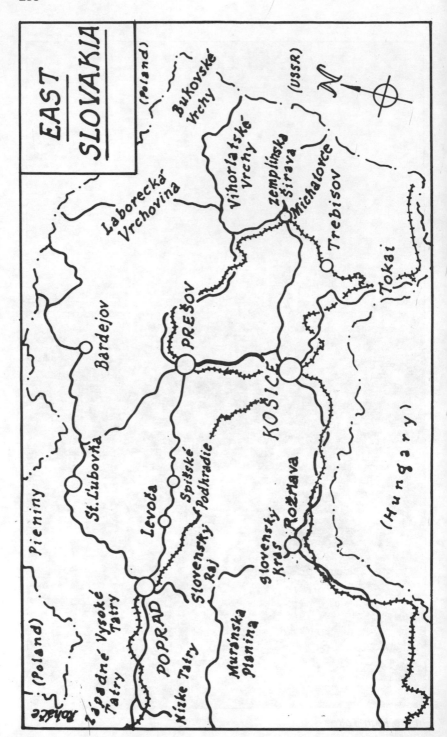

East Slovakia

Once you travel east of the Tatry you have left the mountains of Slovakia, although hills still abound and the highest peaks are still over 1000 metres. There are areas of outstanding natural beauty such as Slovenský Raj and Slovenský Kras, and villages and towns with visible evidence of their long history. Not as many tourists reach as far east in Czechoslovakia, and those you meet are mostly from the neighbouring countries. Even fewer people can speak English than in the rest of Czechoslovakia. The people here are more conservative, especially out in the villages. The Ukranian, Hungarian and Gypsy minorities are strongly represented in the population, and the Gypsies in particular suffer from racism.

PIENINY
Pieniny is a small but very beautiful area lying on the Polish border, on the other side of Spišská Magura from Vysoké Tatry. Both Poland and Czechoslovakia have created national parks in their part of Pieniny.

The map *Spišská Magura Pieniny* is a detailed map covering Pieniny and Spišská Magura and right out to Poprad, and Stará Ľubovňa.

Pieniny has suffered a shifting fate as the area was passed back and fro between Hungary and Poland.

Červený Kláštor
This is the main centre for the area. There is a Carthusian monastery founded in the 14th Century, now a museum containing a Gothic church, historical and ethnographic exhibitions about the area and a pharmacy exhibition. Open all year, closed Mondays.

To and from Červený Kláštor
From Poprad you can get to Červený Kláštor by bus. If there is no direct bus, change buses at Spišská Stará Ves. Get off the bus at the monastery, not at Červený Kláštor village. There are buses to Červený Kláštor and Lesnica from Stará Ľubovňa.

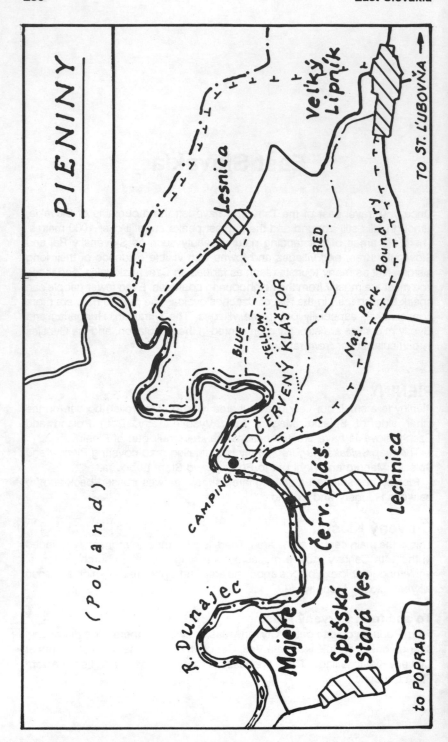

Accommodation
There is a camp site at Červený Kláštor. TU Chata Pieniny at Lesnica is open all year, but is booked up most of the time. At Haligovce, a few kilometres along the road towards Stará Ľubovňa from the monastery, is Motorest Dunajec with chalets (tel. 971 05).

Dunajec river gorge
From Červený Kláštor there are raft trips down the gorge of the Dunajec river, a beautiful trip that can also be made as a 2km walk along beside the river. There are Polish rafts on the same stretch, as the border follows the middle of the river. In fact the Polish raft trip is 1km longer, as they can continue where the river enters Poland. The rafts operate from May to October. Restauracie Stará Lubovňa operate rafts from outside the monastery for Kčs 50 per person and promise that their bus will collect you from the other end. But no bus turned up when I went. Private rafts sail from a landing 100m upstream of the monastery for Kčs 40 and don't promise any bus. From the landing at the end of the raft trip you could walk back along the river, or walk up the road to Chata Pieniny at Lesnica which has nice old wooden houses. From Lesnice there is a yellow marked track to Červený Kláštor, or the occasional scheduled bus out to Stará Ľubovňa. To get back to Červený Kláštor by bus you'll have to change at Veľký Lipník.

In the first weekend in September every year the International Pieniny kayak slalom is held on the river.

Tour
Čedok have a tour from Starý Smokovec that includes a visit to the monastery in Červený Kláštor, the raft trip (weather permitting), lunch at Haligovce, and a visit to the *skansen* at Stará Ľubovňa. All inclusive price about US$28.

STARÁ ĽUBOVŇA
Stará Ľubovňa's main attractions are its castle, most of it in ruins, and its *skansen*. The castle was one of a series of fortresses built to defend the northern border of Hungary and was important for the defence of the Magyars' trading routes, but it has also been in Polish hands at various times. There was once a river port here from which goods, especially Hungarian wine, were transported by raft on the rivers Poprad, Dunajec and Wisla to Warsaw and the Baltic.

The **castle** today consists of an extensive area of ruins. Reconstruction work is underway. The **museum** at the castle must be toured with a guide, but the guide will take you around without waiting for any minimum number of people. During the Second World War the castle was occupied by the Gestapo. The memorial near the well is to their victims who were thrown into the well. The castle is open from May 1 to October 31, the season depending a bit on the weather, from Tuesday to Friday from 9.00am to 4.00pm and at the weekends from 9.00am to 5.00pm; closed Mondays and from noon to 12.30pm.

The *skansen* is by the castle, and the buildings have been moved from villages in the area. Four cultures lived side by side here, the Slovak (Šariš), Rusín (Cis-Carpathian), Goral and German and the buildings have been chosen to represent them. The wooden Greek Orthodox Church dates from 1833. The two people standing outside a house are bee hives! The *skansen* is open roughly May to September (closed Monday) and outside this season you must phone (0963) 239 82 first if you wish to visit it.

Below the castle is the Gypsy village of **Podsadek**.

There are castle ruins in the village of **Plaveč**, east of Stará Ľubovňa.

The river Poprad is much cleaner than most Czechoslovak rivers. Canoes can be hired at Ružbašská Miľava (see *Accommodation*).

To and from Stará Ľubovňa

The Mníšek nad Popradom border crossing to Poland is open for road traffic, and there is a local bus service to the border. The rail border crossing to Poland, Plaveč-Muszyna, is also nearby.

Although there is a railway station, bus is the main means of transport as it is faster than train. There are buses to Poprad (via Kežmarok), Pieniny, Bardejov and Prešov amongst other places.

Orientation and information

The town is situated on one hill, with the castle atop another, while the bus and railway stations are located down by the river between the two. There are occasional local buses from the town to the castle, otherwise walk the few kilometres. There are local buses to Vyšné Ružbachy. The telephone area code is 0963 and the post code is 064 01. The post office is near Hotel Vrchovina. Čedok is on the main square, tel. 219 21, 218 00, as is Slovakotour, tel. 213 92.

Accommodation

Hotel Vrchovina, B, tel. 233 11, is near the centre and a typical rundown Czechoslovak hotel. Bicycles for hire.

Turistická ubytovňa pod Hradom, TU A, tel. 213 01, is just below the castle. Kčs 42 per person, Kčs 5 for a shower. Restaurant, but no guests' kitchen. Book through Čedok, but they might refuse.

Ružbašská Miľava, tel. 918 127, has a camp site, chalets and rooms, and is about 8km from Stará Ľubovňa on the Poprad river and the road towards Poprad. Open all year, but the smaller chalets are closed in winter as they have no heating. Camping summer only, cold water only. Chalets Kčs 52 per person, rooms Kčs 41 per person. No problem with tent space, but the rest gets booked up.

Vyšné Ružbachy

Vyšné Ružbachy is a peaceful spa with fresh air situated west of Stará Ľubovňa in the Spišská Magura foothills, and including the strange geological formation known as the Crater. In the summer the thermal swimming pools are open daily except Monday and Tuesday. The temperature has been getting cooler in recent years, and was about 22°C in 1989.

Just below the town is an open air exhibition of sculpture in a disused quarry where an international gathering of sculptors was held. There are ski lifts above the town. The skiing season is December to March.

Accommodation
There are two C category hotels beside each other below the spa in the village: **Hotel Magura**, tel. 918 120, the smaller of the two; and **Hotel Kráter**, tel. 918 114. Whatever camp you see on maps here closed down years ago.

SLOVENSKÝ RAJ (SLOVAK PARADISE)
From a distance Slovenský Raj, located southeast of Poprad, looks deceptively like an area of gentle rolling hills. But in its depths is hidden an area of spectacularly beautiful scenery. The area consists of Triassic and mesozoic chemically pure limestones which have been eroded by streams to form narrow canyons, cascades and waterfalls. In the winter these become frozen. They are accessible to walkers, with the aid of ladders, steps and chains. Since 1964 Slovenský Raj has been a "protected landscape zone", and in 1988 became a national park. Numerous protected and rare species of plant and wildlife are found here, and there are beautiful flowers.

There is a detailed map of the area: *Slovenský Raj*. A guide book by Karol Hric and others is published by Šport, but only in Slovak and German. Other books with a resumé in English, but consisting mainly of photos: *Slovenský Raj* by Ladislav Jiroušek & Karol Hric, Kčs 94; *Slovenský Raj* by Ladislav Deneš; *Chodníkmi Slovenského Raja* by Dionýz Dugas, new edition 1989, Kčs 85.

Dobšinská ľadová jaskyňa (Dobšiná ice cave)
Of the many caves in the area, Dobšinská ľadová jaskyňa is the only one open to the public. A visit to it is fascinating, but cold. The best time of year to visit the ice cave is in the spring, when there is new ice. Tours begin at 9.00am, 11.00, 1.00pm and 3.00pm between May 15 and September 15. During the rest of the year, and every Monday, the cave is closed. Cost: Kčs 8, Kčs 4 students and children under 15.

Access, centres, accommodation and eating
Bases to explore this area from are Člngov, Dedinky, Dobšinská ľadová jaskyňa, Kláštorisko, Hrabušice-Podlesok, Spišská Nová Ves, or, if you have a car, even Poprad, the High Tatras or Levoča.

Hrabušice-Podlesok
Although not terribly easy to get to, I feel that Hrabušice-Podlesok is the most convenient place to stay. It is well-situated in relation to the most interesting area to walk in, and although a long way from Dobšinská ľadová jaskyňa, a pleasant day trip can be made by walking over the hills to it.

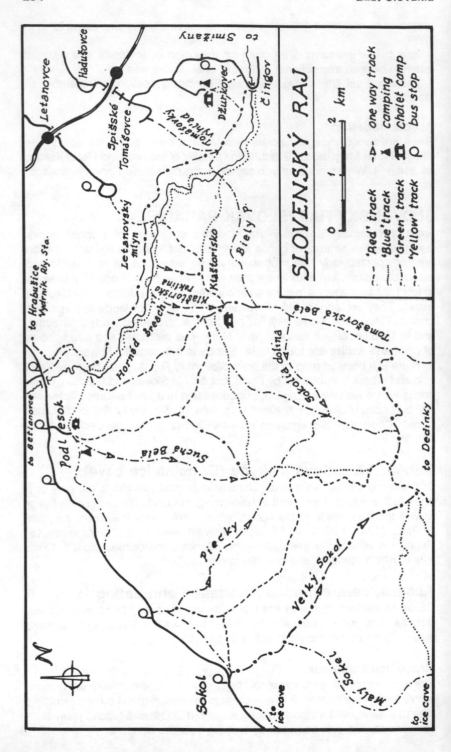

There are some direct buses from Poprad. Otherwise change from a long distance bus at Spiš. Štvrtok to a local bus to Hrabušice-Podlesok. By train get off at Vydrník. There are occasional buses from Vydrník to Hrabušice-Podlesok, otherwise it's a one hour walk. If there is no bus to Hrabušice-Podlesok for a long time, you can catch a bus to Hrabušice razc. – Betlanovce from where it is only 1km further to walk. There are also buses between Podlesok and Spišska Nová Ves. Hitching may be possible. There is a car park at Hrabušice-Podlesok.

Autokemping Podlesok, 053 15 Hrabušice, tel. Spišska Nova Ves 916 281 is the main accommodation centre here. There has been building activity here in the last few years, but on my last visit there were still no showers, no hot water and no flush toilets. Compensation for these conditions are the friendly atmosphere of the place, the view of the Vysoké Tatry on a clear day, and the fact that you can walk straight out of the camp into the most interesting part of Slovenský Raj. Price for camping per night is Kčs 16 per tent, plus Kčs 8 per person, plus Kčs 2 per person tax. For camping it is open from June 1 to September 15. There are four-bed bungalows for Kčs 150 which are open all year round.

Spišska Koliba (CHO A, B), 053 15 Hrabušice-Podlesok, tel. Spišska Nová Ves 916 326. Chalets.

Eating: Meals are served in the restaurant Spišska Koliba (sk.III) from 7.30am to 9.00am, 12.00am to 3.00pm, and 6.00pm to 9.00pm. There is a little stall with some groceries behind the restaurant. There can be long queues here in the morning — quicker to eat breakfast in the restaurant. Between the camp and the *koliba* is a barrel shaped stall selling beer and sweets.

Kláštorisko

Kláštorisko is situated on a mountain meadow. The road up to it is closed to the public, who must walk the 1¼ hours up from Hrabušice-Podlesok. The people of the Spiš region found refuge here during the Tatar raids on Hungary in the period 1241-42. In thanksgiving for their protection, they built a monastery here in the 14th Century, which became a home for Carthusian monks. This was abandoned by the monks in the 15th Century, but local robbers camped in the ruins for many years, terrorising the surrounding villages. An archaeological excavation is underway. Skiing in winter.

There are chalets at Kláštorisko costing Kčs 100 for two people, but they have no heating, so the *bufet* is the only warm place in spring and autumn. Camping in tents is no longer allowed. Address: Chatová osada Kláštorisko, 053 15 Hrabušice, tel. Spišska Nová Ves 916 307.

Čingov

There is a car park at Čingov, and some buses, otherwise it is a ½ hour walk to Čingov-Ďurkovec from Spišské Tomášovce railway station.

The campsite at Čingov-Ďurkovec is not as crowded as the camping ground at Hrabušice-Podlesok. It is spread over a hill, with a view over the surrounding towns and farmland (not over Slovenský Raj). Sanitation leaves a lot to be desired. Cold water only, including shower. Cheaper than Hrabušice-Podlesok. Open June 15 to September 15.

Besides the camp there are a couple of chalet colonies and dormitory accommodation. A restaurant is open some of the time, and there is a nice *vináreň*, that also sells coffee and soft drinks; it seems too flash to wear tramping clothes in, but everyone does. The toilets under the restaurant have warm water. In another part of Čingov, Smižany-Čingov, is Hotel Flora, a B class hotel, with A class chalets. Address: 053 11 Smižany-Čingov, tel. Spišska Nová Ves 932 27.

Spišska Nová Ves

The place to go if you want more comfort is **Hotel Metropol** (B*), Dukelská ul. 1/1936, 052 01 Spišska Nová Ves, tel. 222 41. Spišska Nová Ves is the main centre for public transport to the northern part of Slovenský Raj.

Dedinky

Dedinky (793m) lies on a hydro lake in the southern part of Slovenský Raj. There is tent camping, chalets and a mountain hotel, Hotel Priehrada (B). The phone number for all of them is Rožňava 943 69, and the postal address is Dedinky, 049 25 Dobšiná. A chairlift operates all year.

Dobšiná

The town of Dobšiná (468m) lies outside the national park to the south of Dedinky. There is a good view from the road junction at Dobšinský kopec. The tourist office in the centre of town has rooms to let upstairs with access to a kitchen, but space is very limited. They can book the nice chalets and hostel type accommodation within walking distance on the side of the hill above the town. There is also space for a few (very few) tents. If the tourist office is closed, go there direct.

Dobšinská ľadová jaskyňa

There is no camping here. There are two hotels: Hotel Jas, B class, by the track to the cave; and Hotel Ľadová, C class, on the main road, and with a restaurant and *bufet*. There are also some A class chalets with 5 to 6 bunks. The postal address for all three is Stratená-Dobšinská ľadová jaskyňa, PSČ 049 71, and phone number for all three: Rožňava (0942) 981 32.

Tramping

There is no English on the key on the map. You must keep to the marked tracks, and those tracks marked on the map with arrows on them are one way tracks, which may only be walked in the direction of the arrow. When you get there you'll see why. Many people use them, and it can be rather hard to pass each other on the ladders and other aids to access. Those afraid of heights may need to avoid the most interesting tracks, though the steps, ladders, and chains etc provided make it quite safe. The main rule to remember in tricky places is to keep three points of contact, ie use both hands and both feet and only move either one hand or one foot at a time. If you are afraid, look up, not down. Take extra care in wet weather. There are also some beautiful easier walks: avoid one way tracks and canyons if you are looking for these. The walking times on the signposts are quite realistic, so if you found you were cutting the times in the Vysoké Tatry short, don't necessarily expect to here. Don't judge times by distance on the map; there is a vast difference between the time it takes on some straight and flat tracks, to the time it takes on those that twist and clamber through canyons. A lot of the tracks are in stream beds, so be wary after lots of rain. I recommend wearing boots, which will also keep your feet dry most of the time.

Part of the yellow marked track on the map through Kyseľ behind Kláštorisko has been closed, because a fire here made the boulders unstable. The blue marked track behind Kláštorisko is now two way.

The following is written using Hrabušice-Podlesok as a starting point, because of its convenient position.

From Podlesok you can get straight into an incredible gorge by following the green marked track up Suchá Belá. It takes 2 hours to the top, and can get crowded. It is a one way track, so from the top you must decide on another way back.

Another green marked track from Podlesok leads along the road below the camp, then up a valley. Part of it is a nice walk along the river, but a lot of it is along the road. When you come out on the entrance road to the youth camp, turn right. After 1 hour, you come to the bottom of Piecky, and after 1½ hours to the bottom of Velký Sokol. The road continues over to Dobšinská ľadová jaskyňa, but the occasional bus service reaches only as far as Sokol. Hitchhiking is difficult. Continuing on the green marked track from Sokol leads you to Dobšinská ľadová jaskyňa after another 2½ hours walking. There are many other possible walking routes to Dobšinská ľadová jaskyňa, but this is the most simple. Coming back one could catch the Poprad bus as far as Vernár, then follow the red marked track over the hill then back to Podlesok via Sokol (3¼ hours).

The Piecky route leads up a stream. Suddenly there is a little canyon ahead. The track doesn't go up it, but turns to the left, where there is the first tall ladder up beside a little waterfall. People always gasp when they see it. When you reach the first roadway, you are not at the top. Cross it and keep climbing. Between here and Malá Poľana (992m) there are in season many raspberries, often each with its resident worm. Watch out for the nettles among them. This trip takes 2 hours, again on a one way track. From Malá Poľana it is 1¼ hours to Kláštorisko, or 3½ hours right out to Smižany.

The Velký Sokol track is two way as far the junction where Malý Sokol enters it. As Malý Sokol is two way, a round trip is possible here, by going up Velký Sokol, following the blue marked track across the tops, and dropping down Malý Sokol (5 hour round trip). Malý Sokol is less developed, and not quite as spectacular as some of the other valleys, but it makes an interesting rock-hop. A lot of the stream is underground, but you may get your feet wet.

Heading in the opposite direction from Podlesok, past Spišská koliba, the blue marked track leads you, after 15 minutes, to Hrdlo Hornádu, the entrance to the Hornád Breach. Here is the rather strange sight of the Hornád River running into the hills rather than out of them as rivers tend to do. The canyon used to be only accessible in winter on ice or in summer by boat. Now there is a track all the way down the river to Čingov (3½ hours) or Smižany (4¼ hours) where there are more buses than from Čingov, and a railway station. Some of the way the track is on metal steps in bluffs far above the water. This is a good river for kayaking (permission is needed). Take something to drink with you, as the Hornád River flows into the hills from farmland, and is dirty. A good round trip is to follow the river down to Čingov, and return via the yellow marked track over Tomášovský Výhľad, a viewpoint on top of a bluff. This return route is quicker and very different, with wide open ridges and nice views, but it is quite a grunt where it drops down to Letanovský Mlyn then climbs back up again. Čingov to Podlesok on the yellow track takes 2½ hours.

Other walking times (in hours) in the area of the Hornád Breach are:
From the bottom of Klaštorisko Roklina, 1 hour downstream from Hrdlo Hornádu:
• Kláštorisko, (green) 1
• Kláštorisko (yellow) ¾.
From Letanovský Mlyn, 2 hours downstream from Hrdlo Hornádu:
• Kláštorisko (red) 1
• Čingov (yellow) 1¼ – Tomašovský Výhľad (yellow) ¾
• Letanovce railway station (red) ½
• Hrdlo Hornádu (yellow) 1
• Hrabušice village (yellow) 1½
From where Biely Potok meets the Hornád, 2¾ hours downstream from Hrdlo Hornádu
• the bottom of Kyseľ (green) ¾
• the bottom of Sokolia dolina (green) 1¼
• Klauzy (green) 2
• Kláštorisko (blue) 1¼
• Tomášovský Výhľad (green) ¾
• Spišské Tomášovce railway station (green) 1¼
From the camp site at Čingov-Džurkovec:
• Čingov (green) ¼
• Tomašovský Výhľad ¾
• Spišské Tomášovce railway station ½.

LEVOČA

Levoča is a beautiful medieval walled town founded in 1245. A lot of it is under restoration, a lot is falling down, and some is deserted, but there are some beautiful buildings, and it evokes an atmosphere of the past. Levoča was one of the most important towns in the Magyar Kingdom. Today it has a population of 11,000.

The church of St James in the square dates from the 14th Century and is the second largest Gothic church in Slovakia, (the largest is in Košice). It houses a carved and gilded altar piece created by Master Pavol. At 18 metres high and 6 metres wide, it is the largest of its kind in the world. The altar piece dates from the early 16th Century, and was restored in the 1950s. For Kčs 1 you can hear a recording about it in English. The church is open in daytime from Monday to Saturday as a part of the museum, which is in the Town Hall. The Town Hall itself has a Gothic core surrounded by Renaissance extensions. You'll recognize it by its arches. The museum in it includes an art gallery and a history of Levoča. The square is surrounded by Renaissance houses.

Just inside Košická brána (Košice Gate), one of the original town gates remaining and the main entrance to the town from the highway, is Novy Minoritský kostel, a church which belonged to the monastery. The *gymnázium*, just west of the square, has a fantastic tower. In fact the building itself is worth a look at. There is a church, Gymnaziálny kostel, attached. Another church stands in the forest on the hill above the town. In winter there is skiing in the valley.

Information

Čedok and Slovakoturist both have offices on the square. Post code: 054 01. Telephone area code 0966.

To and from Levoča

Levoča is on the main road from Poprad to Prešov. The main bus stop is outside the walled town, just up the road from the main town entrance. Buses on the route Poprad – Prešov stop here. The last bus to Prešov leaves at about 7.15pm. Easily visited as a day trip from Vysoké Tatry, Slovenský Raj or Prešov.

Accommodation

Hotel Družba, C, cesta Slobody 22, tel. 2335.
Hotel Biela pani, C, Nám. Mieru 36, tel. 2896. The sign "Hotel C" is easier to see than the hotel name over the front door. On the 2nd floor. Doubles Kčs 153, same price for 1 person alone.
Autokemping Levočská dolina, tel. 727 01. Camping ground and chalets 3km up the valley from Levoča.

Eating

There are various places to eat and drink. For a quick feed, there is a *samoobsluha* at the top of the square. Down the back streets you'll find local pubs (*hostinec*).

SPIŠSKÉ-PODHRADIE

Overlooking the village of Spišské-Podhradie, atop a craggy hill, lie the ruins of one of the most impressive castles in Czechoslovakia, **Spišský Hrad**. A fantastic sight. The oldest records of a castle on this site are from 1209. It developed gradually, and between the 13th and 18th Centuries it was rebuilt several times . The castle was of great strategic importance as the central point of the Spiš region. It was the largest castle complex in Central Europe, with five courtyards, extensive fortifications and a vast outer bailey. In 1780 the castle was burnt out and since has gradually fallen into decay. Restoration began in 1969.

In my opinion the castle is more impressive from a distance than when you actually visit it. The entrance to the castle is from a turning past Spišské-

Podhradie on the main road to Prešov. There is also a walking track up from Spišské-Podhradie. It is open from May 1 to October 31, daily except Mondays, from 9.00am to 5.00pm (last entry 4.15pm). There is an information leaflet in English (or at least a valiant attempt at English!).

There are a number of legends attached to the castle. One of them concerns Juraj Thurzo, the young lord of Spišský Hrad. He was a man who loved company, good fun and, above all, pretty girls. He decided to arrange a feast, and sent messengers to invite all the local noblemen. During the feast Thurzo took a fancy to Dorothy, the young daughter of the landlord Révay. The more wine he drank, the more lustful he became. He asked her to dance, and while they danced he planned to seduce her. "It is rather stuffy here. Would you like to take a stroll to catch a breath of fresh air?" he asked with practised nonchalance. Once outside he expected to see some sign of worry or fear, something that never failed to excite him. But instead the girl calmly said: "My mother asked me not to leave the hall. I have heard about your amorous adventures. But I trust you. . . " At that moment something broke in Juraj Thurzo. He was overcome by a feeling of shame, and a feeling of great love which he had not known before. "You are too good and too lovely for me to be worthy of you," he whispered in her ear. The following month Spišský Hrad was the scene of a grandiose wedding. (From *Slovak Spas & Health Resorts*, No. 13).

The southern extension of the castle hill is the **nature reserve of Dreveník.** An instructional path leads you around the more interesting parts of it. Among the most remarkable formations are the gorge Peklo (Hell) and Kamenný raj (Stony Paradise), which with imagination resembles a rocky townlet. There are a number of caves, often concealed, which were once inhabited by cave men, and in the southwest part of Dreveník is an ice cave.

Spišské-Podhradie itself developed from a settlement below the castle. From the 12th Century it was an important crafts centre.

Spišská Kapitula, now a part of Spišské-Podhradie, is a fortified town built by ecclesiastical dignitaries. It is centred on its cathedral, which, despite a few Gothic alterations, is a noteworthy example of Romanesque architecture. But count yourself lucky if you can get into it. The Renaissance bishop's palace was built in 1652.

Towards Prešov from Spišské-Podhradie the main road ascends Branisko via a series of hairpin bends. From here there are glimpses of Spišský Hrad. The marked tracks in this forested area are shown on a map at the highest point on the road.

Getting there
Spišské-Podhradie is situated just off the main Poprad – Prešov road. Buses on this route stop there.

Accommodation
The only accommodation is a C category hotel: Hotel Spiš, 053 04 Spišské-Podhradie, tel. 85 21. Has hot and cold water, and central heating.

PREŠOV

Prešov is the economic and cultural centre of the Šariš ethnic region, as well as being an important Ukrainian cultural centre. There are also many Hungarian speaking people living in the town. Though an ancient Slav settlement existed here, the first written records of an urban settlement date from 1247. Prešov attained the status of royal town in 1374. Today it has a population of 72,000, and is not overrun by tourists.

To and from Prešov

Straightforward driving from Poprad (European highway no. E50, Czechoslovak highway no. 18), Košice (E50, 68) and Michalovce (18). Hitchhiking is reasonable on these roads, but it is difficult to hitch out of Prešov itself. Buses are generally more convenient than trains. Bus service from Poprad and frequent buses between Prešov and Košice. Trains and buses to Bardejov. The bus and train stations are beside each other.

Orientation and getting around

From Poprad follow the signs to "Centrum" and they'll bring you to Slovenskej republiky rád. No street map of Prešov is available, but there is a plan of the historic centre on the back of the map *Východné Slovensko*, number 14 in the *Poznávame Československo* series.

Buy tickets for local town buses beforehand from kiosks or machines. Many of the local buses pass the bus station. At Trojica bus stop, in the centre, is a big bus orientation plan.

Accommodation

Prešov's post code is 080 01 if writing to any of the following, and the area code for phoning is 091.

Hotels

Dukla B*, ul. Slov. republicky rád. 1, tel. 227 41, opposite Čedok. 122 beds. US$15 to 25 per person per night.
Šariš B*, Leningradská ul. 1, tel. 46351-52. 150 beds. Town bus to Trojica stop.
Savoy B, ul. Slov. republiky rád 50, tel. 310 62. 44 beds.
Verchovina B, Svätoplukova ul. 1, tel. 249 22. 30 beds. Next door to ČSA.
Hotel Sigord B*, 082 52 Kokošovce, tel. 983 02. Out of town.

Other

Motel Stop, 080 02 Prešov-Haniska, tel. 252 20. B class motel and bungalows. Note that is *closed* from July 1 to August 31 every year, when it is taken over by a children's camp. A few kilometres south of town on the old road to Košice. Some buses.
Autokemping, 082 33 Chminianska Nová Ves, tel Prešov 951 90. Open July 1 to September 30. 15km west of Prešov on the road to Poprad. 2km east of Chminianska Nová Ves village. Camping. Bungalows. Camping area floods if there is a lot of rain. Hot water. Bar. Washing machine and ironing in the

"Ladies" — Kčs 5 per hour. Bus from Prešov (last bus about 11.00pm), buy ticket from driver. Bus stop is 10 minutes walk past camp entrance, but if you tell the driver you want the camp he may stop outside.
Chatová osada B v Kúpeľoch Išľa, Prešov 080 01, tel. Prešov 411 00. Northeast of Prešov. Bungalows only. Seasonally open.
Tourist Hostel — Tatran, ul. Pod Kamennou baňou 6, tel. 492 52. 2, 3, 4 and 6 bed rooms. Bus 15 or 22.

Eating

There are restaurants in the hotels. For something cheaper, but nothing special, there is a sk.III eatery at Slov. Republiky rád. 61, open daytime only. It even has a toilet, but you have to ask for the key. In the same street, at no. 21, is a class IV stand up "bufet". The locally bottled beer, Šariš, is good.

Information

Tatratour, Slov. rep. rád. 129, tel. 34300, 34301, 33962. For information and to change money.
Čedok, Slov. rep. rád. 1, tel. 24040, 24141, 24042, 33260. Opposite Dukla Hotel. Open weekdays 8.00am to 4.00pm, (Wednesdays 9.00am to 6.00pm), Saturday 9.00am to 12 noon. Changing money weekdays 8.00am to 3.00pm, Wednesdays 9.00am to 5.00pm, Saturdays in summer 9.00am to 12 noon.
Bank On the corner of ul. Leninova (the continuation of Slov. rep. rád. leading towards the bus station) and ul. Partizánska.
Public toilets, ul. 29 Augusta.
Tuzex, Slov. rep. rád. 38.
ČSA, Slov. rep. rád. 26, tel. 332 35.
Films, Prešov has a lot of cinemas (eg Kino Mier at Svätoplukova 4) with films from all over the world, but check first if they are dubbed or with subtitles.

What to see

The town centres on the street Slovenskej republiky rád, where there is a fantastic **Greek Orthodox cathedral** next door to Čedok. It was founded in the 15th Century, and rebuilt in Baroque style in 1754. In the centre of Slovenskej republiky rád is the **Gothic Church of St Nicholas**. It was built in the middle of the 14th Century, with late Gothic extensions from 1502. On Svätoplukova is the **Evangelical Church**, dating from 1637 to 1642. All the churches in Prešov are really worth a visit. People dress up to enter a church. The local people appear to be more church-going than the average Slovak, though it is mostly older people. On Saturdays there are weddings everywhere.

The old regime was negotiating to sell the beautiful synagogue to a family from Los Angeles, but that has now been dropped.

The museum is at Slov. rep. rád 86. The natural history section is good, but the political history section was just propaganda before the Velvet Revolution — it will be interesting to see if that changes now. Closed Monday. Open Tuesday to Friday 10.00am to 6.00pm, weekends 9.00am to 1.00pm. Entrance Kčs 2.

Prešov is a town for wandering. Though typically rundown, there are some beautiful old buildings and houses with some character preserved here. Others are being demolished or left to fall into decay. If you look through the old archways and into the damp smelly back alleys, you see that it is often only the frontages that are cared for, while what is behind them is falling down.

The suburb of **Solivar** also has a long history. Salt was extracted here as far back as 896AD, and old buildings remain, especially from the 17th Century.

There is a ruined castle above **Kapušany**, just northeast of Prešov.

Prešov can also be used as a base to visit other places. Day trips can be made to **Košice**, **Spišské-Podhradie**, or **Bardejov**.

BARDEJOV

The town of Bardejov lies in northeast Slovakia. During a period of German settlement in the 14th Century it flourished as a trading crossroads and craft centre between Hungary, Poland and Russia, and it still retains its layout and medieval character from this time. It 1376 it became one of the few royal free towns in Slovakia (others were Košice and Levoča). In 1412 and again in 1491 the town fell to the Poles. In 1986 Bardejov won a UNESCO prize for its preservation of its historical character and buildings. The most important buildings are the Church of St Egidius and the town hall. Sections of the town's fortifications remain.

In the 1870s and again in the 1930s there was a lot of emigration due to poverty and unemployment. Today's population is about 30,000 (as against 3,000 in 1427) and it is planned that the population should not exceed 45,000 by the end of the century, so the historic core can be preserved.

Nearby is the spa, Bardejovské Kúpele.

Cigeľská mineral water which comes from a nearby village is supposed to be good for hangovers.

To and from Bardejov

There are trains and buses from Presov, and buses from Stará Ľubovňa.

Accommodation

Hotel Dukla, B, 085 01 Bardejov, is centrally situated. Hotel Mineral, B*, 086 31 Bardejovské Kúpele, is at the spa itself. There is camping near the spa, and another camp at Nižna Polianka, 20km from Bardejov near the Polish border. Out in the hills 25km from Bardejov is T. U. Kříže, a modern hostel which can be booked through Slovakotour in Bardejov.

Information

Čedok is on the square, and Slovakotour is on ulica Slovenská (tel. 82 42). The railway and bus stations are within walking distance of the square. There is a map of the historic core on the back of the map *Východné Slovensko*, number 14 in the *Poznávame Československo* series.

What to see

The **Church of St Egidius** stands on the square. Building began in the 14th Century, and in the 15th Century the church was expanded. The tower was built in 1486, but when the church was damaged by fire in 1640 the tower suffered especially badly, so the bells had to be removed. At the end of the 18th Century St Egidius was reconstructed in the original 14th Century style. The church contains 11 valuable Gothic altar pieces, each of which belonged to a particular guild. Behind the altar St Egidius stands in the middle with St Stephen and St Ladislav. Above them is a description of the coming of Jesus to Jerusalem. To the right, just inside the sanctuary is the executioner's chair. The seats in the sanctuary were reserved for the rich. The Gothic altar piece to the left of the sanctuary belonged to the weavers' guild, the wealthiest guild. The altar piece to the right of the sanctuary is the oldest of the 11. The altar of St Barbara was thought to be the work of Master Pavel of Levoča, because the pain in the face is typical of him, but it has now been established that it is not his work. The church's pews are beautifully carved, and the font is Baroque. In summer there is a guide in the church, so it is usually open, but during the rest of the year it is open only for services.

The **town hall**, which is a blend of Gothic and Renaissance, was built in 1505-11, and is thought to be one of the first (if not *the* first) buildings with Renaissance features in Slovakia. On the outside is a child showing its buttocks and tongue with its head between its legs. This is said to have been carved because the Italian sculptors weren't paid what they were promised. The town hall is in the centre of the square, and is expected to open again in 1991 after restoration.

The houses on the **square** are from the 15th Century and belonged to rich merchants. In the 18th Century the town suffered from fires, so it is not surprising that the statue on the square is of St Florian, the patron saint of firemen. (The present statue is a copy.) The plague in 1678 and fire in 1710 led to the decline of Bardejov. A lot of signs are in Ukranian as well as Slovak. There are many Ukranian villages around here.

In the side streets off the square lived the craftsmen and the poor. At Veterná ul. 10, off the top end of the square, is the **executioner's house**, which included a torture chamber. The executioner's symbol is over the door.

In 1352 the town received the right to build fortifications. There were 23 bastions and three main entrance gates. The system was advanced, with each guild having a bastion to look after. Large sections of the fortification system remain.

People were crucified in Bardejov in the 14th and 15th Centuries, and the hill on which this took place is still called *Šibeňa hora*.

Bardejovské Kúpele

Bardejovské Kúpele used to be frequented by the Hungarian and Polish nobility. The older buildings date from the late 18th and early 19th Centuries. This peaceful spa is surrounded by forest and specialises in digestive and respiratory disorders. Only patients and people working at the spa are allowed to live in Bardejovské Kúpele, and no cars are allowed. The mineral water is not far down in the ground, so care is needed to protect it. Of the different springs, the doctors tell men to drink from the Hercules spring and women to drink from Elizabeth spring. Empress Elizabeth is said to have remarked that she was 20 years younger after her stay here. And, they say, a change of environment should lead to a change of partner.

There is a *skansen*, or open air museum, at the spa with buildings that have been moved here from villages in the region. They include a wooden Greek Orthodox church from the beginning of the 18th Century. Open daily except Monday.

MURÁNSKA PLANINA (Muráň Tableland)

The karst plateau of Muránska Planina (the Murán Tableland) is situated south of Nízke Tatry and southwest of Slovenský Raj. Left largely in its natural state, it is a good area for tramping. Looking up from the village of Muráň there are spectacular bluffs, and you can walk up to the ruins of a castle. There are even free-running horses. You normally meet Czechoslovaks rather than tourists, and although camping is not allowed, you often find people sleeping out.

The map *Slovenské Rudohorie — Stolické vrchy* covers Muránska Planina. The *hostinec*, Jeleň, in Muráň has 10 beds, and cold water only (tel. Revúca 694 54). Another starting point to Muránska Planina is Červená skala, a former smelting hamlet, but there is no accommodation there.

SLOVENSKÝ KRAS

Slovenský Kras, or the Slovakian Karst, covers 800 sq km, making it the largest karst region in Central Europe. Its attractions include wild gorges, abysses, dolines, blind valleys, ice grottos and limestone caves. The most easily accessible of these are the four caves (Gombasecká, Domica, Jasovská and Ochtinská aragonitová – open to the public with guided tours), the beautiful Zadielská valley, and an ice grotto you can walk in to from Silica. It is a good tramping area for those who find karst landscape fascinating, but more perseverance is required than normal in Czechoslovakia because the tracks in the area are generally poorly marked and maintained. There are also castles, both ruined and restored, in this peaceful and friendly part of the country.

The tourist season starts early, as the weather is warmer, and it is very beautiful in spring. As this is a relatively undiscovered part of Czechoslovakia, it can be a problem visiting caves and castles outside the peak season, because the guide will only take people around if there is a certain minimum number of people.

The centre of this area is Rožňava, which was a mining town in the Middle Ages. While the Turks occupied Hungary they made plundering trips into the area. Slovenský Kras borders Hungary, and many of the people living here are Hungarian speaking. Domica, Silická Brezová and Slavec, for example, are Hungarian villages. There are Hungarian schools as well as Slovak ones. During the Second World War it was a part of Hungary.

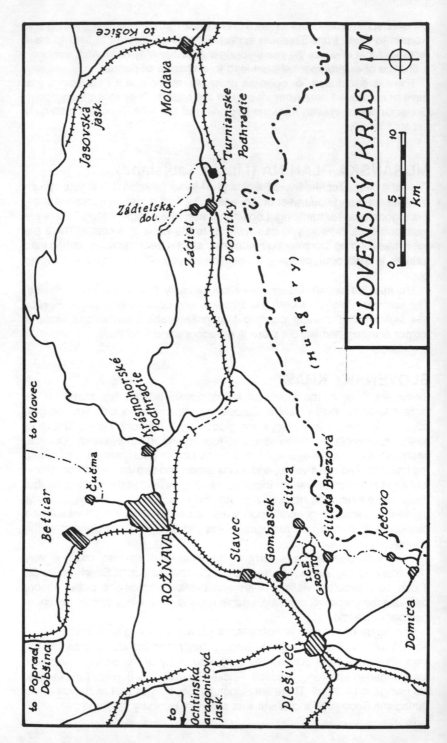

To and from Slovenský Kras

Rožňava lies just off Highway 50, which bypasses it, as does the railway. There is a good view from Jablonovské saddle on the road between Košice and Rožňava (the bus follows this route). Buses to Poprad pass along the southern edge of Slovenský Raj, stopping at Dobšinská ľadová jaskyňa. They leave every few hours, and take 2 hours 10 minutes to Poprad. There is a daily bus connection with Budapest.

Getting around

The main transport hub is the Rožňava bus station, which has moved to a site in front of Hotel Sport until about 1994 when it will move back to its original site in the centre. Rožňava's railway station is out of town, though there is a closer station on a branch line. The centre of Rožňava has recently been closed to cars.

To Domica There is only an occasional bus to Domica. To walk there from Plešivec takes 3 hours. Hitching there is difficult.

Gombasec The Silica bus from Rožňava stops right outside the caves and camp, and is the most convenient way to get there. It has a habit of running early, but also occasionally runs late. The last bus from Rožňava to Gombasec leaves about 10.50pm. Otherwise Gombasec is 15 minutes walk up the road to Silica from the main road, or a 30 minute walk from Slavec Jaskyňa railway station If you do what the locals do and walk down the railway tracks (away from Rožňava) till you come to the road leading to the left to the caves. There is only one station at Slavec, despite what signs and maps may show.

Betliar Various buses stop here. Also railway station on branch line.

Zádielska dolina Catch a bus to Zádielska Dvorníky.

Accommodation

Camping & Chalets

The only tent camping in the area is a camp site at Gombasec, by the entrance to the cave. Open May to September only. It has showers, but cold water only. A nice spot, apart from the racket one can sometimes hear from the quarry across the valley. There is also an A class chalet camp by the cave, open only in the summer season. Address: Chatová Osada a pri Jaskyni, 049 11 Plešivec, tel. Rožňava 921 76.

At Domica there are A and B class chalets, but the police won't allow people to camp with a tent: Chatová osada pri Jaskyni, 049 55 Dlhá Ves, tel. Rožňava 928 215. Capacity 130. Open summer season only.

Up the hill at the top of the village of Betliar, up the road to the right of the chateau, there is a peaceful B class chalet camp. (Tel. Rožňava 811 11). It is a 10 minute walk from the main road. Reception is open only from about 4.00 or 5.00pm to 7.00 or 8.00pm, summer season only. Chalets cost Kčs 23

per person, one person travelling alone must pay for a 2 room chalet (Kčs 46). Since 1983 there has been no tent camping in Betliar.
At the top of Zádielska dolina is a chalet colony. Tent camping is no longer allowed here. There is a restaurant (sk.III), but outside the peak season there is no hot food, just drinks, biscuits, chocolate etc. As the road up Zádielska dolina is closed to vehicle traffic, to drive here you must use the road which turns off near Krásnohorské Podhradie. From where this road comes into Zádielska dolina, the camp is 150 metres up the valley, left across a bridge.

Turistická Ubytovne
Hotel Gemer in Rožňava has a dormitory with 8 beds for Kčs 32 per person. In Plešivec Hotel, Planina and Koruna hostinec both have B class dorms. (See Hotels and UH section below for addresses, etc.)

Motel
There is a B class motel in Krásnohorské Podhradie (tel 5230), with restaurant and snack bar.

Hotels & UH
There are four hotels in Rožňava (post code 048 01):
Hotel Gemer (B), nám. Baníkov 31, (tel. 28 29), is right on the town square. They charge foreigners 100% more than the usual price, (unlike some hotels which charge them 160% extra). They tend to be full from March to August, especially in July and August. Reservations through Čedok. Sk.III restaurant, *pivnice* (beer cellar), 'pub' and a little shop.
Hotel Kras (B*), Šafárikova ul. (ph 2293-4), Sk.II and III restaurants. Car park.
Hotel Šport is by the sports stadium, with restaurant and a pleasant sk.II *kaviareň*. Car park. Bicycles to rent.
Rožňava – Kupele (B), 1km from Rožňava towards Čučma.
   In Plešivec (post code 049 11) is a hotel and a hostinec:
Hotel Planina, C, Železničná 509, tel. 921 59, opposite the railway station.
Koruna, UH, nám. ČA 36, tel. 921 58, cold water only.

Information
Čedok is at nám Baníkov 22, Rožňava, tel. 2343. See the map for the location of post offices, bank, shops etc. The post code for Rožňava is 048 01, and the phone area code 0942.

Caves
Gombasecká jaskyňa is the most easily accessible of the caves for those without their own car. From April 1 to May 15 and September 16 to October 31 there are tours scheduled at 9.00am 11.00, and 2.00pm. From May 16 to September 15 there are tours hourly, with the first leaving at 9.00am and the last 4.00pm. The caves are closed on Mondays, and from November 1 to March 31 the caves are completely closed. The minimum number of people for a tour is eight, and some tours are cancelled because there are not enough people. The tour commentary is in Slovak, with a German summary if requested. A leaflet in English is available. The cave was discovered in

1951. It is easy to walk through; in fact it has been rather overdeveloped for tourists, and one can see green growth around the lights. It is famous for its "straws", created because the cave had no draught. These are stalactites up to three metres in length, but only half a centimetre wide. The red colour comes from oxidised iron, and the black from oxidized manganese.

Domica is one of the 15 longest caves in the world. Only a small part of Domica jaskyňa is open to the public. It used to be possible to buy a special ticket and go underground to the Hungarian side, where the larger part of the cave system lies. As well as the usual limestone formations, this cave is interesting because of the remains found from when Neolithic man inhabited it nearly 5000 years ago. There are sometimes boat trips on the underground river Styx. Leaflet available in English. Open all year. Closed Mondays. From May 16 to September 15 tours at 9.00am, 10.30, 12, 2.00pm, and 3.30pm. During the rest of the year: 9.00am, 11, and 2.00pm. Domica is very close to the Hungarian border. As a foreigner you may have your passport checked by the police.

Ochtinská aragonitová jaskyňa is to the west of Rožňava. It was found during mining operations and opened in 1972 by boring a tunnel as access. It is not a karst cave, but was formed by hydrothermal processes. Hot solutions from lower in the Earth's crust rose and altered the limestone. The unusual crystal formations sometimes resemble flowers. The cave's season, tour times and prices are identical to Gombasec. There is vehicle access to the entrance. By bus get off at the Hrádok stop on the saddle between Štítnik and Jolšava.

Jasovské jaskyňa is closer to Košice than Rožňava. It Is not on the main road. Same times, etc as Gombasec.

For the ice cave Silická Ľadnica see *Tramping*.

Other attractions
Rožňava

This old mining town was already extracting ore in the 12th Century. There is a mining museum at Šafárikovo 43, and a museum of the working class on the same street at number 31. Rožňava has a Gothic cathedral dating from about 1300, and other interesting old buildings. Around the town lie forest clad hills.

Betliar

Set in a large park, Betliar Chateau was founded in the 16th Century, but has twice been extensively rebuilt. It now houses many collections, the most comprehensive being that of hunting trophies. At one time the chateau was a hunting lodge for the local nobility. The chateau is under reconstruction until about 1991-2.

Krásnohorské Podhradie

The medieval castle, **Krásna Hôrka**, dominates the landscape around Krásnohorské Podhradie from its position atop a cone shaped hill. Founded in the early 14th Century, it belonged to several wealthy feudal families. In the 16th Century it was enlarged and fortified at great expense by Peter Andrássy

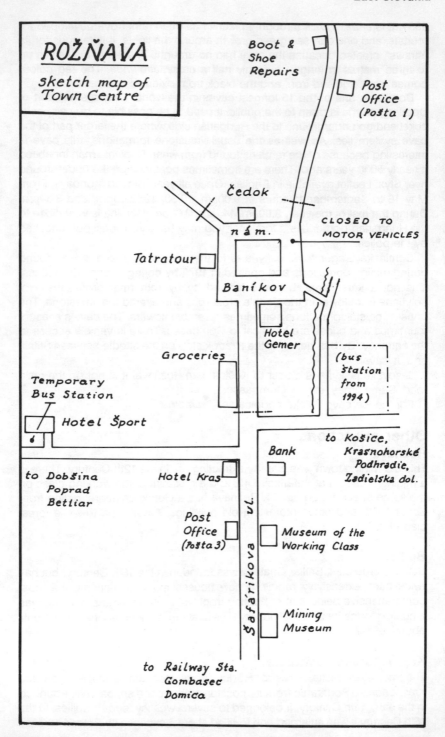

ROŽŇAVA

sketch map of
Town Centre

Boot &
Shoe
Repairs

Post
Office
(Pošta 1)

Čedok

nám.

CLOSED TO
MOTOR VEHICLES

Tatratour

Baníkov

Hotel
Gemer

(bus
station
from
1994)

Groceries

Temporary
Bus Station

Hotel Šport

to Dobšina
Poprad
Betliar

Hotel Kras

Post
Office
(Pošta 3)

Šafárikova ul.

Bank

to Košice,
Krasnohorské
Podhradie,
Zadielska dol.

Museum of the
Working Class

Mining
Museum

to Railway Sta.
Gombasec
Domica

and was in the Andrássy family from this time on. They built several comfortable chateaux, and the castle ceased to be inhabited after a fire in 1817. In 1867 they installed a family museum in it.

In 1770 one of the towers was turned into a chapel. The wife of one of the Andrássys died in 1703. 111 years later the grave was dug up, and it was found that the body had mummified due to infiltration of calcium bearing water. You can see the mummy in the chapel.

Iron from the estate was used to build the suspension bridge in Budapest.

No information on the castle is available in English, so ask if there is someone in the group who could translate what the guide says.

Below the castle in the village is a folklore museum. Last century Dionysius Andrássy had a Jugendstil mausoleum built near the village.

Culture festivals

There is a Hungarian folk festival in Gombasek about the last weekend in June, and a Slovak folk festival in the village of Rejdová on the last weekend of August.

Tramping

Occasionally the map *Slovenský Kras Domica* is available, but it is very hard to get hold of. (Some people I met found a copy in a second hand bookshop in East Germany.) On top of this problem, tracks are generally badly marked.

Walking times from Gombasec:
* Plešivec (green) 1 hour
* Silická Ľadnica (ice grotto, yellow) 1¼ hours
* Jablonovské Sedlo (yellow) 5¾ hours

Silická-ľadnica

It is best to visit Silická-ľadnica in the winter. The most direct way to the ice grotto is to walk in from just before Silica on the yellow marked track (15 minutes). The sign at the top says "Keep to the Path". It is a spectacular drop from here down to the bottom. The path descends to the entrance of the cave — you can't actually go in, but can see the ice all around the entrance. If you are hot it is a cool retreat. The cave is also accessible by track from Silica (½ hour) and Gombasec. The track up from Gombasec goes up from behind the chalet camp, where it is a bit confusing, then it becomes a good track up the line of the power lines to Závozná. This is the top of the uphill grind (½ hour). The track then twists between dolines for some time, until suddenly one comes to a path with railings by the sign (1¼ hours, yellow markers).

Domica — Kerčovo — Silická-Brezová — Silica

Red markers. It is not very easy to find the way, and the caves along the way are difficult to find. Be careful to stay on the track, as the Hungarian border is very close by. There is an occasional bus from Domica to Kerčovo, an interesting looking little rural village, otherwise it is a 30 minute walk. From Kerčovo it is 1¼ hours walk to Silická-Brezová. From the last bus stop in

Kerčovo the way leads through the upper part of the village, then up a valley. When you come to the first building above the village, look up to your right, and you should see a marker on a tree which the track sidles up to. Walk along the top of the high fence. Pass the next building you come to on the left side, then veer slightly to the right. The track then passes through an area of dolines, generally keeping to the right hand side of the open area, by the forest. When it enters the forest, there are still not many markers, but the route becomes easier to follow, and is level. This is a peaceful area, but criss-crossing tractor tracks and the karst landscape make route-finding a little difficult. When you are out of the forest again, the markers follow the right hand side of the open area. When you run out of markers, cut across to the village.

There is an occasional bus out from Silická Brezová, very occasional. To continue to Silica, follow the red markers, if you can find them. A short cut to Gombasec is to follow the power lines that the red track follows for a little way, until you come to the yellow track from Gombasec to Silická-ľadnica, where you turn left. But this route is overgrown and thorny and difficult to follow. There are buses out from Silica. The red marked track continues from here all the way to Zádielska dolina via Jablonovské sedlo.

Volovec
From Rožňava one can walk up the mountain Volovec, where there is a tourist hut. Or catch a bus to the village of Čučma, from where it's a one hour walk.

Zádielska dolina
There is a parking area just above the village of Zádiel, above which the road is closed to motor vehicles. The valley is a nature reserve, and it's a beautiful 1 hour walk up what becomes a narrow canyon with limestone bluffs rising hundreds of metres above. From the top of the valley it is 2½ hours to Hrhov on the yellow marked track, or 8 hours all the way to Domica (if you can find the way) on the red marked track.

An interesting alternative route out from the top of Zádielska dolina is to follow the blue marked track to Turnianske-Podhradie (3½ hours). This follows along the top of the bluffs you have been gazing up at, before dropping down to Turnianske-Podhradie via the ruins of an old castle. This begins with a ½ hour grunt up an obvious track to a track junction (keep following blue). A little further along is a short deviation to a view point over Zádielska dolina. From here the track is quite level (which might surprise you if you'd looked up from the valley below), following along a plateau. Follow the markers, not the vehicle tracks they occasionally follow for a little way, or you'll get led astray. There is a wide area with no markers. Keep heading in the direction of the last one, and you should find them again. Later the route comes out on the clifftop where there is a good view, and follows it to Zadielsky kameň, where there is a great view. Turn to the left: there are not many markers, but there is an obvious foot track. From here the way becomes slower as you descend over rocky terrain. Then climb up the ridge again towards the castle. The blue track heads off to the right, but keep going up the ridge if you want to inspect the castle ruins. They are most impressive at the far end — make your way there through the undergrowth. The modern fortifications are around the vineyards, not the castle: high fences and locked gates. When it reaches the highway, the marked route continues under it following village streets to the railway station.

Eating

The very popular restaurant **Koliba Saroška** on Jablonovské saddle serves Slovak specialities and is always full. There are plenty of places to buy snacks around the centre of Rožňava. The local beer is no good. At Domica there is a sk.III restaurant and *bufet*. In Betliar there is a *bufet* in the chateau grounds open from 7.30am to 8.00pm, and selling beer and sausages, reminding one of Germany. In the main street of Betliar is a restaurant above the shops. See *Accommodation* for further recommendations.

Evenings

THE place to be is the Hotel Kras kaviareň in Rožňava, which closes at 10.00pm, or 11.00pm on Friday and Saturday. There is sometimes music at the weekend, but if this is the case one must be "correctly" dressed. All of the Rožňava hotels have nice *kaviareň*, but they are often closed on Saturday evenings for private wedding receptions. A cultural centre for young people will be opening opposite Hotel Kras on the road to Hotel Šport in 1994.

KOŠICE

Košice, with a population of 203,000, is the second largest town in Slovakia after Bratislava. Included in its population are about 15,000 Gypsies. Košice is situated in East Slovakia, in the valley of the River Hornád, 21km north of the Hungarian border. Its main attraction is its historic core.

Košice's history dates back to pre-historic times. In the Middle Ages the town had 10,000 inhabitants. It was the second largest city in old Hungary. Since the end of the First World War the town has developed rapidly. At the end of the Second World War the new government was formed here after Košice was liberated.

There was no interest in restoring the old town core before 1983, because Košice was a Hungarian city, and the Slovaks were more interested in Slovak towns. Now the inhabitants of the inner city are being moved out to satellite suburbs so the old buildings in the centre can be restored.

To and from Košice

The railway station and bus station adjoin each other between the old town and the river to the east (walking distance). There are frequent buses from Prešov, and hitchhiking shouldn't be too difficult. Bus connection to Michalovce. Buses and trains to Rožňava, but the bus is faster (lot of international trucks, especially Rumanian, on this stretch). Train from Poprad. Several flights a day from Bratislava and from Prague (mostly via Bratislava). Latest check-in at the airport 20 minutes before departure, or in town 45 minutes prior to departure.

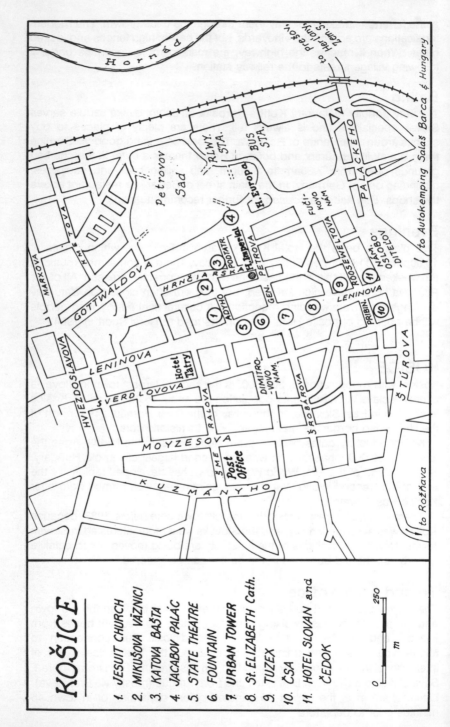

KOŠICE

1. JESUIT CHURCH
2. MIKUŠOVA VÄZNICI
3. KATOVA BAŠTA
4. JACABOV PALÁC
5. STATE THEATRE
6. FOUNTAIN
7. URBAN TOWER
8. St. ELIZABETH Cath.
9. TUZEX
10. ČSA
11. HOTEL SLOVAN and ČEDOK

Accommodation

Camping

Autokemping Salaš Barca, Alejová ul., 040 00 Košice, tel. 583 09. "A" category. Open 15 May to 30 September. Take tram no. 4 to Barca, the last stop. If driving head south from the centre down trieda Sovietskej armády (direction Šebastovce) and turn right when you reach Alejová ul.

Hostels

Slovakoturist have double rooms in student hostels available for their groups, so you could see if they will book individuals in. There is a TU A in Šturova.

Hotels

The following hotels are all post code 040 00 Košice:

Slovan, A* (****), Leninova ul. 1, tel. 273 78, telex 77416, 307 beds, all rooms with bath, singles US$22 to 30, doubles US$19 to 25 per person.

Imperial, B* (***), ul. gen. Petrova 16, tel. 221 44, 60 beds, with bath US$14 to US$23 per person, without bath US$12 to 18.

Hutník, B* (***), Tyršovo nábr. 6, tel. 377 80, 332 beds, rooms with shower and toilet.

Hotel Europa, B, on the street Protifašistických bojovníkov (sic) has recently been restored and is near the railway station.

Hotel Tatry, C, ul. Šmeralova 1 is rundown but cheap.

Information

Ulica Leninova is the main street in the old centre, and offices, shops etc. which you may need are on this street, or nearby. It is open to pedestrians and public transport only. Ul. gen. Petrova leads towards the railway and bus stations, and is a pedestrian precinct. There is a map of Košice in nám. Osloboditeľov, opposite Hotel Slovan. It is occasionally possible to buy a street map of Košice.

Čedok's office is in the Hotel Slovan building at Rooseweltova 1, tel. 531 21, 208 75. Tatratour are at Ulica Šrobárova 6, near the cathedral. They also have an exchange office, and are open from Monday to Friday, and Saturday mornings. Slovakoturist's address is: 040 01 Košice, Jána Bačika 11, tel. 280 53, 277 40, 257 41, telex 077478. CKM's address: 042 12 Košice, Leninova 82, tel. 278 58, 228 03.

ČSA is at Pribinova 4, near Hotel Slovan. Their telephone number is 268 72-3, telegrams to AEROLINIE, telex 077216. The airport telephone number is 235 68. Pragocar rental car company is at Ulica Vrátna 1, just off Leninova (tel. 205 35). There are taxi services at Pribinova 2 (tel. 222 44) and at the railway station (tel. 200 44).

There is left luggage (maximum 15kg) and luggage lockers at the railway station.

The main post office is in Šmeralova and open weekdays and Saturday mornings. The address if you want your mail sent there is: Poste Restante, Pošta 1, 040 01 Košice. Pošta 2 is in the railway station.

Tuzex is at ulica Leninova no. 7.

What to see

In the centre of Košice stands the most outstanding historic building in Slovakia, the Gothic **Cathedral of St Elizabeth**, completed in 1508. The exterior is especially impressive, bringing back memories of St Vitus's Cathedral in Prague. Restoration work by Polish workers will be continuing for many years, but the cathedral is still open. **Urban Tower**, next to the cathedral, was built in the 15th Century in Gothic style, and reconstructed in Renaissance style in 1628. The inscriptions on the old tomb stones around the wall are in German. The tower is now part of Košice museum. Walking past the fountain from the cathedral brings one to another impressive building, the **State Theatre**, which should reopen in 1991 after reconstruction, during which it was connected with empty houses via an underpass to give the actors more space.

At the corner of Leninova and Ulica Adyho, just across from the theatre, is the **Jesuit Church** built between 1671 and 1681 in early Baroque style. Walking down Adyho, and straight ahead at the crossroads brings you to Ulica Pri Miklušovej Väznici. At no. 10, on the left, is **Mikušova Väznici**, two houses which now house Košice's museum, with a permanent exhibition on the history of the town. Until 1550 they were potters' houses. From this date, for a period of about 250 years, they became a prison. They contain cells, a torture chamber and the original interior decoration. Open Tuesday to Saturday 9.00am to 5.00pm, Sunday 9.00am to 1.00pm. Near Mikušova Väznici is **Katova Bašta**, an old bastion dating from the 15th Century. A little further out and to the right from here brings one to **Jacabov Palác** on the corner of Gottwaldova and ul. gen. Petrova. A rich Hungarian had this palace built in 1903 in pseudo-Gothic style. Some of the stone came from the Gothic cathedral during the cathedral's reconstruction. It became the residence of Beneš, Czechoslovakia's president, in 1944, after the liberation of Košice. Now it is used for ceremonies etc.

There are a lot of interesting churches in Košice. One of these lies in **Dimitrovovo námestie**. If you get off the main streets into the back alleys you can see another side of the town. The frontages of buildings that the public sees are painted and looked after, while around the back is often grotty.

There are nearby woods at Košice-krásna, Košický les (on the road to Jahodná, bus 14), or Furča. There is **kayaking** at Anička (bus from the bus station).

There is an international **organ festival** in Košice about May-June every year. Every October a 40km international marathon, established in 1924, is held from Košice to Šaca and back.

Herľany

At Herľany there is a geyser which once every 32 to 34 hours spurts water up to 30 metres above the ground for a period of about 20 minutes. By phoning 116 you can hear a recorded message in Slovak telling you when the geyser will be playing. If you don't have anyone to translate, ask Čedok. There is a bus to the geyser, and if it plays at night it is floodlit.

Eating and drinking

At Leninova 16 Jednota have a complex of different class restaurants, *vináreň, pivnice* and a night bar. There are also places to eat and drink near Jacabov Palác. There are numerous *vináreň* around the old town. There are markets every day in Dimitrovovo námestie where villagers sell their products, but the biggest day is Saturday.

ZEMPLÍNSKA ŠIRAVA & VIHORLATSKÉ VRCHY

Zemplínska širava is a 33.5 sq km artificial lake situated in the far east of Slovakia near the Soviet border. It is known as the Slovak Sea, because Slovakia doesn't have any sea. A few years ago, with its warm summer temperatures, it was a good place for swimming. Now it has become too polluted, although people do still swim in it. In the summer there are cruise boats. You may be able to borrow or rent canoes and dinghies, but not yachts, by asking at club houses. At Vinné is Viniansky hrad, the ruins of a 13th Century castle. The main centre in the area is Michalovce. It has some nice churches, and the Zemplín Museum is next to the bus station. If you walk out onto the road from the bus station, there is a map of Michalovce on your right. From Michalovce bus station there are buses out to the resorts along the northern shores of the lake. If you want to get away from the more developed resorts, head further out along the lake from Michalovce. At Kaluža "high rise" development is starting. There is a Čedok office and a Tuzex shop in Michalovce.

Vihorlatské Vrchy are the volcanic hills to the north of the lake. Although some of the area is now closed due to the military taking it over, there is still public access to Morské oko, a beautiful lake situated up in the forest, and Sninský-kameň, a rather spectacular peak.

Maps

A map called *Vihorlatské vrchy — Zemplínska širava* was planned on my last visit, so see if it is published yet. You may be able to buy a map of Slanské vrchy and Zemplínska širava, but Vihorlatské Vrchy is not on this. A new map, *Bukovské vrchy Laborecká vrchovina* covers Morské oko, but not Zemplínska sírava. There is a street map of Michalovce with a rough map of Zemplínska širava on the back.

Getting there

There are a few buses a day between Prešov and Zemplínska širava. The trip takes 2 hours 20 minutes. There are lots of buses between Michalovce and Košice. On this route you pass over Slanské Vrchy, where there is a huge memorial to Soviet soldiers. There is a direct bus once a day at 8.00am from Michalovce to Rošňava, otherwise change buses at Košice.

Accommodation and eating

There are many camp sites along the lake-shore. Some have on-site tents, and some have bungalows. At Kamanec, there is camping behind the motel.

If you go right down to just before the pier, there is a good spot for pup tents on the left. Also good blackberries. By the motel is a strange looking chalet colony (tel. 245 65). There is a camping area along the lake shore between Kamanec and Klokočoc, but it is rather exposed to the wind and close to the road. Camping at Paľkov, just past Klokočov, is good. There is a large area available for tents, some of it sheltered, and it is not too close to the road. Most of the camp sites are open from mid May to mid September, and most have cold water only.

If you are looking for a roof over your head, rather than a camping spot, there are a couple of hostels in Hôrka, and a *hostinec* with sleeping for 20, cold water only, at Medvedia Hora. Kamanec Motel has B category accommodation. Cold water only. It is open all year (tel. Michalovce 872 08). It has a sk.III restaurant, open from 8.00am to 9.00pm, but meals are served during more restricted hours. There is a B* class hotel, Merkur, in Hôrka (tel. 752 70), otherwise there are three hotels in Michalovce.

Vihorlatské Vrchy and Morské oko

Morské oko is a beautiful lake surrounded by forest, a lovely peaceful spot formed by lava from a volcanic eruption blocking the stream running in the valley. It is now a nature reserve, and camping, fires, swimming and boating are all prohibited. Malé (Little) Morské oko is ½ to 1 hour walk from Morské oko itself, but it has been spoilt by logging operations. If you are a blackberry fan it might be worth walking up the first part of the track (season begins about late August).

Buses to Morské oko operate only in the holiday period between late June and late August. There are only one or two a day, and they run from Micholovce via Úbrež, not via the Zemplínska širava resorts. There is one bus a day to Morské oko in the same season along the northern shore of Zemplínska širava. It leaves Michalovce at about 8.30am, only stops at major stops (eg Kamanec Motel), and doesn't run at weekends. When there is no bus you must walk the last 9km from Remetské Hámre (1½ to 2½ hours, following the blue markers along the road). Hitchhiking is possible, but there is hardly any traffic outside the holiday period. At the parking area there is a *bufet* and a map. From here it is a 15 minute walk up to the lake itself.

Sninský-kameň (1005m) is a fantastic sight. It is a large rock outcrop situated above Morské oko. To get there, follow the track to Tri Tably (821m) from the top end of Morské oko, and then along the ridge to Sninský-kameň. Watch out for track markers on the way up, as logging roads criss-cross the hillside. A board at the bottom explains how the rock was formed. From the signs at the bottom of the rock, follow the red marked track around the rock, and you will come to steel steps leading to the top. Pollution and haze spoil the view, but you can see Morské oko below. From here the red track continues to Strihovké Sedlo, but it is not used much. Following the track towards Zemplínske Hámre for a few minutes brings one to a ladder up onto the other outcrop. From here it is possible to descend to the valley to the north.

The areas around Morské oko and Sninský-kameň are nature reserves, but a lot of the rest of the forest has been spoilt by logging. Even so it is a

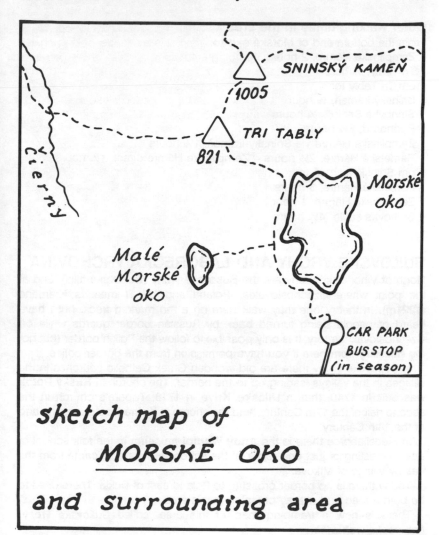

SNINSKÝ KAMEŇ
1005

TRI TABLY
821

Morské
oko

Malé
Morské
oko

CAR PARK
BUS STOP
(in season)

sketch map of
MORSKÉ OKO
and surrounding area

Other walking times in the area
From the bottom end of Morské oko to:
• Zemplínske Hámre, 2 hours
• Tri Tably, ¾ hour
From Tri Tably to:
• Sninský-kameň, ½ hour
• Strihovké Sedlo, 4¾ hours
• Podhoroď, 8¾ hours
• Zemplínske Hámre via Sninský-kameň, 1½ hours
• Remetské Hámre, 2½ hours – Zemplínske Hámre direct, 1¼ hours
From Sninský-kameň to:
• Remetské Hámre, 3 hours
• Zemplínske Hámre, 1 hour
• Strihovke sedlo, 4¼ hours

BUKOVSKÉ VRCHY AND LABORECKÁ VRCHOVINA
North of Vihorlatské vrchy are the Bukovské vrchy (Bukovské hills), and at the point where Czechoslovakia, Poland and USSR meet is Kremenc (1221m). In theory one may walk here on a red marked track, but I have heard of people being turned back by Russian border guards while on Czechoslovak territory. It is only possible to follow the Polish border (but not the Russian) from here if you have permission from the border police.

In Bukovské vrchy there are old wooden Greek Catholic churches in the villages in the valleys leading up to the border. The church in **Ruský Potok** was built in 1740, that in **Uličské Krivé** in 1718, Topoľa's church in the second half of the 17th Century, and the church in **Kalná Roztoka** at the end of the 18th Century.

In Medzilaborce there is the **Andy Warhol museum** in the folk school of arts, consisting of just one room of the school. His parents came from the nearby village of Miková.

Today there is no border crossing to Poland east of Dukla. There used to be both a road and railway crossing in this area.

There is now a tramping map of this area, called *Bukovské vrchy, Laborecká vrchovina*.

THE TOKAI REGION
The Tokai region is in southeast Slovakia, and continues into Hungary. This is one of Slovakia's wine growing areas, and Streda n. Bodrogom, Malá Tŕňa, Viničky, Malý Horeš and Kráľovský Chlmec are all villages involved in wine making. The region has long fine autumns, and according to an old Austro-Hungarian decree grape picking was permitted only after October 24, when the season was over in other areas. Today the picking season starts on St Simon and St Jude's Day (October 28) at the earliest, and finishes in November, sometimes after the first snow has fallen.

INDEX OF PLACES

(Note: This index follows the Czech and Slovak alphabets — č after c, ch after h, ř after r, š after s, and ž after z.)